W9-BJC-602

NIMITZ AT WAR

NIMITZ AT WAR

COMMAND LEADERSHIP FROM PEARL HARBOR TO TOKYO BAY

CRAIG L. SYMONDS

OXFORD
UNIVERSITY PRESS

OXFORD
UNIVERSITY PRESS

Oxford University Press is a department of the University of Oxford. It furthers
the University's objective of excellence in research, scholarship, and education
by publishing worldwide. Oxford is a registered trade mark of Oxford University
Press in the UK and certain other countries.

Published in the United States of America by Oxford University Press
198 Madison Avenue, New York, NY 10016, United States of America.

© Craig L. Symonds 2022

All rights reserved. No part of this publication may be reproduced, stored in
a retrieval system, or transmitted, in any form or by any means, without the
prior permission in writing of Oxford University Press, or as expressly permitted
by law, by license, or under terms agreed with the appropriate reproduction
rights organization. Inquiries concerning reproduction outside the scope of the
above should be sent to the Rights Department, Oxford University Press, at the
address above.

You must not circulate this work in any other form
and you must impose this same condition on any acquirer.

Library of Congress Cataloging-in-Publication Data
Names: Symonds, Craig L., author.
Title: Nimitz at war : command leadership from Pearl Harbor to Tokyo Bay / Craig L. Symonds.
Other titles: Command leadership from Pearl Harbor to Tokyo Bay
Description: New York, NY : Oxford University Press, [2022] |
Includes bibliographical references and index.
Identifiers: LCCN 2021052633 (print) | LCCN 2021052634 (ebook) |
ISBN 9780190062361 (hardback) | ISBN 9780190062378 (UPDF) |
ISBN 9780190062385 (epub)
Subjects: LCSH: Nimitz, Chester W. (Chester William), 1885–1966. |
World War, 1939–1945—Naval operations, American. |
World War, 1939–1945—Pacific Ocean. | Leadership. |
United States. Pacific Command—Biography. | United States. Navy—Biography. |
Admirals—United States—Biography.
Classification: LCC D767.N56 S96 2022 (print) | LCC D767.N56 (ebook) |
DDC 940.54/5973092 [B]—dc23
LC record available at https://lccn.loc.gov/2021052633
LC ebook record available at https://lccn.loc.gov/2021052634

1 3 5 7 9 8 6 4 2

Printed by Sheridan Books, Inc., United States of America

To
E. B. "Ned" Potter
and to
Timothy Bent

CONTENTS

LIST OF MAPS

INTRODUCTION

NEARLY FIFTY YEARS AGO, as a new assistant professor in the History Department at the U.S. Naval Academy, I shared an office suite with Elmer B. "Ned" Potter. Ned had taught at the Naval Academy since before the Japanese attacked Pearl Harbor. He was also the co-editor with Chester Nimitz of the book *Sea Power* (1961), which we all used as a text in the required naval history course that I subsequently taught at the Academy for thirty years. Ned knew Nimitz well, having worked closely with him on *Sea Power*. Ned's biography of the admiral (entitled, simply, *Nimitz*) appeared in 1976, and he kindly gave me an inscribed copy. I still have it.

Since we shared a telephone line, I often took calls intended for him. My favorites were from his wife, Grace, a Virginia lady in every sense of that term. She never identified herself, as in "Hello, Craig, this is Grace Potter." She never had to. When I heard, "Wheyal, halloh thayah"—each word two distinct syllables—it could be no one else. I never got a call from Nimitz, since he had died in 1966, but Nimitz was very much a part of the many conversations Ned and I had about naval history until Ned retired in 1977. We remained friends until he died twenty years later, in 1997. I hope he would have approved of the wartime portrait of the admiral that I offer here.

This is not a biography of Chester Nimitz. It is, instead, a close examination of his leadership during his three and a half years directing World War II in the Pacific Theater when his actions and decisions guided the course of the war and helped determine its outcome, the legacy of which we still live with today. In many ways, it is remarkable that he assumed such a role. National trauma—social, political, economic, and military—produces a cultural tension that can challenge democratic norms. In such circumstances, the loudest, most aggressive voices often assume leadership roles. During World War II, military and naval leaders such as Admiral Ernest J. King, General Douglas MacArthur, Admiral "Bull" Halsey, and General George Patton all rose to prominence. All were talented and competent. All were also larger-than-life figures whose temperament, stubbornness, self-assurance, and impatience characterized their leadership. They were, and are, polarizing figures.

Nimitz, like Generals George Marshall and Dwight Eisenhower, exemplified another leadership style, a quieter one that depended on intelligent listening, humility, and patience. Nimitz did not shrink from hard decisions—he was, at critical moments, as bold as any commander in the war. Yet he believed that ultimate success depended on accommodation as well as determination, on humility as well as aggressiveness, on nurturing available human resources as well as asserting his authority. Rather than impose orders, he elicited solutions; he sought achievement, not attention. He unified. His was a quiet, calm, yet firm hand on the tiller during an existential crisis, and his leadership style reinforced rather than challenged democratic norms. It is a leadership template more relevant than ever.

The focus and purpose of this book is to recreate and evaluate Admiral Chester Nimitz's experiences in the 1,341 days during World War II in the Pacific when he commanded, directed, and supervised the largest naval force ever assembled in the largest naval war ever fought.

———

AS ALWAYS, THERE ARE A NUMBER of individuals who have helped me in the preparation of this work. In addition to the inspiration provided by Ned Potter at the beginning of my career, I am indebted to my editor at Oxford, Tim Bent, who has mentored me during the more recent phases of that career. Tim and I have worked together on several book projects. Despite the inherent tension that exists between author and editor, he has always found the perfect balance of praise and criticism, suggestions and applause, and—like Nimitz himself—he has been patient and encouraging throughout.

Over the many years of our association he has also become a valued friend. This book is dedicated to both Ned and Tim.

There are many others who lent their support and to whom I owe thanks. At the top of the list is Richard B. Frank, who read the entire manuscript carefully and saved me from a number of errors while also suggesting new ways of looking at particular issues. John B. Lundstrom read much of the manuscript and was both generous and meticulous in his comments and suggestions. In particular, he encouraged me to rethink Nimitz's management of the Coral Sea action. Jon Parshall helped me further refine my understanding of the Battle of Midway. Admiral Nimitz's twin grandsons, Chester (Chet) Lay and Richard (Dick) Lay, read all of the manuscript and offered encouragement and advice. Elliot Carlson read the two chapters dealing with Robert Ghormley and directed me to a number of useful sources, and Thomas J. Cutler read the chapter on Leyte Gulf. Barrett Tillman and James Sawruk helped me with technical details concerning U.S. fighter planes. All of them are generous to a fault, and I greatly appreciate their time and expertise. As always, of course, any errors that remain are mine alone.

Others played important roles in helping me find material, which was especially complicated during the pandemic of 2020–21. At the Naval War College in Newport, Rhode Island, where I worked during the first two years of this project, archivists Stacie Parillo and Elizabeth Dalmage were essential in my hunt for documents, and patiently watched over me in the reading room. In the Nimitz Library at the U.S. Naval Academy in Annapolis, where I completed the work, the library director, Larry Clemens, helped me gain reentry to the COVID-restricted campus, and Jennifer Bryan, David D'Onofrio, and Samuel Limneos of the Special Collections Department always had my cart of boxes ready when I arrived. Chris McDougal, the archivist at the National Museum of the Pacific War in Fredericksburg, Texas (Nimitz's birthplace and hometown), was extraordinarily generous in tracking down resources about Nimitz. At the Naval History and Heritage Command in the Washington Navy Yard, I benefited from the help of John Hodges and Dale (Joe) Gordon. And at the Franklin D. Roosevelt Library in Hyde Park, New York, I relied on Kristin Carter,

Cliff Laube, and Paul Sparrow. Janis Jorgenson was indefatigable in tracking down photographs at the U.S. Naval Institute Photo Archive while remaining cheerfully helpful. My longtime friend John Hattendorf gave me a copy of the March 6, 1944, issue of *Life* magazine, which he found in an antique store, the cover of which is depicted in chapter 18. Jeff Ward once again demonstrated his perfectionism in rendering the fifteen original maps in the book. Amy Whitmer and Sue Warga at Oxford University Press saw the manuscript through the publication process and corrected several infelicitous passages for which I am grateful.

Michael Lilly, the author of *Nimitz at Ease* and the grandson of Nimitz's close friends in Hawaii, Sandy and Una Walker, generously made available family letters, papers, and photographs, as well as Una Walker's diary, all dealing with Nimitz's friendship with his grandparents. Samuel P. King in Hawaii shared with me a copy of the unpublished memoir of Sandy and Una's son, Henry A. "Hanko" Walker. Tom Savage, the grandson of Ernest J. King, shared family papers. In addition to their careful reading of the manuscript, Chet and Dick Lay also shared family letters and photographs (including the one used here as a frontispiece) and their grandfather's complete medical history.

At the Naval War College, where (somewhat ironically) I spent the years 2017–20 as the Ernest J. King Professor, I benefitted from several lengthy conversations about the relationship between King and Nimitz with David Kohnen. My colleagues in the Hattendorf Historical Center commented on drafts of several of the early chapters. In addition to David, this included Rob Dahlin, Jeremiah "J" Dancy, Mark Fiory, John Hattendorf, Jamie McGrath, Tim Demy, Nick Prime, Tim Schultz, Geoff Till, and Evan Wilson. All of them were thoughtful and supportive colleagues.

As always, my greatest debt is to my wonderful wife, Marylou, partner of more than half a century, who, in addition to being an insightful and thoughtful sounding board and a meticulous editor, makes everything worthwhile.

Craig L. Symonds
Annapolis, Maryland
Summer 2021

PROLOGUE

A T TEN O'CLOCK IN THE MORNING on the last day of 1941, fifty-six-year-old Rear Admiral Chester W. Nimitz, wearing the dress white uniform that Navy officers still call a "choker," stepped forward on the small deck of the American submarine *Grayling*, tied up to a wharf at the submarine base on Southeast Loch in Pearl Harbor, Hawaii, and prepared to read his orders aloud.

The sub was relatively new, commissioned only in March; it was nevertheless a markedly low-key venue for such a ceremony. There was room on its small deck for only about two dozen men, and the squat black conning tower behind Nimitz provided a melancholy backdrop. Across the harbor, the wreckage of several battleships was all too visible. Several days afterward, Nimitz told a fellow officer that he had chosen to hold the change-of-command ceremony on the *Grayling* because it was very nearly the only American warship still afloat. That was gallows humor, however, because there were actually many American warships still afloat and intact. Instead, Nimitz had selected the *Grayling* because he had spent much of his early career in the submarine service. Indeed, as a lieutenant commander back in the 1920s, he had supervised the construction of that very base.

The ceremony itself was mostly pro forma. Nimitz read his orders, the official act that made him commander of the United States Pacific Fleet—or what was left of it—and at that moment he accepted authority over, and responsibility for, American naval forces throughout the Pacific Ocean. At that moment, too, he advanced in rank from being a rear admiral with two stars on his shoulder boards to a full admiral authorized to wear four stars. To signify that, when Nimitz finished reading, a sailor behind him yanked on a line, and a small square blue flag with four white stars in a diamond pattern broke atop the *Grayling*'s short mast. The promotion was not permanent—it came with the job. When the assignment was over, whenever that might be, Nimitz would revert to being a two-star admiral again like his unlucky predecessor, Husband Kimmel, who had worn four stars on December 7, but who stood now in the small audience on the wharf wearing only two.

After the ceremony, Nimitz awarded medals to half a dozen men who had performed heroically on the "Day of Infamy," then he crossed the brow to the pier to address the small group of spectators. His remarks were brief since in his view it was not a moment for oratory. "We have taken a tremendous wallop," he said, "but I have no doubt of the ultimate outcome." There was a group of reporters present, and one of them asked him, "What are you going to do now?"

Almost certainly, the reporter hoped to hear a stirring call to arms or a vow of revenge—something for a headline in the papers back home. If so, he was disappointed. As Robert Sherrod of *Time* magazine noted, "It was simply not in [Nimitz] to make sweeping statements or give out colorful interviews."

Nimitz considered the reporter's question and replied: *All we can do is bide our time and take advantage of any opportunity that might come along.* It was quintessentially Nimitz: candid but restrained, and delivered in a calm, unpretentious tone.

Nimitz thanked everyone for coming. Then he turned and walked the short distance to his new office at the submarine base, where a tall pile of paperwork awaited him.

PART I

TAKING COMMAND

I am learning what it is all about and in due time hope to become useful in the job.

—Chester W. Nimitz to Catherine Nimitz, January 9, 1942

For Americans, news of the Japanese attack on Pearl Harbor was both ter-rifying and disorienting. For two decades U.S. Navy leaders had planned for a possible war with the Empire of Japan. Virtually all those plans, however, had involved a swift American offensive by the battleship fleet, most of which was now either sunk or seriously damaged. With one au-dacious move, the Japanese had seized naval superiority in the Pacific. The U.S. Navy was not only physically crippled but also psychologically wounded. Moreover, the combination of a "Germany First" Allied strategy and the early successes of German U-boats in the Atlantic—including off the American East Coast—meant that there would be no significant reinforcements for that crippled fleet for some time. For both the nation and the Navy, it was a precarious moment.

O N DECEMBER 16, 1941, only nine days after the Japanese attack on Pearl Harbor, President Franklin D. Roosevelt named Chester Nimitz Commander in Chief of the Pacific Fleet—the Navy acronym for which was CinCPac. Curiously, he had considered making that appointment exactly a year earlier.

In the spring of 1940, in the hope that a show of strength in the Pacific would deter Japanese aggression in South Asia, Roosevelt had "suggested" to the Chief of Naval Operations (CNO), Admiral Harold Stark, that the fleet should conduct its annual exercise in the Central Pacific west of Hawaii. Afterward, the president directed that the fleet remain in Pearl Harbor instead of returning to the West Coast. That greatly annoyed the fleet commander, Admiral J. O. Richardson. A long stay in Pearl Harbor, Richardson argued, would complicate his logistics and interfere with his planned training program. Richardson was further angered when Roosevelt, unwilling to acknowledge that the move was aimed at Japan, announced that Richardson himself had proposed it. Thoroughly disgusted, Richardson flew to Washington to complain. During his conversation with the president, he told Roosevelt "the senior officers of the Navy" did not have "trust and confidence in the civilian leadership of the country."[1]

Roosevelt was shocked. He had served as Assistant Secretary of the Navy during World War I and considered himself a Navy man. He may have decided at that moment to replace Richardson, though, if so, he waited until the winter to do it. His first thought was to appoint Nimitz, who was then Chief of the Bureau of Navigation. Nimitz declined the offer, insisting that he was too junior for such a post and that his appointment would cause resentment among the many admirals who were senior to him. So instead Roosevelt appointed Husband E. Kimmel.* Had Nimitz accepted the job, it is likely that he, and not Kimmel, would have borne the opprobrium resulting from the Japanese attack on December 7 and might well have been shelved—as Kimmel was—for the duration of the war. Now, a year later, with war having begun, Roosevelt told his Secretary of the Navy, Frank Knox, "Tell Nimitz to get the hell out to Pearl and stay there till the war is won."[2]

Nimitz knew the assignment was fraught with difficulty. The Japanese attack had left four U.S. battleships sunk and four more badly damaged; even without those losses, the Imperial Japanese Navy was significantly more powerful than the forces Nimitz could muster to oppose it, and he knew he could not expect any meaningful reinforcements soon. Finally, while Nimitz's predecessors as CinCPac had also been endowed with broader authority as Commander in Chief, United States (CinCUS), Nimitz would lack such authority. In the aftermath of Pearl Harbor, Secretary Knox decided to separate the two jobs. So while Nimitz became CinCPac, the larger job of commanding the entire U.S. fleet worldwide went to Admiral Ernest J. King, a demanding, no-nonsense, and uncompromising officer who became Nimitz's immediate boss. Given that, Nimitz knew that the burden he was about to shoulder would require patience and discretion as well as determination.

TWO DAYS AFTER KNOX TOLD HIM to "get the hell" out to Pearl, Nimitz said goodbye to his wife, Catherine, and their three daughters: Catherine,

---

* When Richardson learned that he was to be replaced, he asked Knox why. Knox told him, "The last time you were here, you hurt the president's feelings."

twenty-seven, called Kate; Anna, twenty-two, called Nancy; and their surprise child, Mary, ten. Their only son, Chester junior, twenty-five years old and called Chet, was a 1936 Annapolis graduate and already in the war. Having followed his father into the submarine service, he was in the USS *Sturgeon* at Mariveles Naval Base on the Bataan Peninsula in the Philippines.

Nimitz could have flown to the West Coast, but instead took the train in order to give himself a few days to study and prepare. He traveled as "Mr. Freeman" (his wife's maiden name) in a civilian suit: a quiet passenger who kept to himself—perhaps a businessman on a trip home to see his family for the holidays. He was accompanied by his aide, thirty-year-old Lieutenant H. Arthur "Hal" Lamar, whom Nimitz had selected for the job partly because Lamar was color-blind and not eligible for a sea command. In the first of the letters that Nimitz wrote to Catherine every day over the next three and a half years,[†] he assured her that Lamar was "a tower of strength" and "a great comfort" to him on the trip, during which Nimitz tried (unsuccessfully, according to Lamar) to teach him to play cribbage.[3]

After a stop in Chicago, where Nimitz got a haircut, the two men transferred to the Santa Fe Super Chief for the three-day trip to Los Angeles. Before they left Washington, Admiral Stark had entrusted Lamar with a canvas bag of briefing documents, including photographs of the Pearl Harbor disaster, telling him not to show them to Nimitz until after they left Chicago. As the train headed west, Lamar pulled them out and Nimitz studied them, including the photograph of the USS *Arizona* aflame and sinking. The *Arizona* had been his flagship when he served as the commander of Battleship Division One just over three years earlier, and seeing it in its death throes was particularly painful.

---

† Not all of those letters survived. After the war, Catherine burned most of those covering 1943 and 1944 as well as all of the letters she wrote to him. Her explanation was that things shared between husband and wife should not be made public. Thankfully, the letters he wrote to her in 1942, early 1943, and during the last six months of the war survived.

At one point Nimitz left the compartment to visit the bathroom. The locks on the bathrooms were secured during station stops, and Nimitz found himself locked in. After repeated pounding and buzzing, the porter finally arrived to let him out, but it was obvious that the porter thought Nimitz simply did not understand how to work the lock. Irked, Nimitz invited the porter to try it himself, and closed him in. After a moment or two, the porter sheepishly knocked on the door and asked to be let out. Nimitz took his time doing so, writing Catherine that the porter finally acknowledged "that I had a good cause to be vexed."[4]

In LA they were met by a car and driver and taken to the Naval Air Station, where Nimitz said goodbye to Lamar, who returned to Washington to serve as aide to Nimitz's replacement at the Bureau of Navigation, Rear Admiral Randall Jacobs. After lunch at the officers' club and a cursory inspection of the coastal defenses, Nimitz headed south alone to San Diego.

His flight from there to Hawaii was delayed by a day due to bad weather, and so it was Christmas Eve when he boarded a PB2Y-2 Coronado seaplane for the seventeen-hour flight to Pearl Harbor. He arrived on a bleak Christmas morning with rain spattering the harbor. As the plane flew in over the harbor, Nimitz climbed up into the cockpit to stare out the windscreen at the hulls of sunken battleships protruding from the oily water. Before he deplaned, he made a point of shaking the hand of each member of the crew to thank them for the sacrifice they made by being away from their families on Christmas Day.[5]

A small boat came out to pick him up. Nimitz's first question to the officer who met him was about Wake Island, the tiny American outpost 2,300 miles west of Hawaii that had been attacked by the Japanese three days after the attack on Pearl Harbor. When he had left California, the island was still holding out and an American relief force was steaming toward it. He learned now that the relief expedition had been recalled and that Wake's garrison had surrendered. Staring silently out over the harbor, Nimitz made no comment.

UNSURPRISINGLY, THE OFFICERS AND MEN OF the Pacific command were curious about their new boss. What they saw was a man five feet ten inches tall with a large square head and a prominent jaw. A few may have noticed that he was missing the ring finger on his left hand, the result of an accident with the gear on a diesel engine years earlier. More likely, they focused on his snow-white hair and light blue eyes, which contrasted strikingly with his tanned and weathered face. Those eyes were especially arresting, and some found their scrutiny unsettling. One officer subjected to his gaze thought it "seemed to penetrate clear through the back of my head."[6]

In addition to his arresting looks, Nimitz's default countenance was an austere, tight-lipped expression that is evident in virtually all of his official photographs (see chapter 1). It was an expression that seemed to suggest disapproval, or at least guarded skepticism. It did not. It was the consequence of poor dental care in his youth. In Nimitz's annual physical for 1941, the doctor marked the following teeth as "missing": 1, 2, 3, 14, 15, 16, 17, 18, 19, 28, 29, 30, 31, and 32. Those are the back teeth, on both sides, both upper and lower. In addition, five of his front teeth had been "replaced by cast gold." A 1942 dental report noted that Nimitz's teeth "did not" meet "Navy standards." Because he was sensitive about that, he generally kept his mouth tightly shut.[7]

Once he spoke, however, that initial impression of severity quickly dissipated. For one thing, he spoke in a soft voice, sometimes so quietly that people had to lean in to hear him. For another, it became evident at once that he was genuinely interested in what people had to say. His instinctive empathy became clear to the members of the staff when he met with them for the first time. Many expected a tongue-lashing about the failures of December 7; some thought that, like Kimmel, they would be sent packing. Instead, Nimitz shook hands with each one, looked them in the eye, and quietly asked for their help. He was new to the command, he said, and would rely on them to help him get his bearings so that together they could recover from this setback and win the war. "I have complete confidence in your ability and judgment," he said. It was Nimitz's particular gift to be able to impart to others the confidence that they could succeed. A senior officer said later that it was as if someone had opened a window in a stuffy room. Not only was it a morale booster, but it was also judicious, since a wholesale replacement of the existing staff would have led to even more confusion.

Still, it was an early example of the fact that, as a longtime friend said of him, "he knew how to deal with people."[8]

When he was a midshipman, Nimitz's Academy classmates had characterized him as "calm and steady going," and three decades later a fellow admiral used almost the same language to describe him as "the calm, collected type that never showed stress or strain." He did not betray anxiety even in tense moments; if he was worried, it didn't show. "I never saw the Admiral agitated," another officer recalled later; "I never saw him angry." Occasionally, if provoked, Nimitz might express his concern by exclaiming: "Now see here!"[9]

While that demeanor was reassuring to subordinates, especially in time of war, it could also make him something of an enigma to strangers. A British officer who visited Pearl Harbor soon after Nimitz assumed command described him as "an old man, slow and perhaps slightly deaf." He was neither the first nor the last to underestimate Nimitz.[10]

Another characteristic of Nimitz's command temperament was his political acumen. He knew, almost instinctively, which administrative battles were winnable and worth fighting, and which simply had to be endured. While he could make bold and independent decisions—a trait that would become evident soon enough—he also had the patience to maneuver quietly and effectively in an environment that required collegiality and cooperation as well as loyalty and obedience. As an admiring staff officer put it later, "He could work with these people with a certain amount of give and take [to] attain what he really started out to do without giving the appearance of giving an order." Even in dealing with his enlisted Marine orderly, instead of giving him a peremptory directive he was likely to ask, "Would you do this for me?"[11]

Some looked upon this dexterity as weakness. In their view, a leader should *command*, not *negotiate*. A few dismissed him as a political admiral, more at ease with administrative efficiency than command responsibility. They mistook their man. Nimitz was "political" in the way that George Washington, Ulysses S. Grant, and Dwight D. Eisenhower were political. That is, he understood that command decisions at every level had to reflect

Rear Admiral Chester Nimitz in a pre-war official U.S. Navy photograph showing his default tight-lipped expression. (U.S. Naval Institute)

political realities as well as strategic and operational goals, and he nurtured a non-confrontational demeanor that allowed him to deal effectively with his superiors even when he disagreed with them. As war correspondent Robert Sherrod said of him, he "conceived of war as something to be accomplished as efficiently and smoothly as possible, without too much fanfare."[12]

He behaved similarly with his subordinates. He regularly invited input from others—from members of his staff, of course, but also from quite junior officers—and when they offered it he listened quietly and patiently without interrupting. If a visitor went on too long, Nimitz might start moving pencils around on his desk, which aides soon learned was a sign that he had heard enough. As one of those aides recalled, he "always gave a person a chance to have his say." He might not accept your advice, the officer recalled, but "you knew you had your full day in court." And when he did overrule a subordinate, he turned it into a teaching moment by explaining why.[13]

He made it a point to compliment others for their contributions because he believed that men responded better to praise and encouragement than to threats or warnings. This was reflected in the way he used fitness reports—those annual report cards on the performance of everyone in the Navy, from seaman apprentice to admiral. Fitness reports are notorious for their overblown accolades—though that phenomenon was less pronounced in the 1940s than it became later. Nimitz offered praise to all, often adding a note at the end about an officer's potential. Then he showed the report to the officer in question, looked him in the eye, and told him that he expected him to live up to that assessment.[14]

Another key aspect of his command demeanor was a puckish sense of humor. He didn't tell jokes, a fellow officer explained; he told stories that had a humorous side. A close friend believed that, like Abraham Lincoln during the Civil War, Nimitz told these stories to "throw off feelings of anxiety and frustration." Nimitz might be listening to a conversation, or perhaps an argument, and he'd say, "That reminds me of a story." Many of them were shaggy-dog stories with a lengthy—some might say interminable—buildup. During dinner parties before the war he sometimes took so long to tell one that his wife, Catherine, would interrupt him: "Let me tell it, you take too long." One of his favorites was about a young doctor who arrived at the home of a nervous father-to-be. "Don't worry at all," the doctor told him. "Leave it to me. Everything will be fine." Then the doctor disappeared into a back room with the expectant mother. After a minute or two he came out and asked for a butter knife, which the husband provided. A few minutes later the doctor was back to ask for a screwdriver. Then it was a pair of pliers, then a stiff wire with a hook on the end like a coat hanger. Depending on the audience, this buildup could go on for several minutes, with Nimitz pausing for dramatic effect. Finally, the prospective father (and perhaps by then Nimitz's audience) could stand it no longer. "Doctor," the poor man asked, "is everything all right?" "Yes, yes, everything's fine," the doctor answered. "I just can't get my bag open." As he intended, Nimitz's folksy stories eased tension at awkward moments or derailed an emerging disagreement.[15]

Many of Nimitz's stories were risqué—or at least what was considered risqué in those more innocent pre-war years. Catherine sometimes stopped him when he began one of these in mixed company, but they became a staple of the all-male dinner parties at his quarters in Pearl Harbor. If his guests moved from the dinner table to the card table, which was not uncommon, he might tell the story of the aspiring woman bridge player who was invited to a bridge party at the home of the local champion. Alas, her husband, who was partnered with the hostess, embarrassed everyone by bidding recklessly, trumping his partner's ace, and even forgetting what suit had been bid. When he excused himself to make a trip to the bathroom, his humiliated wife apologized for him. The hostess graciously waved off her apology, though she had to confess that "this is the first time all evening I've had the faintest idea of what he was holding in his hand."[16]

Humor was central to Nimitz's style of command, and he wielded its power to soothe or divert without losing authority. Once in 1934, while in command of the heavy cruiser *Augusta*, he was holding captain's mast, conducted periodically aboard U.S. Navy warships to administer non-judicial punishment for a wide variety of infractions. On this occasion, a third-class petty officer named Woolley was brought before him. Woolley's division officer explained that he had been caught in a house of ill repute with his uniform half off while he was supposed to be on shore patrol. Now he stood before his captain at attention in his dress whites.

"Well, Woolley," Nimitz said, "what have you got to say for yourself?"

"Well, Captain," Woolley replied, "it was this way." He then related that while carrying out his shore patrol duties, he had inadvertently torn the sleeve of his jumper, and knowing that Nimitz wanted the men on shore patrol to be turned out in proper uniform, he asked a girl he knew if she would sew it up for him. He went up to her room, where she had a sewing kit. "So that was why I was there with my jumper off." Nimitz congratulated Woolley on his creative defense and dismissed the case.[17]

Few recalled ever seeing him angry. When he got mad, one remembered, "he'd sort of just stiffen up a little bit and he'd look at you with those piercing blue eyes and you'd know you'd gone too far." The only recorded time Nimitz displayed genuine anger was 1934, the same year as Woolley's captain's mast, when the *Augusta* represented the United States at the state funeral of Admiral Heihachiro Togo, victor at the 1905 Battle of Tsushima during the Russo-Japanese War. Togo was a national hero in Japan—the Japanese equivalent of John Paul Jones or Horatio Nelson. It was a solemn and formal occasion, and ships representing most of the world's navies gathered to pay respects. As each ship arrived, the others greeted it with an appropriate gun salute and by raising the national flag of the new arrival. At the time, tensions were high between Japan and China, so the arrival of the Chinese cruiser *Ning Hai* was notable. It was flying the flag of a rear admiral and was thus entitled to a 17-gun salute. Every ship was careful to observe precise protocols, yet when the *Augusta* fired its salute, instead of the Chinese flag, the officer of the deck ran up the Japanese flag. It was not entirely his fault, as the flag was mislabeled in the flag locker; still, it was more than embarrassing and had grave international implications. Nimitz had to visit the *Ning Hai* as well as Japanese officials ashore to offer profound apologies on behalf of the United States. Even then, both countries half suspected it had been a deliberate insult.[18]

When Nimitz returned to the ship, the offending deck officer and the signalman reported to the bridge to apologize. Nimitz muttered, "If I wasn't so mad, I'd kill both of you right now."

Yet even then he delivered the remarks quietly; he never raised his voice. As another officer recalled, Nimitz was "always in control of himself" and "calm in any emergency." That self-assurance communicated itself to those around him and acted as a reassuring influence even in the most difficult of times. After all, if the boss wasn't worried, maybe there was nothing to worry about.[19]

ANOTHER RESOURCE NIMITZ BROUGHT TO HIS new command as CinCPac was his experience as head of the Bureau of Navigation in Washington, the job he had held prior to being appointed to the Pacific Fleet. His long tenure in Washington had encouraged some in the Navy to categorize him as a desk admiral—a paper-pusher. His many friends in the Navy had warned him that serving consecutive tours in the nation's capital would damage, if not destroy, his career. The place to win promotion, they reminded him, was at sea.

Yet Nimitz's years in Washington had proven valuable in several ways. First, the pre-war Navy was relatively small—small enough that Nimitz got to know, by record and reputation at least, virtually every senior officer. He had seen and reviewed the personnel file of almost everyone he would deal with in the ensuing war. Second, his tour in Washington made him comfortable with managing a large organization—the entire naval officer corps, in fact—from a desk. That was essentially what he would have to do in Pearl Harbor. It would not fall to him to order course changes, fire salvoes, or launch planes. Instead he would orchestrate the movements of those who did.

Finally, heading the Bureau of Navigation had required Nimitz to deal regularly with both high-ranking officers and senior political figures in Washington, including the president. That experience accustomed him to working comfortably with powerful, opinionated, and often self-important individuals while at the same time bringing himself to their attention. In Pearl Harbor, Nimitz no doubt seemed all-powerful to the thousands of men who were subordinate to him, but he was also responsible to those above him, and it proved valuable—indeed, essential—to know those powerful men and to have learned how to disagree with them without challenging their authority.[20]

In the immediate aftermath of the December 7 disaster, his superiors in Washington looked to him to be a savior. Nimitz knew the accolades would dissipate quickly if he failed to live up to their high expectations. And no one had higher expectations than Nimitz's immediate boss, the new Commander in Chief of the U.S. Navy, Admiral Ernest J. King.

———————————

IT WOULD BE DIFFICULT TO FIND two men who shared the same profession and life experience yet were more temperamentally different than Chester Nimitz and Ernest King. Nimitz was serene, reserved, and solicitous; King was pugnacious, bellicose, and confrontational. So severe was his demeanor, so daunting his persona, that although his middle initial stood for Joseph, some secretly referred to him as "E. Jesus King."[21]

Admiral Ernest J. King was Nimitz's immediate superior. In that capacity, he was demanding, impatient, and occasionally frustrated when Nimitz did not fulfill his insistent expectations. (U.S. Naval Institute)

Tall, slender, and ruggedly handsome, King was a competent and efficient officer who worked as hard as any man in uniform. Men admired him for his expertise, his work ethic, and his ability to get things done. They also feared him for his high expectations, uncompromising standards, and sharp tongue. King was all business; he disdained idle chatter or conventional conversation. As one contemporary put it, "He was logical, cutting, cold, and sparse with words." Another summed him up as "a complicated, brilliant, ruthlessly ambitious man who never suffered fools willingly." He happily—even proudly—embraced his reputation. Once, while introducing himself to a group of younger officers, he declared, "I'm Ernest King. You all know who I am. I'm a self-appointed son of a bitch."[22]

King hated to waste time, and he believed that his time was especially valuable. A fellow officer recalled that at the barbershop, "you could be half way through a haircut, and he decided that he wanted a shave. You got out of the barber chair and waited until he was shaved." King simply took that as his due. Once, leaving his office in Washington to go to the Navy Yard, he strode purposefully out to the curb where a Navy car and driver were waiting. King muttered "Navy Yard" to the driver without looking at him. The driver, who was a recent recruit, pulled open the door and responded, "Your wish is my command." To which King shot back, "You're goddam right it is."[23]

That abrasive manner may have been why, despite a stellar career, King had been passed over for the Navy's top job as Chief of Naval Operations back in 1939, a job that had gone instead to the more congenial Admiral Harold Stark, whose curious nickname, "Betty," had been inflicted on him at the Naval Academy and stayed with him throughout his life.[‡] Having missed the brass ring, King may have wondered if his career was effectively over. Then in December 1940, one year before Pearl Harbor, Stark had recommended to President Roosevelt that King be rescued from his membership on the prestigious but essentially advisory General Board and sent to command the Atlantic Fleet, then engaged in an undeclared but deadly serious naval war with German U-boats in the North Atlantic. Stark told the president that the hard-nosed King was just the man to "lick things into shape."[24]

King took charge of the Atlantic Fleet with his usual energy, instituting wartime protocols, and more importantly a wartime mentality, which would prove invaluable soon enough. Under King, ships operated at full speed, at night as well as in the daytime, and the men went to general quarters (battle

---

‡ Stark got his nickname as a plebe at the Academy when an upperclassman, noticing his name tag, asked him if he was related to General John Stark. Young Stark confessed he did not know who that was, and the upperclassman informed him sternly that prior to the Revolutionary War's Battle of Bennington, General Stark had proclaimed: "We will win today or Betty Stark will be a widow." He then ordered Stark to call out that phrase every time he encountered an upperclassman. He did, and the name stuck. Ironically, General Stark's wife was actually named Molly.

stations) regularly. Consequently, when actual fighting began a year later, Roosevelt called on King again, this time to take the top job as Commander in Chief of the U.S. Fleet and thus Nimitz's boss. King is reputed to have said that when the shooting starts, that's when they send for the sons of bitches.

Gratified as he was to have arrived at last at the top of his profession, King set some conditions before he accepted the post. One concerned the Navy's bureau system. Since the middle of the nineteenth century, administrative tasks within the Navy had been divided up among a number of near-autonomous "bureaus." In addition to the Bureau of Navigation, which Nimitz had led, there was the Bureau of Yards and Docks, the Bureau of Construction, Equipment and Repair, the Bureau of Provisions and Clothing, and so on. King himself had headed the Bureau of Aeronautics in the 1930s and had ruled it with his usual forcefulness. These quasi-independent fiefdoms complicated centralized planning and decision-making. King insisted that to exercise efficient command over the whole United States Navy, he should not have to negotiate with half a dozen bureau chiefs.[25]

Nor did he want to deal with the media. He knew that the man responsible for U.S. Navy strategy and operations worldwide would be under siege by reporters seeking a news story or a good quotation. While accepting that the press had a role to play in a democracy, King wanted no part of it. He hated "the whole concept of public relations." If he took this job, he told the president, he wanted assurances that he would not have to hold press conferences or answer interminable questions from reporters.[26]

Roosevelt declared himself willing to meet both demands. He could not dissolve the bureaus by fiat, he explained, but he promised King that any bureau chief who proved difficult would be replaced. As for dealing with the media, the president, who was a master of public relations, would happily assume that burden. He told King that only under special circumstances would he ever have to hold a press conference.

There was one more thing. King wanted to change the acronym used by the Navy to define his position. The former acronym "CinCUS," for Commander in Chief, United States, sounded altogether too much like "sink us," and after Pearl Harbor that felt like a bad joke. King suggested that he should bear the title "CominCh," for commander in chief. Roosevelt immediately agreed. Later, however, he had second thoughts. He sent his chief of staff, Admiral William D. Leahy, to ask King if he would mind changing his title. After all, Leahy reminded him, according to the Constitution there was only one actual commander in chief, and that was the president. King looked Leahy in the eye and asked if that was an order. No, Leahy responded, but the president would be pleased if King did it. King coolly told him that if the president ordered it, he would comply. Otherwise, he preferred to keep the title. King remained CominCh throughout the war.[27]

THE NAVAL HISTORIAN AND THEORIST ALFRED Thayer Mahan once described the oceans of the world as "a great common." Consistent with that, the executive order that established King's authority declared that "for the purposes of exercising command all oceans must be regarded as one area." King intended to take that literally. Soon after his elevation to CominCh, he circulated an announcement that he would exercise direct command over operations in both the Atlantic and the Pacific.[28]

Two days later, he rescinded the order. King discovered almost at once that he simply had too much on his plate to exercise operational command in both oceans. For one thing, as head of the Navy, he had to meet regularly with the heads of the other services: Army Chief of Staff George C. Marshall; the Chief of the Army Air Forces, General Henry "Hap" Arnold; and soon Leahy, too, a former CNO himself, who served as Roosevelt's chief of staff. Leahy presided over meetings of the service chiefs as chairman. The group had no formal name or assignment, but its members soon began referring to themselves as the Joint Chiefs of Staff (JCS), and the name stuck.

King was also a member of what was called the Combined Chiefs of Staff (CCS), composed of the American Joint Chiefs plus the British heads of service or their representatives. This was the group that, with input from Roosevelt and British prime minister Winston S. Churchill, shaped and directed Allied global strategy. King later estimated that his work on the JCS and CCS took up two-thirds of all his time during the war.[29]

Consequently, King appointed Vice Admiral Royal E. Ingersoll to command the Atlantic Fleet, and acknowledged that Nimitz would exercise actual as well as nominal command of the Pacific Fleet. Throughout the war,

King would send Nimitz broad directives and occasional specific orders, and the two men would meet regularly—a total of sixteen times over three and a half years—usually in San Francisco, halfway between Washington and Pearl Harbor. But King simply did not have the time, or, for that matter, the latest information at hand, to direct the movements of the Pacific Fleet on a day-to-day basis.

He was not entirely happy about it. Nimitz, King knew, was good at navigating the halls of influence in Washington—he was, in King's view, "a fixer," a description not intended as a compliment. King did not perceive patience and accommodation as assets. It was not at all clear to King that Nimitz was tough enough to make hard calls, to take chances when necessary, or to discard individuals who failed to adjust quickly enough to the tempo and the demands of wartime operations. In a phrase, he feared that Nimitz wasn't "a son of a bitch."[30]

Throughout the duration of the Pacific war, there would be moments of frustration for both men. While Nimitz generally accommodated himself to his role as dutiful subordinate, he occasionally had to risk King's wrath by confronting his boss on one issue or another. For his part, King was often annoyed by Nimitz's unwillingness to be more aggressive. He thought Nimitz was too ready to compromise, to see both sides of an issue and seek a middle ground, traits that were entirely foreign to E. Jesus King. "If only I could keep him tight on what he's supposed to do," King lamented privately to a friend. "Somebody gets ahold of him and I have to straighten him out." King discovered, however, that the pressures of defending the Navy's interests from the Army and fending off proposals from the British for diversionary adventures around the world took so much of his time that he had limited opportunities to "straighten out" Chester Nimitz.[31]

That was just as well. Like many others, King underestimated the steel that was at the core of Nimitz's benign exterior. Behind those cool blue eyes, impassive expression, and enigmatic demeanor, beyond the humorous stories and instinctive empathy, lay a resolve and audacity that became especially evident when it was most needed.

A T PEARL HARBOR, Nimitz was at the center of an enormous theater of war that was characterized by—even defined by—the vast
distances between strategic locations. That fact hugely complicated both
his planning and his logistical challenges, which was precisely why J. O.
Richardson had opposed basing the fleet there in the first place. For one
thing, all of the oil needed to fuel the ships and planes of the fleet had to
come by sea from California, 2,400 miles to the east. Submarines bound for
their hunting grounds in the western Pacific had to travel more than 3,000
miles in the opposite direction, across the International Date Line, just to
begin their patrols. Allied outposts at Samoa, New Caledonia, and Australia
were so distant that supply ships or reinforcements from Hawaii could
take up to a week to reach them. And the ultimate strategic objective—the
Japanese capital of Tokyo—was 3,865 miles away. That was more than six
times the distance from London to Berlin in the European Theater.

Locally, Nimitz found his domestic arrangements little short of idyllic. The Navy provided him with a spacious and well-appointed two-story, four-bedroom house at 37 Makalapa Drive, a short walk from his office down at the submarine base. The house had large windows that overlooked a garden of lush tropical foliage. There was even a grand piano, though he did not play himself, despite being a devoted fan of classical music. Kimmel, who had resigned on December 17, the day after Nimitz was appointed, had moved out of the house that same day. It had then been occupied by Kimmel's temporary replacement, Vice Admiral William S. Pye, who vacated the house when Nimitz arrived. Both Kimmel and Pye had relocated into another house across the street, and Nimitz invited both of them, as well as Pye's wife, Annie, over for Christmas dinner on his first night in Hawaii. He made a point of telling Kimmel that he was not to blame for the disaster on December 7. "It could have happened to anyone," Nimitz said, aware that if he had not turned down the job eleven months earlier, it might have happened to him.[1]

Almost at once, Nimitz developed a routine. He awoke at 6:30, did a few "setting up exercises," and then set out for a brisk three-mile walk. He returned for breakfast around 7:15, after which he walked downhill to his office, on the second floor of the submarine base. He wore a short-sleeve, open-neck khaki uniform, the four silver stars on his collar eliciting smart salutes from everyone he passed. Arriving about 8:30, he attacked the pile of paperwork that had accumulated overnight. At 9:00 every day he hosted a staff meeting—even on Sundays. As one staffer put it, "Sundays didn't mean anything." Nimitz was not a religious man. In retirement, he did occasionally attend church services with his family, and at one service, after his children had filed out of the church, his daughter Mary noticed that their father had not followed them. She went back into the church and found him kneeling in the pew. "Daddy," she said, amazed, "are you praying?" "Hell no," he answered. "I've got a cramp in my leg and I can't get up." On the other hand, Nimitz did often make it a point to be in his office on Sunday mornings at 10:00 a.m., because that was when a powerful San Francisco radio station broadcast a program of classical music.[2]

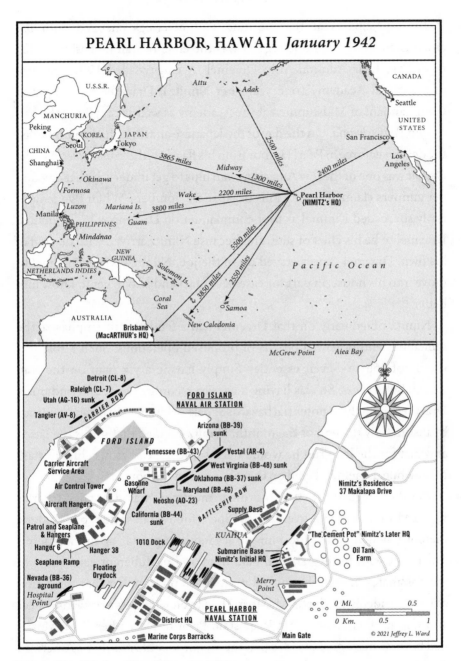

Map 1: Pearl Harbor, Hawaii, January 1942

The participants at the morning staff meetings changed with the circumstances, though one regular was the chief of staff he had inherited from Pye, Rear Admiral Milo Draemel. A craggy-faced 1906 graduate of the Naval Academy (one year after Nimitz), Draemel had served as Commandant of Midshipmen at the Academy as well as captain of the battleship *Pennsylvania*. On the day of the Japanese attack, he had commanded the destroyer force in Pearl Harbor from his flagship, the cruiser *Detroit*. The *Detroit* was one of the few American warships to get underway that day, and her gunners claimed several kills of Japanese bombers. When Pye temporarily succeeded Kimmel as fleet commander on December 17, he invited Draemel to be his chief of staff, and because Nimitz arrived with no staff of his own, Draemel simply stayed on in the job. Nimitz invited Draemel to move into his house, in part for ease of contact and also to get to know him better.

Nimitz noted early on that Draemel had a tendency to emphasize the difficulties and potential pitfalls of proposed operations. Such a role was useful, of course—even essential. Simply having a yes-man on the staff was all but useless. So was having a naysayer. Nimitz needed to find out if Draemel highlighted potential hazards as part of his job or if he was cautious by instinct. By the end of the month, Nimitz decided that it was the latter, and that for the long run he would need someone else as his chief of staff. Meanwhile, Draemel stayed on the job—and in the house.

Another regular at the morning meetings was Captain Charles H. McMorris, known universally as "Soc" (for Socrates) due to his eidetic memory, which had made him an academic superstar at the Academy. Then, too, with his egg-shaped bald head and protuberant ears, some of his classmates thought he looked more like a philosopher than a warrior. A 1908 Academy graduate, McMorris had been Kimmel's war plans officer and was another legacy from Pye's staff. Prior to December 7, McMorris had been dismissive of the idea that the Japanese could attack the American fleet in Pearl Harbor. When Kimmel had asked him, "What do you think about the prospects of a Japanese air attack?" McMorris had answered, "None. Absolutely none." Now, having misread the situation so badly, he was one of the strongest voices for a swift counterattack. That, of course, often put him at odds with Draemel.[3]

At midday, Nimitz sometimes had lunch at the submarine base mess, where he sat at a long common table with his staff officers. That allowed him another opportunity to assess them. Other times he skipped lunch altogether either because he got caught up in the paperwork or because his weight had crept up above 180 pounds. In either case he spent most afternoons in his office, leaving his desk periodically to visit members of the staff and keep tabs on progress. He generally stayed until 5:00 or 6:00.[4]

He tried not to bring work home. Instead, he often undertook a second and much longer walk in the afternoon—sometimes as long as six or seven miles. His father had died of a heart attack at twenty-nine, five months before Chester was born, and, determined to avoid a similar fate, Nimitz made it a point to walk or swim, or both, every day. When he could, he also played tennis or pitched horseshoes, and he was accomplished at both. In part it was therapeutic—an excuse to get out of the office—but mainly he did it to stay fit. After the walk, he often hosted dinner guests, an option made easy for him because of the cook and two Filipino stewards who ran the house, including the kitchen, with quiet and unobtrusive efficiency. In addition to Draemel, both Kimmel and Pye were regular dinner guests during those first few weeks.

Another frequent guest was Lieutenant General Delos C. Emmons, a 1909 West Point graduate. Emmons had replaced Lieutenant General Walter Short in command of the Army forces in Hawaii after Short, like Kimmel, was recalled in disgrace. Nimitz liked Emmons, who had a jovial personality, and they got along well. As military governor as well as Army commander, Emmons had the job of preserving order on the island, and he was conscientious in doing so. In the wake of the Japanese attack, Short had closed all the bars and liquor stores in Honolulu, and Emmons had continued that policy after he took over. Nimitz himself enjoyed a drink before dinner, and it seemed unfair to him to deny that privilege to the soldiers and sailors as well as the entire civilian population. He did not want to intrude on Emmons's command responsibilities, but during casual conversations at

In Pearl Harbor, Nimitz occupied comfortable, even luxurious, quarters that were surrounded by tropical foliage. This view shows the horseshoe pit he had installed on the south side of the house. (U.S. Naval Institute)

dinner in the early days of his command, he wondered aloud about relaxing the order, and eventually Emmons took the hint and did so.[5]

At dinner, Nimitz encouraged general conversation about mundane topics, often leavening them with one or more of his famous stories. He preferred simple and uncomplicated meals—meat and potatoes, bread and butter. After dinner, Nimitz might invite his guests to join him in a game of cribbage. If they demurred, he might suggest that they sit back and listen to classical music, which some appreciated and others merely tolerated. Nimitz was a devoted connoisseur—Brahms was his favorite—and he treasured his extensive collection of records, which in those days were made of hard (and fragile) shellac discs and had survived shipment from Washington. On some nights when he did not have company he turned off all the lights so he could open the windows to the night air and listen, usually in his pajamas and bathrobe, to whatever musical piece he had selected. Or he might walk back to the office after dinner and resume work, staying until 10:00 or 10:30 before returning to the house for bed.[6]

He was not a sound sleeper. He fell asleep readily, then often woke up at three or four in the morning. Sometimes he got up and worked for a few hours, though more often he would simply turn on the light and read. He liked to read biographies and novels. He was a particular admirer of Douglas Southall Freeman, and had read all four volumes of Freeman's 1934 biography of Robert E. Lee. Freeman's Lee was a paragon of virtue, though one aspect of Lee's personality that Freeman listed as "a positive weakness" was his tendency to avoid personal confrontations. In Freeman's view, Lee "chose the role of diplomatist instead of that of army commander" (an assessment that mirrored King's view of Nimitz). In addition to history and biography, Nimitz also enjoyed historical fiction. During that first month in Hawaii he was reading *Oliver Wiswell*, Kenneth Roberts's 1940 novel about the American Revolution, the title hero of which was a British loyalist.[7]

IN HIS OFFICE AT THE SUB BASE, the activity was virtually nonstop as officers rushed in and out with reports throughout the day. A staff officer remembered that "he was busy as the devil, phones were ringing and messages coming in," all day. To Catherine, Nimitz reported, "Our offices are most noisey [*sic*] and nerve wracking, because of the great activity." Many of the messages in his in-box during that first week were congratulatory letters about his promotion. Others were damage reports, status reports, casualty lists, or queries for direction or guidance.[8]

One of the first messages was from King, who urged him to organize a raid against Japanese bases in the Gilbert Islands, which Japan had recently captured from the British, or to "undertake some aggressive action for effect on general morale." Such missives from King would constitute a nearly constant refrain during the war. Despite the official Allied policy of "Germany First," King was eager to strike back at the Japanese as soon as possible and wrest the initiative from them. Nimitz assured his boss that offensive operations were under active consideration, and he brought up the issue at the very first of the morning staff meetings. McMorris was all for it; Draemel was not so sure.[9]

There were, in fact, a number of arguments against it. After all, the American battleship fleet had been devastated—the surface of Pearl Harbor still glistened with oil slicks, and the bodies of American servicemen were still being recovered. Yet, having had a chance to assess the damage in the week since his arrival, Nimitz decided that things were not as hopeless as they looked. As he would write a quarter of a century later, "as bad as our losses were . . . they could have been devastatingly worse." Four battleships had been sunk and four others damaged, and that was a heavy blow, but there were other tools to hand.[10]

For one thing, there were the fleet submarines, including the *Grayling*, on which Nimitz had assumed his new command on December 31. It was a measure of how much the world had changed since the last war that even though the United States had declared war on Germany in 1917 ostensibly for its use of unrestricted submarine warfare, the first operational order sent out from Washington after the attack on Pearl Harbor was to conduct "unrestricted submarine and air war against Japan." An old submarine hand himself, Nimitz expressed no qualms about those instructions.

The problem was that there were few submarines available. Though the United States had ninety-two submarines in the Atlantic in January 1942, it had barely half that number in the Pacific, and most of those had been forced to retreat from Manila when the Japanese attacked, abandoning both their base and their stockpile of torpedoes. That included the *Sturgeon*, in which his son Chet was serving. Nimitz reported to King that he had only "about fifteen" operational boats between Hawaii and the West Coast. Unaware as yet that the torpedoes they carried were unreliable—it would be months before he or anyone else knew that the submarines' primary weapon, the Mark XIV torpedo, had critical flaws—Nimitz dispatched the boats he did have into the western Pacific with instructions to target Japanese supply lines. If nothing else, it would remind the Japanese that despite their astonishing early successes, they were not yet masters of the Pacific.[11]

An even more important resource than the submarines, however, were the aircraft carriers.

AIRCRAFT CARRIERS WERE STILL RELATIVELY NEW in 1942. The first American carrier, commissioned in 1920, had been an experimental version with a flight deck built atop the hull of the coaling ship *Jupiter*, which had become redundant after the fleet converted to oil-fired boilers. In her new configuration, the *Jupiter* was rechristened the USS *Langley* with the hull number CV-1.* She was an odd-looking vessel. Some thought her elevated flight deck gave her the aspect of an old covered wagon, which became her nickname. At the time, her anticipated function was to serve as an auxiliary to the battleships: sending out planes to scout for the enemy. Over the ensuing decade, however, in the wake of the Washington Naval Arms Limitation Treaty (1922), a virtual revolution in carrier design took place.

In conformance with that treaty, all the major powers, including the United States, had agreed to scrap or halt construction on a number of battleships and battlecruisers. Unwilling to let the unfinished hulls go to waste, the United States negotiated a clause that allowed both Japan and the United States to convert two of their unfinished capital ships into aircraft carriers. In 1926, the Japanese converted the battleship *Kaga* and the battlecruiser *Akagi* into carriers (fifteen years later, they would spearhead the attack on Pearl Harbor). The Americans also turned two of their unfinished hulls into carriers, the *Lexington* (CV-2) and *Saratoga* (CV-3), both commissioned in 1927.[12]

These oversized vessels changed the nature and function of aircraft carriers. Whereas the *Langley* had been conceived of as an auxiliary to the battleships, these new carriers—more than twice the size of the *Langley*

---

* In the designation for carriers (CV), the "C" meant that it was a carrier and the "V" signified that it hosted planes that were heavier than air. In the 1920s, when the designation was created, it had seemed to some that lighter-than-air dirigibles offered a viable alternative to airplanes. By 1942, the need to designate airplanes with a "V" was already anachronistic. It continued nevertheless, and U.S. Navy planes were similarly designated. Hence, USN fighters were designated as VF, scout bombers as VS, bombers as VB, and torpedo planes as VT.

This pre-war photo of the *Saratoga* (foreground) and the *Lexington* shows them anchored off Diamond Head. Commissioned in 1927, their size and capability changed the type of missions they could perform, and over time helped transform the character of naval warfare itself. (U.S. Navy photo)

and capable of carrying as many as eighty aircraft each—became powerful striking platforms in their own right.

Young officers looking to take advantage of the new opportunities signed up for pilot training at the Navy's new flight school in Pensacola, Florida. Brash, confident, and daring, they developed their own subculture. Because they wore forest-green uniforms with brown shoes, regular surface warfare officers called them "brown shoe" officers, not intending it as a compliment. In turn, the fliers dubbed the ship drivers "black shoe" officers. While they coexisted well enough on shipboard, they retained their tribal allegiances.[13]

King had recognized this revolution in naval warfare early and, determined not to be left behind, went through the pilot training course himself in 1927 as a captain, though he was nearly two decades older than most of the others in the program. Nimitz did not undergo pilot training. In 1927, he was the commanding officer of the Naval ROTC program at the University of California at Berkeley, a job he loved since he acted as a mentor to scores of bright young aspiring officers, many of whom stayed in touch with him throughout their careers. Nevertheless, despite his status as a "black shoe," and lacking any aviation training, Nimitz fully appreciated the impact of the revolution wrought by the emergence of the oversized carriers. A battleship might fire its big guns at targets fifteen or twenty miles away, but planes from a carrier could strike targets more than a hundred miles away. Moreover, unlike the battleships, the carriers had little heavy armor and were therefore significantly faster. While most battleships topped out at 21 knots, a carrier could steam at 33 knots. That made it impossible, or at least impractical, for battleships and carriers to operate together. The plodding battleships would be an anchor to the speedy carriers and make the entire force both less agile and more vulnerable.

On the other hand, carriers could not operate alone. Because their expansive flight decks limited the number of guns they could carry, they required an escort of cruisers and destroyers both to provide anti-aircraft defenses and to fend off hostile submarines. Grouping a carrier, two or three cruisers, and four or five destroyers together with a fleet oiler to keep all of them fully fueled created what was known as a task force (TF).

In January 1942, Nimitz had three task forces. Two were built around the veteran carriers *Lexington* and *Saratoga*, now fifteen years old but still among the largest in the world, and the third centered on the smaller but newer *Enterprise* (CV-6). A fourth task force would soon be available. Back in April 1941, Roosevelt had secretly transferred the *Yorktown* (CV-5), a sister ship of the *Enterprise*, from Pearl Harbor to the Atlantic to help with the undeclared war against German U-boats. Now, after the Japanese attack, he ordered her back to the Pacific.

The loss, at least temporarily, of eight American battleships during the Pearl Harbor strike had seemed catastrophic at the time, but there were few missions where the lumbering battleships would have been Nimitz's weapon of choice anyway. Battleships were blunt instruments whose big guns could hammer enemy battleships; carriers were rapiers that could deliver the quick, sharp thrusts of a fencer. Which is exactly what Nimitz had in mind.[14]

NIMITZ WANTED TO ENSURE THAT HE had the right people in place to carry out those stabbing thrusts. Alas, most of the officers who were senior enough to command a carrier task force had grown up in the battleship culture. It was not clear in January 1942 which of them could make the transition from commanding a line of battleships and heavy cruisers to the management of a carrier task force—to lay down the cudgel and pick up the foil.

The task force commanders Nimitz inherited were a mixed lot. The oldest and most senior of them was Vice Admiral Wilson Brown (Naval Academy, 1902), who commanded the *Lexington* task force (TF 11). Brown had a distinguished record, having served as the naval aide to two presidents—Calvin Coolidge and Herbert Hoover—as well as a tour as a popular Superintendent of the Naval Academy. Virtually all of his sea service, however, had been in battleships or training commands. Then, too, his health was questionable. Only three years older than Nimitz, he looked at least ten, and had developed a tremor that caused his head to twitch. A few junior officers called him "Shaky" Brown behind his back. Though he lacked experience with carriers, or with aviation generally, his seniority and service record justified his appointment. Only time would show whether he could adjust to it.[15]

The commander of the task force built around the *Saratoga* (TF 14) was Vice Admiral Herbert Fairfax Leary, a 1905 Academy classmate of Nimitz's. Tall and thin, he had a reputation in the service as a diligent worker. He rose at six every morning and worked until late at night, taking time out only for hurried meals. A classmate marveled that "he never seems tired and never spares himself." His success in the service had been more a product of determination and perseverance than brilliance or insight. He had won the Navy Cross for efficient gunnery during World War I, but like Brown he had no experience with aviation or aircraft carriers.[16]

The third of Nimitz's task force commanders was Vice Admiral William F. Halsey Jr. He had graduated a year ahead of Nimitz at the Naval Academy and, like Brown, was three years older than his new boss. In fact, Halsey had briefly outranked Nimitz in 1940 when he was promoted to vice admiral while Nimitz was still a rear admiral.

Halsey's nickname was "Bull." Likely the result of a newspaper typo of his first name, Bill, the name stuck because it seemed to fit both his physical appearance and his pugnacious personality. Like both Brown and Leary, he

Rear Admiral William F. Halsey Jr. was the most experienced and colorful of Nimitz's task force commanders and would emerge as one of the heroes of the Pacific war, though his tenure was not without controversy. (U.S. Navy photo)

had begun his naval service in destroyers and he earned a reputation for aggressive and inspirational leadership as a destroyer skipper. Then in 1927—the year the *Lexington* and *Saratoga* were commissioned—he saw sooner than others that carriers were likely to change the character of naval combat, and he applied for flight school. He was vastly disappointed when he failed the eye exam.

A few years later, however, King, who by then had completed flight training and was serving as head of the Bureau of Aeronautics, offered Halsey the opportunity to command an aircraft carrier if he took what was called the observer's course at Pensacola. Instead of a pilot's gold wings, Halsey would receive an observer's silver wings—and no eye test was required. Halsey enthusiastically agreed. When he got to Pensacola, though now fifty-two years old and still with poor eyesight, he finagled himself into the regular pilot training program and earned his gold wings along with a score of twentysomething ensigns and lieutenants. By 1942, when he commanded the task force built around the USS *Enterprise* (TF 8), he was the only vice admiral in the Navy who wore the gold wings of an aviator.[17]

Unlike King, Halsey was perfectly willing to chat with reporters, and they in turn eagerly sought him out because he was almost always good for a printable quotation (and sometimes an unprintable one). Early in the war, when one correspondent asked him to predict the outcome, Halsey replied that before he was finished, the Japanese language would be spoken only in hell. Later, he answered another query about his plans by replying: "Kill Japs. Kill Japs. Kill more Japs."[†] He declared that he would ride the Japanese emperor's white horse through the streets of Tokyo, which led some admirers to send him bridles, whips, even a saddle. Eventually Nimitz ordered him to stop saying it. Halsey's swagger, his bulldog physiognomy, and his willingness to provide good copy made him a favorite of the print media, and he appeared on the cover of *Time* magazine in November 1942, a month before King did.

In addition to these three task forces, Nimitz would soon have a fourth when the *Yorktown* returned from the Atlantic. Rear Admiral Frank Jack Fletcher flew from Hawaii to San Diego to take command of the task force built around her (TF 17). Fletcher had graduated from the Academy a year behind Nimitz in 1906 and was another "black shoe," having commanded destroyers, battleships, and most recently a cruiser division. His only experience with aircraft carriers was when he had led the aborted effort to reinforce Wake Island in December 1941. The Japanese had attacked Wake three days after the raid on Pearl Harbor. Their initial effort to seize it had been repulsed, and one of Kimmel's last orders before resigning was to send Fletcher with the *Saratoga* task force to relieve and reinforce the beleaguered garrison. Only days later, Pye, in his temporary capacity as Kimmel's

† Referring to the Japanese as "Japs" was virtually universal among Americans in 1942, and indeed throughout the war, in both newspapers and official documents, as well as in conversation. Nimitz did so, too. Not only does Halsey's memoir, published in 1947, use the term throughout, but the index entry for the Japanese is "Japs."

replacement, learned that the Japanese had renewed their assault on Wake and had committed two carriers to the attack. That convinced Pye to order Fletcher to turn around. Upon receiving that order, Fletcher had thrown his uniform cap to the deck in frustration.[18]

Fletcher was a plain-spoken, no-nonsense officer who smoked corncob pipes and gestured animatedly when he talked. Generally imperturbable, he could occasionally be provoked (as he was when got the recall order from Pye). Nimitz knew Fletcher well, not only from their Academy days but also because Fletcher had served briefly as Nimitz's Assistant Chief of the Bureau of Navigation in Washington. Nimitz liked Fletcher and was grateful both that the *Yorktown* was coming back and that Fletcher would command the task force built around her.[19]

Along with the few score submarines, these four carrier task forces with their embarked squadrons were the principal weapons Nimitz had to conduct the war. There would be more later. In 1940 Congress had passed the Two-Ocean Navy Act, which authorized no fewer than eighteen new carriers along with nearly two hundred other ships, though none of them would be coming off the building ways until 1943. Given the "Germany First" policy, one reasonable option for Nimitz was to conserve his scarce resources until those ships became available. That, however, flew in the face of both King's expectations and Nimitz's own instinct. Consequently, Nimitz planned to use his four carrier task forces aggressively, and soon.

THROUGHOUT THE EARLY MONTHS OF 1942, the Japanese continued their rampage across the South Pacific, gobbling up new conquests almost daily. Their decision to go to war in the first place had been driven by a determination to obtain unfettered access to the raw materials—and especially the oil—of the European colonies, particularly British Malaya and the Dutch islands of Java and Sumatra, and that was where they focused their efforts. Their attack on Pearl Harbor had been intended primarily to neutralize the American fleet while they secured these valuable resources. There was little Nimitz could do to interfere with them—other than send his few submarines to the western Pacific—and he found it depressing to arrive at his office each day and find dispatches reporting yet another Japanese conquest.

For many Americans—in government, in the military, and in the general public—this string of Japanese successes was disorienting. Prior to December 7, most Americans had dismissed the Japanese as inconsequential foes in any future war. Now many saw them as supermen who could appear anywhere at any time and in overwhelming force. Some alarmists predicted that they would target Hawaii or the Panama Canal, even the American West Coast.

One particularly vulnerable American outpost was Samoa, exactly halfway between Hawaii and Australia (see Map 2). King told Nimitz that in addition to defending Hawaii, his primary task was to protect the line of communication to Australia. If the Japanese seized Samoa, as they had both Guam and Wake, it would sever that connection. In addition to its location, Samoa also hosted the best deepwater port in the South Pacific, at Pago Pago. Yet in January 1942, Samoa's garrison consisted of only about a hundred men of the 7th Marine Defense Battalion plus another hundred or so local militia known as the Fita Fita (Samoan for "soldier"). As if to demonstrate the garrison's vulnerability, an impertinent Japanese sub skipper surfaced off Samoa that month and shelled the island, though it turned out to be only a nuisance raid. To secure this invaluable outpost, King organized a convoy in San Diego to carry five thousand U.S. Marines there. Since the *Yorktown* was also in San Diego and bound for the Pacific, she and her escorts could accompany the convoy to protect it from Japanese interference.[1]

The imminent arrival of the *Yorktown* in the Pacific was welcome news for Nimitz, and he challenged his staff to develop a scheme for the best use of this new resource, as well as the three other carrier task forces. Though he was never reluctant to make independent decisions, he always sought to obtain as much information as possible before doing so. In addition to Draemel and McMorris, therefore, he invited Pye to the morning conference. Pye had been deeply shocked by the Japanese attack on December 7, and that made him diffident now. He was also in the awkward position of being a senior vice admiral without a command. Both Pye and Kimmel did their best to be helpful—Nimitz wrote Catherine that "everyone wants to help me, Pye and Kimmel most of all"—but they were also sensitive about being in the way.[2]

At the morning meeting, Nimitz outlined the priorities that King had stipulated (defend Hawaii, protect the sea lanes to Australia) and suggested that since the Japanese were likely to be preoccupied with their ongoing offensive in the South Pacific, there might be opportunities to conduct a quick raid against their bases in the Gilbert and Marshall Islands. That would serve the dual purpose of distracting them from the troop convoy bound for Samoa while also reminding them that the United States could still strike back.[3]

The response from the officers in the room was less than enthusiastic. Draemel characteristically sounded a note of caution. With U.S. assets so depleted, was this really the time to launch an offensive? Pye, too, was wary; sensing his skepticism, Nimitz asked him to summarize his concerns in writing.

Vice Admiral William S. Pye temporarily replaced Husband Kimmel as CinCPac when Kimmel resigned on December 17. In January Nimitz gave him command of the battleship force, though in November he left the theater to become president of the Naval War College in Newport, Rhode Island. (U.S. Navy photo)

Pye responded with an eleven-page memo. In it he suggested, first, that the Japanese probably knew about the troop convoy now en route from San Diego because he assumed they had spies in Mexico who would have seen it depart. By implication, at least, that suggested that protecting the convoy should be the focus of most, if not all, of Nimitz's available forces. Second, he did not think the carriers should conduct offensive operations at all until the task forces could be augmented by more destroyers, and unless they operated in close proximity to one another so that they could provide mutual support. Finally, he did not think there had been sufficient reconnaissance of the Japanese islands in the Central Pacific, about which very little was known.[4]

One of Pye's concerns that would appear quaint in retrospect was his sensitivity to the fact that although the Japanese had seized the Gilbert Islands and were building military facilities there, technically and legally those islands belonged to the British. In Pye's mind, that meant that "indiscriminate bombing cannot be done." Whether that was because British citizens might be killed or because British property might be damaged he did not say.

In fact, Pye worried about sending aircraft carriers to attack enemy shore bases at all. The Japanese had successfully attacked Pearl Harbor, of course, but that had been a surprise attack. It was dogma in the naval service that pitting guns afloat against guns ashore was a fool's bet. Pye extended that doctrine to aircraft as well. "An attack by ship-based aircraft against shore-based aircraft except when the element of surprise is present," he wrote, "may result in serious losses." In his view, that made carrier raids against the Gilberts or the Marshalls "unsound."[5]

Nimitz took Pye's concerns seriously. That, after all, was why he had a staff: to provide views that challenged his own. Yet Nimitz was determined to strike a blow—even if it was largely a symbolic one. At the bottom of Pye's memo, Nimitz noted that Pye's concerns about the risk from Japanese land-based aircraft could be minimized by having long-range patrol planes conduct searches in the rear of the task forces as they withdrew. At the January 8 meeting, Nimitz announced his decision: he would employ all four of his carrier task forces in a coordinated operation. Fletcher's *Yorktown* group (TF 17) would see the convoy of U.S. Marines safely to Samoa. There, it would meet up with Halsey's *Enterprise* group (TF 8) for a raid into the Gilberts. At the same time, Brown's *Lexington* group (TF 11) would attack Japanese bases in the Marshalls. That left the *Saratoga* (TF 14) to provide cover for the Hawaiian Islands.[6]

THEN: DISASTER. JUST THREE DAYS LATER, on January 11, the *Saratoga* was maneuvering 420 miles southwest of Oahu when she was struck by a torpedo from the Japanese submarine I-6. The skipper of the I-6 reported to Tokyo that he had sunk her, though in fact the big flattop stayed afloat and made it back to Pearl Harbor under her own power. Nevertheless, a quick inspection revealed that although she had been hit by only one torpedo, there was too much underwater damage for a local repair, and the *Saratoga* would have to return to the West Coast for a full refit. The amount of damage inflicted by a single enemy torpedo was an eye-opener. Nimitz wrote King that Japanese torpedoes "cause greater damage than anticipated." The loss of the *Saratoga* meant that Nimitz was now down to only two carrier task forces plus Fletcher's group coming from San Diego.[7]

At the staff meeting on January 15, Nimitz's advisers, Pye and Draemel in particular, only stated the obvious when they noted that "the Allied position is precarious." The threats were ubiquitous. Not just at Samoa but at Fiji, where the local commander declared his forces "insufficient," and at New Caledonia, which, according to the commander there, was "practically undefended." U.S. bases at Palmyra Island, located halfway between Hawaii and Samoa, and Johnston Island, eight hundred miles west of Hawaii, also called for reinforcements. Australia, too, clamored for support. In response, King ordered Nimitz to send a squadron of patrol planes there. Nimitz objected. Doing so, he replied, would leave Hawaii "dangerously weak against a possible carrier strike." King backed down, noting the "paramount importance" of Hawaii. The bigger question was whether Nimitz could continue his planned offensive in light of the multiple threats and his depleted resources.[8]

It was the first of a number of critical moments Nimitz would face as CinCPac. King urged an offensive; Nimitz's advisers cautioned against it; at least half a dozen American outposts were calling for reinforcements; and one-quarter of Nimitz's offensive capability had just been removed from the chessboard. Meanwhile, no matter how long he spent responding to letters and messages, the pile of paperwork on his desk never got any smaller. In a rare early admission of his frustration, he confessed to Catherine, "It seems to me like I am on a tread mill—whirling around actively, but not getting any where very fast."[9]

Despite the loss of the *Saratoga*, Nimitz decided to go ahead with the raids. He did not do so merely to gratify King, though that was surely a factor; he believed it was essential for morale within the command. For several weeks, the United States and its Allies had endured a series of crushing and disheartening defeats; it was, Nimitz believed, essential to strike back. He directed McMorris to write orders for Halsey's *Enterprise* force to steam south to Samoa and wait there for the convoy. When Fletcher's *Yorktown* group arrived, both carrier groups would proceed west into Micronesia. Fletcher would attack Japanese bases in the Gilberts, and Halsey would raid the Marshalls. That left Brown in the *Lexington* group to defend Hawaii. In Washington, King insisted that it was "essential" that the attacks "be driven home," and Nimitz incorporated that language in his orders.[10]

A particularly frustrating aspect of Nimitz's job throughout his command tenure was waiting for news. Forces at sea routinely maintained radio silence to avoid giving their position away, so once Nimitz dispatched a task force on an operation he had little choice but to, as one staff officer put it, "bravely sweat it out." He did not badger his operational commanders with additional orders, nor did he receive any progress reports. Once the *Enterprise* and its consorts departed Pearl Harbor, it was as if they had disappeared. Even after Halsey reached Samoa on January 20 ahead of the convoy, he did not break radio silence, for he did not want the Japanese to know that an American carrier task force had arrived in the South Pacific.[11]

BECAUSE HIS FATHER HAD DIED BEFORE he was born, Nimitz had been raised by his maternal grandfather, and one piece of advice his grandfather gave him was never to worry about things that were beyond his control. That stoicism became a central element of Nimitz's personality and was a core element of his equanimity. Years later, in retirement, he included that advice in a speech: "Learn all you can, then do your best, and don't worry—especially about things over which you have no control."[12]

So he didn't. On January 22, with all the elements of the planned raid on their way, he got out of the office and spent the afternoon playing tennis. Nimitz was a serious and competitive tennis player who routinely challenged much younger opponents, and he insisted that they play their hardest. Suspicious that younger junior officers would go easy on him, he warned them, "If you ever give away a point, I'm going to kick you out of here." On this occasion he played his aviation assistant, Captain William V. Davis, who was seventeen years his junior. While he almost never recorded the outcome of his matches, he usually won. That night he hosted another dinner in his quarters, writing Catherine afterward, "It was a good get together to talk business."[13]

While he waited for news from Halsey and Fletcher, Nimitz considered another offensive using his sole remaining carrier, the *Lexington*. King had urged him to "give consideration to [the] practicability of raiding Wake Island with additional task force two or three days after [the] attacks on Gilberts or Marshalls," and Nimitz was perfectly willing to do it.[14]

The loss of Wake to the Japanese on December 23, while Nimitz had been en route to Hawaii, had been a blow. The 450 Marines there had conducted a heroic defense, fending off superior Japanese forces for more than two weeks. The recall of Fletcher's relief expedition had been wrenching, especially for the Marine pilots on the *Saratoga* who were preparing to fly to the island to succor their comrades. Even as the *Saratoga* turned around, the Marine garrison on Wake fought on until it was obvious that there was no hope. The last message from the commander of the Marine contingent on the island, Major James Devereux, read simply, "Issue in doubt." In the end, several hundred Marines and more than a thousand construction workers were taken prisoner.[15] Japanese culture, especially Japanese warrior culture, held that people who surrendered, regardless of the reason, forfeited their honor and were not deserving of decent treatment. Nor did they get it.*

---

* The Marines captured on Wake endured years of harsh imprisonment. The Japanese kept many of the civilian construction workers on the island as forced laborers. In 1943, when the Japanese commander, Rear Admiral Shigematsu Sakaibara, feared that the island might be retaken by the Americans, he ordered the survivors lined up and executed by machine gun, a war crime for which he was subsequently hanged.

In the collective mind of the American public, Wake Island was a kind of modern-day Alamo. Already the Hollywood director John Farrow (future father of Mia) was planning a movie based on the Marines' heroic stand. A raid on Wake Island, therefore, would be both operationally meaningful and psychologically satisfying, a factor not to be ignored in such fraught times. The problem was that with the *Saratoga* limping to the West Coast for repairs, and the *Enterprise* and *Yorktown* raiding Micronesia, it meant that Nimitz would have to commit the last of his carriers to undertake it. At a staff meeting on January 21, the day after Halsey arrived in Samoa, several of those present expressed doubts about the wisdom of sending off all three of the carrier groups at the same time.[16]

NIMITZ DECIDED TO GO AHEAD. IN part, he did so because of "the indicated desires of Cominch"—that is, King. In addition, however, Nimitz knew that most of the Japanese strength was engaged in the Dutch East Indies, which meant it was not in a position to carry out another strike at Hawaii. He therefore ordered Brown to conduct an air raid on Wake Island with the *Lexington* and to follow it up with a bombardment by his accompanying cruisers "if practicable." Nimitz may already have been having second thoughts about Brown's tenacity, for he followed up the order with another the next day emphasizing that it was "essential these orders be expedited."[17]

To ensure that Brown had sufficient fuel for the round trip to Wake, Nimitz ordered the oiler *Neches* to rendezvous with him en route. The big carrier and its escorts could refuel while underway thanks to new protocols that Nimitz himself had pioneered during World War I when he had been executive officer and engineering officer on the oiler USS *Maumee*. Even so, underway replenishment ("unrep" in Navy jargon) remained a new and even dangerous exercise. Refueling thirsty destroyers while underway had become almost routine, but side-by-side refueling of carriers from oilers while underway had first been attempted only in 1939, and the longer booms needed to improve safety and efficiency in such precarious circumstances did not exist until 1941. Underway refueling was so delicate, the entire task force had to slow to 5 or 6 knots to effect it, and since carriers could not conduct flight operations at that speed, the entire task force remained vulnerable for as long as it took to refuel.[18]

Once again, a Japanese sub wrecked Nimitz's plan. While the *Neches* was steaming toward the rendezvous, doing so unescorted because of the shortage of destroyers, the Japanese submarine I-72 found her and sent her to the bottom with another of their obviously effective torpedoes. Oilers were even scarcer than destroyers, and Nimitz did not have another to take her place. He cancelled Brown's raid.[19]

Meanwhile, he continued to wait for news from Halsey and Fletcher, who should have been closing in on their targets by now. Despite Pye's earlier admonition that carrier task forces needed to operate in close proximity to one another for mutual support, Nimitz had assigned them targets 250 miles apart, which meant they would operate independently. His greatest concern, however, was the fuel situation, about which he had "considerable anxiety," according to the Running Summary at headquarters. Despite that, he suggested to both task force commanders that they could "extend offensive action beyond one day" if they saw opportunities to do so profitably.

The fleet oiler USS *Neches* (commanded, coincidentally, by Frank Jack Fletcher's son, Commander William B. Fletcher) was lost to a Japanese submarine on January 23, 1942. Her loss forced Nimitz to recall Wilson Brown's raid to Wake Island and exacerbated the shortage of both tankers and oilers in the Pacific theater. (U.S. Navy photo)

He did not define what those opportunities might be, but it was self-evident that if they conducted a protracted raid, it would burn up extra fuel, and with the *Neches* gone, Nimitz had only one other oiler available, the Pearl Harbor survivor *Neosho*.[20]

Nimitz finally heard from Halsey on January 31 (Hawaii time) after twelve days of silence. The need to maintain radio silence ended once the attack began. The first words of Halsey's brief report set off celebrations at CinCPac headquarters: "Attacks by Task Forces 8 and 17 were successfully carried out today, many auxiliaries and aircraft destroyed." Halsey reported that he was now retiring and "in urgent need of fuel." Nimitz ordered the *Neosho* to his coordinates, though as it turned out, the *Enterprise* and her consorts made it back to Pearl without having to refuel.[21]

THE *ENTERPRISE* ARRIVED FIRST. She eased into Pearl Harbor on February 5 to a hero's welcome. Ships blew their whistles, and men lined the rails to cheer and wave their caps. Nimitz did not wait for Halsey to come ashore; he took his gig out to the carrier and was hoisted up to the flight deck in a bosun's chair to shake Halsey's hand. An exultant Halsey showed him a message that he had run off on the ship's mimeograph machine and explained the context. As Halsey had approached the target, he told Nimitz, his radar had identified a Japanese search plane overhead, though it passed by without submitting a report. Halsey wrote a sarcastic message thanking its pilot for being so inefficient, had the note translated into Japanese, and then gave copies of it to his pilots to drop after their bombing runs. It was precisely the kind of stunt that made Halsey popular with his sailors. Whatever Nimitz thought of it, he was not one to depress the celebratory atmosphere. He clapped Halsey on the back, smiled broadly, and told him, "Wonderful. A great show all around."[22]

Later, in private, Halsey offered more details. In addition to the initial targets of Wotje and Maloelap in the eastern Marshalls, he had seized upon Nimitz's suggestion to "extend operations" and attacked the main Japanese base at Kwajalein in the western Marshalls, even launching a second strike when he overheard his pilots reporting (incorrectly) that there were two carriers there. For nine hours, Halsey had maneuvered the *Enterprise* task

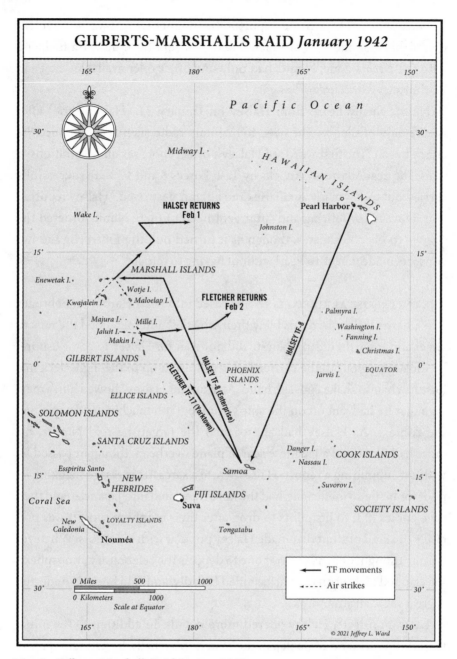

Map 2: Gilberts-Marshalls Raid, January 1942

force within range of four Japanese bases, conducting repeated strikes before he decided it was time, in the words of one of his pilots, "to get the hell out of here." It was almost too late. During his withdrawal, five Japanese land-based, two-engine bombers known as "Nells" attacked him. Near misses caused some concern, and afterward one Japanese pilot tried to crash his crippled Nell into the stern of the *Enterprise*, though the big flattop suffered no structural damage. Two more Nells attacked later that afternoon but with no success.[23]

Fletcher's *Yorktown* group had farther to go to return to base, and his task force did not arrive in Pearl Harbor until the next day. The reception was anticlimactic, fleet personnel apparently having expended all their enthusiasm and emotion on Halsey and the *Enterprise*. Then, too, Fletcher had less to report. The Japanese had only recently seized the Gilberts from the British and they had not yet fully developed their bases there. In addition, poor weather had reduced visibility. Fletcher's planes had bombed targets of opportunity, including a small seaplane base, but the only substantive achievement was shooting down a big four-engine Kawanishi flying boat, which the Americans code-named a "Mavis."[24]

In fact, neither raid had accomplished much. Halsey claimed that his planes had sunk fifteen ships and downed thirty-five planes "for sure," plus inflicting other damage ashore. These estimates, based on the reports of his pilots, were significantly inflated. In time, task force commanders would learn to take pilots' damage reports with a healthy dose of skepticism. Actual Japanese losses were one transport and one sub chaser sunk, plus damage to six other ships, including a cruiser. Unknown to Halsey, however, they had also killed Rear Admiral Yatsushiro Sukeyoshi when a bomb had landed directly on his base headquarters. He was the first Japanese flag officer to die in the Pacific war.

More important than how much damage the Americans had inflicted was the fact that the carriers had executed a planned offensive and returned undamaged. In the long history of the war, this first raid on Japanese bases in Micronesia was a relatively minor skirmish, hardly a footnote in the history of the war. But it was a beginning.

THE RAID INTO THE GILBERT AND MARSHALL ISLANDS had no perceptible impact on the Japanese, who continued their unrelenting offensive, rolling up victories in the Philippines, on the Malay Peninsula, and on the islands of Borneo, Sumatra, and Java. Singapore, which the British considered the Gibraltar of the Pacific, capitulated on February 15. Douglas MacArthur's Filipino-American Army in the Philippines continued to hold out, but because the United States lacked the material resources and especially the shipping to reinforce or resupply it, its ultimate fate was certain. When King asked Nimitz if he could send a submarine to sneak some anti-aircraft ammunition and medical supplies into Manila, Nimitz had to tell him that he did not have a submarine available to do it.[1]

To resist the Japanese onslaught, the Allies in the South Pacific pooled their resources into what was called ABDA, an aggregation of American, British, Dutch, and Australian warships. Unprecedented as that was, it was still no match for the Japanese. Most of the ABDA Naval Strike Force, as it was hopefully labeled, was annihilated in the Battle of the Java Sea on February 27, a calamitous defeat that, along with the Battle of the Sunda Straits a day later, saw the loss of seven Allied cruisers, one of which was FDR's beloved USS *Houston*, on which he had taken several lengthy cruises before the war. There was little now to prevent the Japanese from securing the critical islands of the so-called Malay Barrier, and even threatening Australia.

THROUGHOUT THIS PERIOD OF FRUSTRATION AND disappointment, Nimitz continued his daily letters to Catherine. In all of them, he did his best to be determinedly cheerful, emphasizing the pleasant weather, what he had for lunch, and who came to dinner. He also maintained a stoic demeanor in the office, where his calm countenance set a tone of quiet determination. One officer recalled him walking slowly from desk to desk, "conferring with his captains and his rear admirals on the staff with an almost total lack of emotion." Yet occasionally a glimpse of his frustration slipped through. He acknowledged to Catherine that "I do feel depressed a large part of the time."[2]

He continued to receive regular and sometimes insistent messages from King demanding action. The messages continued after the Gilberts-Marshalls raid, and Nimitz felt obliged to remind King that his own forces were "markedly inferior in all types to [the] enemy." King would have none of it. He fired back that the "Pacific fleet [is] not, repeat not markedly inferior in all types *to forces enemy can bring to bear* within operating radius of Hawaii while he is committed to extensive operations in [the] Southwest Pacific." Fair enough. Nimitz had made much the same argument to Pye in ordering the January raids. But what aggressive move could Nimitz make now that could have any possible impact on halting or even slowing the Japanese advance?[3]

There were really only two alternatives. The first was to send one or more of his carrier task forces into the South Pacific as a reinforcement for the imperiled ABDA command. That was unquestionably bold, but it was problematic on several counts. First, with the *Saratoga* still on the West

Coast, Nimitz had only three carrier groups. Sending one of them to the South Pacific would be no more than a gesture of support, and even if he sent all three, essentially stripping the Central Pacific of its offensive resources, it was unlikely to tip the balance of power decisively and would leave Hawaii dangerously exposed. In addition, Nimitz knew that operating carriers amidst the scores of islands in the South Pacific where the Japanese had multiple airfields dramatically escalated the risk. As Pye had noted in his critique of the January raids, pitting planes from carriers against planes operating from shore bases was an unequal contest.

His other option was to conduct another raid against Japanese possessions elsewhere in the Pacific in the hope that it might distract the Japanese from their central purpose. This, too, was unlikely to have a decisive impact—or indeed any impact. The Japanese had mostly shrugged off the Gilberts-Marshalls raid; their only reaction had been to send a few airplanes there to replace those that had been lost. Beyond that, they maintained their focus on the conquest of the South Pacific.

King suggested a third option. He wanted Nimitz to send a carrier task force to guard the lines of communication with Australia. Though the reinforcements King had sent to Samoa had secured that outpost, fifteen hundred miles west of Samoa was another link in the Allied chain connecting Hawaii to Australia. It was New Caledonia, a French colony whose assembly had voted to defy the surrender of the French government in June and support the so-called Free French under Charles de Gaulle. That made New Caledonia a kind of ally—though in the end it proved a very prickly one, as Nimitz would discover. To garrison it, King organized another troop convoy from the States, and to ensure protection for both the convoy and New Caledonia itself, he wanted Nimitz to operate at least one of his three carrier groups there.[4]

Nimitz found it a curious request. It was not at all the kind of offensive move that King had been urging, for it would tie up a carrier task force—one-third of his offensive assets—in the static protection of sea lanes. In fact, Nimitz wondered if he correctly understood it. Surely, King knew as well as anyone that the value of aircraft carriers was their mobility. In addition, keeping a carrier task force in the South Pacific created a serious

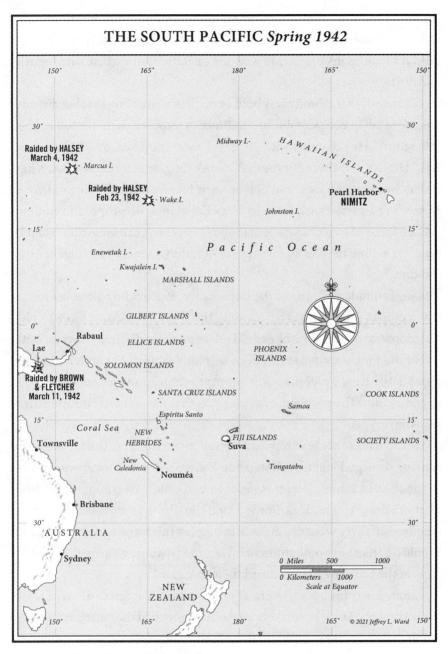

THE SOUTH PACIFIC *Spring 1942*

Raided by **HALSEY**
March 4, 1942 — Marcus I.

Raided by **HALSEY**
Feb 23, 1942 — Wake I.

Midway I.

HAWAIIAN ISLANDS

Pearl Harbor
NIMITZ

Johnston I.

Pacific Ocean

Enewetak I.

Kwajalein I.

MARSHALL ISLANDS

GILBERT ISLANDS

ELLICE ISLANDS

Rabaul

Lae

SOLOMON ISLANDS

Raided by **BROWN
& FLETCHER**
March 11, 1942

SANTA CRUZ ISLANDS

*PHOENIX
ISLANDS*

Samoa

COOK ISLANDS

Espiritu Santo

Coral Sea

NEW
HEBRIDES

Townsville

FIJI ISLANDS
Suva

SOCIETY ISLANDS

New
Caledonia

Nouméa

Tongatabu

Brisbane

AUSTRALIA

Sydney

0 Miles   500   1000
0 Kilometers   1000
Scale at Equator

NEW
ZEALAND

© 2021 Jeffrey L. Ward

Map 3: The South Pacific, Spring 1942

logistics problem, at least until new naval bases could be constructed. The Running Summary kept at Nimitz's headquarters pointedly noted, "The great difficulties in connection with the operations in that area are logistics and the lack of bases."[5]

Because of that, Nimitz was bold enough to write King that his directive would "result in considerable expenditure of resources with no commensurate return." He recommended "against [your] proposal as a guiding directive." His use of the word "proposal" is revealing since it implied that King's orders were suggestions, and in that spirit Nimitz offered his own. Instead of sending a carrier task force to New Caledonia, he proposed sending a surface force of two cruisers and four destroyers. A carrier group could be sent "from time to time," he wrote, "as situation or enemy intelligence may indicate."[6]

King reminded Nimitz of the importance of providing air cover for the troop convoys, but he okayed sending the cruiser-destroyer force to New Caledonia, and told Nimitz he could rotate other ships there "as you see fit."[7]

Nimitz took no satisfaction from this little victory. He understood and appreciated King's eagerness for "prompt action," and was willing enough to gratify him. The problem, of course, was that the demands outnumbered his assets.

He did have other warships in addition to the carriers. The Japanese had sunk or damaged eight battleships on December 7, but there were others in the theater. Nimitz designated seven battleships (including three Pearl Harbor survivors) as Task Force 1 and put Pye in command of it. King wondered if there wasn't some way to employ this force against the enemy. Would a battleship bombardment of, say, the Japanese base on the island of Truk in the Caroline Islands divert their attention?[8]

Nimitz knew his boss was under pressure from Congress to make use of the battleships. Why, lawmakers wanted to know, had the nation invested so much of its treasure in building these "castles of steel" (Churchill's phrase) if they could not be used against America's enemies? In due time, the older battleships, including those that had been repaired since December 7, would fill an important role as platforms for naval gunfire support during American invasions of Japanese strong points from Tarawa to Okinawa. But for now, and especially for the kind of hit-and-run raids Nimitz envisioned, they were more a burden than an asset.

For one thing, the battleships consumed prodigious amounts of fuel. That meant that an oiler—probably two oilers—would have to accompany them for the long voyage to the Central Pacific, and Nimitz did not have two available oilers. He was also short of tankers, which carried the oil from California to Hawaii. King had planned to send Nimitz four new tankers from the Atlantic until the predations of German U-boats off the American East Coast that spring depleted the American tanker fleet and compelled him to cancel the order.[9]

In addition to the fuel problem, the battleships—like the carriers—required destroyers to escort them, and Nimitz was also desperately short of destroyers. King had recalled several of them from Nimitz's command to confront U-boats in the Atlantic and had ordered Nimitz to send a destroyer division to MacArthur in exchange for some World War I–era destroyers. Even before those reductions, Nimitz had only 49 destroyers in the whole of the Pacific Ocean, whereas there were 104 in the Atlantic. When in late January King asked Nimitz if he could provide a destroyer to escort the British liner *Queen Elizabeth* from Nuku Hiva in French Polynesia, 2,400 miles south of Hawaii, Nimitz had to tell him he did not have one to spare.[10]

And even if the oilers and the destroyers could somehow be found, the battleships were simply too slow for a raiding mission. Their stately approach to a Japanese outpost risked early discovery that would subject them to "prolonged air attack before reaching [the] objective." The fate of the British battleship *Prince of Wales*, sunk in the South China Sea by Japanese aircraft on December 10, was sufficient evidence that battleships operating without air support were sitting ducks. And sending a carrier to accompany the plodding battleships would put it in jeopardy. Nimitz took the issue to his staff. Was there any practical way to employ the battleships against the Japanese? After prolonged discussion, the daily minutes noted that "no satisfactory solution of the problem could be reached." Nimitz reported to King that under current circumstances the best use of the battleships was to keep them in San Francisco for escort duty and for training. King was disappointed, writing Nimitz that the "present employment of battleships is unsatisfactory."[11]

Then what about the submarines? Surely they could be dispatched to harass enemy trade. King told Nimitz that "every submarine that can be spared" should be sent "to attack enemy lines of communication." Such advice was hardly necessary for an old submarine hand like Nimitz, and every submarine that was operational was already at sea. Still, Nimitz dutifully acknowledged the suggestion, while the keeper of the Running Summary at headquarters noted loyally, and perhaps with some pique, that "this directive is already being complied with."[12]

King may have begun to tire of Nimitz's explanations of why more could not be done. While Nimitz pondered the best use of his scarce resources, King ordered Brown's *Lexington* group (TF 11) to head south to cover the approaches to New Caledonia. Brown, however, suggested an alternative.

ONE OF THE MANY JAPANESE CONQUESTS in January was the port of Rabaul at the northern tip of New Britain Island (see Map 3). It was four thousand miles west of Hawaii, but only fifteen hundred miles north of Australia. Moreover, soon after the Japanese seized it in February, dozens of ships, mostly transports, began to arrive in Rabaul's commodious harbor, evidence that the Japanese were planning yet another offensive. But where? New Guinea? New Caledonia? Australia? Wherever it was, King wanted to preempt it by attacking the shipping in the harbor. Thus when Brown suggested an air raid on Rabaul, King told him to do it, and because Brown's *Lexington* group had an especially robust escort of four cruisers and nine destroyers, King suggested that he should follow up the air raid by bombarding the harbor with his cruiser force.[13]

In issuing those orders, King effectively bypassed Nimitz and assumed de facto oversight of Brown's task force. Nimitz said nothing about it at the time, though he did ask Pye to fly to Washington to meet personally with King to clear the air about authority and responsibility in his theater. Pye was a good choice. He was one of a very few people in or out of the Navy whom King considered a friend.

As Pye headed east to Washington and Brown headed west toward Rabaul, Nimitz met with Halsey to plan a sortie against a different target. He had been forced to recall the initial raid against Wake due to the loss of the oiler *Neches*. Now he wanted to try it again, this time using both of his remaining carriers. He acknowledged that a raid on Wake Island was unlikely to "divert much strength from the southwest," but it was "as strong an aggressive operation as can be undertaken at this time." It was, Nimitz told Halsey, "chiefly of morale value."[14]

Halsey was willing enough to strike another blow, yet when he got his written orders the next day from McMorris, he was alarmed to see that McMorris had designated his combined command as Task Force 13, and, worse, that the orders directed him to depart on Friday, which was the thirteenth! Halsey sent his air officer, Captain Miles Browning, to see McMorris about it. Browning argued that superstitious sailors would find sailing on Friday the thirteenth an ill omen, though almost certainly it was Halsey himself who thought it was bad luck. In any case, McMorris agreed to change the task force designator to TF 16 and told Browning that Halsey could delay his departure until Saturday the fourteenth—Valentine's Day. Nimitz was willing to indulge such eccentricities until and unless they threatened to jeopardize operational efficiency.[15]

Halsey and the *Enterprise* departed as scheduled on the fourteenth; Fletcher and the *Yorktown* followed them out of port the next day. Once again, Nimitz was compelled to wait for news, not only from Halsey and Fletcher but also from Brown, who was now halfway to Rabaul. Halsey maintained his usual radio silence; once he disappeared over the horizon, it was as if he had vanished. Brown, on the other hand, was positively chatty. On February 19 (February 20 west of the International Date Line), still 350 miles from Rabaul, he radioed that he had been spotted by several Japanese long-range seaplanes. Fighters from the *Lexington* splashed one of them, and downed a second one an hour later. Nevertheless, the snoopers had sent off sighting reports that were picked up by the radio room on the *Lexington*. As far as Brown was concerned, that compromised the mission. Like Pye, Brown believed that carrier raids against land bases could be effective only if they achieved tactical surprise. In his view, "the ever growing importance

Vice Admiral Wilson Brown had a distinguished naval career that included a successful tour as Naval Academy superintendent and service as naval aide to two presidents, though he enjoyed only modest success commanding a carrier task force. (U.S. Navy photo)

and effectiveness of aircraft has not changed the old truism that ships are at a disadvantage in attacking strongly defended shore positions." He therefore announced that he would continue westward during the daytime to keep the Japanese guessing, but that he would turn around after dark and withdraw.[16]

In that same message, Brown also noted that his task force suffered from "an acute fuel shortage"—so acute, in fact, that instead of returning to Pearl, he planned to head south for Sydney, Australia. That set off alarm bells with King, who did not want any American carriers based out of Australia for fear that the Australian government would insist on keeping them there. For his part, Nimitz quietly took note of the fact that for the second time in a month, Brown had been compelled to cut short a projected attack due to fuel concerns.[17]

Brown was right that the Japanese had spotted him. That afternoon, still heading west, he was attacked by seventeen land-based two-engine bombers from Rabaul. His fighters shot down all but two of them—Lieutenant Edward "Butch" O'Hare shot down five by himself—and the Japanese failed to do any damage.* Brown reported all this to Nimitz as well as to King in a series of radio messages. Nimitz may have wondered why, since so many Japanese planes had been destroyed, Brown did not continue with the raid after all, because the attrition of Japanese airpower significantly reduced the risk. If so, he did not suggest it to Brown, for he did not like to second-guess commanders on the scene, and in any case, this was King's operation.

There was another message from Brown, who repeated his need for fuel and added that he also needed six replacement planes, plus six more "for spares." Of course, there were few "spares" of anything in the Pacific Theater that February, and Nimitz wondered, too, about Brown's reported fuel consumption, which struck him as "excessive and greatly beyond previous reports."[18]

There was more. As if to justify his decision to call off the strike, Brown volunteered his opinion that though the raid had been his idea, attacking Rabaul with a single carrier was too risky. Such a valuable target, he now claimed, required the commitment of two carriers. Taking him at his word, King ordered Nimitz to detach Fletcher's *Yorktown* group from Halsey and send it to Brown. Nimitz dutifully obeyed, though it was evident that at some point he would have to clarify the extent of his authority over the disposition of his forces. Meanwhile, when Brown learned that he was to be augmented by a second carrier, he responded that even with two carriers,

---

* Though O'Hare was credited with shooting down five Japanese bombers at the time, an ensuing investigation showed that he actually shot down three, and damaged three others, one of which subsequently crashed. Nevertheless, he was named a Navy "ace" and recalled to the United States, where he was promoted to lieutenant commander and awarded the Medal of Honor. The Navy then sent the handsome and personable O'Hare on a tour to sell war bonds, which meant he missed the Battle of Midway. He returned to active service in 1943 and was killed in November of that year. Six years later, in 1949, O'Hare Airport in Chicago was named for him.

an attack on Rabaul was not a good idea: "I do not recommend it under present conditions." King told him to do it anyway.[19]

Brown's frequent reports contrasted dramatically with the continued silence from Halsey. Every day, Nimitz consulted a chart in his office to trace the likely track of Halsey's task force as it closed on Wake Island. Based on that, he had expected to hear something by February 22, Washington's Birthday, but that day, too, passed with no word. Then early the next morning, radio operators in Hawaii intercepted a sudden frenzy of *Japanese* radio signals from Wake. The Japanese were searching for an American carrier task force that had struck the island that morning. There was still no word from Halsey.[20]

If Halsey couldn't *send* messages without giving himself away, he could still *receive* them, and Nimitz radioed him to suggest that he could steam farther west to raid Marcus Island. He did not order it. Instead, he told Halsey that it was "desirable to hit Marcus if you think it possible." Marcus was not an especially important base, but it was deep within Japanese-held territory, only a thousand miles from the home islands. A strike there was certainly daring, and could possibly provoke alarm in Tokyo, where it might influence Japanese thinking and planning. Like the attack on Wake, it was a form of psychological warfare.[21]

Still maintaining radio silence, Halsey did not acknowledge the order. Did he receive it? Some of Nimitz's staff thought that Bull was keeping silent deliberately to make a point about his operational independence. Caution was one thing, but Halsey's continued silence seemed almost disrespectful. If it bothered Nimitz, nothing in his demeanor or expression reflected it, though others on his staff were annoyed on his behalf. The Running Summary noted testily, "Vice Admiral Halsey has not yet informed CINCPAC of what he has been doing."[22]

Once again, it was the Japanese who provided the information. On March 4, a public radio broadcast from Tokyo reported that thirty U.S. airplanes had attacked the Marianas Islands. Nimitz concluded that the Japanese radio announcers had simply identified the wrong island: it was Marcus, not the Marianas. There was still no report from Halsey, and the Running Summary noted, perhaps with some annoyance, "Task Force 16 still silent."[23]

Meanwhile, despite Brown's protestations, Nimitz hoped that after Fletcher joined Brown on March 6, the two-carrier strike force might yet accomplish something against the shipping at Rabaul. The next day, however, the Japanese ships that had been gathering there pulled up their anchors and headed south for New Guinea, which was now revealed as Japan's next target. Since it was the shipping and not the base itself that was Brown's objective, the two American carriers also moved south, passing around the eastern tip of New Guinea into the Coral Sea.

On March 11 Halsey and the *Enterprise* task force returned to Pearl Harbor and another celebratory welcome. That same day, Brown reported that four thousand miles to the west, he, too, had struck a blow. The Japanese ships from Rabaul had anchored off New Guinea's northern coast and begun landing troops at the ports of Lae and Salamaua. From his position south of the island, Brown launched an attack on the shipping off Lae with planes from both the *Lexington* and the *Yorktown* (see Map 3). Surmounting the nine-thousand-foot crest of the Owen Stanley Mountains along the spine of New Guinea, the Americans caught the Japanese landing force by surprise. Brown reported the results in glowing terms, claiming the destruction of five transports, three cruisers, a destroyer, and a minesweeper. His report caused a stir all the way up the chain of command. Nimitz reported it to King, who passed it on to the president, who wrote Churchill that the raid marked the best day in the Pacific war so far. As usual, the pilots' reports were exaggerated. Still, the Japanese had been surprised, and it was at least possible that the raid would interfere with their so far clock-like invasion schedule. Nimitz sent Brown a congratulatory "Well done" and recommended him for a Distinguished Service Medal. Privately, he feared the strike was unlikely to retard the continuing Japanese advance.[24]

KING CONTINUED TO DIRECT BROWN'S MOVEMENTS from Washington. And since Fletcher was now with Brown, King assumed de facto control of his task force as well. King vetoed Brown's plan to head for Sydney to refuel and ordered him to return to Pearl. Brown protested that he did not have enough supplies for such a long voyage, but King dismissed that out of hand. He told Brown that his men could survive on "beans and hard-tack," like sailors of old. Indeed, he told Brown to transfer any resources not needed for the trip to Fletcher so that Fletcher's *Yorktown* group could stay in the Coral Sea and continue to provide cover for New Caledonia and Australia. King did not prescribe any particular target for Fletcher, telling him he was "free to strike as you see fit," though he reminded him that "our current tasks are not merely protective, but also offensive." The "best way to protect," he wrote, "is by reducing enemy offensive power through destruction of his mobile forces, particularly carriers."[25]

Nimitz was left to manage the logistical details. He directed Brown to detach the cruiser *Pensacola* and the oiler *Tippecanoe* from his task force and send them to Fletcher, and ordered the (now empty) oilers *Kaskaskia* and *Neosho* to return to Pearl. He radioed Fletcher to remind him that he was now serving "directly under Cominch," and he copied King on all these orders, doing so in part to keep his boss informed, but also as a reminder that issuing operational directives from Washington required logistical adjustments in theater.[26]

Whatever King thought of Nimitz's gentle hint, he was growing increasingly dubious about Fletcher as a task force commander. His skepticism had its origins in the failed Wake Island rescue mission in December. En route to Wake, Fletcher had been compelled to refuel the task force while still six hundred miles from the objective. The refueling had been slowed by challenging sea conditions, and by the time the process was complete, Pye had called off the mission. It was not due entirely to the fueling delays, yet the episode convinced King that Fletcher was overly cautious about fueling and insufficiently committed to simply getting on with the mission. It was a point of view he never fully relinquished.[27]

On March 28, Fletcher received a message from King asking him to "report current situation," and Fletcher replied that he was headed for Nouméa in New Caledonia "for provisions." King pounced: "Your [message] not understood if it means you are retiring from enemy vicinity in order to provision." After twenty-four hours to calm down, King relented the next day, telling Fletcher he could proceed to Tongatabu to reprovision, a curious directive in that Tongabatu was a thousand miles farther from the Coral Sea than Nouméa. The episode underscored the awkwardness of King's attempt to manage operations from eight thousand miles away, though if Nimitz pointed this out to him, it is not recorded.[28]

Meanwhile, others in Washington worried about the Philippines. Under pressure from both the president and Army Chief of Staff George Marshall, King ordered Nimitz to load up a convoy of ships with supplies for immediate shipment to Manila. Such an operational directive completely ignored logistical realities. Nimitz patiently responded that the prospect of a convoy making it safely from Hawaii to the Philippines was "remote," and he urged the Joint Chiefs to reconsider. His reply made it all the way to the White House, and in the end, the order was withdrawn.[29]

King returned operational control of Fletcher's TF 17 to Nimitz in mid-April. Still, King's exercise of direct authority over two-thirds of the Pacific strike force led Nimitz to wonder if it reflected a decline in his standing in Washington. When Catherine wrote him that she had recently had lunch with Annie Knox, wife of Navy secretary Frank Knox, Nimitz wrote back that he was glad she had done so. He told her that back in December, when he stopped off in Knox's office to say goodbye before heading west, Knox had been "highly emotional" and had "difficulty controlling his voice." Nimitz feared that Knox was "not so keen for me now as he was when I left." He may have been right. When FDR asked Knox for a list of the forty best naval officers then on duty, Knox convened a group of admirals to help him compile it, and when he delivered that list to the president, Nimitz's name was not on it. Whether Nimitz knew this or not, he wondered if his command tenure in the Pacific would be only temporary, as Pye's had been. To Catherine he wrote, "I will be lucky to last six months. The public may demand action and results faster than I can produce."[30]

Three months before, Nimitz had arrived in Pearl Harbor uncertain of what he might find, and for the first month he had engaged in triage: shoring up sagging morale, patching together a functioning staff, and reacting to serial crises. He had confessed to Catherine feeling like he was on a treadmill making little progress. By March, his confidence had grown. He had restored morale, instituted new protocols, and directed several offensives.

More than once he had pushed back against directives from King and even from the JCS. His biggest accomplishment, however, was establishing himself as the calm eye at the center of the storm. It was not clear that it would be enough. His superiors were impatient, and it seemed possible that, like Kimmel and Pye, he could soon be shelved.

Instead, his command authority was greatly enlarged.

T HE CHANGE IN THE PACIFIC COMMAND was initiated at the highest political levels. Concerned about the vacuum of authority after the demise of ABDA, Roosevelt cabled Churchill to resolve "the complexity of the present operational command setup" in the Pacific. FDR suggested that the British should take the lead in the Indian Ocean, and that "responsibility for the Pacific Area will rest on the United States." In particular, he wrote that "supreme command in this area will be an American." Churchill agreed that "an American should be appointed Commander in Chief . . . in the Pacific area." But which American?[1]

One obvious candidate was Douglas MacArthur, who certainly expected to be tapped for the job. Indeed, he believed he already had it. He was, after all, the most senior American officer in the theater—or in the world, for that matter. The problem was that MacArthur came with a lot of personal, professional, and political baggage. Even George Marshall, who had urged the president to confer the Medal of Honor on MacArthur, was dubious about giving him supreme command. Marshall greatly admired MacArthur, yet, having worked under him in the 1930s when MacArthur had been chief of staff, and now over him as chief of staff himself, Marshall knew that MacArthur's command personality was problematic. Brilliant he may have been, but he also had a tendency to remain aloof—even imperious—and to surround himself with a few close aides collectively known as the "Bataan gang." His extreme self-confidence often morphed into arrogance and fed a conviction that he alone knew how to conduct the war. He also issued regular public communiqués that emphasized—indeed exaggerated—his importance in the war. In Marshall's view, such characteristics made him something of a risk in "supreme command."[2]

General Douglas MacArthur had an extraordinary Army career that included tours as superintendent at West Point and Army Chief of Staff. His escape from the Philippines and his declaration "I shall return" made him a national hero. (U.S. Army photo)

MacArthur was also a political lightning rod. Some Republicans in Congress were already urging him to consider a run for president in 1944, and though MacArthur gave no formal sanction to these suggestions, neither did he appear entirely opposed to the idea. Even without that, Roosevelt had never liked or quite trusted MacArthur since 1932 when the general had violently suppressed the so-called Bonus Army of veterans in Washington, using tanks and cavalry to disperse veterans of the Great War.

In addition to all that, King argued that since the Army was to take the lead in the European Theater, the Navy should have operational control in the Pacific, which was, after all, mostly water. Whatever reservations he still had about Nimitz, King was happy to advocate his elevation to theater

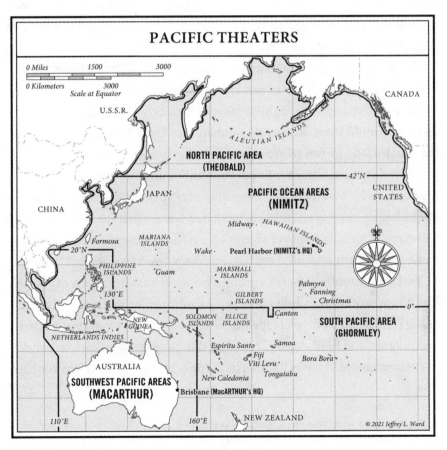

Map 4: Pacific Theaters

command in order to keep it out of the hands of the Army, and of MacArthur in particular. On March 15, King met with the president to talk "at some length" about command issues in the Pacific. Roosevelt, who considered himself a Navy man, likely found King's arguments persuasive.* After some pulling and tugging, what emerged was an agreement to divide the Pacific command not quite in half. MacArthur got command of what was called the Southwest Pacific Area (SoWesPac), comprising the continent of Australia plus the large island of New Guinea, all of the Dutch East Indies, and of course the Philippines. His title was Supreme Allied Commander, but only of a prescribed section of the Pacific. All the rest—more than sixty-five million square miles, three times the size of MacArthur's theater—fell under the command of Chester Nimitz, who retained his title as CincPac, and now added the title CinCPOA: Commander in Chief, Pacific Ocean Area. Roosevelt approved the new setup on March 31. Nimitz found out about it four days later, on April 3.[3]

The new protocol meant that in addition to the U.S. Pacific Fleet, Nimitz now commanded all of the armed forces, including air and ground units, of all the Allied nations throughout his vast theater. According to the agreement, he would exercise "direct command" over all Allied forces north of the equator, and he was to appoint some other officer, who would report to him as well, to command the South Pacific (SoPac) below the equator up to the border with MacArthur's theater at the 160th meridian. King did not relinquish his authority entirely. He reminded Nimitz that the "Chiefs of Staff will exercise jurisdiction over all matters pertaining to operational strategy," and he specifically kept all shore bases under his personal control.[4]

That same month, in fact, King's own position was also greatly expanded. The division of responsibility between a Commander in Chief of the Navy (King) and a Chief of Naval Operations (Stark) proved so awkward as to be unworkable, and FDR decided to clarify things by sending Stark to London as commander of U.S. naval forces in Europe. That cleared the way for King

---

* In a possibly apocryphal story, Marshall is supposed to have said that he did not mind FDR showing favoritism to the Navy, but it bothered him when the president referred to the Navy as "us" and the Army as "them."

to take the CNO's job in addition to that of CominCh, giving him unprecedented authority as both the administrative and operational commander of all U.S. naval forces worldwide. As for Stark, he all but disappeared in London. He was realistic enough to appreciate that because he had been in charge of the Navy on the day of the Pearl Harbor attack, his new job was all that he could reasonably expect.

One of the obligations that came with Nimitz's new assignment was the appointment of someone to command the South Pacific region. Or so he thought. King's initial order directed him to "appoint" a commander, but the next day another message instructed him to "nominate" a commander, evidence that King wanted to keep the final decision in his own hands. Nimitz immediately nominated Pye.[5]

That proposal was dead on arrival in Washington. Pye had been Kimmel's chief of staff on December 7, and in the minds of some, including FDR, he was too closely associated with that event. Moreover, it was Pye, as Kimmel's temporary replacement, who had recalled the Wake Island rescue mission, which to King at least suggested an unfortunate timidity. Pye was simply not acceptable.

Nimitz may have anticipated that reaction, for when King vetoed Pye, he immediately nominated Vice Admiral Robert L. Ghormley, who had the virtue of being entirely untainted by the Pearl Harbor debacle. Indeed, on that fateful day, Ghormley had been as far away from Pearl Harbor as it was possible to get. Back in 1940 when the United States had begun secret discussions with the British to make joint plans in case the Americans got drawn into the war, Roosevelt had sent Ghormley to London to act as an unofficial, and largely clandestine, liaison. He had played a valuable role in that capacity, proving sufficiently nuanced and discreet for strategic/diplomatic conversations at a time when the United States remained officially neutral. With Stark going to London in 1942 to clear the way for King's elevation to CNO, Ghormley became what the British called "spare capacity." He had the appropriate rank and was immediately available, though of course it remained to be seen if he also had the temperament to shift from the diplomatic responsibilities of his job in London to the intense wartime environment in the South Pacific. In any case, it would take some time for him to get to the South Pacific, and one question was who would command SoPac until he arrived.[6]

Some evidence suggests that King wanted to put Fletcher in that job, not because he had changed his mind about Fletcher, but to get Fletcher off the *Yorktown* so that someone else, presumably someone more naturally aggressive, could take over Task Force 17. After Ghormley arrived to assume permanent command in the South Pacific, Fletcher could then be quietly shelved.[7]

Nimitz resisted that ploy, writing King that it was "inadvisable repeat inadvisable" to remove Fletcher from the *Yorktown*. Instead, Nimitz suggested that until Ghormley arrived he should exercise command of the South Pacific himself. King agreed, telling Nimitz to "exercise operational command" of all units in the South Pacific as well as the rest of his command area.[8]

WHILE NIMITZ DEFENDED FLETCHER, HE TOOK a hard look at his other task force commanders. Despite Halsey's penchant for radio silence and his tendency to grandstand for reporters, Nimitz found him entirely satisfactory, and he was happy to keep him in command of the *Enterprise* group (now TF 16). The other two task force commanders, however, were more problematic.

Leary was ashore in Hawaii, at least temporarily, while the *Saratoga* underwent repairs at the Puget Sound Naval Shipyard in Bremerton, Washington. Those repairs could take months, and that effectively made Leary a task force commander without a task force. In King's view, that made him available for other duty, and he transferred him out of Nimitz's theater entirely to take command of what was known as "MacArthur's Navy" (later designated the Seventh Fleet) in the Southwest Pacific. Since it was a theater command, it was a kind of promotion, though Leary actually controlled few ships.

Leary started off his new job on the wrong foot, at least as far as King was concerned, by establishing his headquarters ashore in Melbourne, Australia. Consistent with his determination not to base any U.S. warships out of Australian ports, King immediately ordered Leary to exercise his new command from a flagship at sea. Leary protested. He reminded King that he had to deal with the navies of three countries (the United States, Australia, and New Zealand), which required him to break radio silence regularly, something he could not do from a flagship at sea. King was not swayed by that argument and the orders stood. Leary packed up his Melbourne office and returned to sea.[9]

Leary next notified King that he wanted to establish a reserve force to respond more flexibly to Japanese initiatives. King nixed that notion as well. "Cannot approve withholding ANZAC force from active operations merely to form a reserve," he replied. "This idea is passive." As always, he wanted offensive action. Unsurprisingly, Leary's tenure in command was short. By September he was gone, sent to command the 5th Naval District from a desk in Norfolk, and replaced by Vice Admiral Arthur S. "Chips" Carpender.[10]

Wilson Brown commanded the fourth of Nimitz's task forces. Despite the successful raid against Japanese shipping off New Guinea, Brown's performance in command of the Lexington group led Nimitz to wonder if he might do better in an administrative position. King's proposal to restructure the pre-war fleet organization gave him his opportunity. During the 1930s, the U.S. fleet had been divided into a "Scouting Force" and a separate "Battle Force," which made little sense in an age of carrier warfare. King suggested replacing that structure with a series of type commands: battleships, transports, amphibians, and so forth. Nimitz responded that it was a splendid idea and immediately nominated Brown to command the Amphibious Force, which would have its headquarters in San Diego. Like Leary's transfer, it was ostensibly a promotion. Though the Amphibious Force was small in 1942, it was certain to grow in size and importance once the American counteroffensive began. In the end, though, Brown's tenure in that job also proved temporary, for he became the naval aide to President Roosevelt, a job at which he excelled. Meanwhile, command of the Lexington task force went to Rear Admiral Aubrey "Jake" Fitch, who, though only a year younger than Brown, was more energetic.[11]

IN ADDITION TO THE FOUR TASK FORCE COMMANDERS, Nimitz's responsibility as CinCPOA included literally thousands of Pacific islands in a variety of political jurisdictions, many of them hosting important military facilities. King had indicated that he planned to keep the control of shore bases in his own hands, though it was not clear what that meant since he delegated to Nimitz the responsibility for establishing, supporting, and sustaining them.

Japan's attack on Pearl Harbor forced everyone to engage in a crash course in Pacific geography. Both King and Nimitz had at least heard of places like Palmyra, Efate, Canton, Fiji, and Tongatabu from their study of contingency war plans at the Naval War College. Though war planners in the 1930s had carefully plotted these tiny outposts on the charts, relatively little was known about most of them. King identified several that he believed were critical and gave each of them a code name. That did not always contribute to clarity. Samoa, for example, was code-named "Straw," while other nearby islands were code-named "Strawstack," "Strawhat," "Strawman," and "Strawboard." For some outposts, local authorities generated their own code names. Twice Nimitz asked King for a comprehensive list so that he could decipher references to particular locations in the message traffic, but the number of code references multiplied so quickly that King couldn't provide one.[†] Even so, King ordered Nimitz to send an "appropriate base force detachment" to each coded destination. Nimitz underlined that phrase in the message with his pencil and may well have wondered just what an "appropriate" force was. Apparently that was left to his discretion. Once the base was occupied, Nimitz had to supervise the dredging of channels, the construction of harbor facilities, the building of airstrips, and the laying of protective mine fields.[12]

Orders to send troop convoys to these outposts originated in Washington, and Nimitz received periodic instructions from King to "arrange for protection from San Francisco." Often those orders arrived on short notice and Nimitz's harried staff had to scramble to find suitable escorts. Occasionally the orders were modified in mid-execution. King initially ordered Nimitz to

---

† The number of coded locations eventually grew to several thousand, from Aaron to Zootsuit. A comprehensive list prepared by the Office of Naval History in 1948 is available online as "Glossary of U.S. Naval Code Words," thanks to the curators of the HyperWar site, at https://www.ibiblio.org/hyperwar/USN/ref/USN-NAVEXOS_P-474.html.

develop Suva in Fiji as an "advance operating base." Then, only days later, he cited the "pressure of events" in ordering him to disregard Suva and instead develop Nouméa in New Caledonia. Diplomatically, Nimitz asked King, "insofar as possible," to keep him advised about "plans for south sea bases with advance information," though that was not always possible. Indeed, the orders came in with such frequency throughout the early spring that on March 12, the Running Summary considered it noteworthy to record the fact that "nothing was heard from COMINCH today."[13]

A complicating factor in the development of these new Pacific bases was the role played by the commander of the 14th Naval District, Rear Admiral Claude C. Bloch, who was the administrative commander of the district that included the Hawaiian Islands as well as Midway, Wake, and Johnston Islands. As CinCPac, Nimitz had commanded the ships while Bloch supervised the bases from which those ships operated. Now that Nimitz was CinCPOA as well as CinCPac, he commanded everything, and that made Bloch's role somewhat ambiguous. Their relationship was further complicated by the fact that although Bloch was a rear admiral, he had previously served as CinCUS with four stars, and he had graduated from the Naval Academy six years ahead of Nimitz. At one point in 1937, when Nimitz was commanding Battleship Division One, he had served directly under Bloch. Now Bloch was issuing orders affecting places in his district without consulting or even informing Nimitz.[14]

That was serious enough and was further complicated by the fact that Bloch's perspective on the war was different from Nimitz's. He had opposed the raid into the Gilberts and Marshalls on the grounds that the United States could not afford to risk its carriers. Rather than push the American defensive perimeter outward, as King and Nimitz wanted to do, he sought to contract it. After Nimitz issued orders to construct airfields on Palmyra and Johnston Islands, he was shocked to learn that Bloch had countermanded the orders. Bloch's reasoning was that the Japanese were probably going to seize both of those islands anyway, so why build airfields there?[15]

Nimitz might have pulled rank and ordered Bloch to toe the line. Instead, he invited Bloch to a discussion of Pacific strategy with his staff. There, he outlined King's vision of occupying and developing new bases

Rear Admiral Claude Bloch was the highest-ranking Jewish officer in the U.S. armed forces. During his tenure as CinCUS from 1938 to 1940, he had worn the four stars of a full admiral, though as 14th Naval District commander in 1942 he wore only two. (U.S. Navy photo)

across the Pacific both as a defensive barrier to continued Japanese expansion and as jumping-off points for an eventual American counteroffensive. He then asked the group how they could best execute that vision. By inviting Bloch's input, Nimitz effectively co-opted him, and instead of being an obstructionist, Bloch became a partner in base development. Nimitz thus quietly defused a potentially awkward situation. Within a few weeks, likely at Nimitz's suggestion, King solved the problem entirely by transferring Bloch out of Hawaii and into semi-retirement on the General Board.[16]

In addition to sending "service detachments" to the outposts designated by King and managing the physical improvements, Nimitz also had to "arrange local command relations" (King's term) with the political authorities. Sometimes that proved relatively easy. New Zealand's government, for example, readily granted Nimitz "full and free use of existing facilities" (its naval bases and airfields) for the duration of the war. Indeed, New Zealand authorities were so eager to cooperate, they willingly stipulated that the United States could exercise legal jurisdiction over American military personnel in New Zealand, effectively exempting them from local laws. On Fiji, Nimitz's main problem was adjudicating disputes between the U.S. Army and Navy. Though Nimitz exercised direct command over both services at all these outposts, there were still limits to his authority. King insisted that any transfer of forces from one island to another "must have the OK of the Army or Navy Department." In the margin of that message, Nimitz scrawled a note: "In spite of unity of command." It was a rare but telling glimpse of his frustration.[17]

Nimitz confronted a far more complex set of problems concerning the French. When France fell to the German blitzkrieg in 1940, the terms of capitulation included the establishment of a technically independent though greatly reduced France with a government based in the spa town of Vichy. Technically, the Vichy government was neutral in the war and maintained nominally friendly relations with the United States until 1942. Everyone knew, however, that Vichy France existed only at the sufferance of the Germans, and the Allies deemed it little more than a puppet state.

According to the Franco-German agreement, the Vichy government exercised authority over French colonies worldwide, including those in the Pacific. Not all Frenchmen accepted that. On the island of New Caledonia (Nouvelle-Calédonie), the Colonial Assembly voted unanimously to renounce the Vichy government and adhere to the Free French movement led by Brigadier General Charles de Gaulle.

U.S. relations with de Gaulle were also complicated. Like many Frenchmen, de Gaulle felt a deep humiliation after the 1940 defeat and was extremely sensitive to perceived slights. He was determined that the Anglo-Americans should treat him as the head of an allied government, a full partner to Roosevelt and Churchill. He sent his own representatives to govern French colonies overseas, and for New Caledonia he chose a one-time Carmelite priest named Georges Thierry d'Argenlieu. The former priest had gained notoriety after a daring escape from a German POW train, and de Gaulle had rewarded him by making him a French admiral, though because the French Navy remained under the control of the Vichy government he was an "admiral" with only one vessel: the small (600-ton) minesweeper *Chevreuil*. Like de Gaulle, d'Argenlieu's primary goal in New Caledonia was to ensure full respect for French independence and due deference to French authority. That was the political landscape when American Major General Alexander "Sandy" Patch showed up there with orders from Nimitz to transform Nouméa into an American base.[18]

In the immediate aftermath of the Japanese seizure of Rabaul, the residents of Nouméa had feared they might be next and pleaded for American support. By March, the initial panic had subsided and D'Argenlieu was now at least as fearful of American imperialism as he was of Japanese invasion. When on March 12 a flotilla of gray-hulled U.S. Navy ships carrying American soldiers entered Nouméa Harbor, most of the local residents welcomed them enthusiastically, but d'Argenlieu saw it as evidence of an American plot "to supplant French authority." He also suspected, without foundation, that the French civilian governor, Henri Sartot, was colluding with the Americans in that ambition, and he urged de Gaulle to recall the governor. Ever sensitive to a possible slight, de Gaulle backed d'Argenlieu and ordered Sartot to report to him in London, where de Gaulle had established his government in exile. The recall of their popular governor provoked a general strike by the citizens in Nouméa; swiftly recalibrating his fears, d'Argenlieu now asked Patch to land his soldiers to suppress the strike. Patch appealed to Nimitz: what should he do? Aware that this was at least as much a political issue as a military one, Nimitz referred it all to Washington.[19]

King had no patience for diplomacy. Nouméa's harbor was critical to his plans both to defend Australia and to prepare an eventual offensive. He thought d'Argenlieu was a "devious and surreptious [*sic*]" troublemaker and suggested that Patch place him "under protective custody"—that is, arrest him. The other members of the Joint Chiefs were more restrained, and the Roosevelt administration wanted no more confrontation with de Gaulle than necessary. Perhaps prodded by the president, King sent Nimitz conflicting, if not contradictory, orders. He was to exercise "all due tact and understanding" in dealing with the French, but "without in any way lessening the attainment of matters essential to the conduct of the war." Meanwhile, the administration in Washington reached out to Harold Stark to appeal directly to de Gaulle.[20]

The self-styled leader of the Free French, which he preferred to call the "Fighting French" (Français de combat), was his usual touchy self. He told Stark that the general strike in Nouméa had not begun until the Americans arrived, implying that it was the American presence and not d'Argenlieu's expulsion of the popular governor that had caused the problem. De Gaulle refused to send Sartot back to New Caledonia, appointing another governor, Auguste Montchamp, whom he instructed to resist American imperialism. Meanwhile, the people of Nouméa took to the streets, storming the radio station to demand Sartot's return. At Nimitz's headquarters, the Running Summary noted drily, "The actions of the French in the South Pacific leave much to be desired."[21]

It fell to Nimitz to manage this mini-crisis. He told Patch to reach an accommodation with the French if possible, but authorized him to declare martial law if necessary. In the end, Patch successfully circumvented d'Argenlieu by prevailing upon Montchamp to request American help in restoring order. D'Argenlieu continued to assert that "civil administration will be carried out by a resident designated by me." Nimitz declared that "unsatisfactory" and told Patch to ignore d'Argenlieu's demand. Appreciating that he was playing a weak hand, D'Argenlieu capitulated.[22]

In addition to New Caledonia, King also ordered Nimitz to occupy other French outposts, including the tiny island of Wallis (code name Strawboard). D'Argenlieu accepted the need for such a move, though he insisted that he, and not the Americans, must take the lead. Once again, de Gaulle backed him up, thereby causing delays that were both embarrassing and potentially dangerous. His patience wearing thin, Nimitz engineered a compromise. D'Argenlieu's minesweeper, flying a large French flag but escorted by an American invasion force, would lead an expedition to Wallis Island. There, d'Argenlieu would invite the Americans to land in order to protect the island from the Japanese. The scripted occupation went off as planned on May 27. No shots were fired, no one was arrested, and while the French flag flew over the island, American Seabees got to work turning it into an Allied base. D'Argenlieu wrote Nimitz to thank him for "your excellent plan for the rallying of the Island of Wallis to the Free French."[23]

That was not quite the end of it. After monitoring the broadcasts from Nouméa's radio station, Patch complained to Nimitz that he could not guarantee "either the loyalty or the judgment" of the French radio operators and asked Nimitz's permission to take over the radio station at Nouméa as well as those on Wallis and Bora Bora. King told him to go ahead and do it, which outraged de Gaulle. He would accept censorship, he said, but only by Frenchmen, and he would not allow the Americans to "completely control" the radio stations. He ordered d'Argenlieu "to keep under your control the radio stations of territories placed under your authority." There was even some loose talk about opening fire on the Americans if necessary.[24]

It never came to that. In a lengthy conversation with de Gaulle in London, Stark got the French general to allow U.S. forces to run the radio stations as long as censorship was carried out by Frenchmen.[25]

BY APRIL 1942, NIMITZ HAD CONSOLIDATED his vast new command. He had reorganized his staff and replaced those task force commanders he had found wanting. He did not fire them; he found them new jobs more suited to their talents. He had supervised the occupation of half a dozen island bases in the Central and South Pacific while negotiating with three foreign governments. He had adjudicated disputes between the Army and Navy and defused potential problems with touchy Frenchmen. And he had done it while avoiding an open confrontation with his imperious superior, Ernest J. King. Though his resources remained limited, especially in shipping, he had a fully functioning Pacific command headed by officers he knew and trusted. It was time to get on with the war.

During his first weeks in command, Nimitz met scores of junior- and middle-grade officers, many of whom were previously unknown to him. Many were career officers who had been preparing all their adult lives to command a ship at sea in wartime—the ultimate goal of all their training. Now the moment had come, and one by one they came to him to request transfers to sea duty. As far as Nimitz was concerned, that was exactly as it should be. Before he left Washington, he had urged other senior commanders to assign reserve officers to administrative duties so that the regulars could go to sea.

One regular who came to see him now was Lieutenant Commander Edwin Layton, who had been Kimmel's intelligence officer. A nondescript-looking officer with dark curly hair and owlish glasses, Layton had spent much of his professional life examining and evaluating Japanese language and culture, rotating between sea duty and intelligence work. As Kimmel's intelligence chief, he had naturally faced intensive questioning from the team that investigated the Pearl Harbor disaster. Having satisfied his inquisitors, he was now eager to go back to sea, and he took his request directly to Nimitz. His preference, he told the new fleet commander, was to command a destroyer.

Nimitz sympathized with the request. Were he a thirty-eight-year-old lieutenant commander, he might have asked for a destroyer himself—or more likely a submarine. But destroyer commanders were plentiful—more plentiful, in fact, than destroyers; intelligence officers who could speak and read Japanese and who had a nuanced understanding of Japanese culture were extraordinarily rare. As much as he empathized with Layton's eagerness, Nimitz told him he was needed at headquarters. Layton remembered him saying: "You can kill more Japs here than you could ever kill in command of a destroyer flotilla." Layton acquiesced, and it was a consequential decision, for he would prove to be a key member of the staff.[1]

Nimitz instructed Layton to report to him every morning at 8:00 in advance of the staff meeting at 9:00. Nimitz told him that his job was to channel the thinking of the Japanese high command. Layton recalled him as saying, "I want you to be the Admiral Nagumo on my staff," though of course the man Nimitz really needed Layton to channel was not Nagumo but the commander of the Japanese Combined Fleet, Isoroku Yamamoto. Nimitz put it this way: "You are to see the war, their operations, their aims, from the Japanese viewpoint and keep me advised about what you are thinking about, what you are doing, and what purpose, what strategy, motivates your operations."[2]

It was from Layton that Nimitz learned about Station Hypo.

ACROSS THE ARM OF SOUTHEAST LOCH from Nimitz's headquarters at the submarine base was a bland stucco building that housed the headquarters of the 14th Naval District, where Claude Bloch presided. At each end of the building was an outside set of stairs leading to the second floor. Tucked under the right-hand stairwell was an unmarked door that led to a basement. No sign identified it; no guard stood watch. Yet that stairwell led down to three rooms—known as "the dungeon"—that housed the most secret organization in the United States Navy. This was Station Hypo, the

Lieutenant Commander Edwin "Eddie" Layton was Nimitz's intelligence officer.
During 1942, he played an important role as the liaison between Nimitz and Lieutenant
Commander Joseph Rochefort, who presided over the codebreakers at Station Hypo.
(U.S. Navy photo)

phonetic designation for the letter "H," derived from the radio receiving station at He'eia on the north shore of Oahu. At He'eia, coded Japanese radio
messages were pulled out of the air, transcribed, and then sent to Station
Hypo, where a team of officers led by Lieutenant Commander Joseph
Rochefort tried to winkle some meaning out of them.

There were hundreds of messages every day, the vast majority of them
routine and of little consequence. Only a fraction could be subjected to analysis at all, and from those, only tiny bits of information could be decrypted.
Most yielded nothing. Nevertheless, Rochefort and his team kept at it,
day after day and generally well into the night, and Rochefort passed on to
Layton whatever nuggets of intelligence he found, often adding his own
analysis of what it meant.

Layton and Rochefort were longtime friends. In the early 1930s, they had spent two years together in Japan, primarily to study the language but also absorbing as much about Japanese culture as they could. As Nimitz had pointed out, it was expertise that few others in the U.S. Navy had. Now, a decade later, Rochefort shared with Layton both the raw data and his take on it, and Layton brought that with him when he briefed Nimitz each morning. Almost immediately, Nimitz appreciated that while the information was often sketchy, it was not to be taken lightly and could prove invaluable.

Nimitz became convinced of the value of Rochefort's analysis early on. In mid-January, a week before Halsey and Fletcher conducted the raid into the Gilbert and Marshall Islands, Layton had told Nimitz that Rochefort had noticed that much of the recent Japanese message traffic contained the Japanese character for the letter "R." Rochefort was pretty sure this was a reference to Rabaul. Moreover, Rochefort observed that the *pattern* of Japanese messages showed "a steady decline in enemy activity in the Marshalls." Rochefort concluded that Japan's focus on Rabaul meant that she had pulled her principal striking forces away from the Marshalls and Gilberts. That encouraged Nimitz to radio Halsey, who was already at sea, to extend his attack beyond a single day if he saw an opportunity to do so. It was the first time Nimitz issued orders based on Rochefort's input. It would not be the last.[3]

The Rochefort-Layton-Nimitz protocol worked well, but it also short-circuited the chain of command. Officially, Rochefort's reporting senior was not Layton, or even Nimitz; it was Captain John R. Redman, the Director of Signals Intelligence in Washington, D.C. Redman happened to be the younger brother of the Director of Naval Communications, Rear Admiral Joseph R. Redman. Rochefort was supposed to send the results of his decryption efforts to the younger Redman, whose team would collate them with input from other sources, including Station Cast in the Philippines, so that a comprehensive intelligence estimate could be developed.*

---

* Station Cast, originally at Cavite Navy Yard in the Philippines, moved first to Corregidor, and then to Melbourne, Australia, where it became Belconnen and then FRUMel (Fleet Radio Unit, Melbourne).

Though the Redman brothers had more sources of information, they lacked Rochefort's keen instinct as an analyst and in particular his ability to find a larger meaning in the tiny fragments of decrypted messages. As Redman read the clues in February 1942, for example, he decided that the Japanese might be preparing another offensive in the Central Pacific. He reported this to King, who bombarded Nimitz with a series of messages warning of imminent Japanese threats to "Midway, Oahu, New Hebrides, NE Australia, and possibly [the] West Coast of [the Panama] Canal." Nimitz shared these warnings with Layton, who responded that Hypo had found no evidence of any such thing.[4]

Nimitz took all the warnings seriously, of course, though they often turned out to be false alarms. In early March, King notified Nimitz to expect a Japanese carrier attack on the eleventh. Nimitz dutifully alerted the fleet despite the fact that Layton and Rochefort reported that all of Japan's carriers were in the South Pacific. They were proven correct when March 11 passed with no sign of a Japanese offensive. Still, the alarms continued. Layton found them annoying. "Admiral King was breathing down our necks," he recalled later. "Hardly a day passed without some chivvying message."[5]

The Japanese remained active. In the pre-dawn darkness of March 4, two bombs exploded on the slopes of Mount Tantalus behind Honolulu. Though they did no damage, it was obvious that the Japanese had somehow managed to send aircraft over Oahu without being detected. Layton suggested that they might have done it using long-range seaplanes from the Marshall Islands that were refueled by submarines en route. If so, the most likely rendezvous site was the unoccupied atoll of French Frigate Shoals, located five hundred miles to the northwest, halfway between Oahu and Midway. He was exactly right, and to prevent a repeat of such a stunt, Nimitz ordered the USS *Ballard*, a modified destroyer serving as a seaplane tender, to occupy French Frigate Shoals. That paid dividends two months later when the Japanese sought to conduct a reconnaissance of Pearl Harbor prior to the Battle of Midway and were unable to do so because of the presence of the *Ballard*.[6]

The Army was another source of occasional warnings. On April 23, Marshall reminded Nimitz that April 29 was the emperor's birthday, and that he should be prepared for a Japanese offensive that day. A similar message from King arrived the next day. Again, Nimitz shared the messages with Layton as well as with members of his staff, all of whom were skeptical. The minutes of the meeting stated drily, "This does not agree with our estimate," and again the day passed with no enemy activity. The Running Summary noted, "According to our dope this alert was premature, and so it proved."[7]

Alerts could be evaluated, but directives from Washington were harder to finesse. In mid-March, King ordered Nimitz to keep Halsey available to fly to the West Coast "for a conference." The reason behind this enigmatic message became evident soon enough when just days later, Captain Donald Duncan, King's Air Operations Officer, arrived in Pearl Harbor to brief Nimitz on a plan that had been cooked up in Washington.[8]

FROM ALMOST THE DAY THE WAR BEGAN, both Roosevelt and King had sought some way to retaliate against Japan for the Pearl Harbor attack, mostly for the sake of public morale. The question was how. A direct carrier attack was too risky. Though a Japanese carrier force had successfully crossed the North Pacific in December without being seen, doing so in a time of open warfare was improbable. The American task force would have to steam three thousand miles undiscovered, get to within roughly two hundred miles of Japan's coast, launch its planes, and then wait there for several hours until the planes returned. It was simply too dangerous.

The Joint Chiefs backed a plan to bomb Japan with U.S. Army bombers flying from airfields in China. The logistics of that, however, proved insurmountable. First, the bombers had to fly to airfields in China on a roundabout route—from Hawaii to Australia, across the Indian Ocean to India, and then over the Himalayas. An even bigger problem was maintaining a reliable supply line of spare parts and especially fuel along that same route. The plan called for the delivery of 4,000 tons of fuel per month, yet the planes that were to deliver that fuel burned up seven gallons of gas for every gallon they delivered.[9]

Duncan had come to Hawaii to brief Nimitz on a plan to fly *Army* bombers off of *Navy* carriers. With their longer range, the Army bombers could launch while the carriers were still five hundred miles off Japan's coast, drop their bombs, and then continue westward to land on Chinese airfields. As soon as the planes launched, the carriers could turn around and speed back eastward to be safely out of range before the first bomb fell.

Duncan assured a skeptical Nimitz that it was feasible; he had personally witnessed a B-25 taking off from the carrier *Hornet* off Norfolk. Nimitz did not doubt that it *could* be done, though he was less certain that it *should* be done, for it was a terribly inefficient use of scarce resources. Since one carrier would be loaded down with fifteen dual-engine Mitchell bombers, she would be unable to conduct regular flight operations, and a second carrier would have to accompany her to provide an air defense. In effect, half of Nimitz's total striking force in the Pacific would be committed to what Duncan candidly admitted was a morale-boosting mission. Nimitz would have only two carrier task forces left to fulfill all the other missions King had outlined. Nimitz did not need to explain any of that to King, who would already have taken it into consideration. So rather than raise objections, he sent for Halsey and asked Duncan to brief him on the project. When Duncan finished, Nimitz turned to Halsey and asked him if he thought it would work.

"They'll need a lot of luck," Halsey replied.

"Are you willing to take them out there?"

"Yes I am."

"Good!" Nimitz said. "It's all yours."[10]

Almost at once, the complicated machinery of war began to move: the brand-new *Hornet* got underway from Norfolk and headed south for a transit of the Panama Canal and a trip up to San Francisco Bay while the Army bombers, under the command of Lieutenant Colonel James "Jimmy" Doolittle, prepared to fly across country from Florida to Alameda Airfield to meet her. On April 2, the *Hornet*, loaded with sixteen Mitchell bombers (an extra plane had been added), headed out under the Golden Gate Bridge for a Pacific transit. Six days later Halsey's *Enterprise* task force left Pearl Harbor for a mid-ocean rendezvous with her north of Hawaii. Together with four cruisers, eight destroyers, and two fleet oilers, the combined task force headed west.

Once again Nimitz was compelled to wait for news. Nine days later on April 17 (April 18 Tokyo time), though there was "no dope yet from Halsey," as the Running Summary noted, commercial Japanese radio broadcasts reported air raids on several Japanese cities, including Tokyo.[11]

NIMITZ DID NOT SPEND THOSE NINE DAYS simply waiting for news. Even before the *Enterprise* departed to rendezvous with the *Hornet*, he was dealing with a new issue that was far more important than boosting morale. On April 5, Layton came to him with another tentative analysis from Rochefort. This time, Rochefort's team had discovered a different set of geographical identifiers that were repeated with increasing frequency in the Japanese message traffic. Instead of "R" for Rabaul, Rochefort noted the frequent use of the geographical designator "MO." He suspected at once that it referred to Port Moresby, a city on the south coast of New Guinea. He had concluded back in January that the Japanese were about to seize Rabaul, and now he decided that they were planning to invade Port Moresby. He called Layton on the scrambler telephone and told him that he had, as Layton recalled, "a hot one." "It looks like something is going to happen that the man with the blue eyes will want to know about."[12]

When Layton laid it out for him, it was evident to Nimitz that this was no sure thing. The main Japanese carrier force was then in the Indian Ocean, more than four thousand miles from Port Moresby, savaging British bases in Ceylon. Moreover, in addition to all those references to "MO," the radio intercepts also referred to "the RZP campaign." Rochefort believed that this, too, referred to Port Moresby. To confirm it, the Hypo team redoubled its efforts, comparing vague references in various messages with charts of the Coral Sea. Rochefort's team had already identified two Japanese carriers, *Kaga* and *Ryukaku*, as probable participants in the Port Moresby campaign, and now the British radio intelligence team at Colombo in Ceylon, recently bombed by the Japanese, chipped in with its assessment that it was also likely to involve their two newest carriers: *Shokaku* and *Zuikaku*. That led the codebreakers at Hypo to scan any message concerning those two ships.

The work went on around the clock, and on April 17 Layton told Nimitz that Rochefort and his team were now certain that the Japanese were planning to conduct an amphibious invasion of Port Moresby through the Coral Sea, that it could involve as many as four or even five enemy carriers, and that it would take place sometime in the last week of April or the first week of May.[13]

It was tantalizing to have advance intelligence of enemy intentions, but with Halsey's two carriers three thousand miles away and the *Lexington* in drydock in Pearl, where her 6-inch guns were being removed to make room for more anti-aircraft batteries, that left only Fletcher's *Yorktown* group, still on patrol in the Coral Sea, in a position to handle this new threat.

In spite of that, Nimitz saw as much opportunity as danger in the developing situation. He shared Hypo's analysis with his staff, and the notes from that meeting emphasized that it was unlikely they could send "enough force to be *sure* of stopping the Jap offensive." Since few things in war are *sure*, Nimitz ordered his staff to prepare a detailed "Estimate of the Situation" outlining the strengths of both sides and the options available. The resulting document covered thirty-six typewritten pages.

The Japanese strengths were self-evident: they would have more carriers, more battleships, more cruisers, and more destroyers. Their airplanes had a longer range than American planes, and their aerial torpedoes were "excellent." The principal American strength, thanks to Rochefort's codebreakers, was a "fairly accurate knowledge of [the] enemy advance." Most of the other factors were intangibles. The staff estimate listed the superior "resourcefulness and initiative" of the individual sailor as an American strength, though no doubt the Japanese made the same judgment about their personnel. The summary also touted "the undoubted superiority of much of our equipment," though that ignored the clear supremacy of Japanese torpedoes. Nevertheless, the staff assessment led Nimitz to conclude that he could "accept odds in battle if necessary."[14]

But should he? King's frequent reminders prioritized holding the Hawaii-Midway line, followed closely by the need to maintain the lines of communication to Australia. The central problem was how to respond to this new enemy move while maintaining those priorities. Nimitz cautioned his staff not to underestimate Japanese capabilities. They were "flushed with victory," and their attack on Pearl Harbor had been "a workmanlike job in every way." The staff report had concluded that "only bold and skillful action on our part" could prevent the Japanese from reaching Moresby. "Bold and skillful action" was exactly what Nimitz had in mind.[15]

First, he ordered the work on the *Lexington* accelerated, and he pressed King for permission to send her to the Coral Sea to join Fletcher as soon as possible. King was skeptical. Still hoping to find some way to employ the old battlewagons, he wanted the *Lexington* to remain near Hawaii to conduct maneuvers with the battleships. Only after it became evident that Halsey's two carriers would return safely from the Doolittle Raid did he allow Nimitz to order the *Lexington* to join Fletcher. In fact, Nimitz planned to send both of Halsey's carriers there, too, as soon as they returned. Sending all four of his carriers into the Coral Sea to meet a Japanese offensive that could include four or even five carriers was, in the words of historian John B. Lundstrom, "breathtakingly aggressive."[16]

At least as audacious was the fact that even if Halsey's TF 16 did *not* get back in time, Nimitz was prepared to accept battle in the Coral Sea with only two carriers. He radioed Fletcher to tell him that Fitch was on his way, and that the enemy force he was likely to confront "may eventually include three or four carriers." Nevertheless, he continued, "your task [will be] to assist in checking further advance by [the] enemy . . . by seizing favorable opportunities to destroy ships, shipping, and aircraft." He pointedly did not tell Fletcher to stop the invasion at all costs—that might lead him to rashness. Instead, Fletcher was to do what he could to weaken the Japanese force by attrition. Nor did Nimitz presume to tell Fletcher *how* to accomplish this. He outlined the objective and gave the on-scene commander as much information as he could. It would be up to Fletcher to decide how to use his two-carrier force and how much risk to accept.[17]

Nimitz knew that whatever success Fletcher might achieve depended heavily on his own ability to sustain him logistically. The ships needed fuel; the guns required ammunition; the men had to be fed. To do the first of those, Nimitz had seven fleet oilers, which he believed the minimum necessary to

Rear Admiral Frank Jack Fletcher employed both of his first names to distinguish himself from his uncle, Admiral Frank Friday Fletcher, who served during World War I and after whom the *Fletcher*-class destroyers were named. Frank Jack commanded U.S. naval forces in the first major carrier battle of the Pacific war in the Coral Sea, May 4–8, 1942. (Naval History and Heritage Command)

keep four carrier groups underway. There was no margin for error. The extent to which Nimitz had to manage these issues personally is evident from the message traffic. He calculated that the oiler *Kaskaskia*, which was already in the Coral Sea, could top off the *Yorktown* group with 30,000 barrels and still have 60,000 barrels left to service the *Lexington* when she arrived; then *Kaskaskia* could depart the area. The oiler *Tippecanoe* would stay as an "emergency reserve," and the high-speed *Neosho*, with a full load of 102,000 barrels, would keep both groups supplied. Since the combined task force burned 11,400 barrels of fuel a day, there should be enough for both carrier groups to operate for thirteen days, though if they got into a fight—which was, after all, the whole idea—the kind of high-speed maneuvering needed for launching and recovering planes (or avoiding attacks) would reduce that number significantly. Nimitz sent a detailed message to Fletcher outlining all this but left to him the timing of the refueling and, of course, the tactical details.[18]

HAVING SET THE WHEELS IN MOTION, Nimitz boarded a plane for the fifteen-hour flight from Pearl Harbor to California to meet face-to-face with King. After checking into the St. Francis Hotel, he joined King in the nearby Federal Building, which housed the offices of the 12th Naval District Headquarters. It was the first of sixteen such meetings between the two admirals during the war, and it was not a meeting of equals. To King, at least, it was an opportunity to inform his subordinate of global strategy, including the impact that European operations were likely to have on the Pacific Theater, and to instruct Nimitz about the hard decisions ahead. Nimitz, accepting his assigned role, listened carefully and spoke sparingly. Commander Walter Whitehill of King's staff, who was in the room for much of it, noted later that "King would speak right out, whereas Admiral Nimitz would frequently use some circumlocution to avoid saying unpleasant things." As Whitehill put it, Nimitz always "tried to smooth everything over and make things pleasant."[19]

The first issue on the agenda was the forthcoming operation in the Coral Sea. King expressed some "uneasiness" about it due in part to his uncertainty about Fletcher's suitability for command. Nimitz had more confidence in Fletcher than King did, and since the timetable did not allow a reconsideration of his assignment anyway, the issue was largely moot. Instead of aggressively defending Fletcher, therefore, Nimitz employed what Whitehill no doubt considered a "circumlocution" to suggest that they should wait "until more information is available." That initial discussion was a template for many of their subsequent conversations: King would identify an area of concern, and Nimitz would suggest that it might be best to see how things worked out, especially when it came to making decisions about replacing officers who, in King's opinion, were not performing up to expectations. That naturally confirmed King in his view that Nimitz was reluctant, as Whitehill put it, "to take proper and drastic action about officers whose accomplishment was not up to standard"—in other words, that Nimitz was not "a son of a bitch."[20]

Yet in considering developing events in the Coral Sea, it was Nimitz who exhibited a surprising boldness, for he planned to commit his entire carrier force to a battle with a superior enemy to defend an Australian outpost four thousand miles from Pearl Harbor. The information he had (thanks to Hypo) implied that the Japanese had ambitions beyond Port Moresby— that after capturing that outpost, they intended to move farther east to seize Nauru and Ocean Islands, perhaps even New Caledonia and Fiji. To confront that, Nimitz wanted Halsey to complete a swift turnaround in Pearl Harbor and get out to the Coral Sea as quickly as possible. It was not necessarily to help Fletcher defend Port Moresby—almost certainly he would be too late for that—but to confront the larger Japanese effort afterward. In that respect, Nimitz's plan was at least as much an offensive move as a defensive one. Moreover, Nimitz ordered all of the battleships back to the West Coast, partly to avoid having to supply them with fuel, but also simply to get them out of the way. King was noncommittal. Unwilling to embrace Nimitz's audacious plan, he told Nimitz only that he would consider it.[21]

They also discussed other issues. At one point, King suggested ridding Hawaii of "pessimists and defeatists," which included evicting Hawaiians of Japanese ancestry from the islands. Such a notion was fully in line with administration policy. Two months earlier, on February 19, Roosevelt had responded to alarmist warnings from former Chief Justice Owen Roberts, General John J. De Witt, and Secretary of War Henry L. Stimson, by signing Executive Order 9066 allowing regional commanders to remove "any or all persons" who could be considered a threat from coastal areas. De Witt had acted immediately, instituting a program that eventually relocated some 120,000 Japanese Americans from California and other western states, sending them to what amounted to concentration camps hundreds of miles inland. In March, FDR approved a recommendation to remove the Japanese population from Hawaii as well.[22]

Nimitz thought that was neither necessary nor desirable. It was not out of an enlightened concern for the civil rights of Japanese Americans; he simply recognized the practical limitations of such a policy. There were more Japanese Americans in Hawaii than in California; they could not be loaded onto trains for relocation, and the shipping needed to take them off the island did not exist. Nor, in his view, could Japanese Americans be rounded up and held in guarded camps, as some suggested. Besides, he told King, General Emmons did not consider them a threat. The best solution—indeed the only solution—was to keep a sufficient number of U.S. Army troops in the islands to ensure security. In the end, out of 158,000 Hawaiian residents of Japanese ancestry, only 1,875 were evicted from the islands, barely over 1 percent. It was not because of doubts about their loyalty. Rather, it was because, like American military dependents who were also sent stateside, these particular individuals did not play a critical role in the local economy.

Understandably, what Nimitz sought most in his meeting with King was clarification of his command authority. Sending Pye to Washington to discuss it had helped some, sensitizing King to Nimitz's concern. Yet recently the War Department had ordered Emmons to shift a number of long-range Army bombers from one Pacific outpost to another. Nimitz had not interfered with that order, but now he wanted to know if those bombers were or were not part of his command. King assured him that he had authority "to direct movements of Army troops and planes" within his theater, and he promised to bring the issue up with Marshall at the next meeting of the Joint Chiefs.

King brought up public relations, particularly as they related to Douglas MacArthur. Along with the rest of the Joint Chiefs, King had grown concerned and annoyed by the torrent of "communiqués" that issued almost daily from MacArthur's headquarters, all of which emphasized MacArthur's centrality in the direction of the war. In most of them MacArthur's was the only name included. Nimitz assured King that he preferred to supply the Navy Department with whatever information he had and let Washington decide what should be released to the public. That genuinely reflected Nimitz's preference and his command philosophy. Still, he also knew it was the answer King wanted to hear.

The two admirals also sought to prepare for future events. Before Nimitz had left Hawaii for San Francisco, Layton told him that Rochefort had found hints in the message traffic that the Japanese were planning to change their codes on or about May 1. That could be a routine update, of course, though it could also signal another Japanese offensive, one that would follow their planned assault on Port Moresby. King asked about the security of Midway, and Nimitz told him that Midway was safe against any kind of hit-and-run raid, but that a serious and sustained attack would require him to commit the fleet. King told him that they could at least send additional anti-aircraft batteries there. Nimitz agreed to look into it.[23]

As Whitehill had noted, Nimitz seldom confronted King directly, especially on issues of minor importance. Instead, he saved his ammo for bigger issues, such as his plan to confront the Japanese in the Coral Sea. Years before, when his son, Chet, was freshly commissioned, the younger Nimitz had asked his father how to deal with a bullying superior. Chet recalled his father telling him that a "frontal attack" was seldom effective. Instead, he told Chet, he should "continue to be extraordinarily polite, and don't reveal to him your purpose, and at all times be slowly removing the rug from under him." While Nimitz never pulled the rug from under King, he did occasionally employ a kind of quiet subversion. As an example of that, one of King's more curious enthusiasms was an effort to replace the Navy's khaki uniforms with a nondescript gray uniform, which he thought more in keeping with the deadly seriousness of winning the war. Nimitz hated it. He thought the gray uniforms made officers look like bus drivers and enlisted men like sanitation workers. King's new regulation allowed everyone to continue to wear khakis until the supply was exhausted, and Nimitz simply made sure the supply of khaki uniforms never ran out. It caused an occasional kerfuffle when a newly commissioned officer arrived in Hawaii with a full set of gray uniforms only to discover that no one in the Pacific theater wore them. Even King suffered a moment of embarrassment when, on leaving the Federal Building in San Francisco after one of their meetings, he and Nimitz were met by a gaggle of photographers jostling one another for a picture. One of them, seeing King in his gray uniform, told him, "Get out of the way, Chief, I want to get a picture of Admiral Nimitz."[24]

NIMITZ FLEW BACK TO PEARL HARBOR on April 28. Halsey had arrived there three days earlier with his two carriers, and his ships were already engaged in resupply. Nimitz talked with him at length, explaining the circumstances and his broader objectives in the Coral Sea. Halsey and his two-carrier task force were back at sea two days later on April 30. The next day, Nimitz climbed into an airplane for the lengthy flight out to Midway to assess the situation there.

Upon landing, he was taken aback by the virtual carpet of birds covering the island like a feathered blanket. It was the mating season of the Laysan albatross, known locally as gooney birds, and there were literally millions of them. They were so ubiquitous that to walk from place to place, Nimitz wrote to Catherine, he had "to push them out of the way" with his feet. Moreover, the cacophony of their ululating mating call was deafening. He inspected the island's defenses, awarded some medals, and conferred with the local commanders, staying all afternoon and well into the night. He wrote Catherine that he was "greatly pleased at the high morale & esprit found among the Marines and Navy men." He left the island at 4:00 a.m. and was back in his office that afternoon.[25]

Soon afterward, Hypo intercepted a Japanese message reporting that their seaplane base at Tulagi in the Solomon Islands was under air attack. Fletcher had landed a blow. That was confirmed only hours later when Fletcher broke radio silence to report that planes from the *Yorktown* had attacked Japanese shipping. The pilots reported that they had "positively sunk" two destroyers and five transports, "beached and sunk" a light cruiser, and "badly damaged" four other ships. Once again, the pilots had overestimated the effect of their attack; the strike had claimed only one destroyer and three minesweepers. Nimitz knew by now that most damage reports were inflated, yet he took solace in the thought that, whatever the result, the strike had provided valuable combat training. So far, his gamble was proving fruitful. It was enough, he wrote to Catherine, that "we have inflicted damage and received little in return." The main confrontation with the Japanese invasion force and the carriers covering them was still to come. He told Catherine that he hoped for "more and better news" soon. "You may read about it in the papers in a few days."[26]

O N MAY 5, NIMITZ ENCOURAGED HIS STAFF TO GO HOME EARLY. Get a good night's sleep, he told them, because the next day (May 7 in the Coral Sea west of the International Date Line) was likely to be especially busy.

That day, however, began pretty much as usual. Layton had little to report at the 8:00 a.m. briefing, and the minutes of the subsequent staff meeting noted only, "Fletcher and Fitch should be in position now." By the time the meeting ended, it was full daylight in the Coral Sea. And still nothing. Nimitz forwarded to Fletcher whatever new pieces of information Hypo provided, though he knew that Fletcher, observing radio silence, could not respond or even acknowledge it.[1]

Staff members set up a plotting table of sorts at headquarters by laying a large piece of plywood across two supports and attaching a chart of the Coral Sea. On top of the chart, they placed a thin sheet of tracing paper so they could track the movements of the ships on both sides using a blue pencil for U.S. forces and orange for the Japanese. There was a lot of uncertainty about where to put those marks. U.S. Army bombers flying from Australia reported seeing several enemy ships, though none of their sightings could be confirmed. Nimitz consulted the plotting table periodically, but information remained sketchy. One piece of news that did arrive was that three thousand miles farther west, in the Philippines, General Jonathan Wainwright had been forced to surrender. He had tried to limit his capitulation to the forces on Corregidor, but the Japanese insisted that the surrender include all Filipino and American forces in the islands, threatening to punish Allied POWs if it did not.[2]

In midafternoon, Layton brought Nimitz an intercepted report from a Japanese scout plane pilot who reported sighting an American carrier. That was worrisome because it suggested that the Japanese might get in the first strike. The Japanese pilot reported the coordinates of the sighting, and the staff in Pearl Harbor marked the spot on the tracing paper. It was immediately evident that this could not be Fletcher. The coordinates were, however, very close to where the oiler *Neosho* and its escorting destroyer, *Sims*, were loitering. This was both good news and bad news. It meant that the Japanese had not yet found Fletcher's task force. It also meant that the *Neosho* was in dire peril of an imminent air strike, and her loss would severely damage American logistical capabilities. Oilers were scarce and the *Neosho* was a "fast oiler," which were even scarcer. Soon enough, news arrived that Japanese planes had indeed attacked the *Neosho* and the *Sims*. According to initial reports, both ships were sunk, though the *Neosho* actually stayed afloat for several days, buoyed by her mostly empty fuel tanks, and that allowed the U.S. destroyer *Henley* to rescue most of her crew before she finally succumbed on May 11. Given the carefully calculated fuel needs of Fletcher's command, that was "a hard blow," as the Running Summary put it, though of course it could have been worse.[3]

Finally, late in the afternoon (midday in the Coral Sea), Fletcher broke radio silence to report that planes from his two carriers had sunk the Japanese aircraft carrier *Ryukaku*. The news came as a great relief and provoked a general celebration at headquarters. In fact, the carrier the American pilots had sunk was the *Shōhō*, though Nimitz would not learn

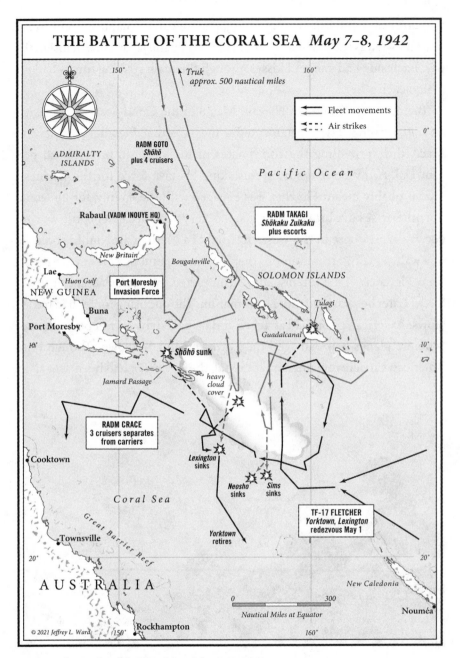

Map 5: The Battle of the Coral Sea, May 7–8, 1942

that until later. It hardly mattered. A Japanese carrier had been sent to the bottom—it was the first major combatant vessel the Japanese had lost in the war. Each side had suffered losses, though the main striking forces had yet to find each other.[4]

The next day (May 7 in Hawaii; May 8 in the Coral Sea) was decisive. At midmorning, Hypo intercepted a message that Fletcher had sent to MacArthur, providing the coordinates of his location, probably to prevent U.S. Army bombers from mistaking his task force for the Japanese. That probably meant Fletcher was engaged with the enemy, for he would not otherwise have broken radio silence. Very likely, a carrier battle was underway somewhere in the western Coral Sea, though all Nimitz could do was wait. Finally, around noon, there was a hopeful but enigmatic report from Fletcher: "First enemy attack completed, no vital damage [to] our force." Later he provided more information. The opposing forces had traded blows: American pilots had attacked and damaged the carrier *Shōkaku*, and Japanese planes had damaged the *Lexington* and *Yorktown*. Though both American carriers remained operational, the *Lexington* had been especially

The Japanese light carrier *Shōhō* in its death throes in the Coral Sea on May 4, 1942. It was initially reported as the *Ryukaku*, and it was some time before Nimitz learned that it was, in fact, the *Shōhō* that Fletcher's planes had sunk. When he saw her go down, the commander of the *Lexington*'s scouting squadron, Lieutenant Commander Robert Dixon, famously reported, "Scratch one flattop." (U.S. Naval Institute)

hard hit. Fletcher reported that he was "retiring to the south." His plan was to transfer planes from the wounded *Lexington* to the *Yorktown* and send the *Lex* back to Pearl for repairs. Here was Nimitz's opportunity to assume operational oversight: either to affirm Fletcher's decision to retire or order him to stay and fight it out. Consistent with his determination not to second-guess his operational commanders, he sent Fletcher a brief message congratulating him on his "glorious achievements." No orders, no suggestions, no advice, only praise.[5]

Then came what the Running Summary at headquarters labeled "distressing news." Fires burning out of control on the *Lexington* had ignited secondary explosions that compelled her commander, Captain Frederick C. "Ted" Sherman, to order abandon ship. By nightfall, one of the largest carriers in the U.S. Navy was gone, sent to the bottom, finally, by friendly torpedoes to prevent the Japanese from towing her off as a prize. Layton remembered that Nimitz was "visibly jolted" by the news. King, too, was deeply affected. Having once commanded the *Lexington* himself, her loss was both a strategic calamity and a personal blow.

There was some welcome news: Hypo intercepts revealed that the Japanese invasion convoy for Port Moresby had reversed course and was heading north. Only later did it become evident that the Japanese had called off the invasion of Port Moresby altogether. Though neither Nimitz nor anyone else knew it at the time, the aborted Japanese thrust into the Coral Sea marked the apogee of their conquests in the Pacific; future maps in textbooks would show the Japanese southern advance halting just short of Port Moresby. The price had been high, but Fletcher had fulfilled the mission that Nimitz had assigned him: "assist in checking further advance of the enemy."[6]

WHAT NOW? SHOULD NIMITZ IMPOSE HIS authority and tell Fletcher to stay in the Coral Sea and continue the fight with his single carrier? Halsey was approaching with both the *Enterprise* and the *Hornet*, and his arrival would give the Americans overwhelming local superiority as well as more aggressive leadership. On the other hand, Halsey could not arrive until May 11 at the earliest, and in the interim the Japanese might find the *Yorktown* and send her, like the *Lexington*, to the bottom. Nimitz decided to husband his carrier strength for future operations. While Halsey continued westward toward the Coral Sea, Nimitz authorized Fletcher to withdraw.[7]

Then he defended that decision in a lengthy message to King. The loss of the *Lexington* and the damage to the *Yorktown*, Nimitz told King, combined with the loss of eighty-one American aircraft, made retirement reasonable, especially since the strategic objective of halting the Japanese invasion had been achieved. It was a matter of calculated risk. The possibility of inflicting more damage on the enemy was not worth the chance of losing another carrier. Nimitz also recommended that Fletcher be promoted to vice admiral and awarded the Distinguished Service Cross.[8]

Predictably, King was not convinced. First, it was not clear to him that Fletcher had done everything he could to attain a decisive victory. He acknowledged to Nimitz that he was "not familiar with all the circumstances," but that it seemed to him Fletcher could have ordered his destroyers to conduct a night torpedo attack against the Japanese fleet after the air battle was over. Some on Nimitz's staff agreed. The Running Summary at headquarters for May 10 noted, "Cominch feels that destroyers should have been able to get in a night attack in the Coral Sea," which was followed by: "Fragmentary reports leads one to agree." When Nimitz read the summary, he crossed out that last sentence in pencil before he initialed it. Still, he felt obligated to follow up on King's query by asking Fletcher if he had considered a night destroyer attack on May 8.[9]

Fletcher, who was already heading eastward with the damaged *Yorktown*, replied in detail. He *had* considered such an attack, he wrote. What deterred him was the fact that he had previously sent a surface force of three cruisers and three destroyers under Australian Rear Admiral John G. Crace to watch the Jomard Passage, off the eastern tip of New Guinea— the most likely route for the Japanese invasion convoy. That meant he had only seven destroyers left to screen the task force.* Moreover, by the

---

* Fletcher's decision to detach Crace's surface force was the focus of much subsequent criticism. Doing so not only deprived his task force of additional anti-air support, but also subjected those surface ships to enemy air attack without air cover. Fletcher's explanation was that if his own carrier force was defeated in the forthcoming battle, he wanted something in place to challenge the invasion convoy headed for Port Moresby.

afternoon of May 8, those destroyers had less than 50 percent of their fuel capacity, and with the enemy more than 135 miles away it was not clear they had enough fuel for a round trip. Then, too, at 25 knots it would take them six hours to get there, which meant that even if their night attack were successful, they would have to return in daylight, when they would be vulnerable to Japanese air strikes. Finally, and decisively, after the *Lexington* went down, the destroyers had been needed to rescue the more than two thousand men of the *Lexington*'s crew who had been forced to abandon ship. By nightfall the destroyers were crowded with survivors; some had more than 300 percent of their complement on board. Fletcher later estimated that having the destroyers perform this duty had saved 92 percent of the *Lexington*'s personnel. Given all that, Fletcher had decided not to risk a night torpedo attack.[10]

Nimitz found Fletcher's answer conclusive. He reiterated to King "with added emphasis" his recommendation that Fletcher be promoted. Whether or not King was convinced, he did tell George Marshall that "on the whole we seem to have gotten the better of it" in the Coral Sea.[11]

King soon redirected his ire away from Fletcher to MacArthur, who in one of his ubiquitous "communiqués" took credit for the outcome of the battle by emphasizing the role that had been played by his land-based bombers. King was infuriated both by MacArthur's grandstanding, and because the role his Army bombers had played in the battle was far from clear. On May 7, while the carriers had slugged it out in the Coral Sea, Crace's surface force in the Jomard Passage had been attacked three times by land-based bombers. The first two attacks came from Japanese planes—first by torpedo planes and then by high-altitude bombers. The third attack came from *American* B-17s based in Townsville, Australia. Both the Japanese and American bomber crews reported substantial results. The Japanese claimed to have sunk a battleship and a cruiser and crippled a second battleship (though Crace had no battleships). For their part, the American pilots reported sinking or damaging a dozen ships. In fact, none of the bombers—on either side—had hit anything. MacArthur nonetheless issued a communiqué announcing that his bombers had turned back the Japanese thrust. When Admiral Leary pointed out to him that the B-17s had actually attacked *American* ships—and missed!—MacArthur not only denied it, he forbade anyone, including Leary, to say so either officially or privately.[12]

Given MacArthur's public claim, King asked Nimitz what role MacArthur's bombers had actually played in the fight. Nimitz was judicious in his reply. "Just how much the action of shore based striking groups and bases assisted Fletcher is indeterminate," he wrote, though he noted that "high altitude bombing against mobile targets" was generally ineffective. Nimitz did acknowledge that Army planes had reported the location of the Japanese battle group that included the *Shōhō*, which allowed Navy planes to find and sink her. Inter-service cooperation had worked on that occasion. Still, Nimitz suggested that relying on Army pilots to identify enemy ships from fifteen thousand feet was problematic. He suggested that King might ask Marshall about putting Navy spotters in Army bombers or, even better, allowing Navy aircrews to fly some Army bombers as long-range scout planes. King promised to get Nimitz more heavy and medium bombers of his own.[13]

Nimitz not only refrained from challenging MacArthur's claims, he made a point of sending him what amounted to a thank-you note: "I greatly appreciate the excellent cooperation furnished by your forces to Fletcher," he wrote. Not to be outdone in courtesy, MacArthur responded in kind, declaring that, in his opinion, Navy forces "were handled with marked skill and fought with admirable courage and tenacity." All that cordiality did not prevent MacArthur from defending his turf. A few weeks later, when he learned that Nimitz had sent a message to his Academy classmate Herbert Leary, who commanded "MacArthur's Navy," he was quick to pounce: "All dispatches pertaining to the coordination of any elements of my command should be addressed to CinC SouWesPac, which is my official designation." He pointedly reminded Nimitz that Leary was governed "by orders issued [by] this general headquarters." The message was signed simply "MacArthur." Nimitz immediately apologized, assuring the general, "I am taking steps to insure [*sic*] that it is well understood that dispatches pertaining to co-ordination of your forces are addressed to you."[14]

QUARRELS OVER PROTOCOL WERE A LOW priority for Nimitz that week; events were moving too swiftly. When Layton came in for his regular 8:00

a.m. briefing on May 10, only two days after the Battle of the Coral Sea, he reported that the Japanese were mustering yet another force composed of at least two and as many as four carriers, plus two battleships and substantial other forces. Rochefort believed the Japanese were preparing another operation that was likely to begin around the end of the month, three weeks away. The target of this new initiative, he said, was Midway.[15]

Layton's report changed Nimitz's thinking about what to do with the wounded *Yorktown*. Initially, he had concluded that it was "undesirable" to attempt making repairs at Pearl and told Fletcher that, like the *Saratoga*, the *Yorktown* should go to Puget Sound for a full refit. The new intelligence from Hypo, however, persuaded him to keep her at Pearl and attempt a local repair. King was skeptical. On May 14, he suggested the *Yorktown* should go to Puget Sound after all "in order to avoid exposure to attack." He also suggested that the air squadrons from both the *Yorktown* and the *Lexington* should be distributed to Allied land bases around the South Pacific where he expected the Japanese to make another offensive.

To Nimitz, that was a curious, not to say shocking, proposal. King had consistently pressed for more aggressive action, while Nimitz had tried to temper his expectations. Now the roles were reversed. In response, Nimitz argued at length that dispersing air groups to land bases was defensive and failed to take advantage of the special skills of carrier pilots. The best way to counter the new enemy initiative, he wrote, was to maintain "our striking forces in a state of maximum mobility to act against advancing enemy forces." If, as Nimitz hoped, the *Yorktown* could be repaired quickly, he planned to supplement her depleted air group with planes from the *Saratoga*, which was still in Puget Sound, and use her "as support for Halsey." King gave way, though he expressed his "regret [that] you prefer not to employ *Yorktown* and *Lexington* personnel ashore."[16]

To mount a credible defense of Midway, Nimitz would need not only the surviving planes and pilots from *Lexington* and *Yorktown*, but also both of Halsey's carriers, which had only just arrived on the eastern edge of the Coral Sea. To recall them, however, would violate King's requirement to keep a carrier force in the South Pacific to protect Australia and New Caledonia. If Nimitz pulled Halsey's carriers back to Midway prematurely, it would expose those places, as well as Nauru and Ocean Islands—located halfway between Australia and Hawaii—to a Japanese assault. On the other hand, if the end-of-the-month timetable predicted by Hypo was accurate and he waited until the Japanese objective became self-evident, it would be too late. As Nimitz wrote to King, "Distance and time . . . make it a fallacy to count on such reinforcement [only] after acute need arises."[17]

When Layton arrived the next morning (May 15) for his usual report, he told Nimitz that there was no longer any doubt that the target of the new Japanese offensive was Midway. The repeated appearance of the designator "AF" in Japanese messages was, in Rochefort's view, decisive. Yet later that same day Nimitz got a message from King arguing that while one target might *include* Midway, it could also be any one of a half dozen other places, "not only Port Moresby, but also either Northeast Australia or New Caledonia and Fiji." He suggested that Midway could be a diversion to disguise the real target in the South Pacific. If so, it would make Halsey's withdrawal from the South Pacific calamitous. King was reinforced in his uncertainty by the British, who reported that they had found no evidence at all of a Japanese offensive in the mid-Pacific. From London, Stark reported British doubts and asked King "on what you base your appreciation," a query that King passed on to Nimitz.[18]

Nimitz acknowledged that "there may well be three separate and possibly simultaneous offensives," including a second attempt at Port Moresby and another aimed at the Aleutians. Nonetheless, he believed a "major landing attack against Midway" was the principal Japanese objective and the one where "the enemy's main striking force will be employed." Because he did not have sufficient strength to oppose all three, Nimitz wrote, he planned to concentrate his forces for a defense of Midway.[19]

To do that, Nimitz employed an uncharacteristically devious gambit. Even before he got Layton's latest assessment, he sent an "eyes only" message to Halsey asking him to maneuver in such a way as to ensure that the Japanese discovered his presence. Dutifully, Halsey steamed to the northwest until he was inside the search area of Japanese planes from Tulagi. Sure enough, Hypo soon intercepted a Japanese message reporting the presence of a powerful American carrier force in the Coral Sea. Nimitz had two purposes in asking Halsey to do this. First, he hoped the news would deter the Japanese from their planned effort to seize Nauru and Ocean Islands, which it did. Nimitz could then use the fact that Halsey had been "discovered" to justify recalling him to Hawaii. It worked. News that the Japanese had reported Halsey's presence led King to lift the requirement that Halsey remain in the South Pacific. Nimitz immediately ordered him to return to Pearl Harbor—and to do so without being seen, if possible. He did not tell King that Halsey was on his way back until after he had arrived at Pearl Harbor.[20]

With Halsey en route, Nimitz outlined his plan to lay a trap for the enemy. At the May 18 staff meeting, he ordered every available airplane—as many as could be fitted onto Midway's small airfield—to fly to that atoll. He also ordered Commander Cyril T. Simard, who commanded the atoll, to initiate searches by long-range Catalina seaplanes with special attention to the northwest, and to continue those searches "until further orders." Third, aware that the Japanese were targeting the Aleutians, and unwilling that any American territory should go undefended, he ordered Rear Admiral Robert A. Theobald to head for Kodiak with a small force of cruisers and destroyers.[21]

Though the pending Japanese thrust at Midway dominated his thinking, Nimitz's job as CinCPOA made him responsible for the whole Pacific Theater, and he had to respond to demands and questions from a half dozen other places. He coordinated the evacuation of New Zealand forces from Fiji, who were then replaced by American GIs; he ordered the establishment of a seaplane base at Efate; and he pushed for a raid on Tulagi by a Marine Raider battalion. Aware that MacArthur was likely to object to the removal of Halsey's carriers from his theater, he reassured him that Crace's squadron, augmented by an additional heavy cruiser, would remain there. This was also the week when Nimitz choreographed the occupation of Wallis Island with the Free French. The Pacific was a giant spiderweb and Nimitz sat at its exact center, disposing of his limited resources in all directions while simultaneously assuaging rivals and fending off doubters and critics. Yet throughout the week, staff members noted that his steady composure never wavered.[22]

Meanwhile, word got back to Hypo that there was skepticism in Washington that Midway was indeed the primary target of the forthcoming Japanese offensive. In the dungeon, Rochefort told Lieutenant Jasper Holmes, one of the cryptanalysts, that they needed to do something to prove to the world that "AF" was Midway. Holmes, who was an engineer by training, suggested that they ask the radio station at Midway to send a message, in the clear, reporting that their salt-water evaporators had broken down. If the Japanese intercepted it and reported that "AF" was short of fresh water, they would have their evidence. Two days later, on May 21, Hypo intercepted a Japanese report that "AF" was short of drinking water. Rochefort waited to let the Allied radio stations in Australia and D.C. intercept the message and report it.[23]

Accepting at last that Midway was, indeed, the Japanese objective, King asked Nimitz to consider—again—making use of the American battleships to defend it. Nimitz responded that he had "given full consideration to employment of battleships in present situation" and that he remained "convinced" that the battleships should be "held in reserve on West Coast." What he really needed, he added, were more fighter planes to defend the carrier task forces.[24]

ALL OF NIMITZ'S PREPARATIONS WERE BASED on the assumption that an effective defense of Midway was even possible. The Japanese were approaching with four, or possibly five, carriers (Rochefort wasn't sure), and Nimitz had only two that were fully operational. *Saratoga* was scheduled to depart the West Coast on June 5. Given the steaming time to Hawaii, however, she would almost certainly arrive too late to take part. Halsey's two carriers would not return from the Coral Sea until May 26, and the *Yorktown* sometime after that. Even if all three arrived on time, and assuming it was possible for them to refuel and resupply in only a few days—no sure thing—they would still confront a superior force.

Nimitz might have reasonably concluded that risking three carriers to defend a tiny outpost of sand and coral against a superior enemy was not only unwise, but foolish. Defending Port Moresby had cost Fletcher the

Lexington. If Nimitz successfully defended Midway while losing two or more carriers, it would leave the Japanese masters of the Pacific.

Another factor was that if the Japanese did seize Midway, Nimitz knew they would have great difficulty holding it. Given its distance from Tokyo (2,200 miles), keeping it supplied would strain Japan's shipping resources to the breaking point. The long sea lines of communication could be assailed by American submarines and make Midway more of a burden to the Japanese than an asset. Letting them have Midway and then savaging their supply lines was arguably the smarter strategic move. Should Nimitz let Midway go by default to conserve his scarce carriers for more important things?

Nimitz concluded that the advantage provided by Rochefort's cryptanalysts could not be thrown away. It is difficult in hindsight to appreciate the boldness of that decision. Twenty years earlier, as a student at the Naval War College, Nimitz had written his thesis on naval tactics. In it, he argued that "great results cannot be accomplished without a corresponding degree of risk." "The leader who awaits perfection of plans, material, or training, will wait in vain," he wrote, "and in the end will yield the victory to him who employs the tools at hand with the greatest vigor." In the last week of May 1942, Nimitz staked everything on an unequal contest with the enemy's main battle fleet. It was a bold decision, but it was not reckless. Having carefully calculated the odds, assessed the circumstances, and considered the prospects, he decided to employ "the tools at hand with the greatest vigor."[25]

HALSEY'S TWO CARRIERS RETURNED ON SCHEDULE on May 26. When Halsey himself showed up at Pac Fleet headquarters, however, Nimitz was shocked by his appearance. He was haggard and worn; he had lost more than twenty pounds and his uniform hung loosely on his frame; his face and neck were covered in an angry-looking rash. Instantly sympathetic, Nimitz ordered him to the hospital. As it happened, Halsey would remain hospitalized for the next two months, first in Hawaii, then in Virginia. Nimitz had counted on Halsey's combination of aggressiveness and calculation to manage the American carrier force in the looming engagement. With

Halsey unavailable, Fletcher would be the senior officer afloat and in charge of the battle. And of course someone else had to be found to command Halsey's task force. Nimitz asked Halsey who that person should be. Having anticipated the question, Halsey immediately recommended that it should be the man who commanded his cruiser-destroyer screen: Rear Admiral Raymond A. Spruance.

Spruance was utterly unlike Halsey. He was composed, reserved, and self-disciplined to the point of asceticism. Nimitz had already decided to request Spruance as his new chief of staff, replacing Draemel, once the immediate crisis had passed. Unfortunately, Spruance, like Fletcher, was a black shoe—a ship driver. He did not wear the gold wings of an aviator (as Halsey did) or even the silver wings of a naval observer. Moreover, a senior aviator

Rear Admiral Raymond Spruance was a conscientious, introverted, and utterly unflappable naval officer. A surface warfare officer (a "black shoe," in the Navy vernacular), he was thrust into the command of Task Force 16 and its two carriers on the eve of a major battle. (U.S. Navy photo)

was available. In March, Rear Admiral Leigh Noyes had arrived in Pearl Harbor from Washington, where he had been Director of Communications. He had the requisite qualifications, including gold wings. But Noyes was new to the theater and a complete outsider to the officers and men of Task Force 16. He was also senior to Fletcher, which would have thrust him into overall command despite having no battle experience. And besides, Halsey's recommendation of Spruance was unstinting. Despite the stark differences in their personalities, Halsey and Spruance had been friends for years, and Halsey's recommendation was so effusive that Nimitz accepted it on the spot. He dispatched a staff officer to summon Spruance to meet him at the submarine base in Southeast Loch.[26]

Spruance got an inkling that something was afoot while en route to the *Enterprise* to make his report to Halsey. As his barge approached the bluff side of the big carrier, he was surprised to see that there were no visible preparations on board for his arrival and that Halsey's pennant was not flying. When he arrived—without ceremony—on the quarterdeck of the *Enterprise*, Halsey's aide ran up to him and told him breathlessly, "Admiral Halsey is in the hospital. They want to see you over at the Sub Base right away. You are probably going to have to take the task force out." There was a moment of silence and then Spruance replied, almost matter-of-factly, "Let's go to the sub base."[27]

When Spruance arrived, Nimitz confirmed what Halsey's aide had told him: he was to take command of Task Force 16 and proceed to sea as soon as the ships were replenished. Nimitz told him that he should leave his own staff behind and rely on Halsey's staff. Given Spruance's lack of experience in carrier command, Nimitz suggested that he should depend particularly on Captain Miles Browning, Halsey's chief of staff, who was an aviator. The *Yorktown* was expected imminently, Nimitz told him, and if it could be repaired in time, Fletcher would assume overall command of the combined force. Their mission, Nimitz said, was to intercept the Japanese carriers north of Midway and reduce its assets by attrition.[28]

There was more. Nimitz told Spruance privately that he was not to take any undue risks. All three American carriers would be committed to the battle, and if they were lost, the Japanese would have unchallenged control of the Pacific. Nimitz emphasized that he should not try to "slug it out" with them. He should instead rely on "the principle of calculated risk," using his judgment about just how much risk to accept. "If things go badly," he told Spruance, you should "withdraw and let them have the place because they can't hold it and we will get it back." Spruance listened quietly, acknowledged both the official orders and the private guidance, and left for the *Enterprise*.[29]

O N WEDNESDAY, MAY 27, 1942, Nimitz devoted the morning staff meeting to what the Running Summary described as "a general discussion of the Midway problem." Spruance was there along with General Emmons and Major General Robert C. Richardson, who represented George Marshall and the JCS. Nimitz had ordered Layton to be sure that Rochefort attended the meeting, too, so that he could present the latest information about Japanese plans. The meeting began, as usual, at 9:00 a.m. sharp, but Rochefort was not there. Finally, at 9:30, he hurried in clutching a sheaf of papers. He explained that he was late because he and his team had been busy collating information that was buried in a dozen different Japanese messages that had arrived the week before but which had defied decryption—until now. The result of their efforts, Rochefort said, "would explain everything."[1]

Nimitz was a stickler for punctuality. Still, he betrayed no annoyance or impatience at Rochefort's tardy arrival. Even so, twenty years later

Rochefort vividly remembered those cool blue eyes looking at him as he made his presentation. Rochefort told him and the rest of the room that the Japanese would commit four carriers to the attack, identifying each of them by name. They would approach from the northwest, he said, and he even predicted where they would be when they launched their planes. Nimitz asked how sure he was that the Japanese would have only four carriers. If they sent all six of their big carriers, the Americans would be outnumbered two to one, or three to one if the *Yorktown* could not be made battle ready. Rochefort insisted there would be only four; the damaged *Shōkaku* and the *Zuikaku* were both still in Japanese home waters.[2]

Nimitz allowed everyone to ask questions, then he outlined the plan. The two carriers of Task Force 16 under Spruance would depart first—the next morning, in fact—and assuming the *Yorktown* could be patched up, she would follow them as soon as possible. The two task forces would steam north separately and rendezvous at a point 350 miles north of Midway. It was to be an ambush. Maintaining radio silence, Fletcher and Spruance would monitor the reports from scout planes out of Midway, and once the enemy carriers were pinpointed, Fletcher and Spruance should time their attack to catch the Japanese aircraft returning from their strike on Midway. That would almost certainly be around midmorning on June 4. According to the Running Summary, Nimitz offered "a very clear explanation of the problem."[3]

After the meeting, Nimitz donned his dress white uniform to visit the *Enterprise.* The ship's company assembled on the flight deck for a ceremony in which Nimitz awarded medals to several fighter pilots who had helped fend off Japanese bombers during the raid on the Marshalls back in February. As Nimitz pinned the Distinguished Flying Cross on Roger Mehle, he looked him in the eye and said quietly, "I think you'll have a chance to do it again in a couple of days."[4]

THAT SAME AFTERNOON THE *YORKTOWN* LIMPED into the Pearl Harbor entrance channel one day ahead of schedule. Her crew had made ersatz repairs topside during the long voyage from the Coral Sea, including patching the hole in her flight deck, but she had suffered significant hull damage below

On board the *Enterprise* on May 27, 1942, Nimitz prepares to present the Distinguished Flying Cross to Lieutenant Roger Mehle (stepping forward) for his actions during the Marshalls raid. The man to Mehle's right in this photograph is Clarence Wade McClusky, who was destined to play a key role in the coming battle. The figure at far right is Navy cook Doris "Dorrie" Miller, who also received the Navy Cross that day for his heroic actions during the Japanese attack on December 7, 1941. (U.S. Navy photo)

the waterline from a number of near misses, and oil was still leaking from her fuel tanks. Nimitz was so eager to begin repairs, he waived the requirement that she discharge her aviation fuel before going into the drydock.[5]

Fletcher came in to make his report and Nimitz, no doubt concerned about losing another task force commander, asked him how he felt. Fletcher acknowledged that he was "pretty tired," which was only to be expected after more than a hundred days at sea and a major battle, and admitted that he was looking forward to a respite while the *Yorktown* underwent repairs. Reassured that Fletcher, though tired, was nevertheless fit, Nimitz broke the news: "We have to fix you up right away and send you out to Midway," he said, explaining what the codebreakers had learned of the Japanese plan.

To meet the new threat, Nimitz told him, the *Yorktown* had to be repaired quickly, making whatever short-term fixes were essential. Her ravaged air group would be brought up to strength with squadrons from the absent *Saratoga*, and she would go back to sea as soon as the interim repairs could be effected. Not only that, but because Halsey was in the hospital, Fletcher would be the senior officer in command during the forthcoming battle.[6]

That was a lot to absorb. And there was more. Nimitz knew that King remained skeptical about Fletcher's combat temperament, and he felt obligated to resolve some of the concerns that King had raised in San Francisco by questioning Fletcher about the action in the Coral Sea. As soon as Fletcher appreciated that he was being effectively interrogated, the conversation became perceptibly awkward on both sides. It was as uncomfortable for Nimitz to act the inquisitor as it was for Fletcher to be cross-examined. Since some of the questions Nimitz asked were quite specific, Fletcher said he would need to consult the ship's log and his own papers. Likely relieved, Nimitz said that would be fine, and he brought the painful conversation to an end.[7]

Meanwhile, *Yorktown* eased into Drydock Number 1, and the next day Nimitz went there personally to examine the big flattop for himself. As the water drained out of the basin and the ship's hull was exposed, Nimitz donned big rubber hip boots and climbed gingerly down into the knee-deep water to inspect the damage. Almost at once he concluded that, as he wrote to King, the damage was "not enough to prevent operations." While Jake Fitch, who had commanded the *Lexington* task force in the Coral Sea, estimated that it would take ninety days to repair the *Yorktown*'s hull, Nimitz informed the inspection party, "We must have this back in three days." He wrote King that he expected the ship to be "ready for operations [in] 48 to 60 hours."[8]

Though he cancelled liberty for all other ships in Pearl Harbor, Nimitz authorized shore liberty for the crew of the *Yorktown*, in part to reward them for their long cruise, and in part to get them out of the way of the hundreds of dockyard workers who immediately swarmed over her hull.

That night Nimitz hosted the principal commanders at dinner. He again outlined the plan, doing so in his characteristic soft, calm voice. He distributed written copies of the order (Op Order 29-42) and reminded everyone that the goal was not to "slug it out" with the Japanese, but to inflict sufficient losses to weaken their offensive capability, and perhaps convince them to call off the operation. To emphasize that, he issued a written order to Fletcher and Spruance directing them "to be governed by the principle of calculated risk," which he defined as "the avoidance of exposure of your force . . . without good prospect of inflicting . . . greater damage to the enemy." Despite his outward calm, he confessed to Catherine in his nightly letter that he was "staying awake night and day trying to figure this thing out." He could not tell her, of course, that the "thing" was a showdown with the swiftly approaching Japanese carrier force.[9]

AT ELEVEN O'CLOCK THE NEXT MORNING (May 28), the *Enterprise* and the other ships of Task Force 16 began exiting Pearl Harbor. The cruisers and destroyers went first, departing one by one at five-minute intervals. The carriers followed, ten minutes apart. Once the entire task force was out to sea, the air groups flew out to join them.

That morning, Nimitz also received a formal written response from Fletcher to the questions Nimitz had asked him the day before. In the letter ("My dear Admiral Nimitz"), Fletcher explained the several factors that had led him to order a withdrawal from the Coral Sea on May 8. "All things considered," he wrote, "the best plan seemed to be to keep our force concentrated and prepare for battle with [the] enemy carriers [the] next morning." Nimitz agreed fully, as he had at the time, and he forwarded Fletcher's letter along with one of his own to King ("Dear King"), to report that he had discussed the Coral Sea operation with Fletcher and that "these matters have been cleared up to my entire satisfaction, and I hope to yours." He added that in his view Fletcher was "an excellent, seagoing, fighting naval officer and I wish to retain him as task force commander." Whether or not King agreed with that fulsome assessment, with Halsey in the hospital and Spruance lacking any experience in carrier command, there was little choice now except to stick with Fletcher. With what amounted to a verbal wink, Nimitz sent King's own words back to him: "We will do the best we can with what we have."[10]

The next day, seawater was pumped back into Drydock Number 1 and the *Yorktown* was refloated. Prodded out into the roadstead by yard tugs while yard workers were still making last-minute repairs, she began taking on supplies and her boilers were lit. Nimitz made a trip out to thank the yard workers for their extraordinary effort and to meet one more time with Fletcher. Since the two carrier groups would operate separately, Nimitz told him that in order to maintain strict radio silence, they should communicate only by short-range TBS radio or by written messages dropped by aircraft.* Nimitz did not prescribe Fletcher's tactics, but he suggested that he might consider using the *Yorktown*'s planes to conduct air searches and provide combat air patrol, while keeping Spruance's two carriers loaded and cocked for a strike as soon as the enemy carriers were positively located. They were not orders, Nimitz told him, only suggestions intended "to assist initial co-ordination"; Fletcher should be guided by circumstances. Then Nimitz wished him luck, shook his hand, and left for his headquarters.[11]

He had done all he could do. Despite the loss of the *Lexington*, the damage to the *Yorktown*, and the loss of his senior carrier commander, he had cobbled together a viable sea force. He had reinforced Midway itself; he had scout planes in the air, a web of submarines in place, and carriers on their way to an ambush position north of Midway, a location designated, somewhat hopefully, as Point Luck. Other than keep the operational commanders up to date with the latest news from Hypo, there was little more he could do now. He confessed privately to Catherine that the next five days would be filled with "anxious waiting," though he added that "we are better prepared than ever before."[12]

Aware that soon enough there would be few leisure moments, and to relieve the palpable tension at headquarters, Nimitz took a group of staff officers over to a swimming beach on the other side of Pearl Harbor at Barber's Point (now called Nimitz Beach) for recreation the next day. Any of those who had accompanied him on one of his walks into the hills behind

---

* TBS (Talk Between Ships) was a short-range VHS radio system that could be used only when ships were relatively close, usually within sixty to a hundred miles depending on atmospheric conditions.

Pearl Harbor knew that "recreation" for Nimitz could prove daunting and strenuous. His regimen at the beach was to swim straight out to sea for a quarter mile or more, then swim parallel to the coast for another mile, sometimes two, before heading shoreward and walking the rest of the way back. Few could, or even tried, to keep up with him. To Nimitz such workouts were restorative. "I expect the next few days to be full and long," he wrote to Catherine that night, "so will bank up some rest." He then confided to her that "some day the story of our activities will be written and it will be interesting—but not for now."[13]

It was not in Nimitz to be idle. In addition to forwarding all the information that Hypo could provide to Fletcher and Spruance, he supervised the air search, tracked submarine contacts, kept an eye on the progress of forces in the Aleutians, and even monitored the amount of aviation fuel available on Midway ("Request immediate check on number of gallons of gas in tanks," he wrote to Simard). He reported to King that "the deployment to oppose enemy in both central and north Pacific is proceeding satisfactorily."[14]

THE FIRST HARD NEWS ABOUT THE Japanese came in at 9:00 on the morning of June 3. The pilot of a PBY Catalina seaplane patrolling five hundred miles west of Midway reported seeing "two Japanese cargo vessels." They were minesweepers advancing ahead of the enemy fleet. Their discovery suggested that the schedule predicted by Rochefort and Layton was nearly spot on. Only a half-hour later, a far more significant report came in from another PBY pilot, Ensign Jewell "Jack" Reid, who was patrolling two hundred miles farther west: "Sighted main body." The enemy formation, he reported, consisted of eleven vessels, including "one small carrier, one seaplane tender, two battleships, several cruisers, several destroyers."[15]

Nimitz was at his headquarters talking with Layton when a courier rushed in with Reid's report. Nimitz saw at once that this was not, in fact, the "main body." Battleships and cruisers supported by a single light carrier were almost certainly escorting the invasion group; the real target was the Japanese carrier force. He consulted Layton, who concurred, then fired off a message to Fletcher and Spruance. He knew their radio rooms would have copied the report from Reid, and he did not want them to go off half-cocked. "That is not, repeat not, the enemy striking force. This is the landing force. The striking force will hit from the northwest at daylight tomorrow." The subtext was clear: Wait. Be patient. To both Fletcher and Spruance he added, "The situation is developing as expected. Carriers, our most important objective, should soon be located. Tomorrow may be the day you can give them the works."[16]

The tension at headquarters built throughout the day, though there was little new information. A handful of long-range and high-flying B-17 Army bombers from Midway headed out to attack the ships that Reid had sighted, and that night Nimitz approved a proposal from the commander of Patrol Wing Two, Rear Admiral Patrick Bellinger, who affixed torpedoes to four of his PBYs and sent them off to attempt a night attack. Improbably, Bellinger's PBYs not only found the approaching ships, but actually managed to hit one, the tanker *Akebono Maru*, though the torpedo did only minor damage.[17]

Nimitz did not return to his house that night, sleeping intermittently on a cot in his office. Consequently, he was there at 5:34 the next morning—still fifteen minutes before sunrise—when the radio room received an electrifying report from PBY pilot Lieutenant Howard Ady: "Enemy carrier bearing 320 [degrees], distance 180 [miles]." At 6:03 another report indicated the presence of "two carriers and battleships." Here was a worthwhile target. On Midway, Simard ordered the pilots to man their planes. Nimitz had sent almost every plane that could fly out to Midway's airfield, and he had told Simard to "go all out for the carriers." Simard therefore kept only two dozen fighters behind for island defense and sent everything else toward the reported coordinates of the two carriers. It was an eclectic collection of Navy, Marine Corps, and Army planes of various types. Since they flew at different speeds and different altitudes, theirs was anything but a textbook attack. Still, Nimitz hoped they could inflict some meaningful damage that might even the odds before the real battle began.[18]

Before all the American planes from Midway were in the air, there was another sighting report: "Many planes heading Midway." The enemy, too, had launched, and Midway would soon be under air attack. That was confirmed at 6:25 when Simard sent a terse report: "Air Raid Midway." After that, there was little hard news for most of two hours. At 8:30, Hypo intercepted a partial message that implied that the Midway-based American planes had suffered serious damage: "Only 3 undamaged fighting planes remain." The good news was that the Japanese had not completely wrecked the defenses at Midway. Simard reported significant damage to the island's power plant, airplane hangars, and other buildings, but the aviation fuel supply remained intact and the airfield was still usable.[19]

Since Fletcher and Spruance were maintaining radio silence, there were no reports from either of them. Still, now and then came bits and pieces of short-range VHF radio chatter—short bursts pulled out of the air by the radio station at He'eia. In one of them, intercepted just past 10:00 a.m., someone blurted out, "Attack immediately!" A staff officer at headquarters claimed to recognize the voice of Miles Browning. What exactly was happening, however, was unclear. If the Japanese carriers were under attack, why were there no intercepted messages from them? Nimitz asked Layton to call Rochefort on the scrambler phone and find out if he had heard anything from the Japanese.[20]

"Don't we have anything on this?" Layton asked Rochefort.

Though Hypo had picked up snatches of earlier messages, Rochefort told Layton there was nothing to indicate that American planes had made contact. "We've tried every frequency that we know."

Years later, Nimitz confessed that his predominant emotion that morning was "anxiety." The word Layton used to describe him was "frantic"—"I mean as frantic as I've ever seen him."[21]

There was one tantalizing bit of information. Just after 11:00, the cryptanalysts at Hypo intercepted a lengthy Japanese message, sent, apparently, by the carrier force commander. Hypo did not have time to decode it, but team members who had become adept at recognizing the particular tempo—called a "fist"—of individual telegraphers did not believe this message had been transmitted by the radioman on the Japanese flagship *Akagi*. One of the analysts said that he recognized the fist as belonging to the radio-man on the cruiser *Nagara*. Why? Was the *Akagi* hurt, even out of action? It

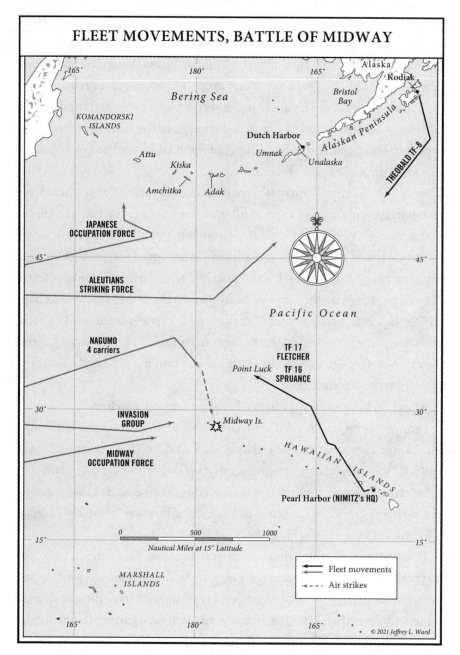

Map 6: Fleet Movements, Battle of Midway

would be several more anxious hours before Nimitz learned the answers to those questions.[22]

——————————

SEVERAL HUNDRED MILES NORTH OF MIDWAY, Fletcher and Spruance had received the same sighting reports Nimitz had. Fletcher noted the distance: 180 miles from Midway. That put the Japanese carriers a little over 200 miles from his position, which was just beyond the effective range of his bombers. Moreover, the wind was extremely light that day—less than 5 knots—and it was coming out of the east. To generate enough wind across the flight deck to allow the loaded bombers to take off, the carriers would have to turn east, away from the enemy, and build up speed to 25 knots. As a result, by the time the bombers got airborne, they would have an additional twenty miles to fly to reach the target. It would be necessary to close the range before launching. On the other hand, every minute that Fletcher waited gave the Japanese an additional minute during which one of their scout planes might find him and eliminate the advantage of surprise.

Another concern was that all of the scouting reports that morning had indicated the presence of only two Japanese carriers at the reported coordinates; presumably there were still two more out there somewhere. Fletcher had launched ten search planes at dawn to cover the unpatrolled sectors to the north. Even if they did not sight any enemy forces, he would have to keep the *Yorktown*'s deck clear until they returned, which meant he could not yet spot the attack planes for a strike. Remembering Nimitz's suggestion, at 6:07 Fletcher ordered Spruance to launch planes from both of his carriers once the enemy was "definitely located." Meanwhile, Fletcher would close the known enemy position until he was within range. If any of his scout planes found the two "missing" enemy carriers, he would go after them. Otherwise he would join the strike against the two carriers that had been located.[23]

In receipt of Fletcher's order, Spruance told Browning to "launch everything they had at the earliest possible moment." Browning suggested they wait another forty-five minutes to close the range before turning into the wind to launch. Nimitz had told Spruance to rely on Browning for air operations, so Spruance agreed. Consequently, it was 7:02 when the planes from *Enterprise* and *Hornet* began to launch. It took most of an hour for the fighters and dive-bombers to get airborne. Concerned that time was slipping away, Spruance overrode Browning and ordered the air group commander, Wade McClusky, to proceed without waiting for the late-launching torpedo planes.[24]

It proved to be a crucial decision. So was the one McClusky made two hours later when, finding only empty ocean at the predicted location, he chose to follow a wayward Japanese destroyer northward that led him, at last, to the target. It was another two hours after that when McClusky and his surviving pilots returned to the *Enterprise* with startling news. Spruance broke radio silence to send a message to Nimitz that electrified everyone at headquarters: "All four [Japanese] CV are believed badly damaged."[25]

Nimitz wrote later that the message inspired "jubilation" at headquarters, though it is not clear how fulsomely he joined in. He had grown wary of pilots' reports. Still, it was spectacular news, and Nimitz forwarded it to King in the stilted language of Navy messages: "Believe badly damaged all 4 CV and other ships hit." Though he also had to add: "Our plane losses heavy."[26]

This time the reports from the pilots were only slightly exaggerated. As it happened, all four of the Japanese carriers were operating together that morning and three of them (though *not* "all 4") were indeed "badly damaged." Before nightfall, two of them (*Kaga* and *Sōryū*) would sink, the first a victim of McClusky's planes from *Enterprise*, the second the result of an assault by dive-bombers from the *Yorktown*. Having recovered his scout planes, Fletcher had launched a coordinated strike, and his planes had flown unerringly to the target, arriving entirely by coincidence at virtually the same moment McCluskey's planes did.

A third Japanese carrier, Nagumo's flagship *Akagi*, went down the next morning. As the analysts at Hypo had speculated, Nagumo had indeed been forced to abandon his flagship after a single decisive bomb hit by Lieutenant Richard Best. But despite Spruance's initial report, there was still a fourth undamaged Japanese carrier out there. That became evident soon enough when Nimitz received a disturbing message from Fletcher: "Have been attacked by air."[27]

Nimitz had to wait several hours for details. Unwilling to break radio silence further even now, Fletcher entrusted his full report to a pilot who flew it to Midway so that the news could be forwarded to Pearl Harbor on the secure submarine cable. The *Yorktown* had been hit "by at least three bombs, badly damaged, [and was] dead in water though apparently seaworthy." Fletcher proposed that his screening ships should "protect and salvage *Yorktown*" while Spruance's two carriers carried on the battle. Nimitz immediately agreed, and he ordered Simard to send air support for the *Yorktown* "as practicable."[28]

By the time Nimitz read that message, however, circumstances had changed again. Soon, there was another message from Fletcher, this one sent in plain, uncoded English: "Am being heavily attacked by air." With almost their last operational aircraft, the Japanese had returned to assail the *Yorktown* again, this time with their Kate torpedo planes. The *Yorktown*'s damage control teams had been so efficient after the first attack that the pilots of the torpedo planes believed they were attacking a different, undamaged carrier.[†] Spruance could not go to Fletcher's aid because his carriers were engaged in nearly constant air operations, either launching or recovering planes or rotating the Combat Air Patrol (CAP). After the Japanese put two more torpedoes into *Yorktown*'s port side, Fletcher reported to Nimitz that the *Yorktown* was now "apparently sinking."[29]

Yet another report from Fletcher that afternoon revealed that although the *Yorktown* was dead in the water and listing badly, she remained afloat and appeared to have stabilized. Fletcher asked Nimitz if he could send tugs from Pearl to tow her to safety. Nimitz did dispatch tugs with salvage crews from Pearl, though he also ordered the minesweeper *Vireo* to steam toward Fletcher from French Frigate Shoals, which was closer.[30]

Meanwhile, Spruance readied another strike to find and sink that fourth Japanese carrier, the *Hiryū*, whose planes had now twice attacked the

---

† In addition to sinking the *Sōryū*, one important and unplanned contribution of the *Yorktown* that morning was that she absorbed the full attention of the Japanese, so Spruance's two carriers in TF 16 could carry on the battle undetected and unmolested.

After the USS *Yorktown* was struck by three bombs and two torpedoes, her skipper, Captain Elliott Buckmaster, ordered abandon ship. Later, when she stabilized, he sent a volunteer crew back on board in an effort to save her. The destroyer USS *Balch* stands by to assist. (U.S. Naval Institute)

Yorktown. Sensitive to the fact that Fletcher remained in overall command, Spruance radioed him to ask, "Have you any instructions?"[31]

By then, Fletcher had transferred his flag to the cruiser *Astoria*, and he was realistic enough, and selfless enough, to know that it was no longer practical for him to exercise effective overall command. He replied at once: "Negative. Will conform to your movements." With that, he left the battle against the *Hiryū* in Spruance's hands so that he could concentrate on saving the *Yorktown*.[32]

Spruance's afternoon strike against the *Hiryū* was successful. In quick succession, Dauntless dive-bombers landed four 500-pound bombs on her forward flight deck. The pilots reported that they left the *Hiryū* still afloat but "burning fiercely" and incapable of flight operations. Spruance passed the news on to Nimitz, and Layton recalled that as he read that message, Nimitz smiled broadly.

That evening, General Emmons arrived at Nimitz's headquarters with a broad grin of his own and bearing a gigantic jeroboam of champagne decorated with blue and gold ribbons. Behind him, a staff officer carried a box of champagne glasses. Emmons had been a skeptic about accepting battle with the Japanese carriers, and this was his way of admitting that he had been wrong. Nimitz ordered small portions of champagne served out to each of the seventy-four people at headquarters and joined them in toasting the success of the day.[33]

The battle was not over. In his report to King that night, Nimitz wrote that he expected the Japanese would still attempt to land on Midway. Recalling King's criticism of Fletcher after the Battle of the Coral Sea, Nimitz reassured King, "We are executing night attacks with appropriate types."[34]

That was not the case. Spruance did *not* order his destroyers to conduct night torpedo attacks on June 4, or on June 5. Calculating that a surface engagement with Japanese battleships and heavy cruisers risked throwing away everything that had been gained, Spruance instead heeded Nimitz's instructions to apply "the principle of calculated risk." Once he recovered the planes from the strike against the *Hiryū*, Spruance ordered the ships of Task Force 16 to turn east, away from the enemy. Then he went to his cabin and "fell into a long deep sleep," a sleep so profound that the next morning his staff officers had difficulty waking him up.[35]

Spruance received criticism, both at the time and later, for not pursuing the Japanese that night and attempting to destroy their fleet altogether. Subsequent analysis, however, demonstrated just how risky that was likely to have been. Though neither Nimitz nor Spruance knew it, Yamamoto himself with his heavy battleship force was speeding eastward in the hope of conducting a night surface attack on the remaining American carriers. Had Spruance continued westward, he might well have run into this juggernaut. Even without that knowledge, Nimitz expressed his faith in Spruance's judgment, telling Layton: "I'm sure that Spruance has a better sense of what's going on there than we have."

By morning, Nimitz was more optimistic. All enemy forces, he reported to King, were heading west, and Task Force 16, having turned around at first light, was pursuing. Spruance sent out search planes to look for any remaining Japanese assets, especially the wounded *Hiryū*. They saw no sign of her, so Spruance sent his remaining bombers to find and sink two "battleships" (actually heavy cruisers) that had been reported off to the south. Those planes found and sank one of the enemy warships and damaged the other so badly it took the Japanese more than a full year to effect repairs. That evening, with the pilots returning in the dark, Spruance ordered the lights of the task force turned on, despite the risk from Japanese submarines, to ensure the pilots could make it back to their carriers.[36]

The pilots had not found the *Hiryū* that afternoon because she, too, had sunk, though Nimitz did not learn that until June 19, when the submarine tender *Ballard* picked up a boatful of survivors from the *Hiryū*. Only then did Nimitz know for sure that it had been a clean sweep.

By then, the *Yorktown* had succumbed. Her crew made heroic efforts to save her, cutting away ruined steel, shoring up bulkheads, and counterflooding to bring her to a more even keel. Yet while she was being towed southward at an agonizing 3 knots by the *Vireo* on June 6, a Japanese submarine slipped through her destroyer screen and put another two torpedoes into her, plus a third into the destroyer USS *Hammann*, alongside. That proved too much for the battered flattop, and at 5:00 a.m. on June 7, she slipped beneath the waves.

WELL BEFORE THAT, NIMITZ AUTHORIZED DRAEMEL to release a general order that he had prepared beforehand, giving full credit for the victory to the men who had fought it. "Those who participated in the Battle of Midway today have written a glorious page in our history," he wrote. "I am proud to be associated with you." In the press release he prepared for public distribution, he announced that "Pearl Harbor has now been partially avenged," though he acknowledged that "vengeance will not be complete until Japanese sea power has been reduced to impotence." It may have been a measure of his relief, even euphoria, that he allowed himself a pun: "Perhaps we will be forgiven if we claim we are about midway to our objective."[37] He knew better. The Battle of Midway had been tactically decisive—one of the few naval battles in history that ended with the virtual destruction of an enemy force. In American history, only the Battle of Lake Erie in 1813 and the two naval battles of the Spanish-American War in 1898 fell into that category. Yet Nimitz knew that success in the Battle of Midway did not mean victory, nor was it "midway" to victory. More than three years of hard fighting lay ahead. It did, however, change the trajectory of the war. Until 10:25 on the morning of June 4, the Japanese controlled the momentum of events. They chose both the target and the timing of new campaigns, and despite the hit-and-run raids that Nimitz had executed, the U.S. Navy had been forced to react to Japan's moves rather than inaugurate major campaigns of its own. With the loss of four of their six big carriers, however, the Japanese also lost the initiative in the war.

Nimitz's bold gamble had succeeded.

PART II

THE SOUTH PACIFIC

Things are moving very rapidly now, and as usual there is bad news mixed in
with the good. But we are not downhearted and we are determined to win.
—Chester W. Nimitz to Catherine Nimitz, September 25, 1942

American success in the Battle of Midway marked a turning point in the war. The United States sought to seize the initiative afterward by launching an offensive in the South Pacific. At the same time, the Japanese were determined to demonstrate that the Americans lacked the ability—and in particular the national will—to conduct a sustained offensive across the broad Pacific Ocean when confronted by determined and unyielding resistance. The unlikely pivot in this trial of resources and resolve was a jungle-covered island called Guadalcanal. For six months, that island was a vortex of violence and carnage as both sides committed more men, more equipment, and more supplies in an increasingly desperate effort to claim or retain this dubious prize. The outcome remained uncertain until the end of the year.

O N JUNE 6, 1942, two days after the heart-stopping confrontation north of Midway, the USS *Saratoga* entered Pearl Harbor after a high-speed run from San Diego. She was too late to take part in the fighting, of course, but welcome nonetheless. Nimitz ordered her to complete a quick turnaround and head back out at once to deliver replacement planes for the depleted squadrons on the *Hornet* and *Enterprise*. The *Saratoga*'s arrival underscored the need for a general reshuffling of his task force commanders, though Nimitz had planned to reorganize his task forces after the battle in any case. For one thing, having two carriers in a single task force, as in Spruance's (formerly Halsey's) Task Force 16, was an accidental legacy of the Doolittle Raid; Roosevelt himself had indicated that he wanted America's task forces to operate with one carrier each. The loss of the *Yorktown* and the expected arrival of the *Wasp* in a few weeks made a reorganization essential.

Nimitz's initial plan was to confirm Jake Fitch, who had brought the *Saratoga* out from San Diego, as the commander of her task force (TF 11), and he informed King that Fletcher would come ashore for a well-earned rest and then take over the *Wasp* group when it arrived. Within days, however, he changed his mind and, since Halsey was still in the hospital recovering, he gave Fletcher Halsey's former job as commander of the *Enterprise* group (TF 16) and designated Leigh Noyes to take over the *Wasp* task force (TF 18). Marc "Pete" Mitscher, the grizzled, weather-beaten skipper of the *Hornet*, would fleet up from that job to command the task force centered around her, which would now be labeled Task Force 17. After clearing the appointments with King, Nimitz announced the new assignments in a general order to the fleet on June 16. Despite Raymond Spruance's performance during the Battle of Midway, he was *not* designated to command a task force. Nimitz had other plans for him.[1]

On June 18, Spruance reported to Nimitz's headquarters as his new chief of staff. Draemel left to take over the Amphibious Force from Wilson Brown, though he eventually ended up as commander of the 4th Naval District in Philadelphia. As Draemel had done, Spruance moved into Nimitz's house, and for the next fourteen months the two men were seldom apart. As Spruance himself put it, "I walked with him down to the office in the morning and back with him each evening." They came to know each other's habits and preferences. Nimitz quickly learned to decline Spruance's offer to make the morning coffee; Spruance made it so strong few others could tolerate it. Similarly, Spruance just as regularly declined Nimitz's offer of a pre-dinner cocktail; Nimitz's special recipe for an old-fashioned packed a wallop. Instead, the abstemious Spruance routinely asked the steward to bring him a glass of tomato juice. During social events, while Nimitz might offer a humorous story, Spruance remained notably quiet. As one officer put it, "Spruance never had any cocktail conversation. He never could master small talk."[2]

Yet for all their differences, they were also companionable, even close. For one thing, Nimitz was delighted to learn that, as he wrote to Catherine, "he likes music as much as I do." What they said to each other during their private conversations during walks and over meals is mostly lost to history. Spruance's biographer, Thomas B. Buell, bemoaned the fact that their exchanges remain "infuriatingly mysterious." Nevertheless, it is inconceivable that they would not have discussed the recent Battle of Midway, including the after-action reports that were submitted by the various participants. And whatever Spruance said about the battle and about those reports, it led Nimitz to change his mind about the command assignments he had just announced.[3]

AS NIMITZ STUDIED THE REPORTS FROM MIDWAY, several things stood out. The old submarine hand was disappointed that American submarines had claimed no victims in the battle. Indeed, only one submarine, the *Nautilus*, ever got within sight of a Japanese carrier. As it happened, the *Nautilus* did play an important role, though not the one Nimitz had envisioned. Its unsuccessful attack on a Japanese carrier led Nagumo to leave a destroyer behind when he turned north, and it was that wayward destroyer that had led Wade McClusky to find the Japanese carriers. While that was not an insignificant contribution, the American subs had drawn no blood on June 4.

One other sub sighted a different element of the Japanese armada on June 5. At 4:00 a.m. that day, the USS *Tambor*, on which Spruance's son, Edward, was serving as a junior officer, sighted four Japanese cruisers. The skipper of the *Tambor*, Lieutenant Commander John W. Murphy, sent in a quick garbled report, then dove without engaging. Both Spruance and Nimitz were disappointed and frustrated by Murphy's performance, and Nimitz cited "Tambor's faulty reporting" as one reason the victory was not more complete than it was. Afterward, Murphy was relieved of his command.

Another disappointment, one with tragic consequences, was the performance of the slow and low-flying Devastator torpedo bombers. Torpedo Squadron 8 from the *Hornet* had been wiped out altogether, and those from the other carriers had fared little better. Of the forty-one torpedo bombers that had launched from the three American carriers that morning, only four survived the strike, and one of those was so badly shot up it would never fly again. And despite the determination and courage of the pilots, none of them had scored a hit. In contrast, the Dauntless dive-bombers had had a field day, especially those from the *Enterprise* under Wade McClusky. His bombers had accounted for the sinking of both the

Akagi and the *Kaga,* while dive-bombers from the *Yorktown* sank the *Sōryū.* The dive-bombers were also responsible for the mortal wounding of the *Hiryū* that afternoon.[4]

A partial solution to the torpedo bomber problem was already at hand: the newer, sturdier, and faster TBF Avengers, which would replace the TBD Devastators. Six of them had flown out from Midway to attack the Japanese carriers on June 4, and while they had had no more success than the other planes from Midway, there were only a few of them, and they had been forced to attack without cooperating bombers or fighter cover. An additional problem with the torpedo bombers remained undiscovered: the unreliable character of the torpedoes they carried. It would be most of another year before that problem was identified and resolved.

Among all the after-action reports that Nimitz received, however, it was the one from the *Hornet* that most puzzled him. The *Hornet* torpedo bombers under Lieutenant Commander John Waldron had been the first to find and attack the Japanese on that historic June 4, though they did so unsupported and as a result were literally annihilated. Yet none of the other squadrons from the *Hornet* had made contact with the enemy at all. They had flown out and flown back and never saw a thing. In the annals of the battle, this misadventure has been labeled the "Flight to Nowhere." Nimitz's effort to understand how it had happened was complicated by the fact that he received only one after-action report from the *Hornet,* the one written by—or at least signed by—her captain, Marc Mitscher.[5]

That was noteworthy in itself because Navy regulations stated unequivocally that the commanders of every unit, including every air squadron, were to submit a written after-action report "immediately upon landing." Nimitz got reports from all the commanders of the air squadrons on the other carriers, but none at all from the *Hornet.* It was understandable that there was no report from Waldron. He and everyone else in his command except the squadron navigator, Ensign George Gay, had been killed. There was no explanation, however, for the absence of reports from the *Hornet*'s scouting squadron, the bombing squadron, the fighter squadron, or the air group commander, Stanhope Ring. Only Mitscher filed a report.[6]

Rear Admiral Marc Mitscher, shown here as a vice admiral, commanded the USS *Hornet* during the Battle of Midway. Mitscher had pale, sensitive skin that burned easily, and to protect it he wore a specially made long-billed baseball cap. In spite of that, a visitor remarked that the fifty-six-year-old Mitscher "didn't look a day over eighty." (Sedivi Collection, U.S. Naval Institute)

Mitscher sent his solo report up the chain of command to Spruance on June 13, the day Task Force 16 returned to Pearl Harbor. In it, Mitscher wrote that the *Hornet* air group, with Commander Ring in the lead, had flown to the southwest on a track similar to McClusky's *Enterprise* group, and that, like McClusky, Ring had found no enemy carriers at the calculated coordinates. According to Mitscher, while McClusky had turned north and found the enemy, Ring and the *Hornet* group had turned south, and had missed the battle by mere chance. It was also mere chance, he wrote, that Waldron's torpedo planes had found the enemy; they had flown at a lower altitude and had somehow gotten separated. Mitscher offered a heartfelt tribute to the men of that squadron: "The conduct of Torpedo Squadron

Eight," he wrote, "led by an indomitable Squadron Commander, is one of the most outstanding exhibitions of personal bravery and gallantry ... in the records of past or present."[7]

Spruance forwarded Mitscher's report to Nimitz, as required. But in his endorsement, Spruance wrote this: "As a matter of historical record, the Hornet report contains a number of inaccuracies." He added, "Where discrepancies exist between Hornet and Enterprise reports, the Enterprise report should be taken as more accurate." He did not openly challenge Mitscher on his report, nor did he quite say that it was false, but his endorsement implied that it was at least unreliable. Nimitz surely would have asked Spruance about it, and about why there were no accompanying reports from any of the squadron commanders on the *Hornet*.[8]

Whatever Spruance told him, it was not complimentary to Mitscher. Not only had the *Hornet's* bombers failed to find the enemy on the morning of June 4, but Mitscher had also fumbled the afternoon attack on the *Hiryū*. First, he was tardy in launching his planes, and then, in the middle of the launch, he had ordered the *Hornet* to turn around and head west with only half of his planes in the air, leaving the rest of them marooned on board. One of those left behind was the air group commander, Stanhope Ring, who had led the "Flight to Nowhere." Mitscher's staff had had to scramble to find out who was senior among the pilots who had managed to get airborne, and then notify him by radio that he, and not Ring, was in command. Finally, on June 5, when Spruance ordered an attack on a pair of Japanese cruisers to the south, Mitscher had defied orders by loading his planes with 1,000-pound bombs instead of the 500-pound bombs that Spruance had mandated. None of this made its way into Mitscher's report.[9]

Mitscher's omission of these events, and the absence of any reports from the squadron commanders, suggested to Spruance that the *Hornet's* after-action report was more than merely unreliable; it was deliberately dishonest. Mitscher declared, "The entire crew of the Hornet [is] deserving [of] high praise for their performance of duty during the subject action." His last sentence stated, "There were no outstanding individuals [despite his praise of Waldron] and there is no cause for censure." Spruance thought otherwise, and it is unimaginable that he did not share his conclusions with Nimitz during their unrecorded conversations.[10]

All that posed a problem for Nimitz, who, of course, had to write his own report on the battle. To do that, he provided copies of all the reports, including Mitscher's, to Commander Ernest M. Eller, whom he tasked with composing the first draft. Impressed by several articles that Eller had published in the Naval Institute *Proceedings*, Nimitz had him transferred from his job as a gunnery officer to act as his staff writer. After a few days, Eller handed Nimitz a thirty-page draft, which Nimitz then painstakingly rewrote. Eller recalled Nimitz wrestling over choosing just the right word. Then Nimitz gave it back to Eller for one more scrubbing. Finally, deciding that it said what he needed it to say and no more, Nimitz tucked it away to hand-carry to King for their next meeting in San Francisco. There was almost nothing in it about the "Flight to Nowhere." The closest Nimitz came to addressing that issue was when he wrote, "HORNET Group Commander [Ring] made the decision to turn south . . . and failed to make contact." The question is why, if he knew that Mitscher's report was false, or at least incomplete, Nimitz did not call him out.[11]

AN EXPERIENCE FROM NIMITZ'S EARLY CAREER suggests a possible answer. Thirty-eight years earlier, when seventeen-year-old Chester Nimitz entered the Naval Academy, he had been required to take a course in naval history— a course that is still required of first-year students, called plebes. His text- book was a brand-new edition of Edgar S. Maclay's *History of the United States Navy*, the third volume of which covered the recently concluded Spanish-American War. Maclay's narrative included detailed accounts of both George Dewey's victory at Manila Bay in May 1898 and the Battle of Santiago that July.[12]

At Santiago, Maclay wrote, the American squadron under Rear Admiral William T. Sampson had blockaded the Spanish squadron of Admiral Pascual Cervera in the harbor. On July 3, however, Sampson left Commodore Winfield Scott Schley in charge of the blockade and steamed off to the east in the armored cruiser *New York* to discuss the campaign with his Army counterpart, Major General William Shafter. Observing the departure of the *New York*, Cervera decided to seize the moment and make a break for it.

As the lead ship of Cervera's squadron exited the harbor, it headed directly toward Schley's flagship, the *Brooklyn*. To avoid what he thought might be a torpedo attack, Schley turned hard to starboard, that is, eastward. Cervera, however, turned sharply west, and his ships raced along the coast in an effort to escape. Having turned the wrong way initially, Schley decided that rather than reverse his rudder he would continue his starboard turn to complete a full circle, then set out in pursuit. Doing so caused some confusion in the American squadron, but soon enough all the warships, including Sampson's *New York*, joined the chase. Eventually the swifter American ships overtook the fleeing Spanish vessels, and one by one either sank them or drove them ashore. It was a spectacular one-sided victory, but not without controversy. Why had Schley turned right instead of left?

In the textbook assigned to Midshipman Fourth Class Nimitz in 1901, Maclay gave full credit for the victory to Sampson and excoriated Schley, who in Maclay's view had behaved like a coward, "deliberately turning tail and running away." Schley was outraged and demanded a court-martial to clear his name. Senior naval officers took sides, and the dispute descended into a months-long public spectacle. Instead of celebrating a victory, the Navy became an object of ridicule. Eventually, President Theodore Roosevelt himself stepped in to order an end to "further agitation on this unhappy controversy."*

---

* The controversial third volume of Maclay's *History* was recalled, and existing copies of it destroyed. As a result, it is difficult to find today. There are copies of the first two volumes in the Nimitz Library at the Naval Academy and in the Eccles Library at the Naval War College, but the original volume 3 is missing from both collections. In a replacement volume, published in 1902 during Nimitz's youngster year, Maclay regretted the use of "certain expressions" in the earlier edition, but he did not back down altogether. He wrote that Schley's conduct betrayed "certain failures . . . particularly in regard to the retrograde movement from Santiago." That Sampson ended up the "winner" of this controversy is evidenced by the fact that the building then under construction to house the Naval Academy's History Department was christened Sampson Hall, the name it bears still.

Midshipman Fourth Class Chester Nimitz in 1901 when he took the required class on U.S. naval history at the Naval Academy. The seventeen-year-old Nimitz was dismayed by the so-called Sampson-Schley Controversy and resolved that he would never contribute to that kind of public squabbling. (U.S. Naval Institute)

Nimitz never forgot the ugliness of that public dispute, and years later he told E. B. "Ned" Potter, his first biographer, that he had "made a vow then and there that, if ever he was in a position to prevent it, there would be no washing of the Navy's dirty linen in public." He did not tell Potter, or anyone else, that the memory of this episode influenced his response to the "Flight to Nowhere." In fact, he never publicly acknowledged that he suspected Mitscher of falsifying his report and remained silent about the incident for the rest of his life.[13]

Nimitz may also have wondered whether he had contributed to the "Flight to Nowhere." Though all four Japanese carriers operated as a unit that morning, Nimitz's plan for the battle (Op Plan 29-42) stated that "one or more [Japanese] carriers may take up close-in daylight positions" to attack Midway while "additional carrier groups" remained behind to deal with U.S. surface groups. Indeed, the last information that Nimitz passed to his carrier commanders that morning was that U.S. search planes had seen "only 2 carriers" at the reported coordinates and that two others remained undiscovered and at large. Almost certainly Mitscher decided to send his entire air group to the west and not to the southwest, as he claimed in his report, in the expectation of finding those two missing carriers. Waldron, leading Torpedo 8, had defied those orders by flying his own course to the southwest—and to his martyrdom.[14]

Mitscher's erroneous report may have been motivated by the best of intentions. He, too, remembered the Sampson-Schley controversy from when he was a midshipman, and by the time he sat down to write his after-action report for Midway he knew that the U.S. Navy had won one of the greatest victories in its history—one that surpassed even the victory off Santiago. Mitscher may have calculated that exposing the errors and blunders of the *Hornet's* role in that battle would only tarnish that victory. Nimitz agreed with those motives. Rather than confront Mitscher on the inaccuracy of his report—or the missing reports of his subordinates—he chose instead to draw a curtain across the embarrassment of the "Flight to Nowhere," writing only that "the performance of [all the] officers and men was of the highest order."[15]

Yet while he may have understood, and even sympathized with Mitscher's motives, Nimitz could not ignore the fact that his report was inaccurate—even dishonest. Mitscher kept his previously scheduled promotion to rear admiral, but he lost command of the *Hornet* task force. Only five days after announcing the new task force commanders (and three days after Spruance joined the staff), Nimitz wrote King to suggest an entirely different lineup. In this new scheme, Fletcher would take the *Saratoga* group, and Thomas C. Kinkaid would get the *Enterprise* group as a placeholder until Halsey was well enough to return to duty. That made Fitch available to take the *Hornet* group in Mitscher's place. Mitscher got orders to command Patrol Wing 2, the PBY squadron at Kaneohe on Oahu's north shore.[†] King approved all the proposed changes, telling Nimitz that he could make "such assignment of Mitscher as you see fit," which suggests that King may have been aware of the situation.[16]

As a face-saving ploy, the word was put out that as a brand-new rear admiral, Mitscher lacked the seniority to command a task force. That fig leaf was stripped away when the *Hornet* task force subsequently went to George Murray, who had been captain of the *Enterprise* at Midway. Murray was naval aviator #22 and Mitscher #33. However, Murray was two years younger than Mitscher and had graduated from the Academy a year behind him. Mitscher himself knew that "he had been shelved," as his biographer put it, and suspected that his naval career was over.[17]

It might well have been but for the fact that Nimitz believed in second chances. Once again it was an experience from his early career that may have influenced him. As a twenty-three-year-old ensign in 1907 commanding the destroyer *Decatur*, Nimitz ran the ship aground on a mud bank in the Philippines. Nimitz managed to get her off the mud bank, and the *Decatur* suffered no material damage. He might simply have kept quiet about it, for grounding a ship was a potentially career-ending event. Yet Nimitz reported it to his superiors and endured a court-martial that sentenced him to a public reprimand. It did not end his career, however. Now, thirty-five years later, he did not discard Mitscher; he kept track of him and made sure to invite him to dinner with some regularity, especially when visiting flag officers or high-ranking officials arrived.[18]

BESIDES NAMING NEW TASK FORCE COMMANDERS, Nimitz also had to rebuild the air squadrons on the carriers. The critical element in every squadron—regardless of airplane type—was the aircrew. Given American

† Interestingly, Mitscher took Stanhope Ring, the *Hornet's* air group commander who had led the "Flight to Nowhere," along with him to his new command, appointing him his chief of staff. At a minimum, that demonstrated that Mitscher was not displeased with him for going the "wrong way" on June 4, and suggests strongly that Ring flew west in obedience to Mitscher's orders.

industrial superiority, it was virtually certain that in time the country would produce the thousands of planes needed to overtake and eventually overwhelm the Japanese. But planes without trained pilots are useless, and the loss of trained and experienced pilots in the Coral Sea, at Midway, and elsewhere was a serious problem.

Nimitz visited with many of the surviving pilots to talk with them about the battle. He made a point of going to the hospital to see Ensign George Gay, the lone survivor of Torpedo Squadron 8 from the *Hornet*. It had become something of a joke among Nimitz's staff that the boss had a tendency to extol the virtues of Texas. When talking about the vast distances in the Pacific, for example, he was likely to note in passing that the Pacific was almost as large as Texas. Now, shaking hands with Gay, Nimitz asked him where he was from, and when Gay replied, "Texas, sir," the whole group burst out laughing.[19]

To provide a nucleus for the reconstructed air squadrons, it was a natural temptation to rely on those veteran pilots and aircrews who had survived the battle. King suggested using the orphaned pilots from the *Yorktown* to "fill in" the depleted squadrons on *Hornet* and *Enterprise*. While Nimitz acknowledged the immediate need for stopgap measures, he emphasized the importance of augmenting the total number of pilots with new flight school graduates. "Long continued intensive operations at sea," he wrote, were wearing on his veteran pilots. Instead of keeping them in Hawaii, therefore, Nimitz sent seventy-four of his best and most experienced pilots—veterans of both Coral Sea and Midway—back to the mainland both for some well-deserved R&R, and to serve as flight instructors for pilot trainees. It was a critical decision.[20]

The Japanese also lost a significant number of pilots and aircrews, plus a serious loss of aircraft mechanics and other specialists, though they made the opposite decision. By keeping most of their trained pilots on active service, the Japanese suffered a continuing attrition over the ensuing months. In 1941, Japan's carrier pilots had been the best in the world, but the losses they suffered in the first six months of the war, combined with an inability to replace or supplement them with new pilots, swiftly eroded both the number and the quality of Japanese carrier pilots. Sometime during the second half of 1942, the upward trend of American pilot excellence crossed the downward trajectory of Japanese pilots.[21]

———————

NIMITZ WAS NOT AT ALL SURPRISED to hear from King that he thought destroyers "should have been used in night attacks during the Battle of Midway." It was the same complaint he had voiced after the Battle of the Coral Sea.[22]

This time, however, instead of asking for explanations from his task force commanders, Nimitz replied with a lengthy message of his own that read in places like a tutorial. It was an audacious move: a former submarine officer lecturing a senior aviator about carrier warfare. While Nimitz conceded that destroyers could still be useful in night torpedo attacks, he noted that the new dynamic of modern warfare had "greatly curtailed such attack opportunities" and in some cases made them "prohibitive." This was especially true when American carriers had a limited number of destroyers to protect them, and sending some of them off on an offensive mission necessarily weakened the defensive screen; "to date such excess over minimum requirements has not been available." Then, too, the greater distances involved in carrier warfare meant that the gas-guzzling destroyers could seldom get to and from the target without refueling. The "fuel situation for destroyers is usually precarious even without high speed at night," he wrote, and the shortage of both tankers and oilers only exacerbated the problem. Finally, sending off destroyers to conduct a night attack could easily mean that they would fail to get back by daylight, "which situation is entirely unacceptable." He assured King that his task force commanders "can be counted on to exploit favorable opportunities" but that such opportunities were rare. The key, he wrote, was "the destruction of enemy carriers, which has already taken place, and the ability to us of [building] more carriers and destroyers." That, he concluded, "should give added impetus to our aggressive operations."[23]

There is no record of what King thought about Nimitz's dissertation, and in any case, King had already moved on from encouraging destroyer night attacks to planning a counteroffensive in the wake of the Midway victory. With the Japanese back on their heels, King was eager to sustain the momentum by launching an American offensive.

He was not alone; MacArthur, too, saw an opportunity. MacArthur wrote directly to the Joint Chiefs (with a copy to Nimitz) suggesting that the victory at Midway made it possible for him to initiate an offensive in the Southwest Pacific. He urged the JCS to transfer a division of troops "trained in amphibious operations" and "a task force including 2 carriers" to his theater. With such a force, he declared, he could conduct a swift advance to seize the Japanese citadel at Rabaul. "Speed is vital," he wrote. "I cannot urge too strongly that the time has arrived" for "offensive operations in the Southwest Pacific area."[24]

King heartily agreed; he urged the Joint Chiefs to sanction an offensive in the Pacific, and soon. But he had plans of his own for those amphibious troops and carriers. Nimitz had twice before suggested an offensive to recapture Tulagi, which had been seized by the Japanese during the Battle of the Coral Sea. Now, when King broached the idea to the Joint Chiefs, it met with general agreement, though Marshall said that MacArthur should command it. King vociferously disagreed. He pointed out that the troops for such an operation would be Marines, and that they would be transported to the target by Navy ships and protected by Navy carriers. The Tulagi operation, he told Marshall, "must be conducted under the direction of CINCPAC and cannot be conducted in any other way." Marshall capitulated.[25]

On June 24 Nimitz received orders from King to arrange for the seizure of the island of Tulagi in the Solomons and Ndeni in the nearby Santa Cruz Islands. King made a point of telling Nimitz to handle this information with "utmost secrecy." Secret from whom, he did not say: from the Japanese, to be sure, and perhaps also from MacArthur. At the staff meeting the next morning, Nimitz told his people to begin "active preparations" for an offensive against both Tulagi and the Santa Cruz Islands.[26]

TO DISCUSS IT, NIMITZ FLEW TO San Francisco on July 2 for another meeting with King, carrying his Midway battle report in a briefcase. He almost didn't make it. Boosted by tailwinds, the seaplane carrying him and his staff arrived early, and the area of San Francisco Bay off Alameda where it was scheduled to set down had not been cleared of debris. As it was landing, the plane struck a floating log and flipped over. Nimitz had been playing cribbage with his plans officer, Captain Lynde McCormick, and both men were hurled across the cabin. McCormick received a serious head wound and two cracked vertebrae; others endured broken bones; the co-pilot was killed. Nimitz himself was badly bruised. The medical report listed contusions of the chest, spine, and both legs, plus "lacerations of both hands" and "contusion of nose." Nimitz's initial concern was for the brief-case containing his report on Midway. After securing it, he then tried to assist the more seriously hurt before climbing down into a rescue vessel. As it pulled away from the wreckage, he stood up to look back at the sinking plane. The coxswain shouted at him: "Sit down, you!" Then, realizing who it was, he tried to apologize, but Nimitz told the coxswain that he was absolutely correct, and obediently sat.[27]

Catherine had been alerted about his arrival in the Bay Area and she was there to meet him as he emerged, dripping, bruised, but intact, from the rescue boat. Because King was delayed with JCS matters, they had a few days together. Despite his injuries, he and Catherine walked about the city, rode the cable car, and window-shopped. Catherine had brought civilian clothes for him so that he could do it all incognito.

Nimitz met with King at the 12th Naval District offices on July 4—one month to the day after Midway. They discussed the battle, Nimitz's report of it, and the changes in command that Nimitz had directed. King assured Nimitz that the Bureau of Personnel would accept and process his revised list of task force commanders. Almost certainly, King asked Nimitz what should be done about Mitscher, for the minutes indicate that Nimitz told him, "Mitscher's assignment is okeh [sic]," meaning, presumably, that he could stay where he was at Kaneohe—for now.[28]

Another topic was Captain Morton T. Seligman, the erstwhile executive officer on the *Lexington*, who had foolishly allowed a *Chicago Tribune* reporter to see documents revealing that the United States had broken Japan's codes. When the *Tribune* published the story after the battle, it jeopardized one of the most important secrets of the war. King wanted both Seligman and the reporter arrested, tried, and shot. Cooler heads prevailed. After all, if the Navy arrested the reporter or shut down the paper, it would imply, at least, that the story was true. For now, therefore, Seligman, like Mitscher, was placed "in escrow."[29]

After that, they turned to planning the offensive against Tulagi, the Santa Cruz Islands, "and adjacent positions," one of which was the large island across the Sealark Channel from Tulagi called Guadalcanal. Rear Admiral Richmond Kelly Turner, who was present, noted that while Guadalcanal had no military facilities, it did have a large flat area on its north coast that might be suitable for an airfield. Then, even as King and Nimitz conversed, they learned that the codebreakers were reporting a large Japanese convoy headed for Guadalcanal with the evident intention of building an airfield there. Immediately, the conversation shifted from seizing Ndeni in the Santa Cruz Islands to capturing Guadalcanal, and doing so before the Japanese completed the airfield.[30]

Nimitz wondered aloud how MacArthur would respond to having a Navy–Marine Corps team carry out a major offensive inside his command area. King told Nimitz that the theater boundaries were not "a Chinese wall." Just because units of Nimitz's command crossed some invisible line, that did not mean they fell under MacArthur's authority. Still, to avoid complications, King prevailed on the Joint Chiefs to move the theater boundary one degree to the west to put the new target inside Nimitz's (actually Ghormley's) command theater.

Setting up a major offensive in the Solomon Islands on such short notice was a challenge. The month before, when Ghormley had stopped off in Washington on his way to the South Pacific, King told him candidly that "the resources were not available" for him to accomplish all that was necessary. King's mantra had always been to "do the best we can with what we have," and he expected Ghormley to do the same.[31]

Nimitz and King continued their conversation the next day. Kelly Turner, who would command the amphibious flotilla for the Guadalcanal operation, expressed confidence that he could effect a successful landing there as long as he achieved surprise and the carriers could provide air cover over the beach. The question was how long air cover would be needed. Nimitz told Turner that it should take "about three days" to land the men and supplies, and Turner expressed satisfaction with that. Soon afterward, Nimitz left to fly back to Hawaii.

Before he had left for San Francisco, Nimitz told his staff to prepare a planning document for the Tulagi operation. Now on his return he told them to expand the plan to include Guadalcanal. The planners did not make light of the difficulties. The Running Summary stated flatly, "We must expect and be able to afford disproportionate losses in gaining our objective." And there was a hint of caution, even a warning, in the observation that "if we are not prepared to lose ships and men yet, then the time is not ripe."[32]

Ripe or not, King set a target date of August 1, 1942, for the invasion. That was only three weeks away.

T HE FIRST HALF OF JULY 1942 was frenetic ("exceedingly busy," as Nimitz put it in a letter to Catherine). Aware that the campaign for Guadalcanal would have to go forward with marginal resources and a tight schedule, Nimitz and his staff scrambled to assemble the necessary shipping.[1]

The individual who had to execute the invasion was not Nimitz but his subordinate: Vice Admiral Robert L. Ghormley, commander of the South Pacific Area. Ghormley had superb credentials. He had graduated from the Naval Academy a year behind Nimitz in 1906, but because he had spent three years at the University of Idaho before going to Annapolis, he was actually three years older than his new boss. He had been both the Director of War Plans for the Navy and the Assistant Chief of Naval Operations. His most immediate prior service was as Roosevelt's clandestine representative in London (his official title was "Special Observer") during the period of American neutrality. He had performed well in that role, which, of course, involved a far different set of responsibilities.[2]

Ghormley had passed through Hawaii en route to his new assignment in May, but that had been during the hectic preparations for Midway, when few were thinking about a South Pacific offensive. Nimitz talked with him only briefly before Ghormley flew on to Auckland, New Zealand, where King had ordered him to establish his headquarters. With the pending offensive in mind, however, King ordered him to move closer to the front, and Ghormley set up new headquarters onboard the old (1918) Army transport ship *Argonne*, moored in Nouméa Harbor at New Caledonia. Ghormley arrived there without a staff and then almost at once received orders to prepare America's first major counteroffensive of the war. Nimitz, too, had arrived in Pearl Harbor without a staff back in December, but he had inherited a staff from Kimmel; Ghormley had to cobble one together from scratch.

The command relationship between Nimitz and Ghormley was not unlike that between King and Nimitz. Ghormley managed operations in the theater,

Vice Admiral Robert Lee Ghormley, commander of the South Pacific Area, had to mount a major offensive in the Solomon Islands both quickly and with marginal resources. (Navy History and Heritage Command)

and Nimitz provided guidance and oversight from a distance. In his student thesis at the Naval War College back in 1923, Nimitz had written that effective command required senior officers to identify the objective and then endow their subordinates with "authority, responsibility, and great freedom of initiative." He wrote to Ghormley on July 7 to define the objective: "Capture Tulagi, Gavutu, Florida, and Guadalcanal Islands on Dog Day, approximately 1 August." He enumerated the available forces and suggested conducting rehearsals at Fiji. Two days later, Nimitz wrote again to outline some of the logistical details, including fuel arrangements, and told Ghormley that he would "from time to time issue further instructions." Nonetheless, the thrust of his communications was to assure Ghormley that he had "full confidence in your ability to carry this operation to [a] successful conclusion."[3]

That confidence may have been shaken the next day when Nimitz received a copy of a lengthy and somewhat alarming message that Ghormley and MacArthur had written and sent to King. In it, the authors flatly declared that the timeline for the invasion of Guadalcanal was unrealistic. The message included the word "doubtful" twice and "improbable" once, and expressed the "gravest doubts" about conducting the operation at all. King suspected immediately that this was MacArthur's handiwork. Less than a month before, the general had insisted that he could go all the way to Rabaul if the Navy sent him a division of amphibious troops and two carriers; now he declared that occupying one of the intervening islands was all but impossible.

Perhaps because he suspected that MacArthur was the primary author, King was uncharacteristically restrained in his response to Ghormley. He explained to him that the "world situation" made it impossible to provide him with everything he needed, but circumstances made it necessary to proceed nonetheless. Ghormley dutifully replied that the forces he had were "sufficient." Still, the letter from MacArthur and Ghormley was worrisome, for it suggested that Ghormley had allowed MacArthur to bully him into protesting his orders.[4]

OF THE MANY SHORTAGES GHORMLEY FACED, the most critical was shipping. There was simply not enough of it, and what there was consisted mostly of holdovers from peacetime. The men of the 1st Marine Division (about nineteen thousand men altogether) were carried to the targeted islands by an eclectic collection of seventeen transports, many of them repurposed merchant ships that were now designated, somewhat aspirationally, as "attack transports." From them, the Marines would climb down into small wooden boats that were called "landing craft" but which were essentially surfboats that lacked the subsequently familiar drop-front bow. When the boats nudged up into the shallows, the men in them had to climb out over the side to make their way ashore.

An even greater concern was how to sustain the invaders once they got ashore. Nimitz's staff noted pointedly that everything the Marines needed—"fuel, ammunition, weapons, aircraft, food, clothing, spare parts, repair manuals, and general supplies"—had to be brought to the island from Nouméa by those same transport and cargo ships making repeated and lengthy round trips. Neither Nouméa nor Guadalcanal had the kind of facilities needed to load or unload them. As a result, Ghormley requested—and got—a postponement of D-Day from August 1 to August 7. Even then it would be a race to meet the deadline.[5]

Nimitz worried that expectations in Washington were overly optimistic. He was confident the Marines could seize their initial objectives, especially if they obtained tactical surprise; the bigger problem was sustaining them afterward. He also suspected that as soon as the Japanese learned of the American initiative, they would immediately launch a counterattack. "It is unsafe," he wrote to King on July 17, "to assume that the enemy will not exert every effort to recover the positions we may take from them." If the invasion force endured any significant loss, especially in shipping, it was entirely possible that "we may be unable to hold what we have taken." He did not expect King to reconsider the operation, but he felt obligated to state his views.[6]

Nimitz also worried about the effect of the operation on the Central Pacific as a whole. To initiate and sustain the assault on Guadalcanal, Nimitz had to commit virtually every transport ship that could be rounded up, plus the escorts needed to protect them, as well as three of his four aircraft carriers—*Saratoga*, *Enterprise*, and *Wasp*—all under Frank Jack

Fletcher, now at last promoted to vice admiral. (Halsey was still in the hospital.) Nimitz wondered whether the buildup in the South Pacific would tempt the Japanese to take another shot at Midway. He ordered the construction of a second airfield at Midway using what were called Marston Mats: perforated steel matting that could be used in place of tarmac. He worried about other outposts, too, and flew to Johnston Island, eight hundred miles to the west, to inspect defenses there personally.* The good news was that Rochefort was fairly certain that Japan's carriers were still in Japanese home waters.[7]

That, however, was very nearly the last piece of inside information that Rochefort and Hypo were able to provide for some time. In mid-August, the Japanese changed their codes again, and Hypo could no longer read their messages. The codebreakers could make informed guesses about Japanese movements based on traffic analysis—the number and location of messages sent—but as the scribe of the Running Summary put it, "we are no longer reading the enemy mail." That was particularly worrisome given that Ghormley had written Nimitz two weeks earlier to tell him that he would "lean heavily on intelligence reports from you." He had asked Nimitz to "keep me fully aware" of "vital information." Now, there was no information to share.[8]

IN THE MEANTIME, NIMITZ MAINTAINED HIS daily routine, including the morning staff meetings. He made frequent visits to the naval hospital, often with General Emmons, walking slowly between the rows of beds and talking quietly to men who had been wounded at Midway. He continued to host lunches and dinners in his home, sometimes with a dozen or more guests, making a point of including junior officers whenever he could. These were not just social events; they allowed him to keep his finger on the pulse of officer morale and hear views from outside the circle of official advisers on his staff. As one junior officer recalled later, "He never minded questions from his subordinates and in fact encouraged them." When he hosted a dinner,

---

* Nimitz made it a point to fly to most of the islands within his far-flung command. It is a window into the Navy's bureaucratic requirements that every time he did so, he had to write orders to himself authorizing the trip, and approve an allocation of six dollars of per diem pay while he was away from his assigned duty station.

Nimitz (like FDR in the White House) liked to mix the drinks himself. His specialty was an old-fashioned constructed from his own recipe. He put a sugar cube in the bottom of the glass, added one drop of Angostura bitters, then added just enough hot water to melt the cube. That was followed by cracked ice, two ounces of bourbon, and, to top it off, an ounce of rum, which made it particularly lethal. He called this powerful concoction a "CinCPac."[9]

Nimitz also continued his strenuous afternoon walks into the hills behind the naval base, almost always with Spruance striding alongside. For these hikes, Nimitz simply removed the four-star insignia from his collars and walked in his khakis. Spruance, however, had a dedicated hiking outfit consisting of faded trousers, a civilian shirt, Marine field shoes, and a beloved and battered Panama hat. Thus attired, he not only kept up with Nimitz, but was likely to push the pace and continue farther than Nimitz might have done had he been by himself.

About once a week the two admirals piled into the big staff Buick and headed over to the north shore for a swim. Hardly a typical "day at the beach," it was another opportunity for challenging exercise. Though a number of younger junior officers on the staff found the admiral's regimen daunting, some of them giving up and straggling back, Spruance had no difficulty. On some occasions during the ocean swim, Nimitz turned shoreward and Spruance churned doggedly onward.[10]

On July 23, Spruance's son showed up at headquarters. Like Nimitz's son, Chet, Edward Spruance had chosen submarine duty after graduating from Annapolis, and he had been on board the submarine *Tambor* during the Battle of Midway. Nimitz invited Edward to come along on their afternoon walk; perhaps taking it as an order, Edward quickly agreed. Nimitz noticed immediately that the relationship between father and son was cool and correct; Edward later described his father as "austere, remote, and inflexible." The three men walked seven miles mostly in silence, though later Nimitz wrote Catherine that "every turn of the road gave us a marvelous view of the harbor and the ocean."[11]

THAT SAME WEEK, FOUR THOUSAND MILES to the south, the men of the 1st Marine Division conducted a practice landing on Koro, in the Fiji Islands.

It did not go well. As one Marine platoon commander observed, "Ship-to-shore communications were slow, navy coxswains were inexperienced, marines were slow to embark, and there was confusion among the destroyers' artillery groups." Simultaneously, Fletcher hosted a pre-invasion conference aboard the *Saratoga* with the principal commanders. Those included Marine Major General Alexander Archer Vandegrift (who disliked his first name and preferred to go by Archer), Richmond Kelly Turner, commander of the transport force (who also used his middle name), and Rear Admiral John S. "Slew" McCain, who commanded the land-based air forces.[†] Ghormley did not attend. Though King had told Ghormley to "command in person in the operating area," and Nimitz had reiterated those instructions a week later, Ghormley believed he could not relinquish the reins of theater management in Nouméa even for a moment, and so he sent his chief of staff, Rear Admiral Daniel Callaghan, in his stead. Callaghan conceived of his role as that of an observer and note taker and let Fletcher run the meeting, which quickly turned contentious.[12]

Turner was at the center of the friction. Physically, Turner was whippet thin, but he had the temperament of a pit bull. An acolyte of King, he shared many of King's confrontational characteristics. The historian John Lundstrom characterized Turner as "arrogant, abrasive, irascible, and domineering." The dispute during the meeting on the *Saratoga* concerned the length of time that Fletcher's carriers would provide air cover over the landing beach at Guadalcanal. Fletcher said that he planned to keep his carriers within striking range of the beachhead for two days before maneuvering independently. Both Turner and Vandegrift vehemently objected. Despite his assertion in San Francisco that three days would be sufficient, Turner now wanted Fletcher to commit to five days, and Vandegrift wanted Fletcher to stay until the airfield ashore was operational.[‡] Had Ghormley been present, he might have adjudicated the disagreement, but he was not,

---

† John S. "Slew" McCain was the grandfather of the future Arizona senator and presidential candidate.

‡ As it happened, the first Marine Corps planes did not land on the airfield until August 20, a full two weeks after D-Day. Given that, it would have been unrealistic for Fletcher to remain off the beachhead until the airfield was operational.

Rear Admiral Richmond Kelly Turner (in foreground) discusses the Guadalcanal campaign with the U.S. Marine commander, Major General Archer Vandegrift, on board Turner's flagship, the attack transport *McCawley*. Turner's abrupt and querulous manner earned him the nickname "Terrible Turner." (U.S. National Archives)

and Callaghan remained largely passive, which may have contributed to the bitterness and acrimony that emerged later.[13]

Fletcher acknowledged that while he certainly needed to provide air cover for the initial landing, his primary responsibility was the protection and preservation of his carriers. Like Nimitz, he was convinced that the Japanese would respond energetically to the American landing and would very likely commit their carrier force. If so, he needed to be ready to meet it. Committing his own carriers to a static defense of the beachhead for more than two days not only wasted their primary attribute as mobile platforms but would also leave them vulnerable to enemy land-based air and submarines. Still, Fletcher agreed to extend his commitment from two days to three.[14]

Turner remained unhappy and he complained to Ghormley, who tried to adjudicate the dispute long-distance by sending Fletcher a plan for his "consideration." He suggested that Fletcher should leave two fighter squadrons on the Guadalcanal airfield—"assuming field is ready"—before he left. It was unlikely, however, that the field on Guadalcanal would be ready so quickly, and in any case Ghormley undermined his "suggestion" by telling Fletcher that if "hostile carriers" came into the area, they should become his primary objective. As a result, Turner thought he had assurances that Fletcher would cover the landing beach until the airfield was operational, and Fletcher believed he had approval to maneuver independently as necessary.[15]

While Ghormley failed to bring clarity to the invasion plans, Nimitz pursued a pet project of his own, one that he hoped would distract the Japanese from the Guadalcanal landings. For some time he had encouraged the development of specially trained Marine Corps Raider battalions to conduct hit-and-run raids on Japanese outposts to keep the enemy off balance. The idea did not originate with him. It was President Roosevelt, encouraged by William "Wild Bill" Donovan, Director of the Office of Strategic Services, who pushed the idea. King was dubious, but Nimitz embraced it. Initially he thought that Wake Island or Tulagi would be an appropriate target for such a raid, though he eventually settled on tiny Butaritari Island in Makin Atoll, the northernmost of the Gilbert Islands. Two hundred or so Marine commandos would be carried to the target by two oversized submarines (*Nautilus* and *Argonaut*) and landed at night in rubber boats. Once ashore, they would blow up fuel depots and other installations, then withdraw the way they had come. Nimitz's notion was that the threat of more such pinprick attacks would compel the Japanese to disperse their defenses. He set a target date of August 17 for the raid—ten days after the Guadalcanal landings.[16]

D-DAY IN THE SOLOMON ISLANDS WAS August 7 (August 6 in Hawaii). Once again, Nimitz waited for news at his headquarters. Waiting was more stressful than usual because for two days there was no news at all. Turner sent off regular messages to Ghormley, but due either to atmospheric interference or to a glitch in Turner's radio equipment few of them got through. Nimitz first heard of the landings from intercepted Japanese radio reports, and twenty-four hours passed before he got anything official from his own officers. Naturally, that fed a rising level of anxiety at headquarters.[17]

Finally, two days later, Fletcher forwarded the gist of several incomplete and garbled messages he had received from Turner. It was not good news. The Marines had gotten ashore with little difficulty, but in the pitch-dark early morning hours of August 9, a Japanese surface force had attacked the Allied cruisers and destroyers guarding the beachhead in what came to be known as the Battle of Savo Island. The cruiser *Chicago* had been hit; the Australian cruiser *Canberra* was "on fire"; the cruisers *Quincy* and *Vincennes* had both been "sunk by gunfire and torpedoes." Casualties, Fletcher reported, were heavy. The staff duty officer, Ralph Ofstie, brought Nimitz the news. He recalled that Nimitz showed little emotion, merely telling him "to draft a dispatch of encouragement" to the men of the 1st Marine Division, who were holding the lines on the island.[18]

An embarrassed and angry Kelly Turner blamed the disaster on Fletcher's decision to withdraw his carriers. It was an unfair accusation since at the time of the battle Fletcher's carriers were still in their covering position south of the island, and in any case the battle took place at night, and none of Fletcher's planes had the avionics or radar needed to allow them to operate in the dark. Nevertheless, Turner's complaints further eroded King's confidence in Fletcher as a fighting admiral.

Ghormley learned about the disaster the same time Nimitz did, and his initial response was reflexive, if not panicky: he ordered Allied naval surface forces at Guadalcanal and Tulagi to withdraw to Nouméa, nearly a thousand miles away. He told Nimitz that he could not protect his sea lines of communication to Guadalcanal and requested "immediate air reinforcement." Crucially, however, he did *not* call off the operation. The men of the 1st Marine Division were already ashore, and extracting them now would be chaotic, if not disastrous. Ghormley had an additional 4,800 men of the 2nd Marine Regiment and other units in reserve but, unsure of their immediate status, he issued a set of conditional orders that betrayed his uncertainty about what was going on. If the men of the reserve force had already

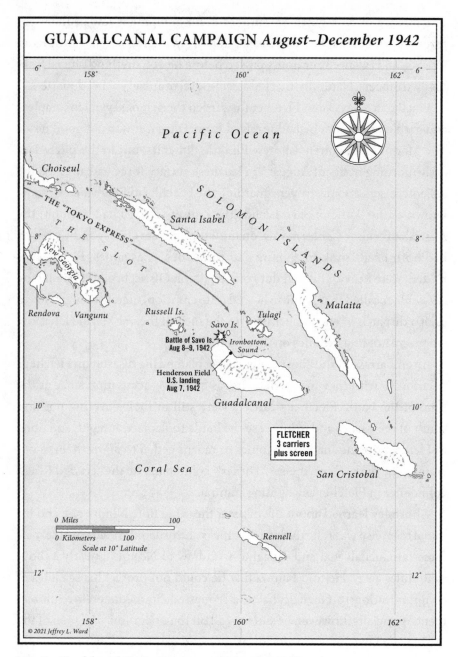

Map 7: Guadalcanal Campaign, August–December 1942

started landing on Guadalcanal, Ghormley ordered, they should continue with that. If they were headed for their secondary target of Ndeni in the Santa Cruz Islands, they should turn around and go back to Guadalcanal. If they had already started landing on Ndeni, they should stay there. He also reached out to MacArthur to ask him to send whatever submarines he could into the area and to continue with reconnaissance flights, though he probably did not endear himself to McArthur by employing the abrupt ending "Action MacArthur," which implied that Ghormley was sending him orders.[19]

Nimitz did not want to interfere from 3,600 miles away, but he immediately responded. He arranged for two Marine fighter squadrons and one carrier squadron to head for the South Pacific as soon as possible, though he knew that it was unlikely any of them could get there before mid-September.[20]

Meanwhile, things got worse. Though Hypo was still unable to read enemy messages, it reported that traffic analysis indicated the Japanese were vectoring substantial surface forces to the Solomons from across the Pacific, even from the home islands. Meanwhile, the shortage of Allied shipping and the abrupt withdrawal of most of that shipping to Nouméa meant that Vandegrift's Marines could not expect reinforcements or supplies for seven to ten days. Nimitz told Ghormley to do what he could to interdict the Japanese convoys, and he urged Fletcher's carrier planes and MacArthur's bombers to "detect and report" the movement of enemy convoys.[21]

Ghormley finally got a status report from Vandegrift that night, which he forwarded to Nimitz. The news from ashore was better than the news at sea. After "bitter fighting," Tulagi was firmly in American hands; U.S. casualties were "about 450," and Japanese casualties were "100%" since they had fought literally to the last man. The Marines on Guadalcanal (code name Cactus) were "digging in" to create a "perimeter defense" around the unfinished airfield. It was evident to all that completing the airfield as soon as possible was "imperative." The difficulty was that the Marines did not have earthmoving equipment, Marston Mats, or most of the other equipment needed for airfield construction. The invasion planning had focused so heavily on getting ashore that the need to ensure swift completion of the airfield was insufficiently considered. The Marines got to work using abandoned Japanese equipment, though the work proceeded slowly. While Vandegrift considered his position "secure," he emphasized that he had few tools and "no barbed wire."[22]

From Pearl Harbor, Nimitz coordinated the collection and distribution of construction equipment, trucks, Marston Mats, hoists, fuel, and ammunition. The bottleneck, as usual, was the shipping needed to carry all of it to Guadalcanal. With shipments there resumed, Ghormley suggested that the ships should arrive at Guadalcanal at night and be unloaded in the dark so that the scarce and valuable transports could avoid air attacks. The Japanese made the same calculation, and what emerged was a race to see who could get the most men, equipment, and especially food ashore the quickest.[23]

King again raised the question of employing the battleships. This time, Nimitz was fairly curt in his reply: "I will not send any of the slow battleships South unless so directed by you." There was nothing for it, he insisted, other than to shuttle men and supplies into the beachhead as fast as possible.[24]

ONE BRIGHT NOTE IN THIS WEEK of continuous crisis was the arrival in Pearl Harbor of Hal Lamar, who had been Nimitz's aide in Washington and had accompanied him on the train to Los Angeles. When Nimitz had headed south for San Diego and the flight to Hawaii, Lamar, as noted, had returned to D.C. to serve as aide to Nimitz's replacement at the Bureau of Navigation, Rear Admiral Randall Jacobs. Nimitz had been trying to get him back ever since. Jacobs wanted to keep him and resisted Nimitz's pleas. On August 15, however, Lamar showed up. Nimitz was delighted, and Lamar became a constant presence both in Nimitz's quarters, where he had his own room, and at headquarters. He was not universally popular at headquarters. He was susceptible to a condition common among flag aides of assuming the authority of his boss, and that annoyed other staff officers, a few of whom referred to him privately as "Stinky." On one charged occasion, Nimitz's assistant chief of staff, Captain Bernard Austin, told Lamar that he was behaving like a little boy and that if he didn't act like a grown-up he would personally spank him. Nevertheless, Nimitz appreciated his aide's loyalty and commitment, and Lamar stayed with him until the end of the war.[25]

About this time, too, Nimitz and his whole staff, including Lamar, moved their offices from the submarine base to a brand-new building farther up the slope of Makalapa Hill. Built of concrete and supposedly bombproof, this charmless building, which almost everyone called "The Cement Pot," would be Nimitz's professional home for the next twenty-eight months. His office, a corner room on the first floor, was open and airy, with colorful drapes that matched the cushions on the bamboo furniture. Lamar tacked campaign maps to the walls, and Nimitz worked at a large wooden desk covered by a sheet of clear glass on which he kept a few mementos plus two framed photographs. One was of the president ("For Admiral Chester W. Nimitz from his old friend, Franklin D. Roosevelt"). Like most naval officers, Nimitz had initially registered as a Republican, but he had changed his registration in 1932 to vote for Roosevelt, and he appreciated FDR's strong support for the Navy. The other photograph was of Douglas MacArthur. It was not a portrait photo; it had been clipped from a magazine. Nimitz was coy when asked why he kept it there, though at least one officer believed it was a cautionary reminder not to make "Jovian pronouncements."[26]

Nimitz also acquired a dog. He had grown up with dogs in Texas, and in Washington he and Catherine had owned a spotted cocker spaniel named Freckles. Freckles's claim to fame was that whenever Catherine sat down to play the piano, he would jump up on the bench next to her and accompany her with a series of howls, which always made Nimitz laugh out loud. His new dog was a dark brown schnauzer whom he named Makalapa after the hill, but whom he and everyone else called simply Mak. The animal accompanied Nimitz on most of his lengthy walks and spent much of the rest of his time curled up at Nimitz's feet under his desk. To most visitors he was benign, though for some he would raise his head, show his teeth, and emit a low growl. Nimitz was unable to discern the source of his selective discrimination. For the rest of the war, Mak, like Lamar, was a regular fixture at headquarters.[27]

Soon after the move into the new building, Lamar noticed a slight tremor in Nimitz's hands. Lamar consulted the staff physician, Dr. Elphege Gendreau, who suggested it might be nerves. Gendreau speculated that despite Nimitz's outward calm, his body was beginning to betray the pressure

Nimitz at the pistol range that Hal Lamar had the Marines build for him outside the new headquarters on Makalapa Hill. Nimitz often visited the range, occasionally challenging the Marine sentry to a shooting match, with a Coca-Cola as the stakes. (U.S. Naval Institute)

he was under. He suggested that shooting a target pistol could help, since it required the shooter to clear his mind and calm his hands as he squeezed the trigger. Lamar approached the Marine unit attached to Nimitz's head-quarters (colloquially called the "Palace Guard") and asked them to build a pistol range outside the new headquarters building. Once it was completed, Lamar challenged the instinctively competitive Nimitz to a match, with a dime as the stakes. Nimitz accepted the challenge, and after that, he regularly visited the pistol range, often right after the morning staff meeting or whenever he wanted to blow off some steam. Lamar noticed that the tremor soon disappeared.[28]

A KEY TURNING POINT IN THE Guadalcanal campaign came on August 20, when the first Marine Corps fighter planes and scout bombers, ferried there by the escort carrier Long Island, landed on the now-completed airstrip, which the Marines had named Henderson Field after Major Loftus "Joe" Henderson, who had been killed at Midway. The presence of those planes gave the Americans daytime air superiority over the beachhead, and that allowed U.S. supply ships from Nouméa to arrive by day as well as at night, whereas the Japanese continued to smuggle in their reinforcements only at night, doing so with such regularity that the Marines nicknamed their convoys the "Tokyo Express."[29]

While the Marines defended their ground perimeter against fierce and ever larger Japanese assaults, Fletcher maneuvered his carriers south and east of the island seeking an opportunity to strike a blow against Japanese carriers. On August 24, he found it. To cover the landing of a large reinforcement convoy carrying five thousand soldiers, the Japanese assembled a substantial force of carriers and battleships, and Fletcher moved north to intercept it.

As the opposing forces converged on each other a few hundred miles northeast of Guadalcanal, Nimitz again waited for news. Early reports were worrisome: the Enterprise had been hit by two bombs (actually three), and though the crew got the ensuing fires under control, Fletcher decided to send her south, out of the battle, directing her planes to Henderson Field. There was good news as well. Planes from the Saratoga had inflicted serious damage on a smaller Japanese carrier, probably the Ryūjō, which appeared to be in extremis, though the extent of the damage was unknown.[§] As the

---

§ Though Nimitz did not learn of it until 1943, the Ryūjō sank soon after the American planes departed.

picture became clearer, it was evident that this third carrier battle of the war, labeled the Battle of the Eastern Solomons (August 24–25), was very nearly a clone of the Battle of the Coral Sea, four months earlier. Now, as then, American planes sank a small Japanese carrier and inflicted damage on one of their big carriers, while Japanese planes severely damaged an American carrier, though in this case the *Enterprise*, unlike the *Lexington*, managed to stay afloat. Most importantly, as in the Coral Sea, the Japanese reinforcement convoy, hit hard by planes from Henderson Field, was forced to turn back, thereby slowing the Japanese buildup on the island. Arguably, the battle had been both a tactical and strategic victory for the United States.[30]

King did not see it that way. Though he had eventually accepted that the Battle of the Coral Sea had been a success, he decided that this confrontation in the Eastern Solomons was a disappointment, even a defeat. In his view, Fletcher had again failed to press the issue. King noted that the American pilots claimed to have shot down eighty Japanese planes, which, if true, meant that the enemy carriers were all but defenseless. Under those circumstances, King concluded, Fletcher could have continued the battle with little risk. In fact, the Japanese had lost only thirty-three planes, yet King saw Fletcher's decision to withdraw as part of a disturbing pattern. In his view, the U.S. Navy could not afford the luxury of a carrier group commander who was hesitant, maybe even timid. Twice before, King had deferred to Nimitz's robust defense of Fletcher, yet after the Battle of the Eastern Solomons King decided that Fletcher had to go.

On August 31, the *Saratoga* was maneuvering in the channel between the Solomon and Santa Cruz Islands when a Japanese submarine worked its way past the screening destroyers and put a torpedo into her; Fletcher himself was slightly wounded. The big ship stayed afloat, though it would have to go into the yards—again—for a refit, and while the *Saratoga* underwent repairs King ordered Fletcher to Washington for "temporary duty."

Nimitz did not object. As a rule, he believed that senior officers who bore heavy command responsibility required periodic recuperation (though he never took leave himself). A few weeks later, when he met with Fletcher in Pearl Harbor, he thought Fletcher seemed well enough except for "a slightly strained expression about the eyes." He told him to get a good rest and to report in November to resume his command. Nimitz subsequently told McCain that Fletcher was tired and needed "a blow," and as soon as he was himself again, he would be happy to have him back. It didn't happen. Fletcher never again commanded a carrier task force.[31]

A UGUST AND SEPTEMBER IN HAWAII are characterized by a hot, sticky climate the locals call "kona weather." It did not affect Nimitz's routine. He continued to walk three miles before breakfast, arrive at the office about 7:30, meet with Layton at 8:00, and host the morning staff meeting at 9:00. After that, he sometimes went to the pistol range before tackling the accumulated paperwork, taking periodic breaks to walk from office to office and look in on his staffers to see what they were working on, mostly to ensure that everyone was on the same page—a practice that business schools have subsequently labeled MBWA, management by walking around.

Throughout those sultry weeks, Nimitz continued to receive regular messages from Ghormley, sometimes more than one a day, almost all of them pleading for reinforcements for Guadalcanal (Cactus), especially fighter planes. The twelve scout bombers and seven fighters of VMF-223 that landed on Henderson Field on August 20 constituted the initial increment of what came to be called the Cactus Air Force. They were soon reinforced by two more Marine squadrons as well as a squadron of Navy Wildcats from the *Saratoga*. That helped, though it was not a permanent solution since keeping trained carrier pilots on shore squandered their specialized expertise. Vandegrift also had fourteen Army P-39 Aircobra fighters, which performed poorly at high altitude. Ghormley claimed that only two of them were operational.

And it wasn't just the planes; it was also the aviation fuel needed to keep them flying. AvGas was so scarce on the island that the Marines took to siphoning whatever was left in the tanks of wrecked airplanes—literally sucking it out with a tube—to use in the steadily declining number of planes that could still fly. And because there were no fuel pumps, the fifty-five-gallon drums then had to be manhandled up onto a plane's wing and the fuel poured into the tanks by hand. Nimitz forwarded all of Ghormley's appeals to Washington with supportive endorsements, telling King that the island needed "a steady flow" of "suitable Army aircraft." He even played cheerleader: "Let's give Cactus the wherewithal to live up to its name. Something for the Japs to remember forever." At the same time, however, he also urged Ghormley to be more active. In a message addressed to all Pacific commanders, though certainly with Ghormley in mind, Nimitz wrote, "We cannot expect to inflict heavy losses on the enemy without ourselves accepting the risk of punishment."[1]

Ghormley's fundamental problem was that the seizure of the Guadalcanal beachhead had been undertaken in such a hurry and with such marginal resources that there was barely enough shipping to sustain it. And, as Nimitz had foreseen, the Japanese had immediately initiated a major effort to take it back. Indeed, it was central to their understanding of the war. They had never expected to win the war outright. Their vision of "victory" was based on an assumption that a stalwart defense of their island empire would eventually convince the feckless Americans to accept a negotiated settlement. Now that the Americans had begun their counteroffensive, the Japanese were determined to prove the validity of their assumption.

On the last day of August, three weeks into the Guadalcanal campaign, Nimitz received another message from Ghormley, laying out his plans for the next several days. It was clear, however, that—as the Running Summary put it—"Admiral Ghormley is having a hard time finding out what his forces are doing." In part that was because the chaotic situation in the Solomons changed almost daily. In part, too, it was because Ghormley was unwilling to leave his headquarters ship in Nouméa to inspect and supervise what was happening at the front. Nimitz began to wonder whether Ghormley might be in over his head in dealing with the stressful situation in which King's impatience and Japanese determination had placed him. To discuss that and other issues, Nimitz boarded a seaplane for the long flight to San Francisco and another conference with King. This time, no doubt, he buckled his seat belt.[2]

NIMITZ MET WITH KING FROM SEPTEMBER 7 to 9. There was much to discuss, and as usual personnel issues were at the forefront. Halsey was finally out of the hospital and able to resume his duties as commander of the *Enterprise* task force; his seniority would also make him commander of carrier forces in the Pacific. Halsey was in San Francisco that week and sat in on some of the discussions.[3]

A more complicated personnel issue concerned Rear Admiral John Henry Towers, who was Chief of the Bureau of Aeronautics. Towers was an active and vocal champion of naval aviation who saw it as his duty to defend aviators from the prejudice of the so-called Gun Club of battleship admirals. He was also politically adept, and he maintained a close relationship with the powerful chairman of the House Naval Affairs Committee, Carl Vinson of Georgia, as well as James V. Forrestal, the Undersecretary of the Navy. King, who liked to keep the levers of command in his own hands, found Towers troublesome. He also suspected him of planting stories in both the *Washington Post* and *Collier's* magazine about how foolish it was to put aircraft carriers under the authority of non-aviators. Back in December, when King had asked Roosevelt for independence from the bureau chiefs, it was very likely Towers he had in mind.[4]

King sought to bring Towers to heel by announcing two orders that restructured the Navy so that Towers came under his direct authority. He did not clear the plan with either the president or Secretary Knox, however, and when FDR found out about it, he was furious. In a letter to Knox countermanding King's orders, FDR wrote, "The more I think of the two orders, the more outrageous I think it is." The president considered calling King in to give him "a good dressing down," though there is no record of such a meeting.[5]

That gambit having failed, King then sought to find a job for Towers outside Washington. His solution was to send him to Nimitz as his deputy commander for air. Nimitz was not happy about it, for he had his own troubled history with Towers. "Never mind," he wrote to Catherine. "We will get along fine."[6]

Another personnel issue was in the North Pacific, where Rear Admiral Robert A. Theobald was feuding with his Army counterpart, William O. Butler. Theobald's nickname was "Fuzzy," though a more apt moniker would be "Prickly," for, as one fellow admiral put it, "he is continually arguing or reciting his woes in contentious fashion." His dispute with Butler concerned a tiny group of islands in the middle of the Bering Sea called the Pribilofs. Theobald insisted that he, and not Butler, should be in charge of their defense. As far as Nimitz was concerned, it was a tempest in a teapot. Still, after some discussion, King and Nimitz decided to support Theobald, though they also decided that if such problems persisted, he, too, might have to be replaced.[7]

Nimitz reported the results of the raid on Makin Atoll. It had gone off as scheduled on August 17 when a Marine battalion (known as Carlson's Raiders after the commander, Evans Carlson) landed in rubber boats from their oversize submarines. After blowing up some Japanese defenses, they were supposed to extract the same way. Instead, the raiders found themselves engaged in a brisk firefight. The Marines fought their way back to the beach, but heavy surf overturned most of the rubber boats. Only about a quarter of the men made it to the subs that night, leaving more than 120 of them stranded on the island, including both Carlson and his second in command, Lieutenant Colonel James Roosevelt, the president's son.* They and

---

* Carlson was so rattled by this he seriously considered surrendering, and likely would have done so if he had found any living Japanese to whom he could surrender.

most of the other Marines successfully evacuated the next morning, leaving behind a ruined enemy outpost and nearly ninety dead Japanese at a cost of forty-four Americans killed or wounded. Only later, after everyone was back in Pearl Harbor, did anyone realize that they had left nine men behind, all of whom were subsequently beheaded by the Japanese.[8]

Enough had gone wrong to cast doubt on the whole idea of conducting more such hit-and-run raids, but Nimitz wanted them to continue, seeing it as a way to compel the Japanese to disperse their forces and to keep them off balance until large-scale operations became feasible. In that respect, it was not unlike what Winston Churchill sought to do with Allied raids on the periphery of Europe.

The two admirals discussed other issues: their annoyance at having to deal with the press, and (equally annoying) the regular "communiqués" issued by MacArthur that inflated MacArthur's role and sometimes revealed classified information.

The main topic of conversation, however, was Ghormley. Both King and Nimitz noted the tone of anxiety—even desperation—that had crept into many of Ghormley's messages. It was not unjustified. Turner later confessed, "We were living from one logistic crisis to another." King was frustrated that the campaign was dragging on so long. For a man whose mantra was to do the best you can with what you have, he found Ghormley's constant requests for more support annoying as well as troubling. Unrealistically, King had envisioned a swift seizure of the lower Solomons (Task I), followed by the conquest of the north coast of New Guinea by MacArthur (Task II), and then the capture of Rabaul (Task III). Instead, operations seemed to have bogged down at Task I. It did not help that Ghormley wrote King that he should "anticipate intensive air action for months to come." Months! King remarked ruefully that "Tasks 2 and 3 apparently go out the window."[9]

Both King and Nimitz wondered if Ghormley was temperamentally suited for the job he held. Of all their concerns, at the top of the list was Ghormley's ability to assess how much risk to accept and under what circumstances—what Nimitz called "calculated risk." They began to discuss possible replacements for him should it become necessary. Nimitz wondered if Turner might be an acceptable replacement, and of course Halsey was now available, too. Randall Jacobs, who had taken Nimitz's old job as Personnel Chief, was in the room during the conversation, and asked if he should mention the possibility to Halsey. No, Nimitz told him. Not yet. First, Nimitz said, he would fly out to Nouméa to see Ghormley personally and assess the situation for himself.

NIMITZ RETURNED TO PEARL ON SEPTEMBER 11. When he arrived, there was another message from Ghormley describing the situation on Guadalcanal as "extremely critical." Heavy rains had rendered Henderson Field unreliable; the food situation was precarious; sealift problems continued; and, as always, he was short of aircraft. Ghormley said there were now only eleven Wildcats and three Aircobras still operational. He was sending the 7th Marine Regiment to Cactus to reinforce Vandegrift, but the outlook remained grim. As the Running Summary put it, the Japanese appeared to be "concentrating everything they have" in the Solomons.[10]

For Nimitz, there were occasional respites from the press of work. Halsey's namesake son, who was serving as an ensign on the *Saratoga*, came by headquarters to say hello on September 12. Nimitz took him along to a scheduled lunch party at the palatial estate of wealthy industrialist Walter Dillingham. Admiral Halsey was there, too, and father and son enjoyed a happy reunion. Dillingham's estate on the slope of Diamond Head had both a tennis court and a pool, and though Nimitz was disappointed by the lack of tennis competition, he enjoyed a swim and a nice meal. Afterward, he returned to the office, staying until nearly midnight "reading dispatches."[11]

That night, as Nimitz read those dispatches, a convoy carrying the 7th Marine Regiment was steaming westward toward Guadalcanal. Given its priceless human cargo, it had an especially powerful escort, one that included two aircraft carriers—the *Hornet* and the newly arrived *Wasp*—as well as the new battleship *North Carolina*. A second battleship, *South Dakota*, would have joined the convoy had she not been damaged when she struck a submerged reef at Tongabatu. Unlike pre-war battleships, these new "fast" battleships could make 28 knots, which meant that the carriers

The USS *Wasp* in extremis after being struck by Japanese Type 95 torpedoes on September 15, 1942. Her loss, combined with the earlier damage to *Enterprise* and *Saratoga*, left Nimitz with only one fully operational aircraft carrier in the Pacific theater. (U.S. National Archives)

had to slow only a little to allow them to keep pace. Moreover, the new battleships bristled with anti-aircraft guns that provided additional protection from Japanese air attacks.[12]

The threat, however, came not from above but from below. The next day, on September 15, Takaichi Kinashi in the submarine I-19 fired a six-torpedo spread into the American convoy. It was one of the most devastating torpedo salvos of the entire war. No troopships were hit, but one torpedo hit the *North Carolina*, another hit the destroyer *O'Brien*, and at least two struck the *Wasp*. The battleship survived, but the destroyer and the carrier did not.[†] The loss of the *Wasp*, combined with the earlier damage to both

---

[†] The *O'Brien* did not sink immediately; she broke apart and sank several weeks later while making her way back to Pearl Harbor for repairs.

Enterprise and *Saratoga*, meant that the *Hornet* was now the only fully operational American aircraft carrier in the Pacific. In the language of the Running Summary, "The situation is not hopeless but it is certainly critical."[13]

Critical as it was, it could have been worse had Turner lost his nerve and recalled the convoy, as the Japanese had done after the Battle of the Eastern Solomons. Instead, the convoy continued on to Guadalcanal and successfully landed 4,157 men of the 7th Marine Regiment, bringing Vandegrift's total force to over 20,000. That convoy also landed 147 vehicles and 4,323 barrels of precious aviation fuel. Though that helped, Nimitz remained concerned, writing Catherine, "We must face this period with grim determination and courage."[14]

NIMITZ HAD TOLD KING HE WOULD visit Ghormley to assess the situation in the South Pacific personally, and so on September 25 he climbed into another plane for the long flight south to Nouméa. Since it was to be a general discussion of the whole South Pacific campaign, he invited Turner as well, though not Vandegrift, who could not be spared from Guadalcanal. Nimitz also invited MacArthur, who declined, though he did send his two most trusted subordinates: his chief of staff, Richard K. Sutherland, and his air commander, George Kenney.[15]

Nimitz's journey was interrupted when an engine burned out a bearing and his plane had to put down on Canton Island, about a third of the way to Nouméa. While Nimitz waited for another plane to be sent from Hawaii, he talked with the men of the island's small garrison, finding them "a fine bunch, with high morale." He arrived in Nouméa on September 28. The first thing he noticed was that the harbor was positively crowded with shipping—more than eighty ships were at anchor. That was particularly curious since a dearth of shipping was the principal bottleneck in the effort to keep Vandegrift's Marines supplied. He soon learned that the logistics effort backing up the invasion was a complete muddle.[16]

The supply chain began in San Francisco, where the ships were loaded. More often than not, however, they were not combat-loaded. Instead, cargoes that should have been shipped together were broken up and loaded willy-nilly into different ships; some ships arrived without even a manifest to indicate what they carried. A member of Nimitz's staff noted, "There'd be seven crates in the bottom of the hold [of one ship], and the important center of the whole assembly was in another ship." As Turner explained it to Vandegrift, "We could not find out what material most of the ships still had on board." Consequently, the cargoes had to be unloaded, identified, counted, catalogued, reorganized, and then reloaded before being sent on to Guadalcanal. Yet Nouméa had only one dock and no heavy-lift equipment. Some ships that arrived in Nouméa from San Francisco had to backtrack to Auckland to be reorganized, adding thousands of miles to their journey. Ghormley had requested "weight handling" equipment and other machinery to help him break this absurd logjam, but, like everything else, it was in short supply. Nimitz saw firsthand why so many of Ghormley's messages betrayed frustration.[17]

Nimitz was not the only four-star officer visiting Nouméa that week. Hap Arnold, Chief of Staff of the Army Air Force, was there, too. The white-haired, cherubic Arnold, who got his nickname from his ubiquitous smile and cheerful demeanor, was visiting each of the command theaters in the Pacific. He had already been to Hawaii to see Nimitz, and then to MacArthur's headquarters in Brisbane, Australia, and now he had come to see Ghormley. In Brisbane, Arnold had been taken aback by MacArthur's profound despondency. Though the Japanese overland advance toward Port Moresby had stalled, MacArthur had fallen victim to the perception that the Japanese were unconquerable. Striding back and forth in his office and gesticulating with his pipe, he had told Arnold that the Japanese were better fighters than the Germans, that he lacked the necessary force to hold them back, and that they were likely to seize all of New Guinea, including Port Moresby, as well as the Fiji Islands. He declared that they would soon "control the Pacific Ocean," at which point they would attack Hawaii. Arnold concluded that MacArthur was suffering from "battle fatigue."[18]

Arnold found similar pessimism at Ghormley's headquarters. Without increased air support, Ghormley told Arnold, the Marines on Guadalcanal would be driven into the sea. Arnold's reaction was that "everybody on that South Pacific Front had a bad case of the jitters." He appreciated that the Marines wanted more air support—so did everyone else. He reminded

Ghormley that his theater was only one front in a global war. Arnold himself was fully committed to the Germany First strategy. He believed that any available aircraft should be sent to Europe and "used against the Germans." In addition, the chaotic state of logistics in Nouméa may have eroded Arnold's confidence that planes sent to Ghormley would be used efficiently.[19]

When Nimitz arrived on the *Argonne*, he was surprised by Ghormley's appearance; he was pale and had lost weight. Though Ghormley had been deemed "physically qualified to perform all the duties at sea" by the Navy medical examiner in September, the doctor had noted some dental problems. Those problems worsened. Ghormley was now in near-constant pain from severely abscessed teeth. He also lived aboard an old ship with no air-conditioning. Nimitz asked him why he didn't move his headquarters to more comfortable quarters ashore. Ghormley replied that the French had been unwilling to offer shore accommodations; aware of the precarious relationship with the Free French government, he had not wanted to force the issue. So he made do.[20]

The meeting took place in the *Argonne*'s wardroom, which had been gussied up by spreading a green baize cloth over the table. Nimitz presided, and he began by asking Ghormley to outline the current situation. What was keeping Cactus in Allied hands, Ghormley insisted, was airpower. Without American air superiority over the island, the Japanese would be able to pour in unlimited and likely irresistible numbers of reinforcements. So far, the handful of fighters and bombers on Henderson Field had forced the enemy to run the "Tokyo Express" only at night. If the Americans lost control of the skies over the beachhead, Ghormley warned, the Marines would not be able to hold their enclave. MacArthur's two emissaries were, if anything, even more defeatist. They argued that all available men and materiel in the Pacific should be sent at once to Australia to blunt the Japanese thrust on New Guinea.[21]

Nimitz asked Ghormley why, if the situation on Guadalcanal was so precarious, he had not sent some or all of Major General Patch's Army division on New Caledonia to the island. Ghormley replied that Patch's men were not trained for either amphibious operations or jungle warfare. Twice during their conversation, a staff officer arrived to hand Ghormley a dispatch, and after reading it in silence, Ghormley muttered, "My God, what are we going to do about this?" Nimitz could empathize—he knew how it felt to be handed one more requirement when his scarce resources were committed elsewhere—but it also suggested that Ghormley was near the end of his rope.[22]

After the meeting in Nouméa, Nimitz flew to Guadalcanal, something Ghormley himself had not done. The flight proved to be an adventure—"hair raising," in the words of one staffer. The pilot did not have up-to-date charts and attempted to fly by dead reckoning. Soon it became evident that he was lost. Eventually someone on the staff came up with a map of the Solomon Islands torn from *National Geographic* magazine, and the pilot used it to pick out landmarks glimpsed through the heavy cloud cover. At last, amid a driving rainstorm, they found Henderson Field. Despite the conditions, Vandegrift was there to greet Nimitz and take him on a tour of the defensive perimeter. Nimitz asked to visit the hospital, where he talked with many of the sick and wounded, and that night he met with Vandegrift and his senior officers. Unlike the mood in either Brisbane or Nouméa, Nimitz noted that the men on the ground who were doing the actual fighting were in good spirits, even enthusiastic. Nimitz promised Vandegrift that he would send him all the support he could, and in a subdued ceremony the next morning awarded him and several others the Navy Cross.[23]

Nimitz's misadventures with air travel continued the next day when he boarded a B-17 for the return trip to Nouméa. Hoping to get a clear view of the island, he climbed into the Plexiglas bubble at the nose of the plane. Heavy rain had so muddied the runway that the bomber failed to achieve liftoff speed, and the pilot had to hit the brakes and shut down the engine to keep it from sliding into the Lunga River. Had it done so, Nimitz would almost certainly have been killed. That afternoon, on a drier runway, the same plane, with Nimitz now tucked safely in the back, successfully got off the ground, as did a second plane carrying the rest of his staff that lifted off twenty minutes later.

Nimitz's plane landed safely on Espiritu Santo, halfway to Guadalcanal, but after half an hour, the second plane was still not in sight. Hours passed

Nimitz presents the Navy Cross to Colonel Merritt A. "Red Mike" Edson as Vandegrift (behind Nimitz) looks on and the ubiquitous Hal Lamar (at right) prepares to hand the certificate to Nimitz. Edson's eight-hundred-man 5th Marine Regiment had held off repeated attacks by as many as five thousand Japanese, an achievement for which Edson subsequently received the Medal of Honor. (U.S. Naval Institute)

and it grew dark. Half of Nimitz's staff was somewhere out over that dark ocean and probably lost. As Spruance had done after Midway, Nimitz ordered one of the big 30-inch searchlights turned on and aimed straight up into the night sky as a beacon. A half-hour later the second plane, dangerously low on gas, landed safely.[24]

Two days later, Nimitz hosted another meeting in Nouméa, where he reported the optimism he had seen on Guadalcanal and pressed Ghormley to act more assertively. Ghormley's reply was that it was first necessary "to get Cactus stabilized." Nimitz pressed him about committing Patch's occupation force, now labeled the Americal Division. Ghormley again demurred. What about using New Zealand troops? Nimitz asked. Ghormley expressed doubt that the New Zealand government would allow it. Nimitz ordered him to find out and noted pointedly, "To win this war, we must use every resource we have."[25]

BY OCTOBER 5, AFTER BEING GONE ten days, Nimitz was back at his headquarters on Makalapa Hill. Buoyed by the visit to Vandegrift, he told his staff that he thought the situation in the South Pacific was "generally favorable." If Guadalcanal had become a vortex, absorbing a disproportionate amount of American assets, it was doing the same to the Japanese, who were losing more men, more planes, and more pilots than they could sustain. This was tactically valuable and had a strategic impact as well, because continual American pressure on Guadalcanal kept the enemy from initiating offensives elsewhere. The key, Nimitz asserted, was to shuttle reinforcements and equipment to the island as fast as possible.[26]

Several members of Nimitz's staff had accompanied him on the trip and had witnessed Ghormley's appearance and demeanor. Nimitz's logistics officer, Bill Callaghan, volunteered that "Admiral Ghormley was a very tired man." That encouraged others to speak up, and the criticism of Ghormley soon became pointed—even personal. Generally, Nimitz let staff members talk out disputes while he listened impassively. This time, Layton recalled watching Nimitz's eyes turn from sunny blue to steel gray until he finally interrupted. "I don't want to hear, or see, such gloom and such defeatism," he told them. "Our job here is to provide them with everything they need on Guadalcanal to fight this battle. We aren't going to do any good sitting here moaning or wailing or wringing our hands." Still, the tenor of the remarks was concerning. When the meeting ended, he asked a few key members of the staff to stay behind. Which among them, he asked, thought Ghormley should be relieved? They all did.[27]

Two nights later, as Nimitz was preparing for bed at about 10:00, an orderly told him that a group of officers wanted to see him about an urgent matter. Already in his pajamas and robe, Nimitz told them they could have five minutes. They argued that Ghormley was in over his head and suggested that Halsey should take his place. Nimitz heard them out, thanked them for speaking so frankly, and bade them a good night.[28]

That late-night visit may have influenced the tone of the letter Nimitz sent to Ghormley two days later. After thanking him for "a pleasant and profitable visit" and providing him with an itinerary of visitors who were headed to his area, Nimitz made a number of specific suggestions about Ghormley's disposition of forces. At its core, the letter suggested that Ghormley was being overly cautious. Nimitz acknowledged that the loss of the *Wasp* made the *Hornet* the only operational American carrier in the Pacific, so of course she should not be exposed thoughtlessly, but Ghormley had sent her so far from Guadalcanal that it would be impossible for her to "act quickly on favorable opportunities." Ghormley had also left the brand-new battleship *Washington* at Tongatabu, so far away that "she might as well have been in Pearl or San Francisco." Third, Ghormley had created a cruiser-destroyer surface force christened Task Force 64 under Rear Admiral Norman Scott, and then had positioned it to the south and east of Guadalcanal, where it was unlikely to encounter any Japanese resupply convoys. It would be better, Nimitz suggested, if Scott operated "to the westward and southwest of Cape Esperance," where it would be "in a position to strike the enemy." Finally, Nimitz urged Ghormley to visit Guadalcanal personally, and soon. Before he sent that letter, Nimitz radioed a copy of it to King to make sure he wasn't asking Ghormley to accept too much risk, though given King's own predilections, he knew that was unlikely.[29]

Never before or ever again did Nimitz offer such specific advice to an on-scene commander. He promised Ghormley that he would forward all the support he could, including a "stevedore battalion" to help with the loading and unloading at Nouméa, but there was an implied warning, as well as a plea, in his entreaty "to take such *calculated risks* as may be warranted to continue the attrition which we are now inflicting on the enemy's sea and air forces."[30]

His advice yielded immediate results. Ghormley relocated Scott's surface force to the west of Guadalcanal exactly where Nimitz had suggested it should be, and two days later it ambushed a group of Japanese warships off Cape Esperance. Scott reported sinking four enemy cruisers and two destroyers while losing only one destroyer himself plus serious damage to the cruiser *Boise*. As usual, the estimates were inflated; actual Japanese losses were one cruiser and one destroyer sunk plus another cruiser so badly shot up it barely made it back to Rabaul. Still, victory in the Battle of Cape Esperance (October 11–12) felt like suitable vengeance for the humiliation of Savo Island back in August, and Nimitz suggested to King that the results of that earlier battle, which the government had kept secret from the public until now, could safely be released.[31]

The victory off Cape Esperance slowed but did not stop the Japanese buildup on Guadalcanal, and over the next several days Nimitz received more distraught messages from Ghormley: the Japanese were approaching with another large convoy, he wrote, and his present forces were "totally inadequate" to meet them. For the first time, the Japanese committed battleships to the bombardment of Henderson Field, and the big shells from their heavy guns briefly made the field unusable. It was clear that, as the Running Summary put it, the enemy was "making an all out effort in the Solomons, employing the greater part of their Navy." At the same time, Nimitz's staff expressed alarm at the "panicky and desperate tone" of Ghormley's dispatches. Nimitz was alarmed as well, writing Catherine that he was "uneasy and worrisome over our situation which is not at all to my liking."[32]

One source of King's occasional frustration was his belief that Nimitz was unwilling to sacrifice well-meaning officers who were not performing up to scratch, preferring to give them a second chance. Now, however, despite his instinctive empathy, Nimitz began to believe that "the interests of the nation" required Ghormley's removal. He also worried that Ghormley was suffering both physically and mentally from the strain. Years later, he told Ghormley's son that he feared his father had been "on the verge of a nervous breakdown." Because Halsey was making a tour of the South Pacific that week in advance of reclaiming his old job on the *Enterprise*, he was close enough to assume the command immediately. When Nimitz radioed King to tell him he had it "under consideration" to replace Ghormley with Halsey and asked what he thought, King fired back a one-word response: "Approved."[33]

Nimitz composed another carefully worded message to Ghormley thanking him for his "loyal and devoted efforts" in pursuit of "a most difficult task," but telling him that in order to take advantage of Halsey's "talents and previous experience" Halsey would "take over the duties of ComSoPac as soon as practicable." It had not been an easy decision. Nimitz wrote Catherine, "It was a sore mental struggle, and the decision was not reached until after hours of anguished consideration." What had finally tipped the scales was his belief that "Ghormley was too immersed in detail and not sufficiently bold and aggressive at the right times." Hard as it had been to make the decision, once he did, he felt better immediately.[34]

When Halsey's seaplane splashed down in Nouméa Harbor on October 18, Ghormley's aide came out in a small boat to meet him and, without comment, handed him a sealed envelope. In it was a succinct message from Nimitz: "Immediately upon your arrival at Noumea, you will relieve Vice Admiral Robert L. Ghormley of the duties of Commander, South Pacific Area and South Pacific Force." Halsey read it twice to make sure he understood it, then, handing it to his intelligence officer, Marine Corps Lieutenant Colonel Julian Brown, he said, "Jesus Christ and General Jackson! This is hottest potato they have ever handed me."[35]

IN SOME RESPECTS, GHORMLEY HAD SIMPLY been unfortunate. He had arrived late in the theater; he had been compelled to assemble a staff from scratch; King had ordered him to move his headquarters to a forward base that lacked the logistical capabilities he needed, and then had ordered him to execute a major offensive in barely over three weeks. Yet Ghormley had also contributed to his own problems. He did not assert himself with the French to demand better facilities ashore; he never called his subordinate commanders together to adjudicate disputes personally or to ensure that each understood his part in the overall scheme; and he had failed to go to the front to investigate problems for himself. He had reported frequently and candidly to his superiors, but in the end he lost his job because of King's impatience and Nimitz's concern for both the success of the operation as well as Ghormley's own well-being.

That concern didn't end after he relived Ghormley of command. "I am very fond of G," Nimitz wrote to Catherine, "and hope I have not made a life enemy." When Ghormley arrived in Pearl Harbor a week later on his way back to the States, Nimitz made a point of meeting his plane and inviting him to stay in his home during the stopover. Ghormley was subdued but friendly, and that night in private Ghormley asked Nimitz why he had felt compelled to relieve him. "Bob, I had to pick from the whole Navy the man best fitted to handle that situation. Were you that man?" "No," Ghormley replied. "If you put it that way, I guess I wasn't." Nimitz told Catherine that "no one could have borne the disappointment better."[36]

Nimitz also heard from Frank Knox that week. The Navy secretary sent him a long, chatty letter that concluded with strong praise: "All of us here are very proud of the way you are handling your job." To Catherine, Nimitz wrote, "Perhaps I can last out the year."[37]

N EWS OF HALSEY'S APPOINTMENT did wonders for American morale. On Guadalcanal, Marines jumped out of their foxholes and
slit trenches and, as one of them recalled, ran around "whooping like kids."
Yet Halsey was not a magic bullet; all the logistical and supply problems
that had plagued Ghormley were still there, and it would be months before
most of them—or indeed any of them—were resolved. Instead, the next
five weeks marked a period of tension and uncertainty—in Nouméa and
on Guadalcanal as well as in the Cement Pot on Makalapa Hill. From mid-
October, when Halsey assumed command, until the end of November,
the Japanese hurled one force after another at the American toehold on
Guadalcanal, and the fate of the campaign for the Solomons, and indeed
of the Pacific war, hung in the balance. From day to day it was never clear
if the enemy's latest push would be the one that proved decisive. Nimitz
revealed his state of mind in a letter to Catherine: "I am not so busy as
I am mentally churned up. My imagination is very vivid and I realize my

helplessness so far away. No one knows better than I do the difficulties that confront Halsey and Vandegrift & the superiority enjoyed at present by the Japs. I am so much aware of what might happen that it keeps me very much preoccupied."[1]

Nimitz got a new director of communications that week: Captain John R. Redman, who, as previously noted, was the younger brother of Rear Admiral Joseph Redman, the Director of Navy Communications (DNC) in Washington. The younger Redman remembered later that Nimitz "received me very nicely," though in fact their relationship began badly. Nimitz knew that both of the Redmans considered Rochefort an obstacle to a centralized intelligence gathering system. Nimitz was not opposed to centralization in principle. Nonetheless, as he told King, he did not want to jeopardize the personal relationship and working protocols that were already in place in Hawaii. Whispering in King's other ear, however, were those who felt Rochefort was getting too much of the credit for the success at Midway, and who saw Rochefort, and Layton, too, as obstacles to their centralization plans. They couldn't get rid of Layton, who was on Nimitz's staff, though they did hope to replace Rochefort, whom they referred to dismissively as "an ex-Japanese language student." To effect that change, they arranged for Commander William Goggins to take his place.[2]

Nimitz was willing to accept Goggins, but he modified Goggins's orders so that he would become Rochefort's executive officer rather than his replacement. John Redman sought to circumvent that. Though he was now on Nimitz's staff, he sent secret messages to his brother in Washington, in one of which he urged that Goggins's orders should specify that he was to be the "Officer in Charge." He also suggested that to clear the way, Rochefort should be recalled to Washington. Deceitful as that was, he made it worse by sending those messages on Nimitz's personal radio net with a code that Nimitz did not have. When, inevitably, Nimitz found out about it, he was furious. "It came as quite a shock to me," he wrote the deputy CNO, "to find that one of my staff, using my call letter, could communicate with other individuals in the Navy in a code which I did not possess." He strenuously complained to

Captain John R. Redman, seen here in a post-war photo as a rear admiral, got off to a rocky start as Nimitz's communications officer by participating in what amounted to a cabal to remove Joe Rochefort from his position at Station Hypo. (U.S. Naval Institute)

the head of the Office of Naval Intelligence, Rear Admiral Harold Train, that the decision to remove Rochefort had been made without consulting him or even informing him. To King, Nimitz attributed the whole sorry mess to "bickerings and jealousy between the Washington and Pearl Harbor" radio intelligence units. Nimitz did not fire Redman, as perhaps Redman himself expected, though it was weeks before he spoke to him again.[3]

Nimitz's protestations did not save Rochefort, who received orders to fly to Washington, D.C., for "temporary duty." As Rochefort fully suspected, the change turned out to be permanent. He ended up supervising the construction of a drydock in Washington State, and Goggins took command at Hypo.* Layton urged Nimitz to demand that King reverse the decision. Disappointed as Nimitz was, he knew which battles he could win and which he could not, telling Layton, "If you know anything about Admiral King, you know that when he has made up his mind, it is made up." Nimitz did register his unhappiness to King at their next meeting in San Francisco, where King dismissed it as a closed matter.[4]

In time, Redman worked his way out of Nimitz's doghouse. He remained on the staff for two full years and eventually became a devoted admirer of his boss. He even learned to play a creditable game of cribbage, a sure path back into Nimitz's good graces. Because Redman was in charge of communications, when Nimitz flew out to one or another remote island to establish a new base, Redman usually went along to set up the radio station. On many of those long flights, Nimitz and Redman played cribbage for a penny a point. During one flight, everything broke Redman's way and, somewhat to his embarrassment, he won every game. "Try as I could," he recalled later, "I couldn't lose." By the time they arrived at their destination, Nimitz owed Redman more than four dollars. Sometime later, when Nimitz admired a knife that Redman had purchased, Redman simply gave it to him. Nimitz offered to pay him for it, but Redman told him that he needn't bother because he was sure to win back its value at cribbage. Nimitz stared at him deadpan, then said, "Get the hell out of my office."[5]

In addition to Redman, another new arrival that week was Vice Admiral John H. Towers, who reported as Nimitz's deputy commander for air on October 14. If it had pained Nimitz to say goodbye to Ghormley, his primary reaction to the arrival of Towers was resignation. Towers was confident, brash, generally dismissive of juniors, and sometimes even openly rude; he and Nimitz were like oil and water. In San Francisco, King had

---

* After Goggins took over at Station Hypo, its name was changed to the Fleet Radio Unit, Pacific, or FRUPac. Eventually it came to employ more than a thousand people.

reminded Nimitz that he had done him a favor by replacing the meddlesome and difficult Claude Bloch as 14th Naval District commander with the more cooperative David W. Bagley. Now he expected Nimitz to repay that favor by accepting Towers as part of his command so that King did not have to deal with him in Washington.[6]

Towers was the most senior naval aviator in the service—officially he was Naval Aviator #3. He had won headlines in 1919 by leading a group of oversized seaplanes on the world's first transatlantic flight (with one stop in the Azores), doing so eight years before Charles Lindbergh's more famous nonstop solo flight. Towers had also commanded the Navy's first aircraft carrier (*Langley*) and later the *Saratoga*. What made him a problem for King,

Vice Admiral John H. "Jack" Towers was the first U.S. naval aviator to reach flag rank and believed that only aviators should be permitted to command carriers or carrier task groups. He continued to advocate for aviators throughout the war, first as Commander Air Forces, Pacific, and later as Nimitz's deputy commander. (U.S. Naval Institute)

and for Nimitz as well, was his insistence that naval aviators should not be subject to the command authority of non-aviators. He had once advocated making naval aviation a separate service like the Marine Corps. Though he subsequently backed away from that position, he continued to insist that it was not only inappropriate but actually illegal for non-aviators—men like Fletcher and Spruance—to command carriers or carrier task forces. He based that argument on the findings of the so-called Morrow Board, which had been chaired by Senator Dwight Morrow.[†] In 1925, that board had recommended that the command of aircraft carriers and other aviation commands "should be confined to" naval aviators. It did not quite have the force of law, but Towers believed it was the will of the government.[7]

Towers also thought it was disgraceful that an aviation pioneer like Pete Mitscher was cooling his heels in Kaneohe commanding a patrol wing instead of a carrier task force. Mitscher had been part of Towers's team during the 1919 transatlantic flight and had served as his deputy at the Bureau of Aeronautics (BuAer). Towers was even suspicious of those, like King and Halsey, who had become aviators in mid-career, referring to them dismissively as JCLs, short for "Johnnys-come-lately."[8]

Nimitz, too, had tangled with Towers. In 1938 when Towers was leading BuAer, he had challenged the authority of Nimitz's Bureau of Navigation to oversee aviators. When Towers himself failed to be promoted from captain to rear admiral later that year, he chalked it up to the prejudice of the "Gun Club," which he believed included Nimitz. One incident in particular widened the gulf between them. On June 10, 1940, with the world reeling from the breathtaking success of the Nazi blitzkrieg and Mussolini's declaration of war against France, both Towers and Nimitz were called to testify before Carl Vinson's House Naval Affairs Committee about a proposed 11 percent expansion of the Navy. After Towers argued for a commensurate increase in the number of aviation captains and rear admirals to command the Navy's growing air arm, Nimitz spoke against it, suggesting that it would make the officer corps top-heavy. Towers won the argument, but he remembered

† Dwight Morrow was the father of Anne Morrow Lindbergh and the father-in-law of Charles Lindbergh.

Nimitz's opposition and told his wife that Nimitz was "very Dutch, very thick-headed." Nimitz was equally unimpressed, confiding to Catherine that Towers was vain and self-important, with "a disagreeable disposition."[9]

When Towers got his orders to the Pacific in the fall of 1942, he tried to repair the relationship by sending Nimitz a friendly note, writing "Dear Chester" to tell him how "delighted" he was to be joining his command. The bonhomie seemed forced, however, and may have done more harm than good. When Towers arrived, Nimitz was polite and collegial, and even managed to suppress his annoyance that Towers had brought along a large group of staff officers. It is noteworthy that while Nimitz called Halsey "Bill" and Spruance "Ray," he never called Towers anything but "Admiral." Members of Nimitz's staff sensed that "he just didn't care much for Admiral Towers."[10]

Towers set up shop at the opposite end of the Cement Pot from Nimitz's suite of offices, and Nimitz left him to manage his duties unmolested. As Nimitz's press officer, Waldo Drake, put it, Nimitz handled Towers with "a blend of psychology, his native courtesy, and patience." Occasionally, however, their mutual antipathy emerged into the open. Towers became irritated that submarine skippers were awarded medals after successful patrols while, in his view at least, aviators were overlooked. To rectify this perceived inequity, he began awarding medals to pilots and squadron commanders on his own and then issued press releases announcing it. When he learned about it, Nimitz "hit the ceiling," as one staff officer put it. Ordinarily, he might have walked over to see Towers. This time he dispatched a Marine orderly to summon Towers to his office.[11]

"Towers," he said when the admiral reported, "I don't want you or any of your staff that you've brought over here having anything to do with awards and decorations." Then, after a pause, he added: "Or public relations." It was as close as he ever came to losing his temper. Nimitz promised Towers that he would make sure aviators got their share of decorations, but the summons was also a reminder of the chain of command.[12]

Towers remained unhappy. He could accept Halsey as commander of the South Pacific (even if he was a JCL), but it was absurd, in his view, that Rear Admiral Thomas C. Kinkaid, who was another black shoe, had moved up to command the carrier force there after Halsey's elevation to theater command. The man who should hold that job, Towers told Nimitz, was Pete Mitscher, who, not incidentally, agreed with Towers that only "experienced aviation men" should be in charge of carrier training and operations. Nimitz did not explain to Towers why he was loath to make that appointment; instead, he thanked Towers for his advice and left Kinkaid in command.[13]

Towers asserted himself where he could. He authorized Mitscher to send a group of PBYs to the South Pacific even though their crews were still in training. Mitscher was happy to do it, perhaps imagining that it could lead to his own transfer to an active theater, which eventually it did.

MEANWHILE, IN THE SOUTH PACIFIC, HALSEY was also asserting himself. Where Ghormley had been reluctant to intrude on French sensibilities by claiming space ashore for his headquarters, Halsey simply insisted that it was necessary and did it, even though, as the Running Summary noted, it caused "some trouble . . . from the French Governor." King backed him up, telling Betty Stark in London to inform de Gaulle that Halsey was authorized to "establish headquarters ashore at Nouméa immediately." Halsey set up offices in the abandoned Japanese consulate and also took over a nearby warehouse and two Quonset huts that everyone called the "Wicky-Wacky Lodge."[14]

Halsey did another thing Ghormley had not: on November 7 he flew to Guadalcanal to see things for himself. The Marines were thrilled to see him and took it as evidence that they had not been forgotten or abandoned. Halsey had a populist touch that Ghormley lacked. He especially praised the Marine pilots of the Cactus Air Force, telling reporters that they were "the most superb gang of people I have ever known." It was during this visit that he told reporters that his plan for the war was to "kill Japs, kill Japs, and keep on killing Japs."[15]

Only a few days into his new command, on October 21, Halsey learned from an Army search plane that the Japanese were sending another reinforcement convoy to Guadalcanal covered by a combat force that included at least two carriers. The enemy's reported course and speed indicated that the carrier force would be in position to strike the island the next morning.

That triggered immediate concern not only in Nouméa, but also in Pearl Harbor, where the Running Summary noted that "they can throw more ships, planes, and troops into the vital area than we can," and that "the next three or four days are critical." Nimitz used similar language in his letter to Catherine that night. As a rule, he sought to downplay his anxiety in his letters. This time, however, his concern was palpable. "The next week or so will be very critical," he wrote, "and I pray that what we have been able to assemble will hold them off."[16]

When Halsey learned of the approach of the Japanese, he demonstrated his combative temperament by flashing a brief and unmistakable order to Kinkaid: "Attack. Repeat, Attack." That initiated what became known as the Battle of the Santa Cruz Islands (October 25–27, 1942). Simultaneously, Japanese Army units ashore launched an all-out ground assault on Vandegrift's Marines. Both at sea and on land, a climactic battle for Guadalcanal was about to begin.

As ever, Nimitz waited uneasily in Pearl Harbor for reports. Unlike Midway, when he had known a lot about the relative balance of forces and had some idea of how events could play out, this time he was mostly in the dark. Scout planes reported as many as five different Japanese forces converging on the island, and early reports were "very confusing." He wrote Catherine, "It makes me feel restless and wide awake waiting for news at this great distance." He told her that "tonight and tomorrow will be critical in our history—and pray God they will be successful for us." His invocation of the deity in consecutive letters was unusual for him and suggested his extreme concern. As usual, no one at headquarters noted it.[17]

Early reports the next day (October 26) were encouraging. Planes from Kinkaid's carriers had put three 1,000-pound bombs into the *Shokaku*, forcing her to retire northward. Though that inspired hope, Nimitz suspected "it was not enough to be decisive." And, sure enough, the Japanese struck back hard. They focused first on the *Hornet*, which was hit by three bombs and also by two crippled Val dive-bombers that deliberately crashed into her—one into the ship's island, the other into her port bow. In a subsequent attack, Japanese torpedo planes also put two torpedoes into her. The *Hornet* lost power and was dead in the water.[18]

Even as he monitored reports of a major battle three thousand miles away, Nimitz's job often required him to take time out to welcome visiting delegations. The one that arrived on October 25 was composed of British flag officers led by Admiral Denis Boyd, who until recently had commanded British carriers in the Mediterranean and who was now headed to the Indian Ocean. Nimitz hosted him and his senior staff members at a dinner that included both Spruance and Towers. It was an interesting evening, and Nimitz listened to Boyd's take on the global war with genuine interest. At the same time he fidgeted in his chair until they left and he could "go down and read dispatches."[19]

The news was uniformly bad. Kinkaid had ordered the cruiser *Northampton* to tow the crippled *Hornet* to safety, but the big carrier had taken on so much water it put an unsustainable strain on the towline, which repeatedly parted. Meanwhile, another flight of Japanese planes arrived to finish her off. Concluding that she could not be saved, Halsey authorized Kinkaid to scuttle her.

By then the *Enterprise*, too, had been hit. Two Japanese bombs put her number one elevator out of commission, and she was several feet down by the bow. The battleship *South Dakota* had also been hit. With the loss of the *Hornet*, however, it was the damage to *Enterprise* that was most worrisome. Kinkaid ordered the *Enterprise* southward, out of the battle, and that made him a carrier task force commander with no operational carriers. The only positive news was that the Marines on Guadalcanal had managed to smash the Japanese ground assault and still held Henderson Field. Nimitz sent Vandegrift a congratulatory message and expressed his appreciation of the men holding the lines.[20]

Halsey put the best light he could on the sea battle by emphasizing that the Japanese had lost a disproportionate number of aircraft. He reported that U.S. pilots had shot down 116 enemy planes "for certain" and another 45 "probable," for a total of 161. If true, it meant that Japanese carriers had been virtually stripped of their offensive capability. As usual, the pilot estimates were high—the Japanese actually lost 99 planes, which was about half their total complement. American losses were sobering as well. As Nimitz reported, "This battle cost us the lives of many gallant men, many planes and two ships that could ill be spared." Still, the Japanese had again been turned back. Nimitz hoped that their heavy losses, especially in aircraft, would buy the time needed for Halsey to rush more men, supplies, and airplanes onto Guadalcanal. He urged Halsey to take advantage of the "lull after intense activity" to place "strong reinforcements on Cactus that will permit offensive action." Halsey replied that he was "in complete agreement."[21]

Over the next several days, as Halsey sought to bolster Vandegrift's Marines, the loss of the *Hornet* raised several questions at Nimitz's headquarters in Pearl Harbor about the decision to abandon her, as well as about the effectiveness of American torpedoes. Charles P. Mason, who had been captain of the *Hornet* during the battle, arrived in Hawaii on November 8 and Nimitz invited him to the staff meeting the next morning. There, Mason explained how, after the *Hornet* was abandoned, American destroyers had closed in to sink her to prevent the Japanese from towing her away as a prize. The destroyers fired a total of sixteen torpedoes at her. Seven of them missed. Given that they were shooting from close range at a large and immobile target, that was worrisome. But equally disturbing was the fact that after nine torpedoes *did* hit her, she remained defiantly afloat. The destroyers then tried to send her to the bottom with their guns, firing more than three hundred rounds of 5-inch shells into her. And still she floated. Eventually the destroyers left her there, a derelict but still floating wreck, and that was how the Japanese found her. They fired two more torpedoes into her, and that finished her off. Whether that was because she was already close to sinking or because Japanese torpedoes were significantly more powerful was unclear. Perhaps both. With the *Saratoga* still undergoing repairs in the drydock at Pearl Harbor, the loss of the *Hornet* made the crippled *Enterprise* the only U.S. carrier left in the Pacific. On her flight deck, crewmembers posted a large sign: "Enterprise vs. Japan."[22]

Towers attributed the whole catastrophe to the decision to put the carriers under the command of a black shoe like Kinkaid. As a result of that, he said, the United States was now without a single fully operational aircraft carrier in the whole of the Pacific Ocean.[23]

Almost as bad, at least from Towers's point of view, was the fact that Kinkaid continued to fly his flag in the crippled *Enterprise* while she made her way to Nouméa for repairs. Towers renewed his argument that only aviator admirals should command carrier task forces. Once again, Nimitz thanked him for his views and continued to appoint those men he believed were best suited to command. Limiting the command of task forces to aviators, he replied, would stifle the ambition, expectations, and morale of career officers like Fletcher, Spruance, and Kinkaid.[24]

Still, the sobering outcome of the Battle of the Santa Cruz Islands led Nimitz to reassess the campaign and in particular Halsey's decision to attack. Barely three weeks before, Nimitz had encouraged Ghormley to take greater risks with his marginal resources, including the *Hornet*. Aware of that, Halsey had sent both the *Hornet* and the *Enterprise* out to challenge a superior Japanese force. Now the *Hornet* was gone and the *Enterprise* disabled for an uncertain period. If that led Nimitz to rethink the advice he had given to Ghormley, or the free rein he had given to Halsey's pugnacious instinct, he left no record of it. More likely, he applied his grandfather's advice not to worry about things he could not change. The *Hornet* was gone, and it was simply necessary to carry on.

The loss of the *Hornet* continued to cause Nimitz pain, however. Because Roosevelt did not want to be accused of withholding bad news on the eve of a midterm election, he authorized the Navy Department to release the fact of her loss to the public. Nimitz regretted that. He feared that the announcement came before the families of all the crewmembers had been notified, as had been the case with the loss of the *Wasp* a month earlier. Still, what was done was done, and rather than complain, he turned his attention to confronting the next enemy assault. To Catherine, he wrote, "We have again held them off at some cost to us but greater cost to them." They would try again, he wrote her, and when they did, he would "endeavor to be ready for them."[25]

IT WAS A PRECARIOUS MOMENT. The Marines still held Henderson Field, but they had been in near-continuous combat for almost three months and many were showing the strain. The logistics remained fraught. Nimitz's staff hardly needed to remind him that the difficulties of sustaining the Marines remained "a cause for serious concern," adding the rather obvious fact that "movements of fuel, food, and equipment to Guadalcanal area are extremely difficult and undertaken with considerable risk."[26]

Of the American aircraft carriers in the Pacific, only the *Enterprise* and *Saratoga* still floated, and both were undergoing repairs. King offered to send three vessels that had been converted from tanker hulls into small escort carriers, but they were scheduled to participate in the invasion of North Africa, which was still two weeks away and halfway around the world. The British offered to send the small (23,000-ton) *Illustrious* from the Indian Ocean, but with the Japanese holding the Strait of Malacca, off Singapore, she had almost as far to go as the escort carriers in the Atlantic, and then her crew would have to spend weeks, if not months, adjusting to the American system.[27]

Before any of that could happen, the Japanese struck again. In the second week of November, the Japanese made a supreme effort to crush the American enclave around Henderson Field. Short of pilots, the Japanese gave the job of grounding the Cactus Air Force to a pair of battleships— *Hiei* and *Kirishima*—which were to shell the airfield with their 14-inch guns. That was supposed to allow a Japanese reinforcement convoy to deposit thousands more soldiers, and especially supplies, on the island. With no carriers available to confront this new threat, Kelly Turner sent Rear Admiral Dan Callaghan, lately Ghormley's chief of staff, with a scratch force of cruisers and destroyers to interpose itself between the enemy battleships and the critical airstrip. It was a near-hopeless mismatch.[28]

The result was the Naval Battle of Guadalcanal (November 12–15, 1942). The first phase of it took place in the middle of the night in a violent thunderstorm. Reports were even more fragmentary than usual, in part because both Callaghan and his second-in-command, Norman Scott (the recent victor in the Battle of Cape Esperance), were both killed early on. As a result, Nimitz passed the night without any definitive information either way. The next morning, an American search plane flying over the scene of the battle reported seeing two destroyers circling and leaking oil, an unidentified "large vessel" on fire, and a destroyer dead in the water and apparently abandoned. Not for two more days did Nimitz hear anything official. Finally, on November 15, Halsey sent him a list of the ships that had been lost: "Atlanta, Monssen, and Laffey sunk, Cushing and Barton missing . . . Juneau torpedoed and sunk." Yet at the same time the ferocity of the battle had led the commander of the Japanese battleship force, Admiral Hiroaki Abe, to call off the bombardment of Henderson Field. Nimitz saw at once how crucial this was. As long as Henderson Field remained operational, American pilots retained air superiority over the island.

And indeed, as soon as it was light on November 14, planes of the Cactus Air Force took off in search of Abe's retreating battleships. They found the damaged *Hiei* circling helplessly, her broken rudder jammed at full starboard, and they repeatedly attacked her, supported later in the day by planes from the partially repaired *Enterprise*. Sometime during the night, the *Hiei* sank. Halsey then sent Rear Admiral Willis Lee with two of the new fast battleships (*Washington* and *South Dakota*) after the other Japanese battleship, the *Kirishima*. Though the *Kirishima* sank several of Lee's escorting destroyers and damaged the *South Dakota*, Lee made effective use of the *Washington*'s new radar-controlled gunfire to sink the *Kirishima*.[29]

Nimitz could exhale. Measured solely by the number of ships sunk, the Japanese claimed victory in the Naval Battle of Guadalcanal, but in fact their loss of two battleships and a heavy cruiser was devastating. Moreover, as in the Battle of the Coral Sea, it yielded them no strategic advantage since their reinforcement convoy was all but annihilated by the Cactus Air Force. The Running Summary at Nimitz's headquarters noted that "while we have suffered severe losses in ships and personnel, our gallant shipmates have again thwarted the enemy. If so, this may well be the decisive battle of this campaign."[30]

King certainly thought so. He immediately seized on this success to urge (again) that it was time to pull the Marines out of Guadalcanal, replace them with an Army garrison, and move on to the next offensive. Nimitz thought that was premature. He believed the Japanese would make "one more major effort" on Guadalcanal. In that he was mistaken. The Japanese did plan another offensive, though after further consideration, they decided to invest no more resources in trying to push the Americans off the island, and instead laid plans to conduct an evacuation.

Even so, Japanese and American surface ships tangled one more time in the seven-mile-wide passage between Guadalcanal and Savo Island, where the two sides had fought three times already. In the Battle of Tassafaronga (November 30–December 1, 1942), Japanese torpedoes again proved the decisive weapon, as they sank the cruiser *Northampton* and severely damaged three other cruisers while the Japanese lost only one destroyer in exchange. The addition of the *Northampton* to the ships already lying at the bottom of that passage solidified its nickname as Ironbottom Sound.

Nimitz was puzzled by the uncanny success of Japanese torpedoes. They proved so effective at such great distances that he wondered if some of them had come from nearby but unseen Japanese submarines. In doing so, he was guilty of underestimating the enemy's technological prowess. Still, the only available countermeasure he could see was to improve tactics and training, and so he urged "training, *training*, and MORE TRAINING."[31]

THOUGH IT REMAINED UNCLEAR WHETHER THE Japanese would launch yet another offensive, it was unarguable that the weary veterans of the 1st Marine Division had more than earned a respite after fighting almost continuously for 123 days in appalling conditions. On December 9, Vandegrift officially turned Guadalcanal over to General Patch and the Army, and the Marines filed aboard troopships bound for Australia. The fighting was not over, nor had the logistical problems been resolved—Patch's soldiers also had to be fed and supplied. Indeed, the total number of Americans on Guadalcanal continued to increase until by the end of the year they numbered more than fifty thousand.

By then, the Japanese had begun a carefully planned and stealthily executed withdrawal. For once, American radio intelligence analysts failed to penetrate enemy intentions, and only afterward did it become clear that the Tokyo Express runs from Rabaul were not bringing in reinforcements but extracting survivors. The last of them, ragged, emaciated, and starving, left in the first week of February, and the campaign was finally over.[32]

Costly as it had been for the Americans, the battle for Guadalcanal had been nothing short of disastrous for the Japanese. The Americans lost nearly seven thousand men; the Japanese lost four times that many. The Japanese had also lost thirty-eight ships and nearly eight hundred aircraft, including, for the most part, their aircrews. It was a blow from which they would never fully recover.

The military historian Russell Weigley once posited that the dominant characteristic of "the American Way of War," as he called it, was to amass overwhelming resources in order to deliver vastly superior firepower against the enemy. After all, America's great advantage over her foes, at least since the middle of the nineteenth century, has been superior wealth and industrial productivity. Because of that, the United States could afford to expend dollars rather than the blood of its citizens to secure victory.[33]

Not on Guadalcanal. There, the United States had leapt into battle with barely enough men to fight off repeated enemy ground assaults, barely enough shipping to keep them supplied, and barely enough air cover to protect them. More than once it had seemed that "barely enough" would not be sufficient. Had the campaign failed, it is possible that, as the historian Richard B. Frank has suggested, King would have been relieved of command. Nimitz, too, might have found his position in jeopardy. Instead, due to a combination of Japanese impatience, the perseverance of the Cactus Air Force, the steadfastness of the U.S. Navy, and of course the determination and grit of the Marines on the ground, King's gamble to seize the unfinished Japanese airstrip on Guadalcanal paid off. Central to that success was Nimitz's steady and careful management of both personnel and resources.[34]

CHAPTER 13

T WO WEEKS AFTER THE NAVAL BATTLE OF GUADALCANAL, Nimitz
got a new houseguest. Rear Admiral Thomas C. Kinkaid was a 1908
Academy grad with formal manners (a contemporary described him as
"somewhat courtly") and distinctive black eyebrows. Much to Towers's
annoyance, he had been commanding Halsey's carrier forces in the South
Pacific. On November 23, however, he surrendered that job to Rear Admiral
Ted Sherman, who was junior to him in rank but who was a naval aviator. It
was done not merely to gratify Towers; King had tapped Kinkaid to be the
theater commander in the North Pacific to replace Robert A. Theobald.

The rotation of officers was like a game of musical chairs, or perhaps a
slide puzzle: Kinkaid took over from Theobald, who headed to Boston to
command the 1st Naval District, while Sherman took over for Kinkaid
in the South Pacific. Meanwhile, Herbert Fairfax Leary, commanding
MacArthur's naval forces, left that job to replace Pye as the battleship commander, and Pye headed to Newport, Rhode Island, to become president

of the Naval War College. Fletcher, instead of returning to command a car-rier task force, as Nimitz had hoped, went to Seattle to head the 13th Naval District. And to complete the circle, Ghormley returned to Hawaii to be-come Nimitz's neighbor as the 14th Naval District commander.[1]

In all this shuffling, Mitscher, too, got a new assignment, albeit not the one he coveted. As far as Spruance was concerned (and very likely Nimitz as well), he was still on probation—or as King and Nimitz had put it during their conversations in San Francisco, "in escrow." He did, however, return to a combat theater with a new job as commander of air forces in Nouméa, a potential stepping-stone to the command of all aircraft in the Solomons (AirSols), including the Cactus Air Force. Halsey had missed the Battle of Midway, so he was unaware of Mitscher's missteps there. He personally requested Mitscher for the job, claiming later that he knew he was "a fighting fool" and just the man he wanted to command his air forces.[2]

En route to Alaska, Kinkaid stopped off in Hawaii for several days and moved into Nimitz's house. Nimitz's habit of hosting visiting flag officers in his home helped him develop personal as well as professional relationships with his Pacific commanders. By sharing meals and conversations, they became more at ease with one another—more open, more trusting, and, critically, more candid. Nimitz's discussions with Kinkaid focused on the Aleutians, where the Japanese occupied two islands they had seized during the Midway campaign: tiny Attu, at the tail end of the Aleutian chain, and slightly larger Kiska, two hundred miles farther east.

When the Japanese first seized those islands back in June 1942, it was not clear whether they had done so as a first step toward the conquest of Alaska, or simply to acquire two more defensive outposts on the northern flank of their maritime empire. Nimitz suspected that the daunting weather and the burden of keeping the garrisons supplied would compel them to evacuate the islands on their own soon enough. Even after it was clear that they in-tended to stay, Nimitz thought the best strategic option was simply to ignore them and let the Japanese bear the burden of trying to keep them supplied. On the other hand, he recognized that because the islands were American soil—however barren—it was necessary, as the Running Summary put it, that "the Japs must be expelled."[3]

Nimitz was unwilling to take resources from Halsey to do it, however, especially with King pressing for a swift renewal of the offensive in the South Pacific. The challenge, then, was to mount a new campaign in the far north while continuing, and even expanding, operations in the south. It is possible to imagine Nimitz and Kinkaid bending over a chart of the Aleutian Islands spread out on Nimitz's worktable. Kiska was the nearer target, but it was held by more than five thousand Japanese soldiers. Kinkaid wondered if he could bypass Kiska and attack Attu, where intelligence estimated there were only about five hundred Japanese; in fact, there were at least three times that many.

Meanwhile, King pressed Nimitz to accelerate the campaign in the Solomons. Now that Patch and the Army had replaced Vandegrift's Marines there, King considered Task I completed. It was therefore time—indeed past time—to move on to Tasks II and III. When he had put that program forward early in 1942, King had not expected Task I to take four months, and he was frustrated that the campaign had "bogged down" (his term). He even floated a plan to skip Tasks II and III altogether and jump past Rabaul all the way to the Admiralty Islands, a thousand miles to the west. Nimitz may have been shocked by such a notion. He replied carefully that while both he and Halsey shared King's eagerness for a swift advance, Guadalcanal itself was not yet "sufficiently secured," and the forces necessary to execute the next phase were not yet at hand. A renewal of the offensive in the Solomons was not possible, he wrote, until "the late spring of 1943."[4]

This revealing exchange constituted the background for their next face-to-face conference in San Francisco, which took place a week later, on December 12. Nimitz brought Kinkaid along, so the initial topic of conversation was the Aleutian campaign. Once King blessed the idea of bypassing Kiska and attacking Attu, Kinkaid excused himself, and King and Nimitz turned their attention to other issues. Over three days, they addressed a wide range of subjects, skipping about from topic to topic. A running theme, however, was King's eagerness to accelerate the campaign timetable, and Nimitz's efforts to temper his boss's expectations. King insisted it was time for big and bold steps. He reminded Nimitz that the first products of the Two-Ocean Navy Act, passed back in 1940, would be arriving that summer. Though Nimitz had only two carriers now, King told him, he was likely to have seven by May—in five months. That would give him the force he needed both to speed up the campaign in the South Pacific and to initiate a Central Pacific campaign into the Marshall Islands. No more baby steps, King insisted. "Let's not nibble."[5]

Nimitz reminded King that the campaign for Guadalcanal was still ongoing, which he insisted was a good thing. Yes, the campaign was taking longer than expected, but if it was frustrating for the Americans, it was positively disastrous for the Japanese. For them, Guadalcanal had become a meat grinder, eroding their human and material assets at a rate they could neither afford nor sustain. Along with MacArthur's campaign in New Guinea, Halsey's campaign in the Solomons, and soon Kinkaid's offensive in the Aleutians, the combined strain on the Japanese would become insupportable. Nimitz argued that opening yet another front in the Marshall Islands, especially in consideration of the many airfields the Japanese had there, not only was unnecessary but would constitute "a frontal attack which would not be as profitable as a continuation of campaigns where we are now."[6]

Nimitz also brought up Joe Rochefort's reassignment and the amalgamation of Hypo into a new and much larger organization labeled the Joint Intelligence Center, Pacific Ocean Area (JICPOA). Though he knew the issue was not open to reconsideration, he felt compelled to tell King that, in his view, removing Rochefort from codebreaking duties had been a mistake.[7]

On other issues, they reached a kind of consensus. King accepted that a thousand-mile leap to the Admiralties was too ambitious—for now—and Nimitz pledged to push the campaign in the South Pacific more aggressively. Nimitz explained Halsey's need for more planes as well as more of the large amphibious ships known as combat loaders. To meet those needs, King promised to "take a stand" with the JCS to raise the percentage of assets dedicated to the Pacific from the current 15 percent to "between 20 and 35 percent."[8]

THE CONSENSUS WAS FLEETING. Nimitz had barely returned to Hawaii when he received another prodding message from King reiterating his frustration with "the progress of the war in the Solomons" and urging him to wrap things up and get on with it. Nimitz again pushed back. Guadalcanal had demonstrated that "we have been too optimistic," he wrote, about how swiftly Japanese positions could be overcome. And in a gentle reminder that the Guadalcanal campaign had been launched without sufficient preparation, he insisted that American troops should never again be asked to conduct a campaign without the tools necessary to be successful.[9]

As if to underscore that, Nimitz was also receiving daily reports from Halsey, who described circumstances in the South Pacific as far more precarious than King or the other members of the Joint Chiefs seemed to assume. Indeed, the same day Nimitz received the harassing message from King, the Running Summary at headquarters noted that "many signs point to an early major [Japanese] push toward Guadalcanal," and three days later it stated that "signs continue to point to an impending attack in the Guadalcanal area."[10]

Such contradictory messages forced Nimitz to mediate between the urgent calls for action from King and the JCS and the sobering reports from his commanders at the front. Even as he sought to curb expectations in Washington, he also called upon Halsey to accelerate his timetable if possible. It was a role that required exactly the kind of command dexterity that had led King to conclude—not admiringly—that Nimitz was "a fixer."

Nimitz did have one happy duty to perform that month. His son, Chet, now the executive officer on the submarine *Sturgeon*, had been awarded the Silver Star "for conspicuous gallantry and intrepidity," and since the *Sturgeon* was in Pearl Harbor that month, Nimitz had the satisfaction of pinning it on him personally.

OF ALL THE PROPOSALS FROM WASHINGTON, the most absurd was one the Joint Chiefs had labeled Operation Setting Sun: an attack on tiny Chichi Jima in the Bonin Islands, more than four thousand miles west of Hawaii and nearly three thousand miles north of Guadalcanal. The idea, perhaps generated by Hap Arnold, was to seize that island to build an airfield from which U.S. Army planes could bomb Japan. While

On January 28, 1943, Admiral Chester Nimitz congratulates Lieutenant Chester Nimitz on being awarded the Silver Star medal for his service on the submarine USS *Sturgeon*. (U.S. Naval Institute)

nearby Iwo Jima would become an American target more than two years later, the idea of an American offensive in the Bonin Islands in January 1943 was preposterous. Nimitz knew that instead of simply saying no to Washington, it was important to explain *why* the answer was no, and perhaps use the opportunity to educate the members of the JCS about logistical realities in the Pacific. He therefore ordered his staff to assess its viability. Not surprisingly, the ensuing report concluded, "The plan is not feasible."[11]

On January 15, 1943, Secretary of the Navy Frank Knox arrived in Hawaii on the first leg of a tour of the South Pacific. FDR had chosen Knox as Navy secretary because he wanted a bipartisan cabinet and Knox was a Republican. In fact, he had been the Republican vice presidential candidate in 1936. Knox was also a former newspaperman (he was part owner of the *Chicago Daily News*), and he had been a "Rough Rider" under FDR's "Uncle Theodore" during the Spanish-American War.

It was almost certainly in anticipation of Knox's arrival that Nimitz ordered his staff to prepare an "Estimate of the Situation," summarizing current conditions in the South Pacific, including the prospects for another advance. The report characterized the situation on Guadalcanal as "favorable" though not yet "satisfactory." The "liquidation" of Japanese forces on the island was still ongoing, it said, as were scheduled improvements to the airfield including "adequate unloading facilities and roads." In short, Task I was "not yet completed." As for future operations, the report insisted that the Marines who had been pulled out of Guadalcanal could not be employed again until May, and there were not enough Army soldiers who had been trained in amphibious operations. It concluded that when an advance did begin, "operations in the Solomons and New Guinea should be simultaneous." Alas, the prospects for a simultaneous advance were dashed almost immediately by a lengthy message from MacArthur that Nimitz received that same day.[12]

MacArthur's message—in five parts—was addressed to "Nimitz and Halsey only," though it is virtually certain that Nimitz shared it with Knox. In it, the general claimed to be as eager as anyone to begin an offensive. His experience in confronting the Japanese on New Guinea, however, had convinced him that "a much stronger force than originally anticipated will be required." The key to any successful campaign, he insisted, was a "progressive advance," moving forward incrementally and building airfields at each new position. Because of that, he wrote, "it is not now immediately possible to undertake a further offensive in the Southwest Pacific Area." Knox had planned to fly to Brisbane to see MacArthur, but after reading MacArthur's message, he instead decided to accompany Nimitz to Nouméa to see Halsey.[13]

Secretary of the Navy Frank Knox and Nimitz during the secretary's visit to Pearl Harbor in January 1943. The drinks they are holding may well be Nimitz's signature cocktail, the "CincPac," a volatile mix of bourbon and rum. Note the missing ring finger on Nimitz's left hand. (U.S. Naval Institute)

First, however, on January 16, Nimitz and Knox boarded a plane for a trip to Midway. It turned out to be an adventure. Soon after takeoff, two of the plane's four engines quit, and the pilot had to turn around and land in the water in Pearl Harbor. The plane began to sink, and the whole party had to scramble out through a narrow hatch. Knox, who had an ample posterior, had difficulty making it and had to be shoved through. The individual assigned that duty was not identified.

Undeterred by this mishap, the official party boarded a relatively new PBY and took off again. They arrived safely at Midway after a long flight and toured the facilities there, but as they prepared to return, they learned that this plane, too, was compromised: it had a hole in one of its pontoons, and a full day would be required to repair it. Back in Pearl Harbor, Towers offered to send the Boeing Clipper that was used to deliver mail to the front. Unwilling to interfere with the delivery of mail, Nimitz turned down the offer. All they could do was wait. It was, Lamar recalled, a "horrible day," with nothing to do but observe the antics of the omnipresent gooney birds, a pastime that quickly became more tedious than entertaining.[14]

When they finally left Midway, they did not return to Hawaii, but flew instead to Espiritu Santo, where Halsey joined them. Then the whole group flew on to Guadalcanal. Another passenger on the flight was Rear Admiral McCain, who had taken Towers's former job as Chief of the Bureau of Aeronautics and who had come out from Washington to assess Halsey's urgent requests for more airplanes.

After landing on Henderson Field, Nimitz saw at once how dramatically conditions on Guadalcanal had improved since his last visit four months earlier. Indeed, the island had been transformed. There were now two airstrips, one of which was an all-weather field, as well as substantial new facilities. That night, Knox and Halsey occupied quarters ashore while Nimitz slept aboard Jake Fitch's command ship, the seaplane tender *Curtiss*, anchored offshore.[15]

The next day, January 22, the whole group flew from Guadalcanal to Halsey's headquarters at Nouméa, where Nimitz presided over a general discussion of future operations. Nimitz made it clear at the outset that the purpose of the meeting was to discuss options, not to reach a final decision. His goal was two-fold. He wanted to demonstrate to Knox that Guadalcanal was not yet secure and that operations remained active and ongoing. On that very day, as it happened, a bitter fight subsequently labeled the Battle of Gifu took place on the ridge beyond Henderson Field. At the same time, he wanted Halsey to appreciate the sense of urgency in Washington. Almost at once, the discussions turned into a dialogue between Nimitz and Brigadier General DeWitt Peck, Halsey's deputy chief of staff and the senior Marine present. Nimitz asked Peck how long it would take to wrap up operations on Guadalcanal. Peck estimated that the island should be fully secured by April 1. That was more than two months away, and perhaps for Knox's benefit, Nimitz expressed the hope that it would be sooner.[16]

Peck asserted that it was necessary to build more facilities on Guadalcanal to turn it into a fully functioning base before making the next move. Nimitz challenged that. Channeling King, he told Peck that the idea was *not* to turn Guadalcanal into a permanent base but to use it as a jumping-off point for a renewed offensive. Task I would be complete, he said, when the Japanese were "eliminated from Guadalcanal," with or without the scheduled improvements to the facilities.[17]

The next major Japanese base beyond Guadalcanal was Munda on New Georgia Island, just over two hundred miles to the west, and Nimitz asked Peck directly, "When do you think that you can move against Munda?" Peck was consistent: April 1. Halsey suggested that in the interim, it might be possible to seize the Russell Islands, roughly a third of the way to Munda. That could be done within the month and would constitute a useful stepping-stone. After some discussion, Nimitz gave his approval. He surveyed the group to ensure that everyone understood and acknowledged the timetable. Then he briefly summarized operations elsewhere, including the Aleutians, touched on the issue of press censorship, and adjourned the meeting. He had accomplished his goal: Knox had a clearer appreciation of the impediments to a swift advance, and Halsey had a better understanding of the mood in Washington.[18]

NIMITZ AND KNOX FLEW BACK TO Hawaii without incident on January 28. By the time they landed, Nimitz was feeling worn out—"quite weary," as he admitted to Catherine. Despite that, he hosted a luncheon the next day in Knox's honor with forty attendees. Knox was supposed to leave for the mainland that afternoon, but bad weather kept his plane grounded. Given that he had to stay over another day, he told Nimitz that he wanted to visit a beach. Nimitz called for his black Navy Buick and took Knox (wearing a suit and tie) and Fuzzy Theobald up the narrow road behind Honolulu and over the green peaks of the Koʻolau Range toward the north shore. Just before reaching the ocean, a turnoff onto a grass driveway led between high hedges that "suddenly opened to a wide lawn and panoramic garden surrounded by tropical trees and Spider Lilies." This garden paradise was the oceanfront home of H. Alexander Walker, known as Sandy, and his wife, Una. They had named it Muliwai, which is Hawaiian for "a river breaking through a sand bar into the sea." As one of the Walker grandchildren later described it, "To drive into Muliwai was to leave the everyday world behind and enter an enchanting and peaceful Garden of Eden."[19]

The Walkers were one of the "big five" families that had dominated Hawaiian politics and society between the wars. Nimitz had met them two decades earlier when, as a thirty-five-year-old lieutenant commander, he

Nimitz with his friend H. Alexander "Sandy" Walker, who along with his wife, Una, owned two houses on Oahu that Nimitz visited often, especially Muliwai, the Walkers' beachfront house on Oahu's northern shore. (U.S. Naval Institute)

had supervised the construction of the submarine base at Pearl Harbor and had lived near them in Manoa Valley. When he returned to Hawaii twenty years later as CinCPac, the Walkers reached out to him, offering their hospitality for lunches, dinners, or a swim in their pool. Nimitz's growing intimacy with them is evident in his notes, all of which they saved. In the first of them, dated December 15, the salutation was, "Dear Mr. and Mrs. Walker." Ten days later, it was "Dear Walker family." By the spring, it was "Dear Sandy and Una." Interestingly, whatever the salutation, he signed all of his letters "C. W. Nimitz" rather than "Chester."[20]

Muliwai had a private beach for walking and swimming and a spacious lawn with a paddle tennis court surrounded by lush tropical flora. The Walkers welcomed Knox graciously and hosted him at a kind of mini luau. Nimitz did not stay. Feeling increasingly weary, he left Knox in the Walkers' care and returned to the Cement Pot to answer dispatches. Knox returned from Muliwai at 6:30, and Nimitz saw him off to the West Coast the next morning. Then, still feeling quite tired and pressed by his staff, he went to the hospital, where the doctors diagnosed acute malaria.

With a temperature oscillating between 100 and 105 degrees, Nimitz remained in the hospital for a week. Frustrated by his confinement and idleness, he chafed at being told to stay in bed. Not wishing to cause alarm—or to encourage anyone to think that perhaps Towers should become acting CinCPac in his absence—he ordered Lamar to continue to fly his four-star flag at headquarters to give the impression that he was still on the job. And he was. His physician complained that despite Nimitz's illness, "there was a stream of people consulting him."[21]

A happy and unexpected consequence of Knox's visit was that due to the several aerial mishaps experienced during their travels, the secretary sent Nimitz a new command airplane. It was a modified DC-54 Skymaster with a private office and room for his staff. Nimitz used it on most of his subsequent trips to outlying islands.[22]

If Nimitz hoped that Knox would be able to temper King's impatience, he was soon disabused of that notion. The very day Knox arrived back in Washington, King fired off a hectoring note "for Nimitz and Halsey only," complaining that the "campaign continues in current status of delay, linger, and wait." He complained that Halsey "appears not to see [the] necessity of operations in central Pacific as well as in Southwest Pacific." The idea, King noted, was to "whipsaw" the enemy "rather than enable him to concentrate in Solomons." Nimitz, still in the hospital when the note arrived, might have felt that he was the one being whipsawed.[23]

Meanwhile, the Solomons remained an active theater. Following yet another confrontation at sea (the Battle of the Rennell Islands, January 28, 1943), Nimitz, who was now out of the hospital, learned that the cruiser *Chicago* had been damaged in that battle. Afterward, as the *Chicago* was proceeding slowly back to Pearl Harbor for repairs, she was attacked by Japanese planes and sunk. Infuriated by the failure to provide adequate air cover for her, and determined to prevent the Japanese from exploiting their success, Nimitz ordered his staff to keep her loss a secret. "I've never said this in my life before," he declared at the morning staff meeting, "but if any so-and-so lets out [news of] the loss of the Chicago, I'll shoot him."[24]

Soon afterward, on February 21, Nimitz flew to San Francisco for another meeting with King. By then, the Guadalcanal campaign was over. Patch radioed Halsey on February 9 that "the Tokyo Express no longer had a terminus on Guadalcanal." King wondered if the Japanese might be tempted to use the forces they had extracted from Guadalcanal to attack Samoa, though in reality none of those troops was in any condition to do so. Still, at their meeting, King suggested to Nimitz that he could forestall such a move by seizing one or another of the Gilbert Islands. Nimitz was not averse to the idea. The problem, as he had written to King in January, was not *capturing* an island, it was *holding* it afterward. "I do not think we can expect to seize more enemy territory and hold *repeat hold it*," he wrote, "until we have a superiority in sea, air and land forces," which would not be the case until the arrival of the new-construction warships that summer. In this, he got unexpected support from Towers. In a long memo to Nimitz, Towers insisted that shifting the campaign into the Central Pacific at this moment was "impossible," and that the best strategy was to continue with progress in the Solomons.[25]

AS AGREED AT NOUMÉA, HALSEY'S NEXT target after the Russell Islands was the Japanese base at Munda on New Georgia Island. Munda was inside MacArthur's command theater, and to ensure cooperation between Halsey and MacArthur, Nimitz ordered Halsey to fly to Brisbane and consult with the general. It was a meeting fraught with potential hazard. Both Halsey and MacArthur had oversized personalities, though of very different types: MacArthur was coldly aloof and imperious, while Halsey was boisterous and assertive. Though they had never met, each had a negative impression of the other. Halsey had previously written to Nimitz that he thought MacArthur was "a self-advertising son of a bitch." It did not auger well for their prospective partnership.[26]

And yet when they did meet it was very nearly a love fest. "Five minutes after I reported," Halsey wrote later, "I felt as if we were lifelong friends." Almost certainly that was because MacArthur made a deliberate effort to charm the admiral—when MacArthur wanted to charm someone, he could be very persuasive. MacArthur likely calculated that he could obtain more of what he wanted by accommodating Halsey than by bullying him. He may even have thought that he could transfer Halsey's loyalty from Nimitz to himself. In his subsequent memoir, Halsey wrote, "I have seldom seen a man who makes a quicker, stronger, more favorable impression."[27]

MacArthur was less impressed. Afterward, he told his air commander, George Kenney, that while Halsey was not dumb, he was also not brilliant. Interestingly, and with no apparent sense of irony, he told Kenney that Halsey was something of a grandstander, that he liked a headline, thought a lot of himself, and was a showman. Kenney concluded that they got along because MacArthur knew how to handle him.[28]

Whoever was handling whom, in the spring of 1943, as Kinkaid prepared to launch Operation Crowbar against Attu, five thousand miles to the north, these two men—so different yet so alike—undertook the completion of Task II, code-named Operation Cartwheel.

CHAPTER 14

F ROM EARLY SPRING and into the summer of 1943, as Kinkaid supervised the invasion of Attu and Halsey launched his attack on Munda, Nimitz continued to monitor the performance of American submarines. His interest was partly a product of his own lengthy career in subs (and because his son, Chet, was serving in one), but beyond that he was convinced that severing Japan's maritime supply lines was a central, even critical aspect of the Pacific war. Japan was an island and, like Britain, dependent on imports to survive. Her decision to go to war in the first place had been grounded in her determination to secure a reliable source of raw materials. Now that she had done so, however, the raw materials themselves—the rubber, bauxite, copper, zinc, and especially oil—all had to be shipped to Japan by sea. Nimitz believed that cutting that supply line would prove far more strategically meaningful than the seizure of one or another Pacific island.

To ensure that the subs remained focused on that crucial mission, Nimitz occasionally had to fend off requests by both King and MacArthur to employ them on other duties. Nimitz had sent a dozen subs to Halsey in the South Pacific, but when MacArthur urged King to send six more to his theater, Nimitz objected, telling King that it would reduce the number of submarines in the "fruitful Empire area." MacArthur pushed his request to the JCS level, and, pressured by Marshall, King ordered Nimitz to do it anyway. Only afterward did King learn that MacArthur had made his request without consulting Leary, his naval commander, and worse, that the area where MacArthur wanted them to operate was shoal water, where they would have to remain on the surface much of the time. After that, King determined that while MacArthur could have more PT boats, he would get no more subs. MacArthur saw that as another example of the Navy's antipathy to his success.[1]

Rear Admiral Robert H. English commanded the Pacific submarine force until January 1943, when he was killed in an airplane crash in California. To take his place, Rear Admiral Charles A. Lockwood, who had been commanding the subs out of western Australia, flew to Pearl Harbor, arriving on February 14—Valentine's Day. Almost at once Nimitz and Lockwood began a productive collaboration that lasted throughout the war. Lockwood moved into the house across the street from Nimitz and became one of his closest confidants. A fifty-three-year-old 1912 Academy graduate, Lockwood was one of those whom Nimitz almost invariably asked to remain behind after the morning staff meeting.[2]

The two men frequently discussed the allocation of subs to various patrol areas as well as their latest exploits. Much of their attention, however, was focused on the malfunctioning American torpedoes. The American Mark XIV torpedo had a new and highly secret magnetic exploder designed to detonate when the torpedo passed under a ship and recognized the magnetic anomaly of the hull above it. By exploding directly beneath the ship, the torpedo was more likely to sink it. Far too often, however, the torpedoes either exploded prematurely or didn't explode at all. Pre-war testing had failed to reveal these flaws in part because the tests often consisted of firing dummy torpedoes up onto a sloping beach so that they could be recovered and used again (they cost $10,000 each, about the same as fourteen

Rear Admiral Charles A. Lockwood commanded Pacific Fleet submarines as COMSUBPAC from February 1943 until the end of the war. He became such a close friend of Nimitz that after the war, the two of them, along with Spruance, were buried in adjacent plots in Golden Gate Cemetery near San Francisco. (U.S. Naval Institute)

jeeps). In addition, the torpedoes responded differently in the warm South Pacific than they had in the chill waters of Newport, Rhode Island, where the torpedo testing station was located. Frustrated sub skippers returning from patrols reported that many of the torpedoes simply ran under the target without exploding. As one of them noted, "It's a helluva thing to go all the way to the China Coast to find out your damned torpedoes won't work." The experts at the Bureau of Ordnance were skeptical, suggesting that the complaints were an attempt to excuse bad shooting or a failure to provide proper maintenance. That, of course, further infuriated the sub commanders. Lockwood believed his skippers, and after conducting more tests, he discovered that the torpedoes ran eleven feet deeper than the settings indicated. During an April 1943 trip to Washington, D.C., he told the Bureau of Ordnance that if they could not produce torpedoes "that will hit and explode," they should provide "a boat hook with which we can rip the plates off the target's side."[3]

Nimitz was as frustrated as Lockwood; according to one staffer, he "backed Lockwood 100% and was very indignant about it." He was especially annoyed that Rear Admiral Ralph Christie, who had helped design the magnetic exploders, refused to acknowledge their shortcomings. To his son, Nimitz confessed, "I can stand anybody who's dumb. I can stand anybody who's stubborn. But I can't stand somebody who's dumb and stubborn." Nimitz asked Lockwood why he did not deactivate the magnetic exploders and rely on the contact triggers. Lockwood said he didn't have the authority to do that, but "I wish you would." Nimitz replied, "I can and I will," and the order went out on June 24. Alas, the contact triggers proved imperfect as well. Often when a torpedo hit flush on the side of a ship, the impact broke the triggering mechanism and the warhead still didn't explode. Lockwood conducted more tests that revealed the torpedoes worked best if they struck the ship at an acute angle. Until replacement torpedoes became available, Lockwood ordered sub captains to try to hit their targets at a 45-degree angle, though of course that greatly complicated their firing solution.[4]

Though Nimitz studiously refrained from involving himself in operational details, he made an exception for the submarines. On those nights when he had trouble sleeping, he sometimes walked to the office at 3:00 or 4:00 a.m., when sub skippers operating west of the International Date Line sent in their reports. On one such occasion, he read a message from the captain of the new *Gato*-class submarine *Darter* requesting a change in his patrol area. Having recently watched the 1939 screwball comedy *Yes, My Darling Daughter*, Nimitz puckishly replied: "Yes, my darling Darter, you shouldn't oughter, but it's approved. Go ahead." The whimsical reply circulated throughout the sub force and did wonders for morale.[5]

Nimitz also assigned submarines to sow mines in enemy waters. This served a dual purpose. Even when the mines did not sink ships, they compelled the Japanese to conduct extensive minesweeping operations, an activity that used up not only ships and men but also copper wire and rubber, materials that Japan had to import from the South Pacific, adding to the strain on her maritime supply lines.

Occasionally Nimitz violated his own principle that submarines should be used primarily, if not exclusively, against Japanese shipping. As one example, he continued to support the Marine Raider battalions that employed submarines to execute stealth attacks like the one on Makin Atoll. On other occasions, however, he was fiercely protective. When MacArthur asked for a few submarines to smuggle supplies to guerillas operating in the Philippines, Nimitz resisted. He expressed himself "heartily in sympathy with [the] project to aid guerillas," but insisted that such missions were "secondary to sinking ships." MacArthur persisted. If American subs were headed for the western Pacific anyway, he asked, why couldn't they carry some supplies en route? It wouldn't be much, he argued, "not over ten tons." Clearly, MacArthur had no conception of how crowded a submarine was, especially one outbound for a war patrol. When Nimitz again demurred, MacArthur likely concluded that here was another example of the Navy's insularity and narrow-mindedness. Later in the war, when submarines were more plentiful, Nimitz did assign several of the larger boats to perform this duty.[6]

As CominCh, King coordinated the war against German U-boats in the Atlantic, and he wondered why American submarines did not deploy in hunting packs the way the Germans did. Nimitz discussed it with Lockwood, who responded in a lengthy written explanation. He had tried using a three-sub hunting pack in January, he wrote, and though it had produced good results, concentrating them into packs in the broad Pacific was ineffective overall because it left vast sections of the ocean unpatrolled. Lockwood concluded that King's suggestion could not be implemented until more submarines were available. Only with the arrival of the first of the new *Balao*-class subs in the spring of 1943 was he able to establish what were officially called Combined Action Groups (CAGs) but which nearly everyone called "wolfpacks."[7]

THE CODEBREAKERS AT HYPO CONTINUED TO monitor Japanese message traffic, and their input occasionally allowed Lockwood to vector his subs toward worthwhile targets. But Hypo also made other contributions. On April 14 Layton strode purposefully into Nimitz's office carrying an intercept that had just been decrypted that morning. It was the travel itinerary of Admiral Yamamoto, who was conducting a tour of Japanese bases. On the first leg of that tour, he would fly down the length of the Solomon Islands from Rabaul to Bougainville. The flight was scheduled for April 18—just four days away. After Nimitz read it and looked up, Layton asked him, "Do we try to get him?"[8]

Nimitz turned the question back on Layton. Was killing a specific individual a military strike or an assassination? Layton insisted that Yamamoto was a legitimate military target; he was the guiding hand of the Japanese Navy and killing him, he argued, would be comparable to the Japanese killing Nimitz. Whatever Nimitz thought of that comparison, he was initially skeptical of deliberately killing the Japanese Combined Fleet commander. Employing a British euphemism, he declared that assassinating a particular individual wasn't quite "cricket." And there was another consideration. The sudden appearance of an American fighter squadron exactly where the Japanese naval commander in chief was scheduled to appear might lead the Japanese to suspect that their code had been compromised. If so, they would change the code and Nimitz would be deprived of an invaluable intelligence source.[9]

Despite that risk, Nimitz concluded that this was an opportunity not to be missed, and he ordered Halsey to arrange an ambush. Halsey was enthusiastic and gave the assignment to Mitscher, who was now the AirSols commander. Three days later, a squadron of P-38 fighters equipped with external belly tanks to extend their range intercepted and shot down Yamamoto's plane, killing him. Years later, long after the war was over and the story had become public, there was speculation that Nimitz had asked Washington for guidance, and that Roosevelt and Knox had discussed the moral implications of the ambush in a secret midnight meeting. While that is of course possible, there is no surviving evidence that such a discussion took place. Moreover, the timing of Nimitz's orders to Halsey suggests that he made the decision unilaterally.

Afterward, Nimitz authorized an announcement that an American fighter squadron had been dispatched to the area because an Australian coast watcher had radioed in a report of Japanese planes flying the length of Bougainville. The cover story stood up; the Japanese did not change their code. For their part, the Japanese kept the news of Yamamoto's death a secret, perhaps out of concern for its impact on public sentiment, or perhaps because of behind-the-scenes maneuvering in selecting his replacement. Finally, on June 5, they staged an elaborate state funeral for him in Tokyo. It was exactly one year after the Battle of Midway.[10]

MEANWHILE, THE CAMPAIGN IN THE ALEUTIANS got underway. As we've seen, Nimitz had never been enthusiastic about it; he knew that so long as the Japanese kept garrisons on Attu and Kiska, their transport fleet, already stretched to the limit, would have to supply them, and that American submarines could go after those convoys. And not just the submarines. Six weeks earlier an American surface force of two cruisers and four destroyers under Nimitz's former plans officer, Soc McMorris, had intercepted an Attu-bound convoy guarded by a substantial escort of two heavy and two light cruisers plus four destroyers. Seeing that he was outgunned, McMorris withdrew southward, pursued by the Japanese. McMorris put up a bold front, making smoke and firing torpedoes, and somehow convinced the Japanese to call off the pursuit. More importantly, they also recalled the supply convoy. After this engagement, known as the Battle of the Komandorski Islands (March 27, 1943), the Japanese gave up on using surface convoys and relied on submarines to supply the garrison on Attu. That kept their subs from more fruitful service, and the small cargoes they carried were barely enough to sustain the garrison. As Nimitz had suspected, the Japanese were finding their newest conquest burdensome.

Nevertheless, on May 11 elements of Major General Alfred E. Brown's 7th Infantry Division landed on the beach at Attu—if an icy slab of frozen tundra could be described as a "beach." Kinkaid assigned command of the covering force to Rear Admiral Francis W. Rockwell, who requested some battleships for the fire support mission. Nimitz had consistently opposed

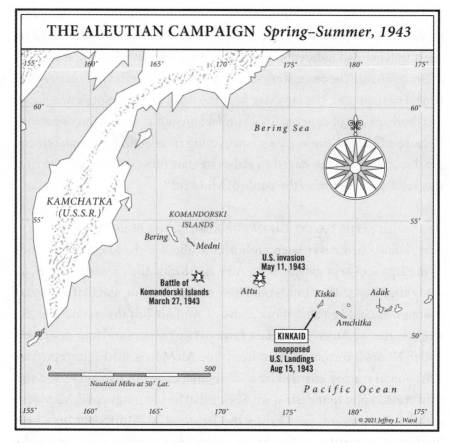

Map 8: The Aleutian Campaign, Spring–Summer 1943

using the old and slow battleships for raids, but naval gunfire support was a mission perfectly suited to their strengths, and he ordered three of them—*Idaho*, *Pennsylvania*, and *Nevada*, the last two of them Pearl Harbor survivors—to join the invasion force.[11]

Attu was as different from Guadalcanal as earthly terrain could be, though no less daunting. Instead of stifling heat and thick jungle, the invaders encountered sub-zero temperatures and a barren landscape covered by a porous, spongy turf called muskeg that occasionally sucked the boots right off their feet. A nearly constant fog and a cold misting rain provided cover for enemy positions on the high ground, and the campaign became another battle of attrition. It lasted for eighteen days and culminated in a desperate Japanese *banzai* charge that resulted in the virtual annihilation of the defenders. The Japanese lost 2,351 killed, with only 28 men taken alive; the Americans lost 549 killed and 1,200 wounded, plus hundreds of cases of trench foot and frostbite. Nimitz was troubled by the human and material cost of such a dubious prize. Still, he knew that political reality sometimes overruled sound strategy, as it had the year before when he had been tasked with supporting the Doolittle Raid.[12]

EVEN WHILE MANAGING TWO CAMPAIGNS FOUR thousand miles apart, Nimitz continued to meet the social obligations of his position, which as ever included hosting periodic luncheons and dinners at his quarters for visiting flag officers or government dignitaries. He often had as many as thirty or more guests at a time, with cocktails beforehand and music afterward. One change in the household that spring was the arrival of Dr. Thomas C. Anderson, who replaced Dr. Gendreau as fleet surgeon. Nimitz had known Anderson before the war; his son had briefly dated Anderson's daughter. Anderson, whom Nimitz called "Andy" or "Doc," moved into the upstairs guest bedroom next to Spruance. After Anderson conducted his first medical exam of Nimitz, he advised him to stop playing tennis, or at least to stop playing singles, as it was too much of a physical strain. Nimitz obeyed, though he continued with both horseshoes and his regular walks into the hills behind the naval base, nearly always accompanied by Spruance and now by Anderson as well.[13]

These activities provided a diversion from his daily routine, yet on many, if not most, of those occasions, the talk invariably turned to the war. To escape that, Nimitz sometimes asked his driver to take him, and usually both Anderson and Lamar as well, to Muliwai, the Walker family's beachfront home, where he had taken Secretary Knox back in January. There, in what was virtually a different world, he could hike, swim, play paddle tennis, and try to forget about the war. The Walkers even constructed a horseshoe pit for him and set up a scoreboard to keep track of the games. In the evenings, Nimitz, attired in shorts and an aloha shirt, might sit in on penny-ante poker games.[14]

The trips to Muliwai were respites for Nimitz. He, Anderson, and Lamar relaxed with Sandy and Una, as well as the Walkers' three children and two grandchildren, who were often in residence. Ginger, the oldest of the Walker children, was the divorced mother of two daughters whom Nimitz christened "the gremlins," naming seven-year-old Maile "Major Gremlin" and four-year-old Sheila "Minor Gremlin." Nimitz came out of his shell with children. His future son-in-law recalled that you could "give him a watermelon and a deck of cards and a bunch of kids and he was in seventh heaven." Besides card tricks, another way he engaged with children was to tell them conspiratorially that he could pull off his finger. When they looked skeptical, he grabbed his left hand and pulled hard at his ring finger. Then he showed them his left hand where, indeed, the ring finger was missing. That almost always broke the ice. Soon the gremlins were treating Nimitz as a favorite uncle, roughhousing with him on the broad lawn of Muliwai. "The war never came into the picture," Lamar recalled later of those salubrious days. By the late summer of 1943, Nimitz, Anderson, and Lamar were making regular trips to Muliwai.[15]

Occasionally Nimitz was also able to engineer a veneer of domesticity in Pearl Harbor as well. The dependents of military personnel had mostly been sent stateside, but at Easter in 1943, Nimitz invited civilian families with children to his house for an egg hunt. Excited children raced about the grounds finding hidden eggs. One of the children recalled asking to use the bathroom, and when he got there, he found that Nimitz had three different rolls of toilet paper to choose from, each printed with a different image: one of Hirohito, one of Hitler, and one of Mussolini.[16]

THERE WAS STILL A WAR TO RUN. For a year and a half, Nimitz had sought to temper King's insistent demands for more aggressive action, regularly reminding his boss that the limited resources he had available—especially in carriers—would not support (or, more importantly, sustain) a new campaign into the Central Pacific while he conducted simultaneous operations in the Solomons and the Aleutians.

As an example of how stretched his resources were, the battered *Enterprise* arrived in Pearl Harbor in May after six months of virtually continuous operations. Nimitz went on board to welcome her and award her the Presidential Unit Citation, the first ever given to a carrier. He also had bad news to deliver. "I know that you have been promised a rest," he told the assembled crew, "and God knows that you deserve it, but you also know that we have lately suffered severe losses in ships and men. I have no recourse but to send you back to the battle."[17]

The crew took the announcement with stoic resignation. Changing circumstances, however, allowed Nimitz to give the *Enterprise* crew a respite after all. Only a week later, on June 1, the brand-new aircraft carrier *Essex* (CV-9) entered Pearl Harbor, and just days behind her was the new *Yorktown* (CV-10), named in honor of the one lost at Midway. They were the first of a new generation of warships that had been authorized almost exactly three years earlier. The Two-Ocean Navy Act of 1940 had approved the construction of no fewer than eighteen new aircraft carriers, plus seven battleships, thirty-three cruisers, and 115 destroyers.* It was a force that, by itself, was as powerful as the entire Imperial Japanese Navy. Not all those ships were destined for the Pacific, of course—the Allies continued to pay lip service, at least, to the "Germany First" principle. Yet the arrival of the *Essex* and the new *Yorktown* signaled that the material advantage heretofore enjoyed by the Japanese was ending, and that allowed Nimitz to send the *Enterprise* and her weary crew to Puget Sound for some well-earned R&R and a much-needed overhaul.

The arrival of the new-construction warships that summer also drew a stream of visitors to Nimitz's headquarters. Nimitz was determined to meet every new commanding officer whose ship touched at Pearl Harbor, and there were so many of them now that he asked Lamar to establish a daily time slot for the meetings. Consequently, at 11:00 a.m., nearly every day, Nimitz held a kind of open house for new arrivals. He greeted each new CO personally, whether it was a Navy captain commanding a heavy cruiser or a lieutenant (j.g.) in charge of an LST. One officer recalled that while chatting

---

* The Navy initially ordered a total of thirty-two *Essex*-class carriers, and twenty-four of them were actually built. Only fourteen, however, actually made it into combat in World War II.

The USS *Essex* (CV-9) was the namesake of a new class of large aircraft carriers that had been authorized back in 1940 after the fall of France. Her arrival in Pearl Harbor on June 1, 1943, followed soon afterward by the new *Yorktown* (CV-10), gave Nimitz greater flexibility to consider offensive operations. (U.S. Naval Institute)

with four new destroyer skippers, "he just talked to them like they were his sons," telling them that "he was proud of them" and was positive that they were going to do a great job. "They went away feeling like a million bucks." At the same time Nimitz quietly assessed each of them. Occasionally he would remark to Lamar afterward, "Got to watch that man. He's one of the good ones."[18]

The spectacular increase of these naval assets made possible the creation of an entirely new fleet to execute the Central Pacific offensive that King had been urging almost since the start of the war. It also required a restructuring—or at least a renumbering—of the fleets. King decreed that fleets in the Atlantic would now be identified by even numbers, and those in the Pacific would carry odd numbers—a protocol still in use today. Halsey's fleet in the South Pacific became the Third Fleet, and MacArthur's naval force in the Southwest Pacific (now under the command of Chips Carpender) became the Seventh Fleet. The new force being assembled at Pearl Harbor for the pending Central Pacific Drive was designated the Fifth Fleet.[19]

ON THE LAST DAY OF JUNE IN 1943, Halsey's newly christened Third Fleet renewed the offensive in the Solomons when U.S. Army forces landed on Vangunu Island, just south of New Georgia, and on Rendova, just west of it. Three days later, a much larger force landed on New Georgia itself. Eventually Halsey committed more than 30,000 soldiers and 1,700 Marines to the invasion, yet they made slow progress in difficult conditions against a determined foe. Nimitz received regular reports from the front, though as usual the information was often sketchy.[20]

As had been the case during the Guadalcanal campaign, the Japanese sought to reinforce the threatened area by sea, and that led to a number of surface actions, most of them at night. On July 5, Nimitz learned of the Battle of Kula Gulf, though once again, as the Running Summary observed, "only the bare outline of action" was initially available. Rear Admiral Walden Ainsworth reported that the light cruiser *Helena* had been lost, sunk apparently by Japanese torpedoes, which again had proved deadly. Ainsworth also claimed that his forces sank all seven Japanese ships "except 1 or 2 cripples." Nimitz radioed his enthusiastic congratulations, but, accustomed as he was to overly optimistic early reports, he waited for more conclusive news. Eventually it became evident that only two Japanese destroyers had been sunk, though several others had been damaged.[21]

As Ghormley had done, Halsey reported to Nimitz nearly every day, and, as with Ghormley, a recurring theme in those reports was a concern for his threatened air superiority. Halsey noted that although his assigned fighter strength was 256 aircraft, he actually had 191, and by August, only 125 of those would be operational—half of his presumed total. With such a small number, he told Nimitz, he would not be able to "maintain continuous fighter cover in strength, and almost no shipping fighter cover." He asked Nimitz for "any action you can take" to strengthen his air forces.[22]

The only planes immediately to hand were replacement squadrons for the carriers, and Nimitz was unwilling to transfer trained carrier pilots onto shore bases. Up to now the Army had been reluctant to send planes to the Pacific, and Nimitz asked King—again—to appeal to Marshall and Arnold to "explore [the] possibility of obtaining more Army fighters to ensure continued active progress [in the] Solomons campaign."[23]

Though he was sympathetic to Halsey's circumstances, King had bigger fish to fry. He was loath to spend political capital with his JCS partners to secure more planes for Halsey while he was trying to solidify their support for the Central Pacific campaign. King told Nimitz that he preferred "not to request Army increase of allocations above commitments until and unless situation requires." Indeed, within a month, King was asking Nimitz if Halsey could give up some of the planes he had in order to create more training squadrons for the Central Pacific.[24]

Halsey was also short of destroyers. After the naval battles of Kula Gulf (July 6) and Kolombangara (July 12–13), he wrote Nimitz that his destroyer losses were approaching "the critical stage." He considered it "urgent" that Nimitz return to him the destroyers he had transferred to Kinkaid for the Attu campaign. Nimitz did so. When Halsey requested more submarines, however, Nimitz demurred. He remained committed to using the subs to cut Japanese lines of supply in Imperial waters. "No additional submarines can be allocated you by SubPac," he wrote Halsey, "without withdrawal from more productive area." As the Running Summary noted, "The increasing destruction of enemy tankers by our submarines is gratifying."[25]

In spite of the difficulties, by late July Halsey was able to report meaningful progress on New Georgia. American soldiers conducted "a general advance all along [the] line," he wrote, and the "entire operation [was] progressing according [to] expectation." None of it was easy—nor was it particularly efficient. In the end, it took more than 33,000 Americans five weeks to wrest Munda from 5,000 Japanese defenders. It was a victory, but a costly one. Some 1,200 Americans had been killed, and twice that number wounded. Though the Japanese had lost far more, they had made the Americans suffer. That meshed with their overall strategy of convincing the

Americans that the cost of fighting the Pacific war was too high and compelling them to open negotiations.[26]

While the losses did not cause anyone to consider negotiating with the Japanese, it did encourage Halsey to reconsider his next step. To both MacArthur and Nimitz, he proposed bypassing the next target, the Japanese base of Vila on the island of Kolombangara, and "allow it to die on the vine." He wanted to leapfrog past it to the weakly held island of Vella Lavella. There was no airstrip there, but Halsey said an American Construction Battalion, the CBs or Seabees, could build one, as they had on the Russell Islands. Nimitz thought the idea was "both suitable and feasible," though he was careful not to preempt MacArthur, who, as theater commander, made the final decision. MacArthur, however, not only approved it, but soon claimed credit for coming up with the idea.[27†]

Progress in the Aleutians proved more elusive. After the unexpected difficulty in securing Attu, Kinkaid wanted to postpone the scheduled attack on the larger outpost of Kiska because one element of his invasion force, the 87th Infantry Regiment, had not been trained for Arctic conditions. If it seemed to King that Nimitz sometimes dragged his feet in pushing the offensive, on this occasion Nimitz demonstrated that he could prod reluctant subordinates when necessary. He wrote Kinkaid asking him to confirm that his request for a postponement was simply "to give 87th Infantry additional training, while all other forces mark time," adding a terse: "Comment." Somewhat defensively, Kinkaid replied that "further training . . . is desirable." But "desirable" did not mean "essential," and Nimitz ordered Kinkaid to carry out the landing as scheduled. A chastened Kinkaid replied that "D-Day can and will be advanced."[28]

When the Americans landed on Kiska, they found that further training had not been necessary after all, for the Japanese were gone. Belatedly accepting what Nimitz had anticipated—that such a distant outpost was unsustainable—they had evacuated Kiska in late July. As the Running

† Good ideas often have several fathers after the fact. Towers, too, claimed paternity for the concept of bypassing Japanese strong points. His biographer asserts that "Jack Towers became the principal proponent of the revolutionary idea" (Clark G. Reynolds, *Admiral John H. Towers* [Annapolis: Naval Institute Press, 1991], 423).

Summary boasted, "Kiska is now . . . in our hands a week ahead of schedule with no Japs contacted."[29]

That emboldened Kinkaid to suggest attacking the Kuriles, the chain of islands stretching from the northernmost Japanese island, Hokkaido, to the Kamchatka peninsula. He noted that it was a shorter route to Japan than either the South Pacific or the Central Pacific, and that from the Kuriles, Army B-24s could bomb the Japanese home islands. Kinkaid had fifty thousand men "trained and equipped for amphibious operations in northern climates." With such a force, he wrote, he could invade the Kuriles in the spring of 1944, or possibly sooner depending on the weather.[30]

It was a tempting idea, and Nimitz ordered Kinkaid to prepare a plan for it. As always, Nimitz knew that planning, even if it never led to action, was a valuable activity. On the other hand, Nimitz also knew that King was eager to begin a campaign across the Central Pacific, and that many if not most of Kinkaid's soldiers in the Aleutians were likely to be recalled to Hawaii for an assault on the Marshall Islands. Kinkaid was eager to learn whether or not his plan was likely to be adopted, and to find out, he asked his flag secretary, Commander Bill Leverton, who had once worked for Nimitz, to try to find out. Nimitz told Leverton enigmatically that he was sending Kinkaid a package that would reveal to him what he was likely to be doing over the next few months. When Kinkaid had stayed with Nimitz back in November, they had played several games of cribbage. Now, as Kinkaid unwrapped the package, he knew there would be no invasion of the Kuriles that summer. Inside it was a cribbage board.[31]

An offensive was imminent nonetheless. At the meeting of the Allied Combined Chiefs of Staff in Quebec, labeled Quadrant (August 19–24), King convinced the Joint Chiefs to approve an expansion of Pacific operations. The Combined Chiefs agreed "to push the war against Japan by maintaining unremitting pressure against her from every direction." Thus in addition to MacArthur's campaign in the Southwest Pacific and Halsey's campaign in the South Pacific, the war was now also to be extended into the Central Pacific as well, as King had long advocated.[32]

In mid-October Nimitz suffered a relapse (called a recrudescence) of malaria and checked himself back into the hospital. Once again, he kept his illness quiet, ordering Lamar to continue flying his flag at headquarters. He left the hospital on October 22, "feeling quite well," as he wrote to Una Walker, "but not quite up to strength as yet." He would need all his strength soon enough. Eighteen days later, Spruance's new Fifth Fleet left Pearl Harbor to initiate the Central Pacific campaign, which would begin at a small atoll in the Gilberts called Tarawa.[33]

PART III

THE CENTRAL PACIFIC DRIVE

We are all working hard to consolidate our gains and to prepare for the attacks which we know are inevitable.

—Chester W. Nimitz to Catherine Nimitz, November 29, 1943

The arrival of the first products of the Two-Ocean Navy Act dramatically shifted the balance of naval power in the Pacific. By the fall of 1943, the Americans possessed such a superiority over the Japanese that they could extend their hard-won gains in the Southwest Pacific, even while initiating an entirely new offensive in the Central Pacific. Of course, doing so meant dividing resources between two major campaigns—and it also meant divided command. That not only violated one of the cardinal principles of war, but it also provoked renewed rivalry between the services and triggered a debate about whether it made sense to conduct two separate lines of attack or whether Allied resources should be consolidated and focused on a single line of attack—and if so, where.

CHAPTER 15

T HE IDEA OF A CENTRAL PACIFIC DRIVE WAS NOT NEW. In the 1920s, when King and Nimitz had been students at the Naval War College (though not at the same time) they had studied the secret contingency plans for possible future wars. There were nearly a score of them, each identified by a color representing a different potential enemy (black for Germany, red for Britain, etc.). Since Japan (orange) was the most likely foe, War College students focused particularly—even obsessively—on Plan Orange. Crafted as early as 1911, the plan grew and morphed over the years until it became a lengthy and detailed blueprint. At its core, however, it was fairly straight-forward. It assumed that war would begin with a Japanese attack on the Philippine Islands. In response to that, American and Filipino forces would retire into the Bataan Peninsula across the bay from Manila and hold out there for six months while the U.S. Navy assembled the battlefleet in Hawaii and steamed to the rescue.

There was a lot of discussion about whether the fleet should do this in one lengthy voyage (the "Through Ticket to Manila") or if it would be necessary to secure interim bases in the Japanese mandated islands by amphibious assault (the island-hopping option). Either way, it was assumed that at some point the Imperial Japanese Navy would sortie to oppose the American advance, and when it did, the result would be a gigantic naval battle somewhere in the western Pacific—a battle, it was assumed, that would effectively determine the outcome of the war. In 1939, when it became evident that the United States was likely to face more than one color-coded foe at the same time, Plan Orange was officially superseded by a series of so-called Rainbow Plans, and the one finally adopted was Rainbow 5, which enshrined the "Germany First" principle. Nevertheless, the longevity and familiarity of Plan Orange meant that though it had been officially discarded, it survived like a ghostly shadow in the thinking of most senior Navy officers, including King and Nimitz.[1]

Any chance of reviving Plan Orange when the war began was undone not only by the near destruction of the American battlefleet in Pearl Harbor but also by Douglas MacArthur, who, instead of falling back into Bataan in accordance with the plan, embraced a scheme proposed by Major General George Grunert to confront the Japanese invaders on the beach. When that failed, the Filipino-American army had to fall back into Bataan anyway, though a prolonged resistance became more difficult because MacArthur had declined to stockpile food and supplies, which he believed would be defeatist and would imperil civilian food supplies. President Roosevelt, unwilling to risk MacArthur's capture, ordered him to leave the Philippines in March 1942. His successor, Lieutenant General Jonathan Wainwright, held out for another two months before he was compelled to surrender in May. Consequently, by 1943 there was no longer an American force in the Philippines to rescue or reinforce. Still, with Guadalcanal at last secured, the Japanese purged from the Aleutians, and the arrival of all those new-construction warships, King convinced the Joint Chiefs that the time had come to initiate the campaign that had been at the center of Plan Orange: a thrust across the Central Pacific into the heart of the Japanese Empire.[2]

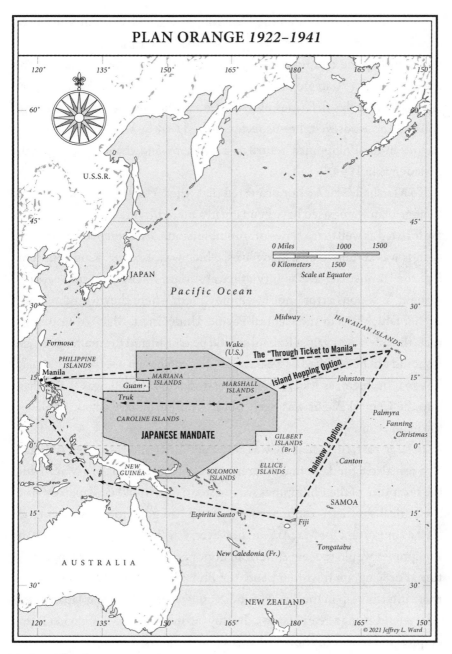

MAP 9: Plan Orange, 1922–41

Not everyone applauded the idea. MacArthur in particular saw the diversion of resources to the Central Pacific as a conspiracy engineered by the Navy to seize control of the war and turn the Southwest Pacific—his theater—into a strategic backwater. He believed that King was the principal culprit in this nefarious plot, but he saw the president as a willing co-conspirator. Roosevelt, he suspected, feared that he would win a decisive victory in the Philippines, return as a war hero, and challenge him for the presidency in 1944.[3]

To Marshall, MacArthur protested that "the factors upon which the old Orange plan were based have been greatly altered," which was true enough. He insisted as well that a series of amphibious attacks through the mandated islands was certain to cost many lives, which was also true. King countered that the "immediate availability of naval surface forces including carriers" made it "a serious error" not to employ them where they would be most useful, which was in the Central Pacific. Undeterred, MacArthur insisted that "the offensive against Rabaul should be considered the main effort, and it should not be nullified or weakened . . . to implement a secondary attack." The real problem, as MacArthur understood all too well, was that a drive into the Central Pacific was likely not to be a "secondary attack" at all, but the main event.[4]

In large part, this squabble was about authority and resources, though it also revealed a fundamental difference in strategic outlook. To MacArthur, the recapture of the Philippines was existential. It would cut Japan off from the critical southern resource base that she had gone to war to secure. At least as important for MacArthur, however, was the fact that reclaiming the Philippines would redeem American honor and fulfill his own pledge to return. For King, on the other hand, the Philippines constituted merely one more interim step in the war. He and Nimitz wanted to defeat Japan's navy. That would avenge Pearl Harbor, destroy Japan's ability to sustain her island empire, and render the home islands all but helpless.

There were disagreements about tactics, too. MacArthur insisted that each new Allied offensive required support from land-based tactical air, which meant that each forward movement should be limited to about 150–200 miles. King disagreed. He acknowledged that MacArthur's "baby steps" (as King called them) would keep American casualties low. On the other hand, it would also prolong the war and result in more casualties in the end. Instead of advancing a few hundred miles at a time, King wanted to take giant leaps of six hundred or a thousand miles. In some ways it was a reflection of how the two services perceived distances. A hundred-mile advance by an army on land was a significant movement, whereas for a navy, especially in the broad Pacific, it represented four hours' steaming.

King had other arguments. He noted that the Central Pacific was a healthier combat environment; it offered a better chance of provoking a decisive confrontation with the Japanese fleet; and, in an argument that appealed to Hap Arnold and the Army Air Force, he observed that occupying the islands in the Central Pacific created an opportunity for Army heavy bombers to attack the Japanese homeland. As MacArthur feared, the war in the Pacific was about to shift to the Central Pacific, where it would be organized, managed, and executed by Chester Nimitz.[5]

MOST EARLY VERSIONS OF PLAN ORANGE had stipulated that the initial step would be an assault on the Marshall Islands. Now that the moment had come, however, Spruance argued that it would be better to begin in the Gilbert Islands, six hundred miles south of the Marshalls. The Japanese had been in the Marshalls for more than twenty years, and they had presumably spent much of that time building up their defenses there; they had seized the Gilberts only in 1942, so those fortifications would be less established. Nimitz agreed, and so the first step in the Central Pacific Drive would be in the Gilberts, with the code name Operation Galvanic.

To conduct the campaign, Nimitz organized an entirely new command that included most of those new-construction warships that had arrived over the summer. Initially called Task Force 50, it was soon renamed the Fifth Fleet in conformance with King's new fleet numbering protocols. Whatever it was called, it was enormous—more than twice the size of Carpender's Seventh Fleet and Halsey's Third Fleet combined. It included several new *Independence*-class light carriers built on the hulls of unfinished *Cleveland*-class cruisers. Though these smaller flattops carried only about thirty planes each, their arrival would give Nimitz strategic control over as many as *twenty* aircraft carriers, three times the number possessed by the Japanese. That undercut MacArthur's argument that no advance could take place without support from ground-based air, since with such a dominant carrier force the invaders could take their air cover with them.[6]

In addition to the carriers, the new Fifth Fleet had a dozen battleships. Seven of them were older (and slower) pre-war dreadnoughts, including repaired survivors of the Pearl Harbor attack, but five of them were new "fast" battleships capable of keeping up with the carriers. The amphibious element of the new fleet included dozens of attack transports (APAs), each theoretically capable of carrying twelve hundred men (though one soldier assigned to an APA said that carrying that many was possible only "if we all held our breath"). There were also attack cargo ships (AKAs), each of which could carry a twenty-four-day supply of food, water, gasoline, and spare parts. And most critical were the Landing Ships, Tank (LSTs), which could carry heavy vehicles—including tanks—to the landing beach and offload them right onto the sand through giant cupboard-like doors in the bow. Screening and escorting this vast armada of carriers, battleships, and amphibious ships were nearly a hundred destroyers. The sheer size of the new Fifth Fleet was testimony to the unprecedented productivity of American industry, and it underscored the folly of the Japanese decision to go to war with the United States in the first place.[7]

To manage all this, Nimitz had to expand his staff, something he instinctively resisted. When he had arrived in Hawaii two years earlier, the staff he inherited from Kimmel had numbered barely two dozen officers. It was small enough that he could remember all their names and have lunch with them at a single long table at the sub base. After his elevation to CinCPOA in the spring of 1942, the staff expanded to forty-five and included some Army officers and even a few British representatives. Now, with the Central Pacific Drive in the offing, that number doubled, then doubled again. Nimitz found it maddening.

One morning Commander Bernard Austin, Nimitz's new assistant chief of staff for administration, came in to ask if he could increase the number of officers assigned to handle personnel transfers from three to six. Nimitz was skeptical. Was it really necessary? To answer that question, Austin came in the next day with two Marine orderlies, each of them carrying a stack of papers two feet high. They were the personnel transfer orders for just that day. Nimitz capitulated. "I think you have a point," he said. Soon, more staffers were added for planning, and still more for logistics. They filled up the office space in the Cement Pot and spilled over into nearby buildings. By the time the Central Pacific Drive got underway in the fall of 1943, Nimitz's staff totaled 245 individuals, and to him it felt more like a faceless bureaucracy than a personal staff. Nimitz accepted the need for it, but it frustrated him nonetheless. His logistics officer, Bill Callaghan, recalled that Nimitz was "staggered" by the size of it.[8]

All 245 members of Nimitz's staff were white males. For all his openness and empathy, Nimitz was a product of his time and his culture. There were no Black officers in the U.S. Navy in 1943 (not until 1944 were the first sixteen Black men selected for officer training). And Nimitz was uncomfortable even with Black enlisted men, preferring Filipino stewards to Black messmen in his quarters. At dinner one night Nimitz referred to "the Negro problem" back in the States, and the context suggested that in his view, the problem was not the oppressive laws and traditions that victimized American Negroes, but the Negroes themselves. One confidant claimed that "negroes are taboo for CinCPac."[9]

Nor was Nimitz interested in having any women in his headquarters. He once told his wife that the Navy's decision to employ women as yeomen

Nimitz particularly valued face-to-face relationships, yet as his staff enlarged in 1943 in advance of the Central Pacific Drive, he found it difficult, if not impossible, to sustain personal relationships with so many. He posed for this photograph with staff members in May 1943. (U.S. Naval Institute)

(essentially secretarial staff) during World War I had been a social experiment that he hoped would not be repeated. But of course it was. In July 1942, only weeks after the Battle of Midway, Congress created the WAVES (Women Accepted for Volunteer Emergency Service). The idea was for them to assume secretarial and administrative duties in order to release men for combat duty. Nimitz endorsed the idea in theory but found the reality disorienting. He believed that the presence of women in uniform was a distraction, and he banned WAVES from his headquarters and even from the Hawaiian Islands. His justification was that Hawaii was still a war zone and unsafe for non-combatants. Lamar believed that Nimitz's attitude was due in part to Catherine's influence. Though she was a vocal and public champion of the WAVES back in the States—even recording a number of radio spots encouraging women to enlist—she, too, feared that their presence in Hawaii would create a volatile social environment, or, as Lamar put it, "that there would be all sorts of illicit sex." After the war, she told an interviewer that "Chester was very wise to say that none of them should come out to the Pacific."[10]

SELECTING THE RIGHT INDIVIDUAL TO COMMAND the new Fifth Fleet was critical. One candidate who possessed all the attributes Nimitz believed necessary was his own chief of staff, Raymond Spruance. As we've seen, the two men were different in many ways: Nimitz was approachable, easygoing, and an affable teller of ribald stories, whereas Spruance was, in the words of one staffer, "prim and neat, rigid [and] all business." Yet Spruance had internalized most aspects of Nimitz's leadership including his work ethic and strategic outlook. He wrote his wife, Margaret, that his boss was "a marvelous combination of *tolerance* of the opinions of others, wise *judgment* after he listened, and *determination* to carry things through," which was an apt summary. Lamar claimed that "they think and talk just alike." Nimitz had recommended Spruance for a third star in April 1943, and that gave him the necessary rank. The drawback was that giving Spruance command of the Fifth Fleet would deprive Nimitz of an efficient chief of staff as well as a companionable housemate and hiking and swimming partner.[11]

Nimitz brought up the subject with Spruance in May as the two men walked to the office together as usual. "There are going to be some changes in high command of the fleet," Nimitz told him. "I would like to let you go, but unfortunately for you, I need you here more." It was the same argument that Roosevelt would use seven months later to inform George C. Marshall that he would not command the D-Day invasion. And Spruance responded to Nimitz's declaration just as Marshall would do. "The war is the important thing," Spruance said. "I personally would like to have another crack at the Japs, but if you need me here, this is where I should be." It was exactly the answer that Nimitz had expected.[12]

If not Spruance, then who? It made some sense to appoint an aviator admiral, and Towers considered himself an obvious candidate. Nimitz's ambivalence toward Towers, however, had not changed since his arrival in October. Whatever gifts Towers might have as a pilot, Nimitz was put off by his vanity and arrogance, and he could see for himself that Towers was not an efficient administrator. Besides which, Towers was certain to be unacceptable to King. Fletcher might have been a candidate had King not effectively shelved him by sending him to Seattle to command the 13th Naval District and the Northern Sea Frontier. Kelly Turner was another possibility, but quite apart from Turner's confrontational—even abrasive—personality, Nimitz wanted him to command the amphibious force.[13]

Finally, there was Halsey. There were a number of arguments in his favor. He had the requisite rank and experience, he wore the gold wings of an aviator, and he was certainly aggressive enough, though he was clearly not Spruance's equal intellectually. The problem was that Halsey was still running the campaign in the Solomons and would not be available for many months. Nimitz knew King would not be willing to put the Central Pacific Drive on hold until Halsey was available. In fact, King had told Nimitz bluntly that "Halsey ought to stay where he is for the time being."[14]

As Nimitz ran through the possibilities, he concluded that Spruance was the best man for the job and that it would be selfish to deny him an opportunity to command the decisive campaign of the war merely in order to keep him at headquarters. After mulling it over most of the night, Nimitz reversed himself. During their walk to the office the next morning, he told

Spruance that he had changed his mind: "Spruance, you are lucky. I decided that I am going to let you go after all."[15]

To replace Spruance at headquarters, Nimitz chose Soc McMorris, his former plans officer, who had displayed boldness and imagination during the Battle of the Komandorski Islands in March. McMorris was spectacularly unattractive—one contemporary described him as having "a face like a fried egg," and a popular nickname for him at headquarters was "Phantom of the Opera." He was also razor sharp and hardworking, and Nimitz quickly came to rely on him as much as he had on Spruance. One difference between the two men was that while Spruance, like Nimitz, generally waited out complaints and concerns from juniors before responding, the impatient McMorris was more likely to blurt out "No!"

Vice Admiral Charles H. McMorris (shown here in a 1945 photograph) replaced Spruance as Nimitz's chief of staff in June 1943. He earned his nickname, "Soc" (for Socrates), at the Academy for his eidetic memory. (Naval History and Heritage Command)

or (less frequently) "Okay" halfway through the pitch. He also tended to delegate what he considered minor issues to others, especially to his assistant chief of staff, Bernard Austin, on whom he became particularly dependent.

Another difference, one that affected Nimitz personally, was that McMorris wanted no part of Nimitz's physical fitness regimen. As Lamar put it, "McMorris wouldn't walk across the street if he could ride." Nimitz never stopped trying to get McMorris to exercise. Periodically, he'd send his Marine orderly over to McMorris's office to tell him that it was a beautiful day and to invite him to go for a walk. McMorris invariably replied, "Yes, it is a fine day for a walk, but I'm not gonna go walking." Consequently, for his walks, Nimitz relied increasingly on Doc Anderson and Lamar, and occasionally, when he was visiting Muliwai, on Una Walker, who, faithful to her surname, could keep up with the men on long-distance hikes. When no one else was available, Nimitz occasionally sent his orderly from office to office to ask who wanted to go for a hike or a swim. When that happened, many staffers sought to make themselves scarce. If they did not literally hide under their desks, they quickly found business that had to be taken care of elsewhere.[16]

SOON AFTER INFORMING SPRUANCE OF HIS NEW ASSIGNMENT, on May 28, Nimitz flew to San Francisco for another meeting with King, who had just returned from an Anglo-American strategic conference in Washington code-named Trident. At that meeting, the Americans had given in to the British insistence on invading Italy in the fall of 1943 in exchange for a British commitment to a cross-Channel invasion of France in the spring of 1944. The Combined Chiefs also affirmed their support for the Central Pacific Drive.

Whatever hesitancy Nimitz had previously felt about opening a new front in the Pacific, he was now fully on board. The arrival of all those new warships—especially the carriers—plus the attrition the Japanese had suffered in the Solomons and elsewhere gave him clear naval and air superiority. He told King that the Japanese had only two full-size carriers left (*Shokaku* and *Zuikaku*), plus "two or three converted carriers used chiefly to ferry planes." He doubted that the Japanese would commit their fleet to defend bases in the Central Pacific. He told King that they would wait until the Americans penetrated their inner defenses before responding. "They would not fight on the fringes," he said.[17]

King approved all of Nimitz's selections for the Fifth Fleet command posts, including Spruance as fleet commander, Kelly Turner for the amphibs, and Major General Holland M. "Howling Mad" Smith to command the landing force. Spruance had specifically requested Smith for that job, and in many ways Smith was a logical choice since he had supervised the training of the Marines who would execute the landings. On the other hand, the newly christened V Amphibious Corps included both the I Marine Amphibious Corps (IMAC) and an Army division (the 27th). It was nearly unprecedented to put Army soldiers under the command of a Marine general, and the proud and touchy Lieutenant General Robert C. Richardson, who had replaced Emmons as the senior Army commander in the Pacific, was dubious about it. Richardson sent multiple letters to Nimitz expressing "considerable anxiety over the command set up for Galvanic." Determined to make this experiment in joint command work, Nimitz knew that it would require finesse and diplomacy, which were not among Howling Mad Smith's strong suits.[18]

Another freighted appointment was command of the carrier force within the Fifth Fleet. Towers was the obvious choice, but he was senior to Spruance as a vice admiral and even he knew that would not do. So instead Towers championed Mitscher for the job. Nimitz might have been ready to give Mitscher another opportunity. Spruance, however, remained unforgiving, and Nimitz did not want to impose Mitscher on him against his will. Nimitz therefore sent Mitscher to San Diego to take over as Pacific Fleet Air Commander, which was largely an administrative post, and brought Rear Admiral Charles A. "Baldy" Pownall from that job to Hawaii to command the Fifth Fleet carriers. Towers was not pleased.[19]

The carriers that made up Pownall's new command had never operated together, so to assess their combat readiness in advance of Galvanic, Nimitz ordered three of them (*Essex*, *Yorktown*, and *Independence*) to conduct another raid against Marcus Island in the mid-Pacific. Towers wanted

Nimitz appointed Rear Admiral Charles A. Pownall to command the carrier force (initially designated Task Force 50.1) within the new Fifth Fleet. Pownall was a veteran aviator, earning his wings in 1927, and he had commanded the *Enterprise* before the war. (Naval History and Heritage Command)

to command it. Given that Nimitz's objective was to see how Pownall performed, he turned Towers down. He reminded Towers that his job was primarily administrative and that if he preferred a combat assignment he could request duty in the South Pacific.[20]

Towers was infuriated. He told Nimitz that his refusal to give naval aviators a greater role in strategic planning and operational command was crushing morale and undermining combat efficiency. Nimitz replied that he believed morale in the theater was actually quite high, especially among the aviators. Towers subsequently complained to retired admiral Harry Yarnell, another aviation pioneer, that Nimitz acted as if "I did not know what I was talking about." A disgruntled Towers continued to resent what he referred to privately as "the battleship gang."[21]

A final element of Nimitz's command team, one too often overlooked, was the Joint Service Force under Rear Admiral William L. Calhoun. A great-grandson of John C. Calhoun, the former vice president (and staunch defender of slavery), Admiral Calhoun never commanded a fleet in battle, yet he was central to success since it was his job to ensure that the fighting forces were provided with the food and ammunition, and especially the fuel, needed to fight the war. Nimitz was acutely aware of the importance of logistics, and he greatly appreciated Calhoun's quiet efficiency. He urged Calhoun's promotion to vice admiral and defended him against occasional critics. Bernard Austin recalled that in addition to appreciating Calhoun's work, "Admiral Nimitz was very fond of Admiral Calhoun as an individual." Calhoun repaid the support with efficiency. The official Navy history of wartime logistics asserts that "no single command contributed so much in winning the war with Japan as did the Service Force of the Pacific Fleet."[22]

ONE COMPLICATION IN PLANNING GALVANIC WAS that with multiple offensives underway across the Pacific, MacArthur, Halsey, and Spruance all wanted—and needed—expanded sealift capability: transports and supply vessels, the shortage of which had nearly doomed the Guadalcanal campaign. Throughout 1943, American shipyards pumped out literally hundreds of new ships, especially those initially labeled EC-2 ships (Emergency Cargo, Type 2) and universally known as Liberty ships. Many of them, however, were destined for the North Atlantic convoys, the supply missions to Russia, or the Mediterranean.[23]

Nimitz also found that the shipping he did have had to be carefully husbanded. Whenever he sent supplies to MacArthur's theater, for example, the ships carrying them seldom returned; MacArthur simply kept them. Some of that was due to limited unloading facilities that kept supply ships loitering far too long at anchor. It was more than annoying, for it upset the delivery schedule, and Nimitz's logistics team complained about it. Nimitz was reluctant to pick a fight with MacArthur, however, so he asked King if he could send more shipping from the States, pointedly suggesting that the "tempo of [the] Central Pacific Campaign [must] not be slowed down by the lack of adequate number of assault bottoms." King replied that the ships Nimitz already had were "the maximum number that can be made available" and that, as always, he should do the best he could with what he had.[24]

Nimitz appealed to King's deputy, Vice Admiral John H. Newton, a former classmate of Nimitz's at the Academy. Newton said he could provide eighteen more Liberty ships, though none of them could arrive in the Pacific until October 15. That was too late for Galvanic, though they would be available for the next operation against the Marshall Islands, code-named Flintlock.[25]

Another key bottleneck was the shortage of tankers and oilers. The Gilberts and Marshalls were more than five thousand miles from the oil wells and refineries in California. King had promised Nimitz seven new-construction tankers (to carry the oil from California to the mid-Pacific), yet as D-Day for Galvanic approached, five of them had yet to complete their shakedown cruises, and two were still on the East Coast. Nimitz was also short of oilers (to refuel the ships at sea). He had thirteen of them, but needed seven more. The best King could do was offer him four civilian contract oilers plus four small (800-ton) and slow (9 knots) tankers borrowed from the Army. Again, Nimitz said he would make do. By now, though, Galvanic began to feel a bit like the Guadalcanal campaign, when the available shipping never quite caught up with the need.[26]

AS HE ORCHESTRATED THE BUILDUP, Nimitz also continued his regular trips out to Muliwai. He often went there for dinner, sometimes bringing along whatever VIP had descended on him from Washington that week. Dinner was generally served on the expansive lanai or veranda overlooking the lush lawn and well-tended tropical gardens and beyond that, the blue Pacific. When dinner ran late, Sandy and Una encouraged Nimitz and his guests to stay overnight. Muliwai had no telephone, however, and Nimitz was unwilling to be out of communication with headquarters overnight. Soon afterward, the Walkers had a phone installed. That was no small adjustment, since it required running a wire all the way across the island. Once it was completed, Nimitz did occasionally stay overnight at Muliwai. When he did, a typical afternoon might include paddle tennis on the Walkers' grass court or a walk on their private beach, followed by a swim, a rinse in the outdoor fresh-water shower, then, after Nimitz and the others changed into shorts and aloha shirts, cocktails on the lanai followed by dinner. The meals were prepared by the Walkers' Japanese chef, Hara, who was invariably cheerful and friendly to Nimitz and to all of the Walkers' guests, though he never wavered in his quiet conviction that Japan would eventually win the war.[27]

After dinner, they might listen to a symphony on either the Victrola or the radio, or play a penny-ante poker game (ten-cent limit, two raises). Then Nimitz and Lamar or Doc Anderson retired to the Walkers' guest cottage, from which they could hear the sound of the surf on the north shore as they fell asleep. The next morning, up early, they returned over the Koʻolau range to the war.

CHAPTER 16

T HE ALLIES WERE ON THE OFFENSIVE EVERYWHERE during that fall of 1943. In September, British and American troops in the Mediterranean landed near Salerno, south of Naples, to begin the Italian campaign, while five thousand miles to the north the Red Army drove the Germans out of Smolensk, triggering a general retreat by the Wehrmacht back to the borders of the Reich. In November, Halsey's forces targeted Empress Augusta Bay on Bougainville in the Solomons, and Spruance's Fifth Fleet prepared to move against the Gilberts later that month. MacArthur, meanwhile, planned an attack on Cape Gloucester, at the southern tip of New Britain Island. All these campaigns were linked by competing logistical demands. The JCS had stipulated that their approval of the Central Pacific Drive was contingent on "the availability of the means at our disposal," so while Nimitz had a green light to take the offensive, he was to do so with the resources he had at hand.[1]

The strategic map was like a giant puzzle, and Nimitz moved the pieces around as needed. Because Halsey's assault of Bougainville came first, Nimitz sent him five carriers, five cruisers, and three destroyer divisions from Spruance's Fifth Fleet with the understanding that they would return in time for the assault on the Gilberts three weeks later. It was a calculated risk because predicting the timetable of war was always perilous, and a delay in the Solomons could postpone their return. Then, too, whenever ships engaged in combat, it was inevitable that there would be some attrition, and just how much of that force would return to Spruance in battle-ready condition was uncertain.[2]

Meanwhile, Nimitz studied the plan for Operation Galvanic, which called for the seizure of two islands in the Gilberts, each of which hosted an airfield: tiny Betio in Tarawa Atoll, at the southern edge of the archipelago, and the slightly larger Nauru Island, four hundred miles to the west. Spruance worried that conducting simultaneous assaults so far apart would strain his already problematic sealift capacity. He suggested dropping Nauru in favor of Makin Atoll, which had been the target of Carlson's raid the year before and which was only 120 miles north of Betio and therefore "within shipping capacity." The JCS initially balked, noting that Makin did not have an airfield. Nimitz argued that the Seabees could build one there, as they had elsewhere.* King backed him up, and the orders were changed. To neutralize Nauru, Nimitz ordered Pownall to conduct a carrier strike on its airfield, as well as a smaller strike on Makin, the purpose of which was to encourage the natives to leave the island for nearby Little Makin Island so that they would be out of the way of the invaders.[3]

The planning went on literally around the clock. "We all worked seven days a week," a staffer recalled. "There were a lot of people in the Headquarters 24 hours a day—and it included the Admiral." Spruance and Turner also worked eighteen-hour days. Holland Smith was at headquarters less often, though when he was there he was sometimes a discordant note. With round wire-rim glasses and a graying brush mustache, Smith's

---

* Validating Nimitz's confidence, the Seabees began constructing an airfield on Makin on D-Day and completed it in less than a month.

THE CENTRAL PACIFIC DRIVE *Nov 1943–Feb 1944*

Map 10: The Central Pacific Drive, November 1943—February 1944

physiognomy suggested that he was perpetually ready for a fight, and not just with the Japanese. Thin-skinned and confrontational, even his own staff grew weary of his complaints about "never having enough of everything." He grew especially quarrelsome when he thought someone was trying to usurp his authority. After learning that the Galvanic plan called for him to remain behind at Pearl Harbor, he charged off to Spruance's headquarters to demand that the orders be changed. His place was with his men, he insisted. He protested again when he saw that Turner was to exercise tactical command during the landings and asserted that "command of the landing force is a function of the Corps Commander"—that is, himself. Again the orders were changed. Still suspicious, he concluded that the Navy leadership—a group that certainly included Nimitz—was making "a determined effort to cut me down to size and show the fountainhead of authority." Like Towers, Holland Smith would have to be handled with patience and tolerance.[4]

One of Smith's concerns was how his Marines were to get ashore at Tarawa. The landing craft designated to carry them from the transports to the beach were officially dubbed Landing Craft, Vehicle and Personnel (LCVPs), though they were universally known as Higgins boats after their designer, Andrew Jackson Higgins. With their drop-front bow, they were a vast improvement over the surfboats the Marines had used on Guadalcanal, yet Smith worried about them anyway. Betio had a coral shelf that extended a quarter mile or more out from its shoreline (see chapter 16). Even at high tide there was only about four feet of water over that shelf, and because the Higgins boats drew three feet fully loaded, the margin for error was small. Nimitz stipulated that the landing must take place at high tide, but Smith was not satisfied. Instead of the Higgins boats, he wanted the Marines carried to the beach in tracked landing vessels commonly called amphtracks, amtracks, or alligators—or, in the Navy's acronym-laden lexicon, LVTs (Landing Vehicle, Tracked). Essentially amphibious tractors, LVTs could crawl over the coral no matter how shallow the water was. Turner did not think they were necessary, but Smith insisted. In his postwar memoir, he claimed that he told Turner that if he didn't get them he would refuse to carry out the landing. The problem was that there were only about a hundred LVTs in the theater, only seventy-five of which were operational. Fifty more of an improved type called water buffaloes (LVT-2) arrived in October just in time to take part. That was still only enough to carry the first three waves of Marines to the beach. Subsequent waves would have to rely on the Higgins boats. Smith didn't like it, ascribing it to "Navy stubbornness," though he realized it was the best he was going to get.[5]

Amid these preparations, visitors continued to show up in Pearl Harbor, expecting Nimitz to host them. On September 19, Eleanor Roosevelt arrived. She was not unexpected. The president had written Nimitz to ask his permission for the visit, telling him that if it was at all inconvenient he should say so. Of course Nimitz said it was just fine. In fact, the First Lady had passed through Hawaii weeks earlier on a fuel stop as she headed west on a tour of the South Pacific Theater. Now she was back, having visited such places as Bora Bora, Aitutaki, and Tutuila—even Guadalcanal. Halsey had initially refused to allow her to tour Guadalcanal since it was still an active combat zone, but after witnessing her indefatigable energy and commitment, he relented. Afterward, he confessed to being "ashamed of my original surliness" and declared that she had accomplished more for morale than any other person who passed through his theater.[6]

In Hawaii, the First Lady split her time between the Army and Navy. Lieutenant General Richardson himself escorted her to various Army

During her tour of the Pacific in the fall of 1943, Eleanor Roosevelt stopped for several days in Hawaii. This photo was taken on September 24 when Nimitz hosted her for dinner at his quarters. (U.S. Naval Institute)

facilities, including Ranger training up in the hills. Nimitz mostly left her in the care of his public relations team, though he did host her for dinner in his quarters. He made a special effort to obtain the makings of a gourmet meal for her, and was pleased with the result until afterward, when Mrs. Roosevelt told him they didn't eat that well in the White House and he felt slightly embarrassed. He left no record of his impression of her, though years later, after both FDR and Nimitz were dead, a reporter asked Catherine what her husband had thought of the late president, and Catherine hesitated only briefly before replying, "Admiral Nimitz felt that the great one in that family was Mrs. Roosevelt."[7]

Two days after the First Lady left on September 23, King arrived. It was his first visit to Pearl Harbor since the war began. He received briefings about the forthcoming operations from both Halsey and Spruance and confirmed his approval to substitute Makin for Nauru. After two days of discussions, Nimitz accompanied him on a flight out to Midway in an Army B-24. Despite a driving rainstorm, they inspected the facilities there, including the new submarine base that Lockwood had convinced Nimitz to build. The only sub in port that day was the *Gato*-class *Sunfish*, so the two admirals climbed down into her for a tour by her astonished skipper, Commander Richard W. Peterson, who probably had never expected to see so many silver stars in his boat.[8]

Nimitz had no sooner said goodbye to King on September 28 than another visitor arrived: Rear Admiral Alan Goodrich Kirk. Kirk had participated in the Allied invasions of both Sicily and Italy and had flown halfway around the world to share what he had learned. Nimitz and Kirk had a history. Kirk had headed the Office of Naval Intelligence before the war when Nimitz ran the Bureau of Navigation, and they had occasionally clashed. Nimitz believed that Kirk was something of a peacock ("a dandy," as Lamar put it) and rather full of himself. Yet he invited Kirk to stay in his home during his visit, included him in all the morning staff meetings, and asked him to brief his team about amphibious landings. The Running Summary laconically described Kirk's presentations as "informative."[9]

In October, Nimitz spent several days in the hospital with a prostate infection, though he managed to meet one more time with Spruance before the Fifth Fleet sailed for the Gilberts. Having reviewed the battle plans, he had no additional instructions for Spruance, though he did remind him that while the Japanese fleet was not likely to sortie in defense of the Gilberts, the concentration of so many American ships there might prove irresistible to their submarines. He suggested, therefore, that Spruance should not linger: "Get the hell in, then get the hell out."[10]

AS PLANNED, HALSEY STRUCK FIRST. On November 1, men of the 3rd Marine Division landed on the south coast of Bougainville near Empress Augusta Bay. The move caught the Japanese by surprise, though as always they responded swiftly, sending a surface force from Rabaul to attack the invaders, just as they had done at Guadalcanal. Thanks to new unloading protocols, the American transports had already been emptied and had withdrawn by the time the Japanese arrived.

Even more crucial to American success was the fact that by now radar had become virtually universal on U.S. warships. That allowed American skippers to "see" in the dark and trumped superior Japanese optics, which had previously given them an advantage in night combat. Nimitz saw at once how important it was to collect and assess incoming data—including radar contacts—in one place near the bridge in order to provide the captain with an electronic overview of the battlespace. In the wake of the confusing battles around Guadalcanal, he had directed the establishment of what was initially called a Combat Operations Center on each ship. By mid-1943 it was renamed a Combat Information Center (CIC), which is the name it bears today. The coordination it provided allowed the Americans to open fire before the Japanese even knew there was an enemy ship in the vicinity. Consequently, in the Battle of Empress Augusta Bay (November 1–2, 1943) the Japanese lost a cruiser and a destroyer while the Americans lost no ships at all and suffered only nineteen mortal casualties. The next day, Nimitz received a message from Halsey that operations on Bougainville were "proceeding favorably."[11]

The Japanese were not done. They dispatched seven heavy cruisers and a light cruiser from Truk to Rabaul for another night attack. To preempt it, Halsey ordered a carrier raid against their Rabaul anchorage. Pilots from the

Saratoga and *Princeton* reported hitting at least five cruisers and possibly a sixth against the loss of only eight planes. Nimitz suspected it was another case of inflated damage estimates, though this time the reports were accurate. A week later, Nimitz himself directed another carrier strike against Rabaul, this one involving the new *Essex*. Japanese planes from Rabaul's airfields swarmed to attack her. In the subsequent air battle, the Japanese lost 40 percent of their planes, while the *Essex* and the other American ships emerged unscathed. After that, the Japanese decided to cut their losses and recalled their warships from Rabaul altogether. That effectively ended the threat to Halsey's beach-head on Bougainville and allowed Nimitz to return to Spruance the ships he had borrowed from him for the assault on the Gilberts.[12]

THAT ASSAULT, CODE-NAMED GALVANIC, BEGAN BARELY two weeks later, on November 20. At 5:00 that morning the ships of the Southern Attack Force—three battleships, five cruisers, and twenty-one destroyers under Rear Admiral Harry Hill—opened fire on Betio Island. For an hour, the Americans fired thousands of tons of high-explosive ordnance, including scores of enormous 16-inch shells, each of which weighed more than a ton, onto the island. The ships lifted fire briefly to allow planes from the five small escort carriers accompanying the invasion force to bomb the island, then the ships opened fire again. Aerial reconnaissance had revealed the presence of four 8-inch Japanese artillery pieces on Betio, and they came in for special attention, though for the most part, the gunners simply aimed at the island—it was so small, they were bound to hit something. For four hours, Betio was blanketed with shellfire. The *Time* correspondent Robert Sherrod, who was on board the battleship *Maryland*, concluded that "no mortal men could live through such a destroying power."[13]

At 9:00 a.m., after four hours of shelling and bombing, the LVTs carrying the first wave of Major General Julian Smith's 2nd Marine Division began heading for the beach.

TARAWA IS ACROSS THE INTERNATIONAL DATE LINE from Hawaii. Hence Nimitz got his first reports about the fighting the day before, on November 19. Julian Smith announced "successful landings" on Betio, though there was a hint that not all was well in the news that he had already committed his reserves and was "still encountering strong resistance."[14]

It became evident almost at once that the naval bombardment, fierce as it was, had failed to knock out the Japanese defenses. Subsequent analysis showed that while U.S. naval guns had wrecked three of the four 8-inch guns on the island, there were dozens of smaller-caliber artillery pieces and machine guns that had not been damaged at all. Consequently, as they approached the beaches, the LVTs came under heavy and accurate enemy fire.

As bad as that was, there was another, even more serious problem. There is a phenomenon known as a neap tide, sometimes called a "spring tide," though it has nothing to do with seasons. It occurs when the sun and the moon are at right angles to the earth. Under those circumstances, the gravitational pull of the moon, which is what causes tides, is cancelled out by the sun's influence, and as a result the high tides are lower than normal, sometimes several feet lower. And as it happened, there was a neap tide at Tarawa on November 20, 1943. Instead of four feet of water over the coral shelf, there was only two and a half feet. It was not entirely a surprise; the operational plan had cautioned that during a neap tide there might be only "one to two feet of water" over the coral shelf.[15]

The Marines in the first few waves, riding the LVTs, were unhampered by the shallow water, though many of the LVTs were so badly shot up they could not be used again. As planned, subsequent waves used the Higgins boats, and when those boats struck the coral shelf, they stopped, unable to go farther. The Marines had to climb out over the side and wade ashore over the coral surface through thigh-deep or waist-deep water while bearing heavy packs. Fully exposed, they took horrific casualties. One Marine who survived that ordeal recalled that the sound of Japanese bullets hitting the water sounded like "a sheet of rain." Some units suffered greater than 70 percent casualties before reaching the island.[16]

Nimitz did not know these details, though the news he did get was sobering enough. At one point Spruance forwarded a message from Julian Smith that was chilling: "The situation is in doubt." The last time such a message had been sent to Pearl Harbor it had come from the commander of

Betio Island and its airstrip. Some of the other, smaller, islands of Tarawa Atoll are visible stretching off to the north. The coral shelf that caused the invading Marines so much difficulty appears white in this wartime photo. (National Archives)

the Wake Island garrison only hours before he capitulated. Nimitz told his PR officer, Waldo Drake, not to release the news: "Let's keep thing this to ourselves until we find out what's going to happen." Drake said later that it was the only time he ever saw Nimitz genuinely worried.[17]

DESPITE THEIR CASUALTIES, THE MARINES GRADUALLY fought their way off the beach. Betio was only two miles long and barely a half mile across—one square mile in all—and there were 4,800 Japanese defenders on the island, which made it quite crowded. As a result, most of the fighting took place at close quarters. Marines crept up to Japanese pillboxes and tossed grenades through the firing slits. The Japanese responded with their signature tenaciousness. American progress was measured in feet.

It took three days for the Marines to overcome resistance, and the killing didn't end until the Japanese were virtually annihilated. Of the 4,800 defenders, only seventeen were taken alive along with two hundred or so Korean slave laborers who looked upon the Americans as their deliverers. The Americans suffered, too. Nearly a thousand Marines, including the Navy corpsmen who served with them, were killed, and twice that number wounded. To endure so many casualties in so small a space and in so short a time was shocking. Small as it was, Betio had been a bloodbath.

Nimitz was greatly relieved to learn that the battle was over and that the island was secured. He flew there at once to assess the battlefield and to show himself to the Marines. With half a dozen staff members, he flew from Pearl Harbor to Funafuti in his Skymaster command plane, then transferred to a smaller DC-3 for the hop to Betio's little airstrip. When the plane arrived over the island, the Seabees had not yet finished filling in the shell holes or extending the runway, and the pilot had to circle for an hour before it could land.[18]

From the air, it was evident that Betio had been pulverized. "Not a coconut tree of the thousands was left whole," Nimitz wrote to Catherine. "I have never seen such a desolate spot." Once he stepped out onto the tarmac, the extent of the devastation became even clearer. Bulldozers were shoving the dead Japanese into piles and covering them with dirt and coral rock. As Marine Major General Julian Smith led him and General Robert Richardson on a tour of the island, Nimitz literally had to step over and around the dead bodies in his path. Lamar later recalled the "bodies lying right in front of him as he walked along." Waldo Drake, who also made the trip, recalled that "there were hundreds and hundreds of corpses" and "people were still floating in on the beach." At one point Nimitz peeked into a wrecked gun mount where there were as many as twenty dead Japanese all piled up one on top of one another three or four deep. Nimitz and Redman looked at each other silently. Even more arresting than this visual nightmare was the smell. At one point, Nimitz turned to Lamar and told him it was "the first time I've smelled death."[19]

It was a relief when it was time to leave Betio for another island nearby where Julian Smith had set up a temporary headquarters. Smith was determined to provide the theater commander with a good meal, and he somehow came up with plates, cutlery, and even a tablecloth. That night, as Nimitz

Nimitz visited Tarawa immediately after its capture in November 1943. Here, Major General Julian Smith, whose Marines seized the island, leads the way, while Army General Robert Richardson explores a Japanese pillbox. (U.S. Naval Institute)

tried to sleep, the shifting tropical winds occasionally brought him a strong whiff of rotting flesh. "The stench," he wrote to Catherine, "was terrific."[20]

Shocked as he was by the loss of life, Nimitz was also impressed by the high morale of the surviving Marines. Far from being dispirited, they expressed an eagerness to get on with the war.[21]

If there was anything positive to come of this nightmare, it was that Nimitz now suspected that his requests for more and improved types of landing craft, as well as supplies and equipment of all sorts, were less likely to be ignored in Washington. No longer would the authorities there, including King, dismiss his requests as a symptom of overcautiousness. The losses at Tarawa also reinforced his insistence that American fighting men should never be sent into battle without overwhelming numerical and material superiority. As the official Army history put it, "Never again in the Pacific war would the assault troops be so handicapped as they had been at Tarawa."[22]

THE REACTIONS CAME SWIFTLY. MacArthur insisted that the heavy losses at Tarawa were incontrovertible proof that the whole idea of the Central Pacific Drive was wrong-headed. He wrote Secretary of War Stimson, "The Navy fails to understand the strategy of the Pacific." He repeated his argument that assaults must take place under the cover of land-based air. To prevent more such disasters, overall control of Pacific strategy should fall to him. "Give me central direction of the war in the Pacific," he wrote. "Don't let the Navy's pride of position and ignorance continue this great tragedy to our country."[23]

Howling Mad Smith was equally censorious. Though he had demanded that he be allowed to accompany the invasion force, his assigned post was on board the battleship *Pennsylvania* off Butaritari Island, part of Makin Atoll. His job as overall ground commander was to advise Turner. It was cruelly frustrating for him to know that his Marines were being slaughtered 120 miles to the south while he cooled his heels on a flagship. "I could do nothing to help them," he wrote later, "except pray."[24]

That frustration may have contributed to his volatile reaction to what he considered the slow-footed progress of Major General Ralph Smith's 27th

Army Division on Butaritari.† The 27th was a New York National Guard division and had received less training than most regular Army divisions, which may have contributed to its deliberate progress. The island had fewer defenders than Betio, and Holland Smith believed his Marines would have taken it in "a few hours." Instead, Ralph Smith's soldiers took most of three days. At one point Holland Smith went ashore, found Ralph Smith's command tent, and ordered him to "get your troops going," insisting angrily (and incorrectly) that "there's not another goddamned Jap left on this island." In a post-war memoir, Holland Smith acknowledged that he used "emphatic language" with his Army subordinate.[25]

When a Japanese submarine slipped through the destroyer screen off Butaritari and put a torpedo into the escort carrier *Liscome Bay*, sinking her and killing 645 American sailors, Holland Smith blamed it on the 27th Division's slow progress. Furious, he ordered Commander Ernest Eller to fly back to Pearl Harbor to tell Nimitz that the Army was failing to do its job. Turner heard about it and countermanded Smith's order. Turner was at least as bellicose as Smith, and he confronted the Marine general about sending messages to the theater commander without going through either Spruance or himself. Eller was an astonished witness as Turner shouted at Smith, "I'll tell Nimitz what I want." Recalling it later, Eller said, "I've never heard a senior officer talk to a senior officer like that." Eller had clearly not witnessed Holland Smith's tirade against Ralph Smith.[26]

Not to be thwarted, Holland Smith pressed Rear Admiral Francis Rockwell to write an "eyes only" message to Nimitz about the Army's failures at Makin and see that it was hand-carried to Pearl Harbor. Nimitz received it at the next morning's staff meeting and was greatly annoyed. This kind of internecine criticism was certain to antagonize the Army, especially General Richardson, who was already unhappy about having soldiers under

---

† It often confuses students of the battle that all three of the principal ground commanders for Galvanic were named Smith: Major General Holland Smith (USMC) was in overall command of the V Amphibious Corps; Major General Julian Smith (USMC) commanded the 2nd Marine Division, which spearheaded the attack on Betio; and Major General Ralph Smith (USA) commanded the Army's 27th Division on Makin Island.

the command of a Marine general. Indeed, it threatened to wreck the precarious inter-service partnership Nimitz had worked so hard to establish. He was also irritated that an airplane and its crew had been detached to fly this complaint to him as if it were time-sensitive critical information.[27]

Here was yet another test of Nimitz's diplomatic skill, another time when he needed to be a "fixer." He was certainly aware that both Turner and Smith were volatile—indeed, their intensity was a key element of their success as commanders—and he did not want to lose either of them. On the other hand, he could not afford to alienate the Army, including General Richardson. Nimitz had to play middleman, soothing Holland Smith, Turner, and Richardson all at the same time. As Eller put it, Nimitz "had this ability to harmonize two very different people" so that they pulled in tandem instead of in opposite directions.[28]

Holland Smith, however, was not to be soothed. In a post-war memoir, he compared the landing on Betio to Pickett's Charge at Gettysburg—a foolish and unnecessary shedding of blood. He blamed Turner, he blamed Spruance, and he blamed the Army. Most of all, he blamed the Navy's high command for ordering the assault in the first place. "Tarawa," Smith concluded, "was a mistake."[29]

The assault attracted controversy on the home front as well. While the number of killed and wounded was appalling, the greatest impact came from photographic images of the carnage. Marine cameramen took black-and-white footage of the Battle for Betio Island. That footage, assembled by United Films, was soon playing in newsreels in American movie theaters. Despite a soundtrack of martial music and a triumphalist narration, it could not disguise the heavy cost the Americans had paid in taking so small a place.

A color film based on footage provided by the Office of War Information and edited by Warner Brothers had an even greater impact. The final product included scenes of dead Americans—on the beach, on the ground, and floating facedown in the water. It was so graphic that many in the government argued it should not be released for public viewing. Nimitz disagreed. It was only right, he declared, that the people should see what the war was like. As Waldo Drake put it, "He believed in telling the American people as much as he could without helping the enemy." Roosevelt agreed, and the film was released for public viewing. Entitled *With the Marines at Tarawa*, it won the 1944 Academy Award for Best Documentary Short Subject.[30]

Far more painful for Nimitz personally was the stream of letters that began to arrive at his headquarters from mothers, wives, and sweethearts of the dead Marines. Some simply wanted to know why the assault had been necessary. Others were more confrontational. One mother from Arkansas began her letter with the sentence "You killed my son on Tarawa." At first, Lamar passed all these letters on to Nimitz, who replied to them personally. According to movie director Frank Capra, who visited Pearl Harbor, Nimitz was deeply moved by the letters: "What am I going to write to their parents?" Capra wrote later that the losses at Tarawa made Nimitz "a tormented soul." As the number of letters increased, Lamar stopped forwarding them and either replied to them himself or simply filed them away. If Nimitz knew about that, he did not intervene. Though he was empathetic to the point of being "tormented," there was still a war to run.[31]

THE MARSHALL ISLANDS are composed of thirty-two coral atolls that sprawl over four hundred thousand square miles of the Central Pacific (see Map 10). Atolls are submerged and extinct volcanoes. Over the centuries, reefs made up of living coral grew atop the rims of those volcanoes, and some of the reefs grew high enough to break the surface of the sea and form small islands. Most of the islands are tiny (hence the collective name "Micronesia"), but some were large enough to support Japanese military bases and airfields. The American plan to attack those bases—Operation Flintlock—called for a simultaneous assault on three of them: Wotje and Maloelap, near the eastern edge of the Marshalls, and the main Japanese base on Kwajalein Island—part of the eponymous Kwajalein Atoll—near the center of the group. All three islands hosted airfields; they were, in fact, the same islands that Halsey had raided two years earlier, in January 1942.

In the aftermath of the alarming losses on Betio, however, there was a lot of second-guessing about whether assaulting all three islands simultaneously might be biting off too much. The Versailles Treaty, which had granted the Caroline and Marshall Islands to Japan under a League of Nations mandate at the end of World War I, specified that Japan was not to fortify them. Virtually everyone assumed that the Japanese had ignored that prohibition. Given that the Japanese had had twenty years to perfect their defenses, their fortifications in the Marshalls were likely to be even more challenging than those at Tarawa, which they had occupied for less than two years. If Flintlock resulted in another bloodbath, it could undermine public and official support for the whole idea of continuing with a Central Pacific campaign. On the other hand, the American experience at Tarawa provided insights into how to improve amphibious protocols and make the next invasion less costly.

One obvious failure on Betio was the pre-invasion bombardment. The official Marine Corps history of the battle noted that "a greater weight of metal was hurled into each square foot of Betio Island than had rained down on any previous amphibious objective." And yet when the Marines went ashore, far too many of the Japanese strong points remained intact. One reason for this was that instead of targeting specific sites, the Navy gunners had simply plastered the whole island in the expectation that such overwhelming firepower did not require careful aiming. In addition, it was evident that American planners had underestimated the resiliency of Japanese fortifications. Built of reinforced concrete covered by layers of coconut logs and topped by several feet of coral rock and sand, they could not be destroyed except by a direct hit from a large-caliber naval gun.[1]

Nimitz undertook two initiatives to address this problem. The first was to prepare a grid with letters along one axis and numbers on the other that could be laid over maps of the target. This would allow the planners to assign specific targets to each ship, perhaps even each turret, at designated coordinates. Under this protocol, deliberate aimed fire replaced sheer volume.

The second initiative grew out of a suggestion by Rear Admiral Harry Hill, who had commanded the battleships off Betio. After reviewing the after-action reports from various ship captains, Hill suggested building pillboxes and other fortifications similar to those found on Betio and using them for target practice to evaluate the effectiveness of naval gunfire.

Embracing that idea, Nimitz ordered the construction of Japanese-style fortifications on the uninhabited Hawaiian island of Kahoolawe, near Maui. Then battleships and cruisers targeted those structures, and after each salvo, inspection teams went ashore to assess the damage and determine how much ordnance—and especially what kind—was needed to take them out. As a result of these experiments, Hill urged the use of armor-piercing projectiles (AP) as well as high explosives (HE), and also that the ships engage from close range.[2]

Another obvious problem at Betio was that there had not been enough LVTs to carry all of the Marines over the coral reef. For all his prickliness, Holland Smith had been right about that. Prodded by Nimitz, the Joint Chiefs directed the War Production Board to shuffle the priority list and double the number of LVTs under construction from a planned 2,055 to more than 4,000. In addition, some of the new LVTs were armored and equipped with a 37-mm cannon, which effectively turned them into amphibious light tanks.[3]

EVEN WITH THESE ADJUSTMENTS, HOWEVER, THE losses at Tarawa—and especially the public reaction to those losses—led many to wonder if the Flintlock plan was realistic. After discussing it among themselves, Spruance, Turner, and Holland Smith all decided that it would be wiser to focus on the two smaller islands (Wotje and Maloelap) and attack Kwajalein at some future date. Nimitz disagreed. He believed that Kwajalein was the key to the whole Marshalls archipelago, and he embraced a proposal from his new deputy chief of staff, Rear Admiral Forrest Sherman, to reverse the proposed sequence—that is, to bypass Wotje and Maloelap and concentrate everything on Kwajalein. Spruance and Turner were skeptical. They worried that given the number of enemy airfields on adjacent islands, supply ships attempting to sustain an American occupation of Kwajalein "would have a tough time of it." To discuss it, Nimitz scheduled a formal staff meeting for December 14.[4]

At that meeting, Nimitz explained his rationale. Capturing the two outer islands would not break Japanese power in the Marshalls, and Kwajalein would eventually have to be taken anyway. On the other hand, if Kwajalein fell, Wotje and Maloelap would be cut off and lose their strategic value. Moreover, photo reconnaissance showed that the Japanese were building a second airstrip on Kwajalein. Nimitz wanted to take the island before it became operational. Spruance and Turner remained unconvinced. Spruance said he could seize Kwajalein but doubted he could hold it. Though the Japanese fleet had not sortied to defend Tarawa, it might do so to defend Kwajalein, and because the American carriers were scheduled to return to the South Pacific after the landings, the invaders would be especially vulnerable.[5]

Always open to other opinions, Nimitz invited the others in the room to state their views. One by one, Kelly Turner, Holland Smith, and everyone else except Forrest Sherman proclaimed a preference for an attack on the outer islands. Nimitz remained silent until everyone had spoken, then paused. "Well, that's fine. We'll hit Kwajalein."*

That should have ended the conversation, but it didn't. Spruance and Turner continued to argue for striking at the outer islands. Turner was especially confrontational, calling Nimitz's plan "dangerous and reckless." Even after Nimitz adjourned the meeting, Spruance and Turner stayed behind to argue further. Finally, Nimitz said to them, "This is it. If you don't want to do it, the Department will find someone else to do it. Do you want to do it or not?" Faced with that ultimatum, they backed down.[6]

Nimitz, usually determined to find consensus and harmony, put his foot down firmly here. He may have become annoyed that Spruance, and especially Turner, were so stubbornly recalcitrant, and knowing that an ultimatum would end their protest, he decided to call their bluff. (He was, after all, a good poker player.) In addition, however, he was motivated by two other factors: first, he believed that the lessons learned on Betio would make the assault on Kwajalein more efficient and less costly, and second, he trusted the information culled from intercepted enemy

---

* The phrasing quoted here is from Waldo Drake's oral history. Others remembered it slightly differently. Edwin Layton recalled Nimitz saying, "We're going into Kwajalein. The Japanese aren't expecting us there," and E. B. Potter, in his biography of Nimitz, renders it as "Well, gentlemen, our next objective will be Kwajalein." However it was phrased, the meaning was clear.

message traffic that the Japanese were unlikely to send their fleet to defend the Marshalls. Even so, he risked a great deal by insisting on attacking Kwajalein against nearly unanimous opposition. Should the attack fail, or even if it succeeded with heavy casualties, Nimitz's tenure as CinCPac and CinCPOA might well be in jeopardy. Turner was likely to tell King that Nimitz had forced his plan on them; Towers would insist—again—that an aviator admiral should be placed in charge; and MacArthur was sure to renew his demand for central direction of the war. If such considerations played any role in Nimitz's thinking, he never acknowledged it. As he had done prior to the Battle of Midway, he listened carefully to all views and opinions, calculated the risks, then made his decision and assumed responsibility for it.

A CENTRAL ELEMENT OF THE FORTHCOMING campaign was the role that would be played by the carrier force under Baldy Pownall. Unsurprisingly, Towers had criticized the performance of the carriers at Tarawa. Sounding a lot like Fletcher at Guadalcanal, Towers insisted that using carriers to protect landing beaches wasted their most important attribute, which was their mobility. Holland Smith complained, too, but for the opposite reason: he thought the carriers should have provided *more* protection for the men on the ground. In fact, Pownall's assigned task for Galvanic had not included ground support. He had been charged with suppressing Japanese air forces on nearby islands and fending off any attempt by the Japanese fleet to interfere. Having accomplished both those tasks, Spruance rated Pownall's performance as "superb," and Nimitz sent him a "Well done." Yet Towers, Turner, and Smith were all unhappy, and Smith in particular claimed that the Marines on Betio had been abandoned by the flyboys.[7]

Nimitz again played peacemaker, though he soon began to develop his own doubts about Pownall. After the battle for Tarawa, Nimitz ordered Pownall to conduct a raid against Japanese shipping at Kwajalein. Pownall was not enthusiastic about it—he thought his pilots needed a rest—though of course he obeyed. His five carriers reached the target area undetected and launched an attack. Afterward, the returning pilots reported that there were only two light cruisers in the harbor plus a number of marus and transports.[†] Pownall's chief of staff, Truman Hedding, and the captain of Pownall's flagship, Joseph J. "Jocko" Clark, each urged him to order a second strike. Pownall wouldn't do it. "I couldn't see the justification for a second strike with tired pilots [and] tired airplanes," he said later. "To commit good airplanes and good pilots to nothing but old merchant ships . . . didn't make sense to me." So he turned his carriers eastward toward Pearl Harbor.[8]

Nimitz read Pownall's report of that raid carefully—carefully enough that he ordered him to remove a reference in it to the Japanese as "bastards." More to the point, he worried about Pownall's tenacity, especially after Sherman showed him photographs that Jocko Clark had brought him revealing rows of two-engine Betty bombers lined up on Kwajalein's airfield—certainly a worthwhile target. Clark had also been upset by Pownall's decision three months earlier not to extend the search for an aircrew that had been lost during the Marcus Island raid, a decision that Clark attributed to Pownall's eagerness to withdraw.[9]

Nimitz's new concerns about Pownall coincided with a revival of the whole issue of who should command carrier forces. Towers had complained to Undersecretary of the Navy James V. Forrestal (who had been a pilot in World War I) that aviators were being denied positions of command responsibility in the Pacific. Forrestal enquired about that, and, feeling pressure from Washington, Nimitz asked Towers for a list of aviator admirals he would recommend for command. Pleased to be asked, Towers again insisted that Pete Mitscher was the obvious candidate. He contrasted Mitscher's "tough and aggressive" attitude with Pownall's "lack of aggressiveness." Aware of Spruance's antipathy to Mitscher, Nimitz asked McMorris to sound out the Fifth Fleet commander about the idea of bringing Mitscher back as his carrier commander. As expected, Spruance opposed it.[10]

That same week, on the day after Christmas, Bill Halsey arrived in Hawaii. He was en route back to the States for an extended leave after his successful campaign on Bougainville. Though Rabaul remained in Japanese hands, the

---

† The Japanese added the word *maru*, meaning "circle," to ship names as a token of good luck. It implies that each ship is a little world (circle) of its own, and also that it will return from its voyage, thus completing a circle. During World War II, the term was used generically to denote non-combat Japanese shipping.

JCS had decided that, like other Japanese strong points, it should be cut off and left behind, its 100,000 defenders deprived of both support and supply. (They were still there, helpless and hungry, when the war ended.) Halsey stayed four days in Pearl Harbor as Nimitz's guest, and doubtless took the opportunity to discuss the issue of carrier command. Halsey had always held a better opinion of Mitscher than Spruance did, and almost certainly he seconded Towers's recommendation. Keeping his options open, Nimitz ordered Mitscher to fly out to Pearl Harbor for a consultation, doing so without telling Spruance.[11]

The next day (December 27), Nimitz invited Towers, Spruance, and Pownall to a meeting. Nimitz suggested to Pownall that he might have been overly cautious during the raid on Kwajalein. A surprised Pownall defended himself. His aircrews were tired, he said, the targets were of minor importance, and lingering too long in Japanese waters was risky. Nimitz heard him out, and replied that there was always an element of risk in war and that little could be achieved without a willingness to accept some risk. As he had reminded both Ghormley and Spruance, it was a question of "calculated risk."[12]

After Spruance and Turner left, Pownall remained behind for a lengthy one-on-one conversation. Sometime during that conversation, Nimitz decided that Pownall did not have a clear sense of "calculated risk" and that he would have to go. Perhaps the time had come to bring Mitscher out of Coventry despite Spruance's antipathy. Before he did anything, however, he would talk to King.[13]

To do that, he flew to San Francisco on New Year's Day, 1944. He suggested to King that Mitscher should relieve Pownall, and that the change should be made immediately so that Mitscher had command of the carriers for Flintlock. King agreed. Pownall would return to California to resume his former job as Commander Air Forces, Pacific. Mitscher would take over Carrier Division 3 (CARDIV3) at once with the prospect of assuming command of all Fifth Fleet carriers if he proved satisfactory.

Mitscher arrived in Hawaii on January 5. It is interesting, and perhaps significant, that, rather than occupy a bedroom in Nimitz's house, he moved in with Towers for a week before being piped aboard his new flagship, the new

Yorktown. In order to encourage a smooth transition, Nimitz asked Pownall to stay on for an indeterminate period and work with Mitscher until Pete felt comfortable in command. Mitscher believed he did not need any oversight, and Pownall, who moved into quarters on Spruance's flagship, felt like a third wheel.[14]

For his part, Spruance was "distressed" by the change. He did not blame Nimitz; he knew his boss was under a variety of pressures. Instead, he chalked it up to the political influence of Towers, who, according to Spruance's biographer, was "one of the few men he ever hated." Yet Spruance was a professional and he would adjust. If Nimitz could learn to live with having Towers on his staff, Spruance could endure having Mitscher command his carriers.[15]

As usual, there were other issues for Nimitz and King to discuss in San Francisco. Most of them concerned mundane topics such as the need for additional dredging at Midway, reports on airplane delivery, and the replacement of Marine garrisons by Army troops. In addition, however, they also sought a more permanent solution to the fraught issue of black shoes commanding aviators. What emerged was a set of guidelines that would henceforth require all black shoe admirals to have an aviator as chief of staff, and all aviators to have a black shoe as chief of staff. Both Spruance and Mitscher resented this forced blending of cultures, and each sought an exemption, but the rule stood. That led to the appointment of Rear Admiral Arthur C. Davis, the former commander of the *Enterprise,* as Spruance's new chief of staff, and Commodore Arleigh Burke, a noted destroyer commander, as Mitscher's chief of staff. Almost no one was happy about it, and Burke in particular was disappointed. He had been scheduled to take command of a new destroyer squadron and instead found himself playing nursemaid, as he might have put it, to an enigmatic admiral he did not know on a ship he barely understood. Time would tell whether the new protocol would prove effective. Meanwhile, there was an invasion to execute.[16]

KWAJALEIN IS THE LARGEST ATOLL IN THE WORLD; its central lagoon is sixty miles wide east to west, and twenty miles across north to south. At the southern tip of the lagoon is the namesake island of Kwajalein, home to Japan's principal base in the Marshall Islands. Twenty miles to the north were the conjoined islands of Roi and Namur, which also hosted substantial military facilities, including an all-weather airfield on Roi.

The American assault got underway at 5:00 a.m. on January 29, 1944, when Mitscher's carriers, now dubbed Task Force 58, began a series of ferocious air attacks. Mitscher had six fleet carriers plus six more light carriers with a combined total of seven hundred embarked aircraft, and those planes conducted repeated and relentless strikes against Japanese facilities on Maloelap and Wotje as well as Kwajalein and Roi. Before the day was over, they had destroyed 155 Japanese planes, most of them on the ground. American plane losses totaled 57. When he heard about it, Nimitz opined that a 3:1 exchange rate was what should be expected in confrontations between Japanese and American aircraft.[17]

Once Mitscher's aircraft had secured control of the skies, Spruance's battleships and heavy cruisers closed in to employ the new gunnery protocols that had been developed since Tarawa. The commander of the gunfire support group at Roi and Namur was Rear Admiral Richard Conolly, who had earned the nickname "Close-In Conolly" while covering the Allied landing at Salerno in the Mediterranean five months earlier. He lived up to that moniker at Roi, bringing his ships to within two thousand yards of the beach to hammer away at his assigned targets using both high explosives and armor-piercing shells. The result was spectacular. By the evening of January 30, there was barely a building or a tree standing. The gunners began to refer to the application of such a focused and sustained bombardment as a "Spruance haircut." Planes from Mitscher's carriers, meanwhile, continued their assaults on nearby Japanese-held islands.[18]

The Marines went ashore on February 1. They secured Roi and its airfield that same day, and took Namur the next. Twenty miles to the south, the men of the Army's 7th Infantry Division encountered tougher resistance on Kwajalein Island and spent three days taking it. Holland Smith saw that as another example of Army timidity.

For the entire operation, the Marines suffered 206 killed, and the Army 142, for a total of 348 mortal casualties. The Japanese lost 8,000 killed, a comparative loss rate of more than 20:1. Farther south, a battalion of Army soldiers seized Majuro Atoll and its expansive lagoon, which Spruance had convinced Nimitz to add to the target list, without losing a man.[19]

DURING THOSE EVENTFUL DAYS, Nimitz did not burden his operational commanders with additional instructions. Having put it all into motion, there was little he could do afterward that did not amount to micromanaging. Instead, during the days leading up to the invasion, he made a number of visits out to Muliwai. On January 15, for example, he, Anderson, and Lamar joined several others there to watch *Lassie Come Home,* a movie perfectly suited to take everyone's mind off the campaign that was about to get underway.[20]

Once Spruance's fleet left Pearl Harbor for Kwajalein, all the ships operated under radio silence, so there were no reports back to the Cement Pot. In conformance with his conviction that it was useless to obsess about things he could not control, Nimitz made more trips out to Muliwai, often bringing guests, including both Ghormley and General Richardson, who had grown increasingly frustrated by his limited authority. Though he was in charge of Army training, discipline, and preparations, Richardson had no operational authority over the employment of his soldiers in combat. Some on Nimitz's staff believed that "there was a little jealousy on Richardson's part that Admiral Nimitz was running the campaign." The disgruntled general also continued to resent Holland Smith's criticism of Ralph Smith's 27th Division at Makin. Nimitz may have hoped that a pleasant day at Muliwai might ease some of that resentment.[21]

The trips had continued even after operations in the Marshalls began. On January 29, the day Mitscher's planes blasted the airfields on Roi and Kwajalein, Nimitz spent the night in the Walkers' guest house. The next morning—as Fifth Fleet battleships and cruisers gave Kwajalein a "Spruance haircut"—he enjoyed what Una Walker described as a "delicious kidney breakfast" before returning over the hills to the Cement Pot to read the early reports from Spruance, who radioed, "The seizure and occupation of Kwajalein is progressing favorably."[22]

As at Tarawa, Nimitz immediately went to the island once it was declared secure, taking Richardson and several staff members along with him. The airfield on Kwajalein was still under repair, so his seaplane landed in the lagoon near Turner's flagship, the USS *Rocky Mount*, and there, on February 4, he held a press conference fielding questions from a gaggle of embedded reporters. Was he surprised by the lack of opposition in the Marshalls compared to Tarawa? Not really, Nimitz replied; "I was optimistic enough to hope for this." What did the victory mean to future U.S. operations? It meant, Nimitz said, "a quickening of the tempo" of the war. Could he be more specific? What was next? Nimitz smiled and said he would "let action speak for itself."[23]

After the press conference, everyone went ashore to tour the wrecked Japanese facilities. Forrestal had flown out from Washington to observe

Nimitz examines a Japanese gun position in this photo by *Life* magazine photographer George Strouck during his tour of Kwajalein with Undersecretary of the Navy James V. Forrestal. (LIFE magazine)

progress, and he rode in the lead jeep with Spruance and Marine Corps Major General Harry Schmidt while Nimitz and Richardson followed in a second jeep. Reporters and photographers trailed behind them in a caravan that wound about the island, stopping periodically to examine destroyed Japanese fortifications. A photographer from *Life* magazine snapped pictures of Nimitz examining a smashed Japanese artillery piece and standing "in solemn reverie" among fresh American graves. At one stop, Nimitz separated himself from the group to approach a group of three soldiers who were sitting on some rocks nearby. Chatting amicably with them, he was impressed by their high morale and eagerness to get on with the next operation.[24]

Nimitz's decision to go straight for Kwajalein, despite the reservations of his commanders, had worked out better than almost anyone had dared to hope. He did not indulge in any I-told-you-so moments, though his buoyant mood was evident when, after returning to Pearl Harbor on February 8, he met again with reporters, this time in his corner office in the Cement Pot. Feeling expansive, he was, as one reporter put it, "unusually candid." He told them that resistance in the Marshall Islands had effectively ended, that Kwajalein, Roi, and Namur were all in American hands, that the outer islands of Wotje and Maloelap had been cut off, and that the prospects for a continued advance were bright. Caught up by his obvious optimism, the reporter for the *New York Times* paraphrased his comments this way: "We have split wide open the outer gate to the real Japanese Empire."[25]

King was a bit annoyed that Nimitz was so open with the press. He wrote to warn him that he was being widely quoted in American newspapers about what the Navy was likely to do next. It verged, he wrote, on "giving aid and comfort to the enemy"—though whether that enemy was Japan or the American press he did not say. "You must watch your step in dealing with the press," he advised, though he also added: "Keep up the splendid work you are doing."[26]

F ROM THE MOMENT IT WAS FIRST ANNOUNCED back in March 1942, the division of command between Douglas MacArthur and Chester Nimitz had attracted public commentary. At the time, Nimitz was largely unknown, whereas MacArthur had been a prominent public figure even before the war, and his dramatic escape from the Philippines and subsequent pledge to return made him a national hero. The flood of "communiqués" that issued regularly from MacArthur's Brisbane headquarters encouraged the popular belief that he was fighting—and winning—the war virtually single-handedly. Though many in Nimitz's orbit resented MacArthur's blatant self-promotion, Nimitz himself never said a word about it. He kept that photo of MacArthur on his desk in the Cement Pot and refused to say anything disparaging about his Army counterpart—except perhaps to King during their tête-à-têtes in San Francisco.

Occasionally, reporters would try to stir up controversy by portraying MacArthur and Nimitz as rivals and adversaries. During one press conference in 1943 when a reporter asked him about it, Nimitz responded, "If you print one word of anything like that now or ever, I will personally see that . . . you will never set foot in this ocean area again." A year later, in December 1944, he reacted angrily to a nationally syndicated column in which Drew Pearson claimed that Nimitz and MacArthur were bitter rivals. "What a trouble maker he is!" Nimitz complained to Catherine, referring to Pearson. "Apparently many people like to read such rubbish." Despite his efforts to suppress any hint of discord, it was all but certain that MacArthur's determination to make the Philippines the central objective of the war would collide with King's insistence that the Central Pacific was a more direct and strategically sound route to victory. When that happened, Nimitz would find himself the man in the middle.[1]

ON JANUARY 27, 1944, TWO DAYS before Mitscher's carriers struck Kwajalein and five days before American soldiers went ashore there, Nimitz hosted a conference at his headquarters in Pearl Harbor. Competing requests by MacArthur and Spruance for the support of Mitscher's carriers made it necessary to make some decisions right away, even before the results of the Marshalls campaign became known. Both Towers and Richardson attended, of course, along with Forrest Sherman and Soc McMorris. Halsey had planned to attend, too, but his plane from San Francisco was grounded by fog, so he was represented by his chief of staff, Rear Admiral Robert Carney, whom Halsey and just about everyone else called Mick.

Nimitz also invited MacArthur. He knew the general seldom left his headquarters, so Nimitz was not surprised when he declined. On the other hand, MacArthur did send all three of his principal subordinates: Chief of Staff Richard K. Sutherland, air officer George Kenney, and his new naval commander, Thomas Kinkaid. Once they arrived in Hawaii, Sutherland and Kenney began a behind-the-scenes campaign to line up as many officers as they could behind the idea of conducting a single line of attack in the South Pacific. Richardson and Towers signed on immediately, and both Kinkaid and Sherman expressed conditional support. Just before the meeting, Towers told Sutherland that Carney, too, was "on board."[2]

At the meeting itself, Sutherland argued forcefully that once the Marshalls were pacified, all American resources in the Pacific—Nimitz's as well as MacArthur's—should focus on an advance through the South Pacific to the Philippines. Richardson, Towers, and Carney all seconded the idea, and so did Sherman and Kinkaid, though less enthusiastically. Only McMorris continued to advocate for continuing with the Central Pacific campaign.

Nimitz knew the proposal would be anathema to King. Three weeks before in San Francisco, King had told him that the Central Pacific Drive should remain his primary focus, with the capture of the Marianas as the capstone. An assault on those islands would likely draw out the Japanese fleet for the climactic naval battle that U.S. naval officers had anticipated for more than two decades. In addition, from the Marianas long-range American bombers could attack the Japanese homeland. King had sold that vision to the Combined Chiefs of Staff at the Trident conference in May 1943, and both FDR and Churchill had signed off on it. Indeed, the CCS had specifically endorsed an assault on the Marianas with a target date of October 1, 1944.

In spite of that, Nimitz did not push back against the alternative now put forward by MacArthur's surrogates. Only a month before, he had overruled the unanimous advice of his own staff about attacking Kwajalein, yet now he did not challenge this far more consequential proposal to reorient the entire strategy of the Pacific war. Instead, at the end of the meeting, he told Sherman to accompany Sutherland to Washington and present the idea to the Joint Chiefs. When Kenney got back to Brisbane, he told MacArthur, "The scheme was in the bag."[3]

It is entirely possible that Nimitz was genuinely convinced by the argument that a single line of approach would be both swifter and more efficient than a dual advance. The unexpectedly high cost of seizing Tarawa was a powerful argument for streamlining the offensive. On the other hand, it is equally possible that he declined to challenge MacArthur's trio of representatives openly, especially when members of his own senior staff supported them. Doing so could provoke an open breach, even hostility. He may have reasoned that since the proposal was likely to be dead on arrival in

Washington in any case, there was no reason to expend energy and goodwill fighting it now. If so, it was another example of his ability to pick his fights carefully. Then, too, he also knew that events in the Marshalls over the next several days would clarify future options, which they did.[4]

Only days later, after the gratifying success in the Marshalls, Nimitz received King's response to the proposal that Sutherland and Sherman had carried to Washington. King expressed his "indignant dismay" at the idea of abandoning the Central Pacific. The Marianas were essential, he wrote to Nimitz, not just to obtain airfields to bomb Japan, or even to draw out the enemy fleet; they were needed to secure a line of communications to the northern Philippines. Going from New Guinea to the Philippines without securing the Marianas, as MacArthur's representatives advocated, was "absurd" and "not in accordance with the decision of the Joint Chiefs."[5]

By the time Nimitz received that letter, the issue had become moot. After the swift success at Kwajalein, Nimitz radioed Spruance, "What do you think, after all, about taking Eniwetok?" (see Map 10). That atoll, another 300 miles farther west, was the hub of the Japanese reinforcement pipeline for the whole region. Having lost so many of their carriers, the Japanese now staged their airplane reinforcements from Japan to the Central Pacific via Iwo Jima and the Marianas to Eniwetok. From there, the planes fanned out to whatever island was under threat. Eniwetok was already on the Allied assault schedule, but not for ten more weeks. Prodded by Nimitz, however, Spruance went to see Turner and Holland Smith, and they all agreed to do it now. Nimitz gave the order. Its capture on February 23 wrecked Japan's island defensive network at least as much as the loss of Kwajalein.[6]

Equally consequential, on the same day the Marines went ashore on Eniwetok, Mitscher's carriers executed an airstrike against the principal Japanese base in the Caroline Islands, another 600 miles farther west, at Truk.

LONG CONSIDERED JAPAN'S GIBRALTAR, TRUK ATOLL had been a central focus of American planning since the 1920s. On February 4, the day Nimitz visited Kwajalein, two American reconnaissance planes reported that there were two enemy carriers and two battleships at Truk—an irresistible target.

Alas, by the time Mitscher's carriers arrived, those ships were gone; the fall of Kwajalein had so unnerved the Japanese high command that they had ordered the fleet back to the Palau Group, another 1,200 miles farther west. Even so, Mitscher's air strike on February 17–18 (Operation Hailstone) was a tremendous success. In his initial report, Mitscher claimed that his planes sank 19 Japanese ships, with 7 more "probably sunk." A week later, after looking over the pilot reports, he elevated those numbers to 23 ships sunk with 6 more "probable."* His pilots also claimed the destruction of more than 250 Japanese aircraft at a cost of only 25 U.S. planes. Instead of the 3:1 ratio Nimitz had suggested as appropriate, American pilots had achieved a 10:1 dominance. The only friendly loss during the operation was a single torpedo hit on the carrier *Intrepid*, which headed back to Pearl Harbor for repairs under its own power. With considerable understatement, Mitscher's chief of staff remarked, "We found that Truk was not as impregnable as we had thought."[7]

Given Truk's reputation, the raid generated a lot of positive comment on the home front. The *New York Times* went so far as to suggest that "a successful neutralizing of the great stronghold may shorten the Pacific war." After reading about it, Nimitz's daughters Kate and Nancy sent him a cable with the playful couplet: "Like Carrie Nation guzzling booze, / When man runs over Truk, that's news."[8]

Even as Mitscher's planes executed that strike, Nimitz received another lengthy radio message from King, who now suggested "pinching off" Truk and advancing past it directly to the Marianas. To investigate the feasibility of that, Nimitz radioed Mitscher not to return to Pearl and instead take Task Force 58 another six hundred miles farther west to conduct an air strike on the Marianas. The purpose, according to Nimitz's planning officer, was "to get as much reconnaissance information as we could on the beaches, so that we could do more detailed planning of the invasion."[9]

It was another "calculated risk." The Marianas were four thousand miles from Hawaii and less than fifteen hundred miles from Tokyo. Moreover, as

---

* The many ships lying at the bottom of Truk (now Chuuk) Lagoon have made it a mecca for recreational divers.

Mitscher's task force approached the islands, Japanese search planes sighted and reported him. Had Wilson Brown or Baldy Pownall been in command, they almost certainly would have aborted the mission. Instead, Mitscher told his staff that he planned to fight his way in.

And he did. Though the Japanese launched "almost continuous air attacks" during his approach, they had little success. One reason was that in addition to effective Combat Air Patrol by fighters from the carriers, an American technological breakthrough called a VT (variable time) fuse dramatically improved the deadliness of the American anti-aircraft batteries. Hitting an airplane at high altitude with a 5-inch shell from a moving ship was extraordinarily difficult, but with the VT fuse, the gunners no longer actually had to hit the target because the new shells exploded when they were in the vicinity of an aircraft.[10]

Planes from Mitscher's Task Force 58 carried out a series of strikes against the three largest islands in the Marianas—Guam, Tinian, and Saipan—on February 22, 1944. (In his battle order that morning, Mitscher quipped, "I cannot tell a lie. D-Day is Washington's Birthday.") Again, American pilots inflicted disproportionate losses on the enemy. Mitscher reported sinking 11 ships and destroying 136 aircraft. "This battle is historic for courage and determination of purpose," he declared. Almost as important, the attackers also brought back scores of photographs of Japanese facilities.[11]

The raid against the Marianas capped a remarkable month for American forces in the Pacific. Official recognition for the Fifth Fleet command team followed almost immediately: Spruance received a promotion to full admiral, and Turner got a third star. Holland Smith was not immediately promoted and complained about it, telling Turner that "you people"—meaning the Navy—got promotions whenever the Marines won them a victory, though soon afterward Smith also got a third star.

Of all of them, however, it was Mitscher for whom the events of February 1944 marked a spectacular redemption. His performance in the Marshalls, plus the raids on Truk and the Marianas, fully justified Towers's persistent advocacy of him. It also won him a third star and confirmation as the Pacific Fleet carrier commander. For most of a year, Nimitz had respected Spruance's aversion to Mitscher by keeping him on the shelf. Once Nimitz gave Mitscher his chance, however, the grizzled and weather-beaten aviator took full advantage of it. Even Spruance came to acknowledge his effectiveness.[12]

The events of that month were celebrated back home, too. In the first week of March, the editors of *Life* magazine declared enthusiastically that "February was the blackest month in the history of the Japanese Empire," and asserted that the successes at "Kwajalein, Eniwetok, and the attacks on Truk and Saipan," showed that "Nimitz's navy seemed to be running virtually unopposed through the Central Pacific." Nimitz himself graced the cover of that issue of *Life*, and the accompanying story suggested that the "taciturn Texan" was the guiding hand behind America's Pacific triumphs. Catherine may have been pleased by the publicity. Her husband was not. For one thing, the photographer had caught him unawares and he looked slightly dyspeptic. Worse, his mouth was slightly open and revealed the glint of a gold tooth. Quite apart from that, however, Nimitz would have preferred not to be presented as the public face of the Pacific war. MacArthur, too, had been featured on the cover of *Life*, but that had been two years earlier, back in December 1941. Nimitz's new fame was not likely to contribute to a smoother partnership.[13]

On February 24, Nimitz celebrated his fifty-eighth birthday. He spent it at Muliwai pitching horseshoes and playing tennis. Having been barred from singles by Doc Anderson, he and Una played doubles against Charles Lockwood and his wife, Betty. Afterward, there was another dinner on the lanai, this time with birthday presents and several glasses of Nimitz's signature cocktail, the "CinCPac." Una's brief diary entry said simply: "Drank plenty."[14]

TWO DAYS LATER, NIMITZ AND SEVERAL staff members, including Forrest Sherman and flag secretary Preston Mercer, boarded a plane for the long flight to Washington; Soc McMorris stayed behind to mind the store. The Joint Chiefs had summoned both Nimitz and MacArthur to resolve any lingering uncertainty about the most desirable route to victory in the Pacific. As usual, MacArthur declined to leave his headquarters. He had come to believe, as he told Halsey, that "Nimitz, King, and the whole Navy [were] in a

vicious conspiracy to pare away his authority." Given those dark suspicions, MacArthur probably should have made the trip—no one could defend his interests more eloquently than he could himself. Instead he once again dispatched Sutherland to represent him.[15]

When Nimitz's plane landed in San Francisco to refuel, Catherine and Mary were there to meet it, bags in hand, and they joined him on the cross-country flight to Washington, where they arrived on March 2. During the ensuing week, Nimitz, Sutherland, and a score of staff officers met daily with the Joint Chiefs, including King, to discuss the competing proposals for the defeat of Japan. At night, Nimitz was able to join Catherine and Mary at the Fairfax Hotel on Dupont Circle.[16]

In the meetings, Sutherland dutifully pleaded MacArthur's case for a single line of approach to the Philippines. The first step, he asserted, would be a westward leap of four hundred miles to Hollandia on the northern coast of New Guinea, a move that would require support from Nimitz's carriers. Nimitz noted that sending the carriers south would delay the westward movement in the Central Pacific, allow the Japanese time to build up their defenses, and perhaps jeopardize the timetable of the war. In conformance with King's earlier suggestion, he proposed bypassing Truk and capturing the Marianas in June. He also suggested seizing Ulithi Atoll, halfway between the Marianas and the Palau Group, and turning it into a fleet base to support future operations.[17]

With strong support from King, the Joint Chiefs accepted most of Nimitz's proposals, though George Marshall insisted on adding Mindanao to the target list. When the discussions concluded on March 11 the Joint Chiefs confirmed a continuation of the dual advance. As a kind of consolation prize, the Chiefs approved MacArthur's move to Hollandia and decreed that Nimitz would use his carriers to support it. After that, however, Nimitz was to continue with the Central Pacific Drive, bypassing Truk and invading the Marianas on or about June 15, three months earlier than originally planned.[†] The JCS also established some longer-term goals: Nimitz was to attack the Palau Group of islands, eight hundred miles east of the Philippines, in September in preparation for an assault on Mindanao in November. Pressed by King, the JCS kept Formosa on the list of future targets after Mindanao, but with no specific date.[18]

With the crucial decisions made, King, Nimitz, and Admiral Leahy—FDR's chief of staff, who presided over the JCS as its chairman—all went to the White House to brief the president over lunch. Roosevelt kept a close eye on operations in the Pacific and he asked several questions, though he did not suggest any changes to the decisions the JCS had made. At one point, he asked Nimitz why he had ordered Mitscher to raid the Marianas immediately after the attack on Truk.

---

† The timing is interesting. The JCS had already approved the invasion of Europe (Operation Overlord) for May 1, 1944. Invading the Marianas only six weeks later demonstrated Allied confidence that it would be possible to assemble the shipping needed to conduct two major invasions on opposite sides of the world within two months of each other. In the end, because the Normandy invasion was delayed, the two invasions actually occurred within two weeks of one another.

The answer, of course, was that Nimitz wanted to test the strength of the defenses there and gather information for a possible future invasion. That explanation, however, would imply that Nimitz had already decided to continue the Central Pacific Drive, and he may not have wanted to open a conversation about that. With a playful grin, he told the president that he would answer his question by telling him a story.

There was a man who needed an appendectomy, Nimitz began. The problem was that the man was elderly, overweight, and something of a hypochondriac, and none of the regular surgeons in the hospital would agree to perform the operation. Somehow, the patient managed to obtain the services of a renowned surgeon from out of state. The doctor was so famous that medical students, and even other surgeons, gathered to observe his surgical brilliance. When the operation was over, the patient asked how it had gone, and the surgeon told him that it went fine.

"But doctor," the patient said, "there's something I don't understand. I have a terrible sore throat."

"Well, I'll tell you," the doctor said, and he explained that the other doctors who had observed the appendectomy were so impressed by his skill that they had burst into spontaneous applause when he finished. "So I removed your tonsils as an encore."

"So you see," Nimitz said, "we hit Tinian and Saipan as an encore."

The president loved it, throwing back his head and laughing out loud, which brought the lunch to a happy end.[19]

It was not the only time that month that Nimitz would employ one of his "stories" to calm the waters of command politics.

WHILE NIMITZ WAS EN ROUTE TO WASHINGTON, MacArthur was making plans of his own in Brisbane. For some time, the JCS had eyed the Admiralty Islands, in the Bismarck Sea, as a possible target; King had suggested seizing those islands as early as December 1942. In addition to further isolating Rabaul, Manus Island, in the Admiralties, hosted a large deepwater anchorage at Seeadler Harbor that would be a valuable staging area for subsequent operations. The JCS had set a target date of April 1 for attacking the Admiralties, but like Nimitz, MacArthur saw an opportunity to accelerate the timetable. On the last day of February (which, in that leap year, was the twenty-ninth), he personally accompanied a reinforced squadron of the 1st Cavalry Division to Los Negros Island, near Manus. Encountering little opposition, he fed in reinforcements until the island was secured. Afterward he toured the island personally, deliberately exposing himself to inspire the troops, making it a very personal triumph.[20]

Eager to capitalize on MacArthur's victory by establishing a fully functioning base at Seeadler, Nimitz suggested to the Joint Chiefs that the Navy should take over the development and administration of Manus Island. When

MacArthur adopts a proprietary stance on Los Negros Island after its capture by forces under his command on February 29, 1944. The figure at left is MacArthur's aide, Colonel Lloyd Lehrabas. (National Archives)

MacArthur heard that, he exploded, interpreting it as yet another attempt by the Navy to steal his victory and diminish his accomplishments. The suggestion, he insisted, implied that he somehow lacked "the capacity to command," a slur that touched not only his "professional integrity" but also his "honor." He ordered Halsey to fly to Brisbane in order to straighten him out.[21]

Halsey arrived in Brisbane on March 3 (the day Nimitz met with the JCS in Washington). There, with several of MacArthur's staff officers standing in silent witness, MacArthur treated Halsey to a blistering tongue-lashing. The Admiralties had been won by the blood of his soldiers, MacArthur told him; it was not only unjust for Halsey and the Navy to assume oversight, it was dishonorable. After a lengthy disquisition, he turned to Halsey, pointed his pipe stem at him, and demanded, "Am I not right, Bill?" To which Halsey replied, "No, sir."[22]

There was an audible gasp in the room. An undaunted Halsey, backed by a courageous Kinkaid, ignored it and explained that since Seeadler Harbor was to be a principal anchorage for the fleet, its administration had to fall to the Navy. The discussion continued all afternoon and into the next day before MacArthur finally relented. "You win, Bill," he said. And he apparently meant it, for he seemed to bear no grudge afterward. It may be that, having grown used to the abject sycophancy of his staff, MacArthur admired Halsey's willingness to argue back.[23]

Meanwhile, Nimitz left Washington and, after saying goodbye to his wife and daughter in San Francisco, he and his staff continued on to Pearl Harbor. When he came into the office the next morning, he found an invitation from MacArthur waiting for him. If Nimitz would come to Brisbane, the general wrote, he would receive a "warm welcome." Up to now, MacArthur had declined all invitations to participate in strategic discussions, mainly because it was unfathomable to him that anyone thousands of miles away might have anything useful to say about what was happening in his theater. Now, however, he wanted Nimitz's support for the movement to Hollandia. He may also have wanted to revisit the question of who would control the Admiralty Islands.[24]

Of course Nimitz accepted. "It will give me much pleasure to avail myself of your hospitality," he wrote, and he prepared for the visit with some care.

His first move was to send a staff officer, Captain Cato Glover, to Brisbane as a kind of advance man to arrange logistics and to open conversations with MacArthur's staff. When Glover got to Brisbane, he paid a courtesy call on MacArthur at Lennon's Hotel, the only modern building in the city, which MacArthur had re-christened "Bataan." (The telephone operator was instructed to answer all incoming calls with "Hello. This is Bataan.") MacArthur and his staff had taken over the whole building, and the general established his office and his living quarters in the penthouse. There, MacArthur greeted Glover warmly and professed enthusiasm about Nimitz's upcoming visit. He acknowledged that there were some differences between the Army and Navy about strategic options, but airily waved off any concerns, adding that he was sure "we could settle our differences promptly." Glover recalled that MacArthur spoke almost nonstop for forty-five minutes and that Glover himself never had a chance "to say a word except to thank him for the meeting."[25]

Back in Pearl Harbor, Nimitz continued to make his own preparations. Aware that MacArthur doted on his wife and son, he told Lamar to find a skilled tailor in Honolulu who could make a Hawaiian-style playsuit for six-year-old Arthur MacArthur, and he asked Una Walker to choose several rare orchids from her world-class garden for Mrs. MacArthur. Thus armed, he and his team left Pearl Harbor for Brisbane on March 23. It was a long flight in any case, and crossing the international date line meant that he arrived on the twenty-fifth. He was gratified and a little surprised to find that MacArthur had come down to the airfield to meet him personally. Though they had nearly a century of combined service between them, it was the first time they had ever met face-to-face.[26]

In private, MacArthur had often been dismissive of Nimitz, referring to him as "*Nee*-mitz," drawing out the first syllable mockingly. But it was a measure of how determined he was to make the meeting a success that he had arranged a formal reception and dinner for his guest, inviting senior officers from all of the services. That was not merely unusual, it was virtually unprecedented, for unlike Nimitz, who regularly socialized with important locals in Oahu, particularly the Walkers, MacArthur routinely declined invitations to dinner or other social activities. His official explanation was that he was too busy. In addition, however, he disliked unstructured gatherings where he was not in control of the agenda.[27]

Prior to the dinner, Nimitz called on MacArthur in his penthouse apartment to present the gifts he had brought. The general was genuinely touched, especially by the custom-made silk playsuit for Arthur. Though the boy had already gone to bed, Mrs. MacArthur wanted him to try it on at once.[28]

The official conversations the next day were also fruitful. Nimitz readily agreed to order Mitscher to conduct air strikes against Japanese bases in the Palaus and the Carolines to cover MacArthur's flank as he approached Hollandia. He was more hesitant about providing direct support for the landings, since that would expose the carriers to Japanese ground-based air. MacArthur's air commander, George Kenney, assured him that his heavy bombers from Australia would neutralize Japanese airpower in advance.[29]

The meetings were all "cordiality and courtesy" (as Nimitz described it to King in a private letter) until the last day, when Nimitz mentioned that, as he understood it, the Joint Chiefs wanted each of them to prepare plans for the next step after Mindanao, which would be either Luzon or Formosa.

At the mention of Formosa, MacArthur "blew up," leaping to his feet and pacing excitedly about the room. He delivered an extended lecture about why Luzon, and not Formosa, had to be the next Allied objective. The United States would have blood on its hands, he declared, if it did not redeem the Filipino people, who looked to the United States for salvation. A swift return to Luzon and the Philippine capital, Manila, was a "sacred obligation" to the Filipinos and to the thousands of American prisoners of war who had been captured in Bataan and were still being held there. The POWs, he insisted, would never forgive being abandoned, nor should they. It was scandalous, he declared, that "those gentlemen in Washington" who had "never heard the whistle of pellets" would try to dictate the course of the war.[30]

Nimitz mostly just listened. When he managed to interrupt, he suggested that "those gentlemen in Washington" "were trying to do their best for the country" and, in his view, were "succeeding admirably." The clash left an awkward silence in the room. To lighten the mood, Nimitz said that it was not unusual for two men in a hotel to puzzle over seemingly irreconcilable problems, and, with a smile spreading across his face, he added that it reminded him of a story.[31]

It seems there were two men in a hotel, perhaps a hotel much like this one, who found themselves pacing back and forth in the hallway, each of them obviously conflicted by a difficult problem. Back and forth they walked, passing each other frequently. Finally one stopped and asked the other what problem he was dealing with. The man replied that he was a doctor and he had a patient in one of the rooms who had a wooden leg that needed to be attached. Alas, the wooden leg had come apart, and the doctor could not figure out how to put the leg together. "Great guns!" the other man replied. One leg apart? That wasn't a problem. "I have a good looking gal in my room with *both* legs apart and I can't remember the room number!"[32] The room erupted with both relief and laughter. Even MacArthur laughed.

It did not, of course, resolve the disagreement. Both Nimitz and MacArthur knew that a final decision about the future trajectory of the Pacific war had yet to be made, and that when it was, it would be by "those gentlemen in Washington."

ARRIVING BACK IN PEARL HARBOR, Nimitz called the Walkers and invited himself to dinner—alone this time, without Lamar or Doc Anderson. It was a quiet dinner on the lanai followed by a cribbage game with Sandy, and likely reflected his need for a little quiet time after a fraught trip. The next day, he was back in the Cement Pot fulfilling his collateral duty of entertaining visiting dignitaries, who arrived now with increasing frequency. In addition to hosting receptions and dinners, and sometimes offering overnight accommodation, he also frequently took his guests to Muliwai, which by the spring of 1944 had become a semi-official hospitality house for visiting VIPs.[1]

On April 1, his visitor was Archer Vandegrift, the hero of Guadalcanal, who had been named Commandant of the Marine Corps in January. Nimitz and Vandegrift took a long walk on the beach at Muliwai during which they almost certainly discussed how to ease the tension between Army and Marine Corps units in Holland Smith's V Amphibious Corps. Smith's intemperate criticism of Army units at both Tarawa and Kwajalein had led General Richardson to demand that Smith's authority be restricted to USMC units, and that a separate corps composed entirely of Army divisions should be created to fight alongside it. That, of course, meant divided command, something Nimitz wanted to avoid.

The next day Nimitz had another visitor. Admiral Thomas Hart arrived at the head of a group of officers who had come to interview witnesses to the Japanese attack on Pearl Harbor twenty-eight months earlier. Husband Kimmel had never accepted the initial ruling of the Pearl Harbor investigation that he had been guilty of negligence, and he fully expected that a court-martial would eventually clear his name. Secretary Knox, who sympathized with Kimmel's circumstances, suggested that because vital witnesses could become victims of the war, their testimony should be collected now, and Hart had come to Hawaii to do that.[2]

Hart and his team immediately got to work interviewing anyone who had been on duty on the Day of Infamy. That included several who were now on Nimitz's staff, though not Nimitz himself, since he had been in Washington that day. On April 3, which was a Friday, Hart interviewed Kelly Turner in the morning, but adjourned the commission at noon for the weekend, and that afternoon Nimitz took him to Muliwai. There, they swam in the ocean and relaxed on the Walkers' expansive lawn in their bathing suits, clowning with the Walker grandchildren. After dinner, they listened to classical music and played several hands of poker.[3]

Two days later, Nimitz brought Richardson to Muliwai. Especially after his conversation with Vandegrift, Nimitz may have hoped that a pleasant Sunday afternoon might temper Richardson's resentments. At sixty-two, Richardson was neither a hiker, like Vandegrift, nor a swimmer, like Hart, so the activity that day was horseshoes, and in place of poker a game of charades. At some point Nimitz found an opportunity to remind Richardson of the importance of unified command.[4]

As Nimitz sought to mend fences and preempt disagreements, Mitscher's carriers executed the raids that Nimitz had promised MacArthur in Brisbane. For three days, American planes hammered away at Japanese

Nimitz poses with two of Sandy and Una Walker's grandchildren (whom he called "the gremlins") during a visit to Muliwai on April 3, 1944. The figure in white swim trunks is Admiral Thomas Hart. (Mike Lilly Collection)

shipping in both the Palau Group and in the Carolines to prevent them from interfering with MacArthur's move to Hollandia later that month. Spruance reported that the raids were a success, and Nimitz passed that news on to Washington. Secretary Knox, however, wanted details; newspaperman that he had once been, Knox wanted to publicize Navy accomplishments whenever he could. Nimitz dutifully radioed Spruance asking him to report more fully, but he got no response. While Nimitz appreciated that Spruance was reluctant to break radio silence, Knox was persistent, so Nimitz ordered Spruance to do it anyway. Still nothing.

On April 6, Spruance's task force entered the harbor at Majuro Atoll and Spruance at last sent in his full report, which Nimitz passed on to an eager Knox. Nimitz flew to Majuro himself two days later, and Spruance explained his reluctance to break radio silence. He had delayed responding, he told Nimitz, because he wanted to verify the pilot reports. Like Nimitz, he knew all too well that preliminary reports often proved overly optimistic. In receipt of the report, Knox immediately released it to the media, and the next day, banner headlines in the *New York Times* reported: "28 JAPANESE SHIPS SUNK, 18 OTHERS DAMAGED."* The accompanying story disclosed that U.S. pilots had destroyed another two hundred Japanese planes. Combined with their losses in the Solomon Islands and in the Central Pacific, the Japanese were quite literally running out of shipping, aircraft, and critically, pilots. Knox was pleased, though he remained a little annoyed that the good news had been delayed.[5]

Three weeks later, Knox himself was dead, felled by a massive heart attack on April 28. He was seventy. Though Nimitz had occasionally wondered about the depth of Knox's support, the secretary had mostly been a loyal advocate and defender. Nimitz wrote Knox's widow, "You have lost a devoted and beloved husband, the Navy has lost the best Secretary it ever had, and I have lost a true and loyal friend." For the most part, Knox had even managed to get along with King, in part because King had a grudging respect for the former Rough Rider, who seemed to appreciate the need for strong leadership in difficult times.[6]

King did not have the same view of Knox's replacement, James V. Forrestal, a handsome and wealthy former bond trader who, as a former pilot himself in World War I, openly championed Towers and the aviation community. As King put it with dry understatement, he and Forrestal "did not see eye-to-eye." In addition to bad chemistry, King disliked and distrusted Forrestal's tendency to be more assertive (King would have said meddlesome) in Navy decision-making. The antipathy cut both ways; Forrestal was not an admirer of King, or of Nimitz either, whom he tended to think of as King's creature. Waldo Drake thought Forrestal harbored a "seething anger" at Nimitz for refusing to give Towers the carrier command he coveted. It was not immediately clear just how much, if at all, this change at the top would affect Nimitz's command authority in the Pacific.[7]

---

* In a sign of the times, that same front page also announced that southern senators were promising "the bitterest and longest of the 'States' rights' battles yet fought in the Senate" to kill a House bill to eliminate the poll tax.

James V. Forrestal served four years as Undersecretary of the Navy before Roosevelt appointed him to the top job after the death of Frank Knox in April 1944. (U.S. Naval Institute)

In addition to a new boss, Nimitz also got a new foe. On May 3, Admiral Soemu Toyoda succeeded to command of the Japanese Combined Fleet following the death of Mineichi Koga, whose airplane went down in a typhoon east of the Philippines. Toyoda had originally opposed going to war with the United States at all, declaring that such a war was unwinnable. Once it began, however, he threw himself into the fight and now fully embraced the plan of his predecessor, which was to hoard Japan's naval resources—especially oil, which was becoming alarmingly scarce—until the Americans attacked the Marianas, and then launch a full-scale assault against the invaders. He labeled the plan Operation A-Go.

INVADING THE MARIANAS WAS EXACTLY WHAT Nimitz had in mind. By this point in the war, the planning process had developed a regular protocol. Nimitz himself drew up the initial outline, laying out the objective, the timing, and the assets available. "He would tell you *what* he wanted to be done," a senior staff officer recalled, "*when* he wanted it done, and *what forces* you would have available, but he would never say *how* to do something." To that initial outline, Nimitz's enlarged staff added specifics, designating and assigning specific ships and units, calculating the logistic support required and the shipping needed to deliver it. Then the blueprint went to Spruance's Fifth Fleet staff, where it was fleshed out with more details—the *how* part of the plan—before pertinent segments were forwarded to Turner, Smith, and Mitscher. Their staffs then wrote the detailed orders specifying which transports would carry which units to the target, which Marine units would make the initial assault, and which squadrons would fly particular missions. By the time it was completed, a typical operational plan might cover a thousand pages or more. One staff officer remembered that the plan for the Marianas (Forager) "was a stack of papers a couple of feet high."[8]

More than any previous invasion, the leap to the Marianas posed herculean logistical problems. The first difficulty was the distance. The island of Saipan, the principal American target in the Marianas, was more than 3,600 miles from Pearl Harbor. Given that, once the operation began, it would be not quite impossible to shuttle reinforcements or supplies there. The invaders would have to conduct the invasion—at least in its initial stages— with whatever they had brought with them, including sufficient fuel oil to keep the hundreds of vessels operating.

The second challenge was the size of the invasion force. Kelly Turner would again command the amphibious force, designated as Task Force 51, which was divided into two groups: one for Guam under Richard "Close-In" Conolly, and the other for Saipan and Tinian under Turner's direct supervision. Their ships—numbering in the hundreds—would carry the 128,000 men of Holland Smith's landing force, which was also divided into separate groups for Guam and Saipan/Tinian. Despite Richardson's lobbying, each landing force remained a mix of both soldiers and Marines, with Marine generals in charge of both landings. On Guam, Major General Roy Geiger would command the III Amphibious Force, and on Saipan Holland Smith would exercise direct command over the V Amphibious Corps, consisting of two Marine divisions (2nd and 4th) plus Ralph Smith's 27th Army Division, the same unit Holland Smith had criticized so harshly for its performance on Makin.

The striking arm of the fleet was Mitscher's Task Force 58, now grown to fifteen aircraft carriers, with a total of nine hundred planes, and escorted by seven battleships, eleven cruisers, and eighty-six destroyers. In support of all these ships was an enormous train of support vessels: cargo ships, ammunition ships, and the essential oilers. Even Charles Lockwood's fleet submarines were pulled off patrol to provide support. It was the most powerful naval fleet ever assembled.[†] Spruance exercised overall command from his flagship, the heavy cruiser *Indianapolis*.[9]

As his staff worked on the details during the first week of May, Nimitz again flew to San Francisco to meet with King. As usual, King began by summarizing operations elsewhere, including the preparations for Overlord, the impending invasion of Nazi-occupied France, which was to be followed by an invasion of southern France (Anvil) and a coordinated drive into the heart of Germany. After Nimitz described the preparations for Forager, the discussion focused on what to do after that. According to the March 12 directive from the JCS, the next steps involved the invasion of the Palau Group, and then Mindanao. After that, King wanted to bypass Luzon and invade Formosa. Doing so would not only cut Japan off from her supplies in the South Pacific but also create an opportunity for closer U.S. cooperation with the Chinese on the Asian mainland. He knew, of course, that bypassing Luzon was sure to provoke outrage from MacArthur.

Halsey also attended the meeting, and all three admirals discussed what role he might play now that the South Pacific campaign was winding down. Halsey was too valuable an asset to be left cooling his heels in Nouméa, yet it seemed wrong to order him to supersede Spruance, who had experienced nothing but success since taking over the Fifth Fleet. It was King's planning officer, Charles "Savvy" Cooke, who proposed a solution. Why not have

---

† The Anglo-American armada being assembled that same month in the English Channel for the invasion of occupied France was numerically larger but had significantly less firepower and, of course, no aircraft carriers. In any hypothetical confrontation between the Fifth Fleet and the Normandy invasion fleet, it hardly would have been a contest.

Halsey and his staff move from Nouméa to Hawaii to write plans for the attack on the Palau Group and Mindanao? That way, as soon as the Marianas were secured, Halsey and his team could take command of the fleet for those operations while Spruance and his team came back to Hawaii to make plans for whatever would follow: either Luzon or Formosa. In effect, Spruance and Halsey would take turns commanding the fleet. When Halsey was in charge it would be called the Third Fleet, and when Spruance took over again, it would resume its identity as the Fifth Fleet. As Halsey expressed it later, "Instead of the stagecoach system of keeping the drivers and changing the horses, we changed drivers and kept the horses." It was pretty tough on the horses, of course, since the crews and the pilots had fewer days of shore leave, but it was unquestionably efficient. The concept was not a product of strategic calculation. It was simply a pragmatic way to take advantage of two talented commanders.[10]

NIMITZ FLEW BACK TO HAWAII ON MAY 8. In a dramatic contrast with his arrival there on Christmas morning in 1941, the harbor was now crowded with hundreds of ships, most of them new: combatants, Liberty ships, and the entire alphabet soup of amphibious ships: LSTs, LCIs, LCTs, and others. More arrived almost daily from the West Coast, all of them filled with supplies, equipment, and ammunition.

Of all the ships needed to conduct a large-scale amphibious invasion, the most critical was the LST. It was not a handsome vessel. As one veteran put it, an LST was shaped like a bathtub, and maneuvered like one, too. Nevertheless, their ability to offload tanks, jeeps, and fully loaded trucks directly from their commodious cargo hold right onto the invasion beach made them invaluable. The plan for Forager called for no fewer than eighty-four of them. Not surprisingly, Allied planners elsewhere were also clamoring for LSTs—as many of them as they could get. Initial plans for the invasion of Normandy called for 230 of them, a number that soon increased. In England, in the Mediterranean, in the South Pacific, and elsewhere, the demand for LSTs exceeded their availability.[11]

That made the accident that occurred on May 17 a strategic calamity as well as a human tragedy. The exact cause is unknown. Sailors on board

LST-353 were offloading 4.2-inch mortar ammunition when one of the mortar rounds detonated. In reporting it to Nimitz, Turner speculated that the ammunition had been stacked too high and had become unstable. Whatever the cause, the explosion ignited the rest of the mortar shells as well as barrels of gasoline stacked nearby. Within seconds, the entire ship went up in a fireball so massive it set off explosions on half a dozen other nearby ships, all of them packed with vehicles, supplies, and more ammunition. Three nearby LSTs had smaller LCTs sitting atop them as deck cargo, and all of them blew up as well. A witness recalled seeing "whole jeeps, parts of ships, guns, equipment, shrapnel, fragments of metal" flying up into the air and then raining down on the waters of West Loch. In addition to the 168 men who were killed, six LSTs and three LCTs were destroyed.[12]

Nimitz knew there was little chance of getting more LSTs from the States—any such vessels there would be headed for England—so he appealed instead to MacArthur. With Hollandia secured, in part due to support from Nimitz's carriers, MacArthur was in a generous mood, and he agreed. That allowed Nimitz to tell King that despite the disaster, "FORAGER target date will be delayed but little if at all."[13]

Indeed, the first elements of the Marianas invasion fleet began to depart Pearl Harbor only two days later, on May 19. The transports and LSTs carrying the invasion force filed out of the harbor one by one and jockeyed into convoy formation while scores of destroyers took up their positions as escorts. Soon the entire formation began a zigzag course westward at a stately 10 knots. Mitscher's Task Force 58 sailed separately. His fifteen carriers were now organized into four task groups (58.1, 58.2, 58.3, and 58.4) of three or four carriers each. Spruance ordered two of those groups to carry out air strikes against Iwo Jima, in the Bonin Islands, before joining the other two off the Marianas. That same week, 3,500 miles to the south, hundreds more ships of the Guam invasion force under Geiger left Guadalcanal.[14]

For more than two years, Nimitz had watched task forces depart Pearl Harbor for the war. In January 1942, he had sent Halsey with a single carrier off to strike at the Marshall Islands; six months later, he had sent Fletcher and Spruance toward Point Luck north of Midway with three carriers and a total of fifteen ships. The fleet he now dispatched to the Marianas consisted of more than six hundred ships, including fifteen of the large fast carriers. He did not worry the force would prove inadequate. If he harbored any concern at all, it may have focused on the temperament and compatibility of the commanders. Despite Spruance's misgivings about Mitscher, the two had worked well together in the Marshalls in February and again during the April raids on the Palau Group. Still, they had very different personalities and priorities. For his part, Kelly Turner was his usual energetic and cantankerous self, but assembling the invasion force had put him under a lot of pressure and he had recently taken to drinking heavily at night. Nimitz asked Spruance about that, and Spruance defended Turner, insisting that his drinking was simply a way of unwinding after a stressful day and that it did not affect his performance. Not to be forgotten was Holland Smith, who continued to harbor doubts about the reliability of the Army units in his command, especially Ralph Smith's 27th Infantry Division. Whether these individuals could work efficiently together remained to be seen.[15]

The ships from Hawaii and Guadalcanal rendezvoused in the enormous lagoon at Kwajalein, and it was there that many of the embarked soldiers, sailors, and Marines heard the announcement piped over the ships' 1MC system: "Now hear this. The invasion of France has started. Supreme Headquarters announced that the landings to date have been successful. That is all." The news provoked loud and sustained cheering and no doubt provided a boost to the morale of those who were about to conduct their own D-Day.[16]

AS THE VARIOUS ELEMENTS OF THE Fifth Fleet resumed their voyage westward from Kwajalein, Nimitz continued the day-to-day activities of his job in Hawaii, both official and social. One evening he invited a large group of officers for dinner with the promise of a movie to follow. To accommodate everyone, the movie would be shown outdoors now that evening blackouts were no longer necessary. Even though a light, steady rain fell all evening, the officers insisted that the movie should be shown regardless, and they all sat in the misting rain to watch Betty Grable in *Pin Up Girl*.[17]

Nimitz also continued with his daily hikes, some of them quite strenuous. On June 11, as Spruance's fleet approached Saipan, and as American, British, and Canadian soldiers fought their way off the Normandy beaches, Nimitz, Doc Anderson, and Una Walker set out on a hike into the mountains behind Muliwai. As the trail snaked upward, it became steeper and narrower, and the drop-off on the seaward side was especially precipitous. About three miles into the hike, Nimitz missed his footing and fell, bouncing and rolling twenty feet down the steep slope before his descent was abruptly stopped by a boulder. Anderson scrambled down to him and saw at once that Nimitz was badly bruised and very likely had some broken ribs, which was later confirmed. Anderson helped him to his feet, and slowly and painfully they climbed back up to the trail. There was no alternative but to hike the three miles back to Muliwai. Nimitz did not suffer any permanent damage from his accident, but he moved gingerly for several weeks, during which a deep breath was painful and a cough excruciating.[18]

News from Spruance was sparse, though Nimitz did get occasional glimpses of what was happening 3,600 miles to the west. Though all of Spruance's ships operated under radio silence, fragments of reports from some of Mitscher's pilots made their way across the ocean to receivers in Hawaii. On June 12, the day after his fall, Nimitz learned that one pilot had reported that "the island beach defenses" remained "unchanged," and that surf conditions on the target beaches were "mild." Another reported that anti-aircraft fire was heavy but inaccurate. Ominously, another pilot reported the next day that the Japanese had placed some heavy guns into the cliffs behind the beach. Nimitz and his staff monitored all these tantalizing scraps of news.[19]

Off Saipan, Spruance's team was also monitoring the radio traffic, and on June 13, a sailor brought him a report from the American submarine *Redfin*, which had been watching the main Japanese carrier fleet at Tawi Tawi near Borneo, 1,800 miles to the southwest. The skipper of the *Redfin* reported that the Japanese fleet had left its anchorage and was headed north.

JUNE 15 WAS D-DAY ON SAIPAN. That morning, the LSTs off Saipan opened their giant bow doors and launched more than eight hundred LVTs, each of them loaded with twenty Marines, into the sea. This time there was no coral reef to cross, for Saipan was not an atoll; it was a full-fledged island twelve miles long and six miles wide with hills and towns—even a railroad. It was the first time an American assault targeted an island with a substantial civilian population. The preliminary naval gunfire from the battleships and heavy cruisers had taken out most of the big guns on the island, but, as at Tarawa, the Japanese defenders had preserved smaller artillery pieces in underground tunnels and caves. Then, too, the size of the Japanese garrison—more than thirty thousand men—was six times larger than at Tarawa. It was soon evident that seizing Saipan was going to be a tough slog—"much tougher than we appreciated," as Holland Smith acknowledged later. Ralph Smith's Army division was supposed to remain offshore as a floating reserve. Instead, fierce resistance led Holland Smith to order it ashore on the second day.[20]

Spruance focused his attention seaward. He had told Nimitz he did not think the Japanese would commit their fleet to the defense of Saipan, though he knew now that the enemy main fleet had sortied from Tawi Tawi. Then, on the fifteenth, even as the Marines landed, Spruance was handed another sighting report from another American submarine. The Japanese fleet had turned east, had passed through the Philippine Islands, and was in the Philippine Sea heading directly toward him. Spruance was still digesting that news when a different American sub reported that a *second* Japanese force, this one made up of battleships and cruisers, was approaching from the south. Two enemy fleets—a carrier force from the east, and a battleship force from the south—were converging on his position.

In Pearl Harbor, Nimitz also had access to those reports as well as to decrypted Japanese reports, and on June 16 he forwarded to Spruance an intercepted message that placed the Japanese carrier force only 350 miles west of Spruance's position. That was beyond the range of Mitscher's attack planes, which was about 200 miles. Yet because Japanese planes had less armor and therefore a greater range, it was just within striking distance of their planes. In theory, they could stand off at that distance and attack the Americans while remaining tantalizingly beyond reach—unless Mitscher steamed west to close the range. There was no news at all about that second

Japanese force to the south. In fact, though no one on the American side knew it, the southern force had joined up with the carriers and the entire collective armada was coming from the east.[21]

Spruance tried to put himself in the mind of his opponent. He mused aloud to his flag secretary, Captain Charles Barber: "If I were the Japanese admiral, I would split my forces to decoy the enemy main force away from Saipan and then strike at the transports with my other force." If that was, in fact, the Japanese plan, and if they pulled it off, it would leave the American landing force stranded on Saipan thousands of miles from any possible support or succor. Spruance did not know the Japanese planned to do this, but he saw that it was possible. He needed to know whether Turner's amphibs and transports could leave the area temporarily, so that Mitscher's carriers could go after the approaching enemy fleet. Rather than use the radio, he took a boat over to Turner's flagship to ask him face-to-face. "The Japs are coming after us," he said. Could the transports unload and depart before the Japanese arrived? Turner told him it was impossible—the landing was not going well and the situation ashore was precarious. He needed to stay. "Well," Spruance said, "I will try to keep the Japs off your neck."[22]

Here was another circumstance that called for the application of "calculated risk." In fact, as both Nimitz and Spruance understood, it was not so much a question of calculation as intuition, which was why Nimitz wanted his subordinates to have the intellectual subtlety to evaluate strategic and operational problems in their full context. Just how much risk was appropriate given the value of the objective and the balance of forces?[23]

The difficulty at Saipan was that Spruance and Mitscher had different answers to that question. To Spruance, the highest priority—indeed, the object of the entire mission—was the capture of Saipan, which required protecting the beachhead and Turner's amphibious fleet. If the invasion failed, it meant defeat, even if the approaching Japanese fleet was destroyed.

Mitscher made a different calculation. Like Spruance, he had received a copy of the decrypted message from Nimitz giving the location of the enemy carrier force, and he saw immediately that it offered a once-in-a-lifetime opportunity to fulfill the U.S. Navy's decades-long dream of a decisive naval engagement with the enemy fleet. It was inconceivable to him that Spruance would not let him seize this opportunity. He sent Spruance a message by short-range TBS radio, and framed it as what practitioners call an "UNODIR" (unless otherwise directed): unless Spruance stopped him, he would steam west toward the enemy carriers during the night and launch a preemptive strike at dawn.[24]

In receipt of Mitscher's message, Spruance conferred with his staff. If Task Force 58 continued west, that second enemy force coming up from the south might slip in behind him to attack Turner's transports. Turner did have other assets, including seven battleships and eleven small escort carriers. Was it enough? Perhaps Mitscher could split his forces and send three carrier groups to attack the Japanese fleet while the fourth remained behind to help Turner defend the beachhead. That, of course, would violate the Mahanian principle of fleet concentration that had been drummed into every officer since his midshipman days. Just how much "calculated risk" was justified here? After some discussion, Spruance decided that he needed to focus on his first responsibility, which was protection of the invasion force. He told Mitscher that he could continue westward, toward the approaching Japanese fleet, during the daylight hours, but he was to reverse course at dusk and steam back toward Saipan at night to ensure that no enemy force got past him in the dark.

Back in Pearl Harbor, Nimitz and others, including Towers, sought to follow events by monitoring the bits of radio traffic that would "skip" under varying conditions of temperature, humidity, and inversion and reach Hawaii. Once it became clear that Spruance had tethered Mitscher's carriers to the beachhead, Towers urged Nimitz to overrule him. Nimitz refused. Waldo Drake remembered him saying, "I've entrusted these fellows with the job of winning this campaign and I don't want them to think I'm butting in." Towers pressed him, but Nimitz cut him off: "I won't do that." For Towers, it was more proof that black shoes should not have command authority over carriers.[25]

A similar conversation was taking place on the bridge of Mitscher's flagship. Mitscher asked Spruance to reconsider his order. Spruance's response was as terse as Nimitz's: "We will proceed with my original orders." Several members of Mitscher's staff wanted him to argue. "No," Mitscher told them. "He's made up his mind, and we'll carry out his orders." He would keep his carriers within 180 miles of Saipan and wait for the Japanese to come to him.[26]

He didn't have long to wait.

J UNE 19, 1944, WAS A BEAUTIFUL DAY in the Philippine Sea; one American pilot said it was "as lovely a day as one could wish to see." Under a cloudless sky, Mitscher's fifteen carriers plus their screening cruisers and destroyers maneuvered 180 miles west of Saipan, dutifully staying within striking range of the invasion beaches. At 10:00 a.m., radar operators on several of the ships reported inbound aircraft coming from the west. As Mitscher suspected, the Japanese commander, Admiral Jisaburō Ozawa, had decided to keep his carriers beyond the reach of American airplanes and send his own bombers in a series of waves to attack the American fleet. The first wave consisted of 69 bombers and fighters, and to confront them, Mitscher launched 140 F6F Hellcat fighters. In addition to having the greater numbers, the American pilots were also better-trained and more experienced than their approaching foes. The losses Japan had suffered in two and a half years of war meant that the pilots now closing in on Task Force 58 were mostly novices. And finally, due largely to Nimitz, the Americans had developed more efficient fighter-director protocols that could vector the fighter pilots to the approaching enemy. Given all that, the outcome was entirely predictable.[1]

The air battle lasted all day. Ozawa launched wave after wave of bombers, escorted by fighters; American fighters met them fifty to seventy miles out. Few Japanese planes managed to fight their way through that intercept and get close enough to an American ship to drop a bomb. By the afternoon, U.S. pilots had shot down more than 350 enemy planes and destroyed a hundred more on the airfields of Guam. The Americans lost just thirty-three. The battle was so one-sided that although it was officially known as the Battle of the Philippine Sea, the pilots took to calling it "The Great Marianas Turkey Shoot."[2]

Yet Mitscher was frustrated. Spruance's order to remain near Saipan had compelled him to play defense all day and denied him the opportunity to find and sink the Japanese carriers. Those carriers did not get away unscathed. Even as Ozawa launched his bombers, the American submarine *Cavalla* got the Pearl Harbor veteran *Shokaku* in its sights and put three torpedoes into her. The big Japanese flattop had survived multiple bomb hits in both the Battle of the Coral Sea and the Battle of the Eastern Solomons, but her luck had run out. She went down bow first with 1,200 of her crew. Another American sub, the *Albacore*, put a torpedo into the brand-new and heavily armored *Taiho*. One torpedo would ordinarily not have been fatal. This one, however, ruptured her fuel tanks, and because of the volatile unrefined fuel the Japanese were compelled to use due to their oil shortage, fumes from those leaking tanks eventually ignited a number of secondary explosions, and the *Taiho*, too, went down. Even without an attack by Mitscher's airplanes, Ozawa lost two of his biggest and best carriers.[3]

By then, Spruance knew that the Japanese surface force coming up from the south had joined the main enemy fleet, and so on June 20, the day after the "Turkey Shoot," he gave Mitscher permission to go find it. Mitscher sent out search planes for that purpose, and late in the afternoon a pilot reported that he had found the enemy fleet, though it was at the absolute maximum range of American bombers. Mitscher launched anyway. Then he learned that the sighting report was in error, and that the target was fifty miles farther

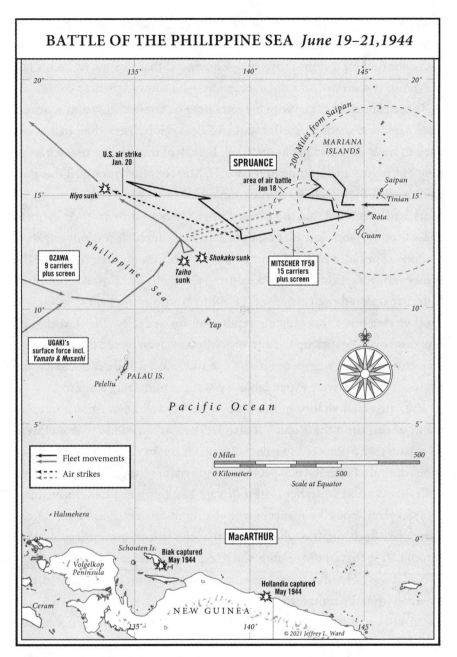

BATTLE OF THE PHILIPPINE SEA *June 19–21, 1944*

20°
135°   140°   145°
20°

200 Miles from Saipan

MARIANA
ISLANDS

U.S. air strike
Jan. 20

SPRUANCE

area of air battle
Jan 18

Saipan

Tinian 15°

15°   *Hiyo* sunk

Philippine

Rota

Guam

OZAWA
9 carriers
plus screen

Sea

Shokaku sunk

Taiho
sunk

MITSCHER TF58
15 carriers
plus screen

10°   10°

Yap

UGAKI's
surface force incl.
Yamato & Musashi

PALAU IS.
Peleliu

Pacific Ocean

5°   5°

Fleet movements

0 Miles   500

Air strikes

0 Kilometers   500

Scale at Equator

• Halmehera

MacARTHUR   0°

Schouten Is.   Biak captured
May 1944

Volgelkop
Peninsula

Hollandia captured
May 1944

Ceram   NEW GUINEA
135°   140°   145°
© 2021 Jeffrey L. Ward

Map 11: Battle of the Philippine Sea, June 19–21, 1944

away than initially reported. Here was another circumstance that required a consideration of "calculated risk." Mitscher was aware that his planes lacked sufficient fuel for a round trip, yet—convinced that this might be his last opportunity to destroy the enemy carriers—he allowed them to continue.[4]

Those planes caught up with the retreating Japanese at dusk and attacked. They sank one medium carrier and two fleet oilers. They then had to get back to their own carriers in the dark. Eighty of them never made it, running out of fuel and landing in the water. Mitscher had discussed this possibility with Jocko Clark, who commanded one of his task groups, and Clark had suggested that the carriers might have to turn on their lights to allow the survivors, low on gas, to find the task force. It was not unprecedented—Spruance had ordered the carriers to turn on their lights for the planes returning from a late strike during the Battle of Midway. Still, when Mitscher ordered the carriers of TF 58 to "turn on the lights," it became another element of his growing reputation for audacity. The next day, he sent destroyers to pick up the aircrews who had been forced down, the vast majority of whom were recovered. Given U.S. industrial productivity, the planes themselves were expendable—it was the pilots that mattered.[5]

The one-sided victory in the Philippine Sea solidified American command of the air in the Pacific. It also left behind a residue of resentment by aviators who objected to rules set by conservative (in their view) black shoe admirals. From the perspective of the aviators—a group that included both Towers and Mitscher—ship drivers like Spruance had no business giving orders about the management of aircraft carriers. Nimitz supported Spruance's decision, though he knew that the fallout from it was another complication that would require him to employ his diplomatic skill.[6]

And it was not the only controversy, or even the most consequential, that emerged from the campaign.

TWO DAYS AFTER MITSCHER'S PILOTS DESTROYED Japanese naval airpower in the Philippine Sea, Holland Smith ordered a general ground offensive on Saipan. He wanted his three divisions to advance northward in a line abreast across the width of the island; the Marines would hold both flanks and Ralph Smith's 27th Army Division would occupy the center. It was a

BATTLE FOR SAIPAN *June 15–July 9, 1944*

Marpi Point
Japanese mass suicides

Philippine Sea

▲ Mt. Marpi

Tanapag Reef

Maniagassa

Tanapag

Tanke Point

reef

Tanapag
Harbor

Muchot Point

Garapan

**2ND
USMC**

Line on June 24

reef

Mt. Tapotchau ▲

Pacific Ocean

Death Valley

Purple Heart Ridge

2ND USMC →

**27TH
USA**

**4TH
USMC**

Afetna Point

*Susupe
Swamp*

Laulau

Mt. Kagman ▲

4TH USMC →

2
xx
4

*Magicinne
Bay*

*Kagman
Peninsula*

**Charan
Kanoa**

**USMC Line on
D-Day June 15**

*Agingan
Point*

*ASLITO
AIRFIELD*

0 Miles   3

0 Kilometers   3

Cape Obyan

Naftan Point

© 2021 Jeffrey L. Ward

Map 12: Battle for Saipan, June 15–July 9, 1944

curious decision, for it required the 27th Division, which Holland Smith already believed was unreliable, to confront the most difficult terrain, and given that, what followed was perhaps all too foreseeable.

Though the assault was to begin at 8:00 a.m., the men of the 27th did not step off until nearly 9:00, and almost at once they ran into trouble. In one sector, nicknamed "Death Valley," a deep gully cut across their line of advance, which required them to scramble down a precipitous slope and then climb back up the other side while under fire. Other elements of the 27th were pinned down by heavy machine gun and artillery fire from higher ground on both flanks. Ralph Smith planned a flanking maneuver to pry the Japanese from their positions. The delay compelled the Marines on both flanks to halt and wait for them.[7]

Holland Smith was disgusted. His doubts about the 27th Division confirmed, he did not visit the scene of combat; instead he went to Kelly Turner and told him that Ralph Smith had to go. Turner agreed, and together they went to see Spruance on the *Indianapolis*. They all knew that for a Marine three-star general to dismiss an Army two-star general in the middle of a battle was sure to have repercussions well beyond Saipan. Nevertheless, after Spruance heard them out he "authorized and directed" that Ralph Smith be relieved of his command. Later, Spruance told Nimitz that, at the time, "no other action appeared adequate." Five days later, Spruance and Holland Smith finally visited several of the forward command posts, and Spruance reported to Nimitz that the men were "cheerful and optimistic" and that the "fighting [was] going much better now."[8]

Perhaps. Yet here was another brushfire that had been kindled by Nimitz's talented but willful operational commanders. And it got worse. Robert Richardson, who had never believed that soldiers should serve under a Marine general, was furious, and he flew to Saipan to look into it. He arrived there on July 12 after the island had been secured, and without consulting or even informing Holland Smith, he reviewed the men of the 27th Division, heaped praise on the soldiers, and awarded medals to the officers. Then he went to see Holland Smith and told him bluntly, "You had no right to relieve Ralph Smith." Nor did he stop there. He accused the V Corps commander of discriminating against the Army and, as Holland Smith remembered it, denigrated the Marines generally as "a bunch of beach runners." Aware of Holland Smith's volatile temperament, Spruance had pleaded with him "to suffer in silence" anything Richardson had to say, and in his subsequent memoir, Holland Smith congratulated himself for his "admirable restraint." After seeing Holland Smith, Richardson went to talk to Kelly Turner on his flagship. Turner was at least as volatile as Richardson, and the two men engaged in a shouting match. Nimitz had worked hard to nurture a cooperative command environment in the Fifth Fleet and the V Amphibious Corps, separately lobbying all the participants, including Holland Smith and Richardson—even Vandegrift—to urge patience and restraint in the interest of unified command. Apparently that had been in vain.[9]

When Richardson returned to Hawaii, Nimitz invited him to headquarters, where he listened patiently as the Army commander ardently defended Ralph Smith, pointing out that Holland Smith had never bothered to inspect the ground in front of the 27th Division and had underestimated the difficulties. Nimitz, however, was less interested in litigating blame than in minimizing the impact. While it surely would have been better had Holland Smith found a less draconian solution to the tactical problem, he hadn't, so it was now necessary to do damage control. Nimitz felt compelled to support Holland Smith officially, though as his assistant chief of staff recalled, "Admiral Nimitz . . . was not too happy with Smith's decision." Another staff member recalled that the whole dispute caused Nimitz "much distress."[10]

Spruance and Turner did not make things any easier. Both men sent Nimitz official complaints about Richardson's high-handedness during his visit to Saipan. Richardson responded with a peevish report of his own accusing Turner of "gross discourtesy," which was pretty much Turner's default temperament. Richardson also convened a board of enquiry in Pearl Harbor that came to be known as the Buckner Board after its presiding officer, Lieutenant General Simon Bolivar Buckner. That board reviewed documents and heard witnesses, and concluded that although Holland Smith had the authority to relieve Ralph Smith, his decision to do so was "not justified by the facts." Holland Smith was dismissive, if not scornful, of the report. It was an *Army* board, after all, and therefore had no authority over him. The real scandal, he insisted, was not his decision to relieve Ralph Smith; it was the fuss that Richardson and the Army were making about it.[11]

All this was enough to challenge even Nimitz's legendary patience, though he set out at once to minimize the fallout. He forwarded all the reports and protests to King, doing so unofficially in a private letter in the hope that they would not trigger a wider dispute. In his cover letter, he told King he would seek to effect a local settlement to keep it from becoming an issue for the Joint Chiefs, where it might provoke a discussion about the practicality of unified command. To assuage Richardson, Nimitz promised him that Army soldiers would never again have to serve under Holland Smith, and to ensure that, he and King secured Holland Smith a new job as Commanding Officer, Fleet Marine Force. It was a step up for Smith, but it was also strictly a Marine Corps command.[12]

Later, when it was time for Nimitz to submit fitness reports on his senior operational commanders, he took special care with Holland Smith's. He did not criticize the decision Smith had made—even now, he was reluctant to second-guess a commander on the scene. He did, however, express his disappointment that Smith had not managed to find a less confrontational alternative to relieving Ralph Smith since doing so was likely to make future joint operations more difficult. Aware that Holland Smith would be wounded by the criticism, Nimitz asked Bernard Austin to show it to him first before it was submitted. Austin hand-carried it to Holland Smith and stood by while the Marine general read it quietly to himself. Soon, Austin saw tears running down Smith's weathered cheeks. When Smith handed it back to Austin, he said, "It wouldn't hurt from anybody but Admiral Nimitz."[13]

As for Ralph Smith, he received orders to Pearl Harbor to assume command of the 98th Army Division, charged with defense of the Hawaiian Islands. When he arrived, Nimitz invited him to Muliwai as his guest at a party that included the actor Laurence Olivier. In doing so, he sought to signal an end to the inter-service feud.* In Washington, King did his best to ensure that the dispute did not drive a wedge between members of the JCS.[14]

---

* The fallout from the controversy made it awkward for Ralph Smith to stay in the Pacific Theater, and he was subsequently sent back to the States, where he trained troops in Arkansas. After the war, he served as U.S. military attaché in Paris.

Nimitz was only partially successful in keeping a lid on the controversy. Almost immediately it became fodder for the press, and for the Hearst papers in particular. William Randolph Hearst, who owned twenty-eight newspapers across the country, was a political foe of President Roosevelt and a champion of Douglas MacArthur. His papers took the Army's side, characterizing the Marines as so rash that their tactics led to "a reckless and needless waste of American lives." Hearst's flagship paper, the *San Francisco Examiner*, asserted that the scandal on Saipan proved that "supreme command in the Pacific" should be given to Douglas MacArthur. Robert Sherrod of *Time* magazine took the other side and claimed that the soldiers of the 27th Division were "hopelessly bogged down," "lacked confidence in their officers," and "froze in their foxholes," too terrified to engage the enemy. That was too much for Nimitz, who endorsed Richardson's request that Sherrod's press credentials be revoked. Unwilling to fuel the conflict, George Marshall quietly tabled the request.[15]

As at Midway, almost exactly two years earlier, American forces had won signal victories in the Philippine Sea and on Saipan. And as at Midway, controversies emerged afterward that threatened to tarnish those victories. The resentment of many of the aviators toward a black shoe commander was unfortunate, as was the bitterness of what came to be called the Smith vs. Smith Controversy. That the disputes did not rise to the level of catastrophe was due in no small part to Nimitz's crisis management.

THE CONQUEST OF THE MARIANAS was the capstone of the Central Pacific Drive. According to the protocol that Nimitz and King had worked out in San Francisco, Spruance would now return to Hawaii, and Halsey would take charge of the fleet to conduct the next steps. In fact, Halsey had already moved to Pearl Harbor, arriving on June 17, the day before the "Turkey Shoot" in the Marianas. He brought with him a large staff, so large, in fact, that Nimitz ordered him to pare it down. Those who remained moved into offices in the Cement Pot on Makalapa Hill.

The JCS had already mandated the next steps: the conquest of the Palau Group in September, followed by a move to Mindanao in November. After that, however, plans were unsettled. MacArthur wanted to use Mindanao as

When Nimitz and King visited Saipan in July 1944, Spruance gave them a tour of the island in a jeep. They wanted to drive to the top of Mount Tapochau, but since the area was not yet secured, the island commander talked them out of it. (U.S. Naval Institute)

a base to conquer the rest of the Philippines, especially Luzon, the biggest of the Philippine Islands and the home of the Philippine capital, Manila. King wanted to leap past Luzon to the island of Formosa, in what he had dubbed Operation Causeway.

To advance that option, King arrived in Hawaii on July 13. As it happened, Bob Hope arrived the same day for the first of his subsequently famous USO shows. A sea of soldiers, sailors, and yard workers turned out to watch it, filling up what was dubbed the Nimitz Bowl. Hope cracked jokes with Jerry Colonna, though the star of the show for the men in attendance was tap dancer Patricia Thomas. The next day, King and Nimitz flew from Hawaii to Kwajalein and then on to Saipan.

During those long flights, King impressed upon Nimitz the importance of resisting MacArthur's obsession with the Philippines. Securing a base on

Mindanao was fine, he said, but after that it was essential not to get bogged down trying to capture the other Philippine islands one by one. The seizure of Formosa would accomplish the same strategic objective faster and with fewer casualties. He ordered Nimitz to work up plans for the occupation of northern Formosa along with a list of forces needed and a timetable.[16]

Spruance met them at the airfield in Saipan, and the first thing King did was offer him congratulations for the "damn fine job" he did in the Philippine Sea. "No matter what other people tell you," King said, "your decision was correct." The three admirals climbed into a jeep for a tour of the island, then met aboard the *Indianapolis* to discuss future strategic options. There, Spruance muddied the waters further by declaring that he did not like the idea of going to Formosa and suggested attacking Iwo Jima and Okinawa instead. Nimitz and King returned to Hawaii on July 20 to engage in more conversations with Towers and with Halsey's chief of staff, Mick Carney. Like Spruance, they were also skeptical of the Formosa option, which King found aggravating and disappointing.[17]

On the twenty-fourth, Nimitz saw King off for his flight back to Washington, and that afternoon he met with his planning group to discuss an invasion of Formosa. The scarcity of service troops and supply ships to sustain the invaders made the logistics of such a move especially precarious. In addition, Forrest Sherman insisted that it would be "ridiculous" to invade Formosa while the Japanese held Luzon. Buckner, who was slated to command the invasion, submitted a written memo stating that he lacked a sufficient force to do it. Based on their input, Nimitz radioed King a long message that same afternoon outlining the additional resources needed. Among them were 208,000 more soldiers, who would have to be carried "in repeated movements of assault shipping" (ten attack transports and twenty-five cargo ships) departing the West Coast every month. He did not say it couldn't be done, but the subtext was obvious: it would not be easy.[18]

TWO DAYS LATER, ON JULY 26, the heavy cruiser *Baltimore* arrived in Pearl Harbor with President Roosevelt on board. Though his trip was supposed to be a closely guarded secret, word had leaked out, and the rails of the warships in the harbor were lined with sailors in whites to cheer the commander in chief. Nimitz, Ghormley, Richardson, and the territorial governor, Ingram M. Stainback, all went out in the pilot tug to greet him even before the *Baltimore* docked directly behind the veteran carrier *Enterprise*.[19]

Ostensibly, the purpose of the president's visit was to discuss Pacific war strategy with his two theater commanders. He had come in person because he knew the political value of being seen with—and photographed with—his successful Pacific commanders (he had been nominated for a fourth term as president just that week). And he had come by sea instead of by plane because he enjoyed long sea voyages and getting away from Washington.

MacArthur initially refused to come. To him, the fact that King, Marshall, and Arnold were not part of the president's entourage suggested that this was a political junket and not a strategic visit. He had no intention of providing a visual backdrop for a Roosevelt campaign poster. But while he could refuse invitations from Nimitz, and even from the Joint Chiefs, he could not refuse the president. Leahy reworded his invitation as an order, and MacArthur grudgingly obeyed. He made a show of it, arriving late in the backseat of an open car that was preceded by police motorcycles with sirens blaring. On the dock, he climbed out of the car and strode purposefully up the brow toward the *Baltimore* wearing a leather flight jacket (in spite of the heat) and his battered field marshal's hat from his time as head of the Filipino Army. Halfway up the ramp, he stopped, turned to the crowd, estimated to number twenty thousand, lifted his cap, and waved. The crowd responded with a rapturous cheer. A witness on the *Baltimore* remembered thinking that "the entire affair was a play and this man [was] an actor taking to the stage to play his part."[20]

The obligatory photo session on the deck of the *Baltimore* lasted some time, with a grinning Roosevelt sitting between his two grim-faced theater commanders. Nimitz was shocked to see how much the president had aged since the luncheon at the White House four months earlier. He had lost weight and his skin was an unhealthy gray. Though FDR was only three years senior to Nimitz, he looked old enough to be his father. After the photo session, the president's aides informed everyone that they would reassemble the next morning for an automobile tour of the island.

Roosevelt and his chief of staff, Admiral William D. Leahy (at right), discuss strategic options with Nimitz and MacArthur in the home of Hawaiian businessman Chris R. Holmes on July 28, 1944. (U.S. Naval Institute)

During that tour, Secret Service agents stood on the running boards of an open car with Admiral Leahy in front beside the driver and FDR, MacArthur, and Nimitz all seated side by side in the back. It was pretty crowded. Nimitz had to sit sideways and lean forward, almost kneeling on the floorboards, so that the three of them fit. The motorcade rolled past naval installations, airfields, and Army camps. At each stop, the president offered a few remarks from the backseat. That night they all had dinner together at the Waikiki Beach home of Hawaiian businessman Chris R. Holmes, where the president was staying. Roosevelt foreshadowed the upcoming discussions by gesturing toward Mindanao on the map and asking MacArthur, "Douglas, where do we go from here?" That was indeed the question.[21]

The next morning, they reconvened in Holmes's living room, where a giant map of the Pacific was propped up on two dining room chairs. Thanks to King's recent visit, Nimitz knew what was expected of him, and he dutifully told the president that after Mindanao, the most efficient next move was to seize Formosa, which would cut the Japanese off from their southern resource base as effectively as capturing Luzon, and could be done faster and more cheaply. Luzon, including Manila, could be bypassed and cut off just as Rabaul and Truk had been.[22]

When MacArthur took the stage, his presentation was less about strategy than about the nation's moral obligations. It was, he said, essential to rescue the Filipino people ("Christian people," he emphasized) from Japanese occupation, and a failure to do so would mean that Asian peoples would never trust the United States again. He reminded the president that the seven thousand American POWs in the Philippines would never forget or forgive being bypassed.[23†]

Leahy was a witness, and he marveled at the way the president "tactfully steered the discussion" so that it "remained on a friendly basis the entire time." Indeed, Leahy found the meetings "much more peaceful than I had expected." Even MacArthur agreed that the president had been "entirely neutral in handling the discussion." In the end, Roosevelt did not announce a decision, saying that a final decision would be up to the Joint Chiefs, though since Leahy was in the room, the arguments each man had presented would be well represented in the JCS deliberations. The long day ended with an outdoor concert under the stars, followed by the obligatory hula dancer.[24]

A buoyant MacArthur, satisfied that he had carried the day, left soon afterward for Hickam Field and a flight back to Brisbane. He had spent not quite forty-eight hours in Hawaii. The president stayed on, and it fell to Nimitz to see that he was engaged and entertained. By now, acting as host to VIPs had become a virtual second job, but FDR was especially high-maintenance. The first activity the next morning was another automobile tour. As they prepared to set off, the president called Lamar over and told him to be sure to have "a nice cold martini" waiting for him when they came back

---

† At the beginning of 1944, there were 11,200 Allied POWs in the Philippines, most of them Americans. Over the next several months, however, the Japanese began shipping them off to Japan, Korea, and elsewhere to do forced labor. By July there were probably fewer than 3,000 American POWs still there.

for lunch. That was the first anyone on Nimitz's staff knew that the president planned to have lunch at Nimitz's quarters. Lamar rushed to make arrangements. Within minutes, members of the Secret Service arrived, and the Seabees began building a new road to the back door, a job that required moving several palm trees. They also added a ramp and widened the doorway to accommodate the president's wheelchair, and they raised the toilet in the bathroom by five and a half inches.[25]

Meanwhile, Nimitz and the president headed over the Koʻolau Range to the north shore of the island, where they observed a training exercise, then drove back over the mountains to Hickam Field, where they met wounded soldiers returning from the fighting on Guam. They also toured the enormous Aiea Hospital, where the president stopped to talk one-on-one with a number of soldiers.[26]

Back at Nimitz's quarters, the number of luncheon guests had ballooned to more than forty, nearly all of them flag and general officers, including Ghormley, Richardson, and Towers. Lamar entertained himself by counting up the total number of stars glittering on the lapels and shoulders of the guests and came up with 136. The president, who was handed his chilled martini upon arrival (eventually he had three of them), seemed to enjoy himself, calling Nimitz "Chester" all afternoon. Nimitz presented him with a gift from the chief of an atoll in the Marshalls. It was a belt inscribed: "What you have taken by force you must be prepared to hold by force."[27]

After the president left, Nimitz ordered all the palm trees put back in place.

———

HALSEY MISSED HAVING LUNCH WITH THE PRESIDENT because he had flown back to the States to attend to his wife, Frances, whom he called "Fan." She had long suffered from health problems and now, after a swift decline, had been diagnosed with advanced dementia. Halsey spent two weeks with her in Delaware, getting her settled in a care facility before flying back to Hawaii. Upon his return, he boarded the battleship New Jersey and broke his flag as commander of what was now officially the Third Fleet.[28]

Many of the subordinate commanders in that fleet also swapped jobs: Vice Admiral Theodore Wilkinson took over the Amphibious

Force from Kelly Turner, and, largely because of pressure from King, John S. McCain stood by to replace Pete Mitscher in command of the carriers—though not yet. McCain was both a "Johnny-come-lately" and coming off a stint of shore duty as King's deputy. Since McCain had not been to sea for more than a year, Halsey thought he should spend some months serving under Mitscher as one of his task group commanders before ascending to the top job. McCain was senior to Mitscher and considered such orders something of a slight. He was bothered enough to protest to Nimitz. Nimitz heard him out, then told him that he should prove the doubters wrong by doing a great job commanding the task group.[29]

Given Japan's recent catastrophic defeats, Halsey's fleet was virtually unchallenged, able to roam the Pacific at will and keep the sea for months at a time thanks to a supply train that now included thirty-four fleet oilers. Mitscher's Task Force 38 was virtually omnipotent. As Mitscher himself put it, "I can go anywhere and nobody can stop me." Here was the apotheosis of the small and battered force that Nimitz had inherited three years before.[30]

Nimitz had always admired Halsey's aggressive instinct even as he recognized that (as his nickname suggested) he could also be the proverbial bull in a china shop. More than once, Nimitz had to ask him to tone down his public comments, in particular his assertion that he would ride the emperor's white horse through the streets of Tokyo. On the other hand, Halsey was just the man to pursue the final destruction of Japanese naval forces. Commander Eller, Nimitz's staff writer, believed that Nimitz preferred using Spruance "for all the major amphibious assaults," and that he turned to Halsey "for the cavalry charges." Nimitz's son, Chet, put it more succinctly: "Where it was blow 'em up and shoot 'em up, that was Halsey." Halsey's new job was not quite a cavalry charge, but there would certainly be opportunities to blow things up.[31]

Meanwhile, Nimitz told Spruance to "go back to California to see your family" and return in "a couple of weeks" to get ready for the next operation, which apparently was going to be Formosa. Spruance's response was blunt: "I don't like Formosa." When Nimitz asked him why, he repeated his preference for Iwo Jima and Okinawa. "Well," Nimitz said, "it's going to be Formosa." It certainly looked that way at the time. Once again, however, events seized control of the timetable from the policymakers.[32]

In early September, three separate American forces put to sea: an invasion force commanded by Wilkinson carried the men of the 1st Marine Division from Guadalcanal to Peleliu, in the Palau Group, for Operation Stalemate; a second invasion force with MacArthur himself on board headed for the island of Morotai, five hundred miles farther south; and, to cover both operations, Halsey and the Third Fleet, including Task Force 38, targeted Japanese bases throughout the western Pacific. During the ensuing week, planes from Mitscher's carriers had plenty of opportunity to "blow 'em up and shoot 'em up" at Iwo Jima, Yap, Peleliu, and Mindanao. On three days in mid-September, those planes conducted 2,400 sorties against Japanese bases in the central Philippines.[33]

What was striking—indeed almost shocking—was that few Japanese planes rose up to contest the American attacks. It was, Halsey wrote to Nimitz, "unbelievable and fantastic." A Japanese pilot who was pulled from the water and made prisoner said they had virtually no airplanes left. The Japanese, Halsey wrote, "were operating on a shoestring" and were "completely neutralized." He proposed that the planned invasions of Yap, Morotai, Peleliu, and Mindanao should all be cancelled and that they should jump straight to the island of Leyte, where, according to local natives, the Japanese had no forces at all. And he proposed that the invasion schedule could be moved up by two months, from December to October.[34]

Nimitz received that message on September 12 (Hawaii time). It was one of a string of off-the-cuff suggestions Halsey had sent him about changing the operational timetable or revising war strategy. To previous such messages, Nimitz had replied by advising Halsey to stick to the task at hand. This time, however, he forwarded the suggestion to King, adding his own view that if MacArthur concurred, an "early movement into Leyte" was feasible. As it happened, the Joint Chiefs were meeting with their British counterparts in Quebec that week, and they approved the idea at once, pending approval from MacArthur. MacArthur was with the invasion force headed for Morotai and maintaining radio silence, so Sutherland answered in his name: "I am prepared to move [to Leyte] immediately."[35]

ONE UNRESOLVED ISSUE WAS THE SCHEDULED invasion of Peleliu. Halsey urged its cancellation, but Nimitz had promised MacArthur he would "provide strategic cover and support" for the move to Morotai, which was already underway. That included suppressing Japanese planes on Peleliu. In addition, by the time the new timetable was approved, D-Day on Peleliu was only hours away. The Underwater Demolition Teams (UDTs), known as "frogmen," were already ashore on Peleliu preparing the landing beaches. Cancelling the invasion now was likely to cause widespread confusion, if not chaos. Nimitz told King that it was not feasible to reorient the forces "as rapidly as Halsey appears to visualize." He radioed Halsey that he should "carry out the first phase of STALEMATE as planned."[36]

It was his biggest mistake of the war.

The strategic objective on Peleliu was the airfield. The Marines seized it on D-Day plus two, though by then it was, in the words of historian Ian Toll, "a burned-out scrapyard." After that, the Battle for Peleliu became a nightmare. When the Marines advanced inland, they discovered that ten thousand Japanese defenders had burrowed deep into hundreds of caves and tunnels. Instead of launching suicidal *banzai* charges, they remained in those caves and defied the Marines to come and get them. The Marines did, but at an enormous cost. This time the hell-for-leather tactics the Marines preferred were unsuitable to the circumstances. After the men of the 1st Marine Division suffered nearly 7,000 casualties in two weeks, the Army's 81st Division relieved them and initiated a more deliberate approach. In the end, it took six weeks to clear the island, with the Japanese again fighting to the last man: 10,000 enemy soldiers were killed and only 200 were taken prisoner. The Americans suffered too, with 8,000 total casualties, including more than 1,500 killed. Those losses were especially tragic in light of the fact that due to the changes in the strategic timetable, the island did not need to be taken at all.[37]

If Nimitz regretted his decision to go ahead with Stalemate, he left no record of it. His grandfather's advice not to obsess over things he could not control made it possible for him to compartmentalize the various aspects of his command responsibilities. That included the need to make life-and-death decisions.

Peleliu was the one island conquest that Nimitz did not immediately visit afterward. Instead, two weeks later, he flew to San Francisco for another conference with King, bringing Buckner along with him. Spruance, who was on leave in Monterey, drove up to join the discussion. They found King still strongly in favor of invading Formosa, convinced that "the only prospect of keeping the Japanese Manchurian army occupied was by the use of Chinese troops."[38]

Nimitz summarized the work his staff had produced. Their report revised the number of soldiers needed to invade Formosa from 200,000 to 500,000, plus an additional 160,000 Marines, and a commensurate increase in sealift capability. Buckner—bravely—told King that he did not think the operation would be successful. Even if it was, he said, friendly casualties could run as high as 150,000. At one point, a frustrated King turned to Spruance, who had so far remained silent. "Haven't you something to say?" King asked. "I understand that Okinawa was your baby." Spruance replied that he supported everything Nimitz had said. King was not accustomed to losing arguments, but he could see that he was going to lose this one. Formosa was out; Luzon was in.[39]

First, however, it was necessary to capture Leyte.

I N THE FALL OF 1944, as the forces under Nimitz and MacArthur converged on the Philippines, their parallel commands began to overlap geographically even as they remained organizationally and administratively separate. Halsey's Third Fleet and Kinkaid's Seventh Fleet were both tasked to support the invasion of Leyte, yet they did not have a common commander. Marc Mitscher, commanding Task Force 38, reported to Halsey, who reported to Nimitz, who reported to King; Thomas L. Sprague, who commanded the escort carriers with the invasion force, reported to Kinkaid, who reported to MacArthur, who reported to George Marshall. Thus there was no authority closer than the Joint Chiefs in Washington who had command responsibility over both fleets. Halsey and Kinkaid were expected to "cooperate." As events would prove, however, cooperation, even with the best of intentions, was a slender reed.[1]

Another inherent difficulty was that in order to keep Kinkaid firmly under his control, MacArthur ordered him not to communicate independently with Nimitz. Worse, he mandated that all radio messages between Kinkaid and Halsey must first be sent to the communications center on Manus Island. From there, the messages would be retransmitted on what was known as the Fox Schedule, which was copied by every ship in both fleets. Once received, the various commands had to scan all the messages to see which of them were pertinent to them, and because virtually all messages were graded "urgent," it was difficult to identify those that genuinely were. All that added at least an hour, sometimes two, to the transmission time and made cooperation awkward at best. It was a circumstance fraught with peril.[2]

THE PHILIPPINE ARCHIPELAGO contains seven thousand islands. The largest (and northernmost) of them is Luzon, home of the capital city, Manila, which in 1944 had a population of over half a million. The second-largest (and southernmost) is Mindanao, which MacArthur had initially selected as the site for his long-awaited return. In between are hundreds of other islands, large and small, including Leyte, just north of Mindanao. Its more central location, the assertion by local resistance fighters that it was only lightly defended, and the large open body of water off its eastern shore (Leyte Gulf) made it an attractive choice for an invasion.

The initial American landings there on October 20, 1944, triggered the largest naval battle in history, one that sprawled across four hundred thousand square miles from the northern tip of Luzon to the South China Sea. It was also utterly decisive. Like Midway and the Marianas Turkey Shoot, the Battle of Leyte Gulf (October 23–25, 1944) was an overwhelming American victory, and, like those earlier battles, it also generated a bitter controversy afterward.[3]

A critical component in that controversy was the aggressive personality of Bill Halsey. As noted, Nimitz's two principal subordinates were a study in contrasts. Spruance was a detail man whose staff generated precise and unmistakable orders; Halsey was a seat-of-the-pants commander whom Nimitz occasionally had to reproach for administrative sloppiness. As the historian John Lundstrom put it, Halsey was fire and Spruance was ice. In spite of that, or perhaps because of it, the two men had been friends for decades, and back in 1942, when Halsey had been too ill to command his task force in the Battle of Midway, his recommendation of Spruance as his replacement was so fulsome that Nimitz had agreed to it at once. Nonetheless, Halsey believed that Spruance had missed the opportunity of a lifetime by being overly cautious in the Philippine Sea.[4]

Halsey had followed the sequence of events off Saipan from the radio reports, and, like Towers, he was disappointed that Spruance had not given Mitscher greater discretion to cut loose from the beachhead and go after Ozawa's carriers. His view was that aircraft carriers were offensive weapons—the slashing sword of naval power—not stationary platforms for the defense of static positions, however important.

As for Nimitz, while he applauded Spruance's performance in the Philippine Sea both in his official report and in person, he, too, wondered whether Mitscher might have accomplished more had he been unleashed sooner. When Nimitz and Halsey reviewed the orders for the campaign in the Philippines, Halsey prevailed upon him to include this key sentence: "In case opportunities for destruction of [a] major portion of the enemy fleet is offered or can be created, such destruction becomes the primary task."[5]

That command guidance was possible, even reasonable, since, unlike Spruance at Saipan, Halsey would not have primary responsibility for the protection of the beachhead in Leyte Gulf. That job fell to Kinkaid. Halsey's task was to fend off the Imperial Japanese Navy, and if he saw a chance to destroy it, he now had the authority to do so.

SOLDIERS OF WALTER KRUEGER'S SIXTH ARMY began landing on Leyte at 10:00 in the morning on October 20 with MacArthur watching from the bridge of the cruiser Nashville. All around him, spread out across the breadth of Leyte Gulf, were hundreds of ships of the invasion force: transports, cargo ships, LSTs, LCIs, and scores of others, many of them borrowed from Nimitz's command and most of them filled with men, equipment, supplies, and ammunition. Farther out were the gunfire support ships, some of them reconstituted survivors of the Pearl Harbor attack, plus several heavy cruisers, all under the command of Rear Admiral Jesse Oldendorf. Farther out still, over the horizon, was a covering force of sixteen small escort carriers (CVEs) arrayed in three groups and designated Taffy 1, 2, and 3, which was their radio call sign. These so-called jeep carriers, all under Rear Admiral Thomas L. Sprague, were small, slow, and all but unarmored. In addition to providing air cover for the invasion fleet, their function was anti-submarine patrol and ground support. Halsey's vastly more powerful Third Fleet carriers were several hundred miles to the north off Luzon.[6]

The landing was not heavily opposed, and that afternoon MacArthur fulfilled his long-standing pledge. He climbed down from the *Nashville* into a Navy landing craft and, after stopping at a transport to pick up Philippine president Sergio Osmeña, he headed for the beach. Due to the shallow beach gradient, the coxswain was unable to push the Higgins boat all the way up onto the sand, and when the bow ramp dropped, MacArthur was annoyed that he had to wade ashore through knee-deep water. He

A scowling Douglas MacArthur splashes ashore near Tacloban on Leyte on the afternoon of October 20, 1944, fulfilling a pledge he had made three years earlier. (U.S. Naval Institute)

suspected this was another Navy trick, and his glowering expression would have made a wary staff officer step back. When MacArthur saw the resulting photograph, however, he was delighted, for his grim expression depicted exactly the image he wanted to project. After splashing ashore, he shook hands with Osmeña, and then, taking up a microphone attached to a mobile transmitter, announced, "This is the voice of freedom, General MacArthur speaking. People of the Philippines, I have returned."[7]

NIMITZ FOLLOWED THESE EVENTS AS BEST he could from Pearl Harbor, though doing so was again problematic. In addition to the six-hour time difference between Hawaii and the Philippines, Leyte was on the other side of the International Date Line. When Krueger's men landed on Leyte at 10:00 a.m. on October 20, it was 2:00 in the afternoon of the previous day (the nineteenth) in Hawaii, and due to the delays in communications, Nimitz learned about it only around 4:00 p.m. Such circumstances made it difficult to track events in real time.*

All that day, as Nimitz worked in his office in the Cement Pot, he periodically headed down to the bombproof operations room one level below, where a large map of the Philippines had been laid out on a table. Staff officers placed markers to indicate where the various elements of American forces were located and—so far as they knew—Japanese forces, too. The news was spotty. The Japanese operated under radio silence, of course, and even the messages they did send defied the efforts of the codebreakers. Many American radio messages were lost as well, since most units used the short-range TBS system, which could be used over distances of only about sixty to a hundred miles, depending on atmospheric conditions. Still, enough messages—or parts of messages—reached Hawaii to allow Nimitz to follow the general outline of the campaign.

---

* It often creates difficulty for modern students of the battle, too. Messages in the Graybook are dated using Greenwich Mean Time (GMT), sometimes called Greenwich Civil Time (GCT). Because of the different times (and even dates) in Greenwich, Manila, and Honolulu, the date/time signatures on the messages do not accurately reflect the local time when the message was sent—or received.

On October 21, he learned from submarine reports that a Japanese surface force comprising at least three battleships and ten cruisers (though no carriers) had sortied from Lingga Roads, eleven hundred miles south of Leyte Gulf, and was headed north. Subsequent reports indicated that this force, which was commanded by Admiral Takeo Kurita, was likely to pass through the Philippines via the Sibuyan Sea, exit via San Bernardino Strait between Luzon and Samar, and attack the American invasion force from the north (see Map 13). The American submarines did more than report. That same afternoon, Nimitz learned that two of them, *Darter* and *Dace*, had drawn first blood by sinking two enemy cruisers and crippling a third before Kurita's force even got to the Sibuyan Sea.[8]

The next day, Nimitz received a message from Halsey outlining his "Battle Plan" to deal with the approaching enemy. It detailed the creation of a new task force, which Halsey dubbed Task Force 34, consisting of six fast battleships, each of them armed with nine 16-inch guns, plus several cruisers and destroyers, all under Vice Admiral Willis Lee. It was large enough to be a match for Kurita's command, including his two super-battleships, *Yamato* and *Musashi*. Halsey instructed Lee to "engage decisively at long range." As usual, Nimitz did not comment on the plan; this was Halsey's battle and he seemed to have a handle on it.[9]

That night, sometime after 8:00 (Hawaii time), Nimitz saw a message that Kinkaid had sent to Halsey, reporting that the battleships and cruisers under Oldendorf were "engaging enemy surface forces in Surigao Strait," south of Leyte Gulf. Apparently, the Japanese were attempting a pincer movement, with their surface forces converging on Leyte Gulf from both north and south. Minutes later, there was more news, this time from Halsey. Planes from Mitscher's carriers had attacked the Japanese battleship force in the Sibuyan Sea and inflicted severe damage. Indeed, the surviving Japanese ships, reeling from the relentless air strikes, had turned around and were retreating westward.[10]

Nimitz also learned that the American light carrier *Princeton* was "heavily damaged and dead in the water," the result of a well-placed bomb from a Japanese plane from Luzon. The cruiser *Birmingham* had gone alongside to

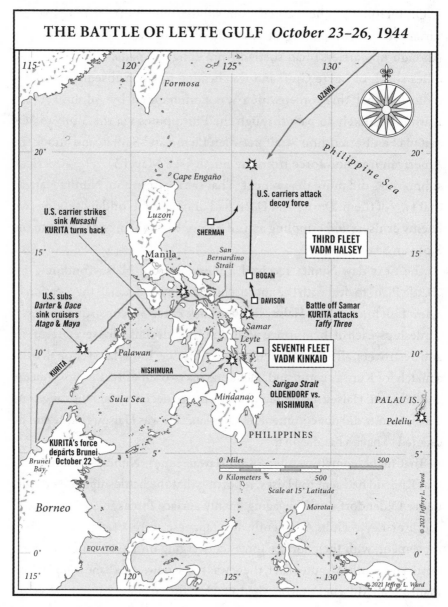

Map 13: Battle of Leyte Gulf, October 23–26, 1944

assist the wounded carrier in fighting the fires, and then both ships had been severely damaged when the *Princeton*'s bomb magazine had exploded. The carrier had to be scuttled; the *Birmingham* limped off out of the battle, eventually making her way to the West Coast for extensive repairs.[11]

Twenty minutes later, the tactical picture became more complicated when Halsey reported that there was a *third* enemy naval force, this one including carriers, approaching from Japan's home waters. In a message addressed to both Kinkaid and Nimitz, Halsey announced that since the Japanese battleship force was in full retreat, he was "proceeding north with three groups to attack enemy carrier force at dawn." Here, perhaps, was the long-awaited opportunity to destroy the Japanese carrier force altogether.[12]

Both Kinkaid, who was five hundred miles to the south, and Nimitz, who was five thousand miles to the east, assumed from Halsey's message that he was taking three carrier groups north, and that the task force of battleships he had established earlier (Task Force 34) remained behind to guard San Bernardino Strait, which was the only passage from the Sibuyan Sea to Leyte Gulf. What neither Kinkaid nor Nimitz knew was that only minutes after Halsey had sent that earlier message creating TF 34, he had sent a second message announcing that the task force would not be formed until he issued an "execute" order. Because that second message had gone out by TBS radio, neither Kinkaid nor Nimitz had received it. And now, though neither Kinkaid nor Nimitz was aware of it, Halsey headed north with all sixty-five ships of the Third Fleet, including three carrier groups and all the ships of the nascent Task Force 34.[13]

THE NEXT MORNING, WHICH WAS OCTOBER 23 in Hawaii, Nimitz got a pleasant surprise. His son, Chet, now a lieutenant commander, arrived in Pearl Harbor for a one-day stopover en route to the West Coast. He had just completed a successful cruise as skipper of the submarine *Haddo*, during which he had sunk 17,756 tons of Japanese shipping, a feat for which the *Haddo* received a Navy Unit Commendation, and Chet himself was subsequently awarded the Navy Cross. He was now on his way back to Kittery, Maine, to take command of a new-construction submarine, the *Sarda* (though as it turned out, the war ended before the *Sarda* was commissioned).

The relationship between Nimitz and his son was more companionable than emotionally demonstrative. Nimitz was "tremendously proud" of his son, as he wrote to Catherine, and Chet subscribed his letters "Your admiring and loving son," but as Chet himself acknowledged later, theirs was not "a close personal father and son relationship." Nevertheless, it was a happy reunion, and before Chet left they even had an opportunity to play a round of golf with Sandy Walker and Doc Anderson. At dinner that night, Chet noted a palpable tension in the room. As he recalled it later: "I noticed Admiral McMorris, Admiral Spruance, and my father and the doctor... were all nervous as cats at supper." As a mere lieutenant commander, he would ordinarily have remained silent in such company, but eventually he felt compelled to ask, "What's everybody agitated about?"[14]

McMorris explained that they were uncertain about the disposition of Task Force 34—whether it was guarding San Bernardino Strait or had gone north with Halsey's carriers. Chet remembered thinking how strange it was that his father would not know that. He believed that such a circumstance could not happen in the submarine service. No sub skipper would

Rear Admiral Clifton "Ziggy" Sprague commanded one of the three escort carrier groups off Leyte Gulf on October 25, 1944. Though this photo is from April 1945, it captures the alarm he must have felt on learning that his nearly defenseless jeep carriers were under attack by Japanese battleships. (National Archives)

act without keeping his boss informed. Listening to the speculation about Task Force 34, he remembered thinking, "Well, Jesus Christ! Don't we have a radio? Why don't we ask them?"[15]

As always, Nimitz was reluctant to interfere in the management of a battle. As Chet put it later, his father didn't want Halsey's team "to think people were looking over their shoulder." In his office the next day (October 24 in Hawaii), Nimitz sought to track what was happening, though the message traffic was frustratingly light. Several times, he asked Bernard Austin to review the radio messages to see if any of them offered a clue about the whereabouts of Lee's battleships. He would not interfere unless it was an emergency.[16]

And then—suddenly—it was. At about 2:00, Forrest Sherman came in to tell Nimitz that they had just received a flash message from Rear Admiral Clifton "Ziggy" Sprague, commanding one of the three Taffy groups off Leyte Gulf.[†] Technically, Sprague was not in Nimitz's chain of command. The content of the message, however, was such that a breach of protocol could be forgiven, for Sprague reported that he was under attack by enemy battleships that were only fifteen miles away and closing! It was, of course, Kurita's surface force, reduced by the losses to *Darter* and *Dace* as well as to Mitscher's planes in the Sibuyan Sea, but still powerful with four battleships, including the massive *Yamato*, plus six heavy and two light cruisers.

At once, everyone in Nimitz's office rushed down to the operations room. Nimitz and the others bent over the table map to locate the various elements of the far-flung battle. The closest American support for Sprague's threatened escorts was Oldendorf's battleship force in Surigao Strait, but those ships were still involved in mopping-up operations there, and in any case they had already fired off most of their armor-piercing ammunition and had only high-explosive shells left, unsuitable for engaging warships. The Third Fleet carriers were several hundred miles to the north, closing in on a Japanese carrier force. And it was now obvious that Task Force 34 had gone with them, for there was no other explanation for the unchallenged arrival of Japanese battleships off Leyte Gulf.[17]

---

† Clifton "Ziggy" Sprague, who commanded the six CVEs of Taffy 3, was no relation to his boss, Thomas L. Sprague, who commanded all three Taffy groups.

That was confirmed only minutes later when Pearl Harbor intercepted a message from Kinkaid to Halsey: "Enemy battleships . . . evidently came through San Bernardino during the night." Layton recalled Nimitz saying that he couldn't understand how that had happened. He was, Layton remembered, "pretty perturbed." Uncharacteristically, he began to pace up and down. As he did, other messages arrived in quick succession, each more alarming than the last.

From Kinkaid: "My situation is critical. Fast battleships and support by air strike may be able [to] prevent enemy from destroying CVE's and entering Leyte."

From Sprague: "Under attack . . . Enemy composed of 4 battleships, 8 cruisers, many destroyers."

From Sprague again, two minutes later: "Still under attack."

From Kinkaid: "Fast battleships are urgently needed."

And finally, in plain, uncoded English, came a plaintive query from Kinkaid: "Where is Lee? Send Lee."[18]

Lee and his battleships were with Halsey several hundred miles to the north, yet there was nothing at all from Halsey to indicate that he was receiving these panicky messages or responding to them. The night before at dinner, Chet had wondered why they didn't just ask Halsey where Lee was. Now, Forrest Sherman made the same suggestion: "We'd better send a dispatch to Halsey and find out."[19]

Unwilling as he was to meddle in the management of an ongoing battle, Nimitz decided that he could at least ask Halsey a question: "Where is Task Force 34?" Nimitz already knew the answer, of course. The question, therefore, was more a goad to action than a query, and Halsey was sure to recognize it as such. Years later, Nimitz acknowledged that the purpose of the message was "as a reminder to Halsey." Nimitz okayed the brief text, and Sherman handed it to a courier for transmission.[20]

In the radio room, the usual protocols were followed: to confuse enemy codebreakers, extra language called padding was added before and after the text and separated from it by a double consonant—in this case, "GG" and "RR"—so that the recipient could peel it away before delivering it. As transmitted at 3:44 in the afternoon (Hawaii time), the message read:

TURKEY TROTS TO WATER GG FROM CINCPAC ACTION COM THIRD
FLEET INFO COMINCH CTF SEVENTY-SEVEN X WHERE IS RPT WHERE
IS TASK FORCE THIRTY FOUR RR THE WORLD WONDERS[21]

Nimitz had nothing to do with choosing the random phrases that
were used as padding. He had no way of knowing that the radio officer on
Halsey's flagship, Lieutenant Charles Fox, despite the telltale "RR," would
leave those last three words in the message.[22]

It was 10:00 in the morning (Manila time) on October 25 when Halsey
was handed that message on the bridge of the *New Jersey*. Two hours earlier
he had sent 130 planes toward the Japanese carriers to the north. The pilots
of those planes reported that the enemy carriers had no protecting fighters,
which should have proved to Halsey that they were more a decoy than a
threat. By then, too, Halsey had seen the panicky messages from Sprague
and Kinkaid about being under attack by Japanese battleships. Years later, he
claimed that his first thought had been to wonder "how Kinkaid had let Ziggy
Sprague get caught like this." At the time, however, he may also have begun
to second-guess his decision to take his entire force northward, including all
of Task Force 34, and leave San Bernardino Strait unguarded. If so, it likely
affected his state of mind when the radioman handed him the clipboard
with Nimitz's message: "WHERE IS REPEAT WHERE IS TASK FORCE
34 RR THE WORLD WONDERS." When he read those last three words,
he exploded, threw his cap to the deck, and stomped on it, hollering, "What
right does Chester have to send me a God-damned message like that!"[23]

Of course "Chester" had *not* sent him a message like that. That it arrived the
way it did was due to the radio room on Halsey's own flagship. Halsey was so
upset that his chief of staff, Mick Carney, had to grab him by the shoulders and
shout, "Stop it. What the hell's the matter with you? Pull yourself together."
Carney led Halsey off the bridge into his nearby flag cabin to calm him down.
They remained there for a full hour—during which the Third Fleet, including
Task Force 34, continued to steam due north, away from Leyte Gulf, at 25 knots.[24]

BACK IN THE OPERATIONS ROOM IN HAWAII, Nimitz continued to study
the map. His flag secretary, Preston Mercer, thought the admiral "was very

disturbed about the situation." As usual, however, Nimitz said nothing, and only his pacing suggested his agitation. At one point, he turned to Captain Truman Hedding, an aviator who worked under Sherman in Nimitz's planning group. "Truman," he said speculatively, "what would you have done if you'd been Commander Third Fleet?"

Hedding recalled later that he was taken aback by the question. "Admiral," he stammered, "you're asking me?"

"Yes."

"Well, I don't know what I *would* have done, but I know what I *wouldn't* have done. I would never leave San Bernardino Strait unguarded."

Nimitz made no comment and returned his attention to the map. At one point he went outside to throw some horseshoes.[25]

––––––––––––

WHEN HALSEY RETURNED TO THE BRIDGE of the *New Jersey*, sometime after 11:00 a.m. local time (5:00 p.m. in Hawaii), he ordered Willis Lee's Task Force 34 to turn around and head south. To provide air cover for it, he sent one of his three carrier groups as well. It was a wrenching decision. He had envisioned Lee's battleships applying the coup de grâce to the Japanese carrier force, sinking any surviving enemy ships with their 16-inch guns.

Halsey must have known that Lee would be too late to join the contest off Leyte Gulf. As it happened, he was also too late to catch the now-retreating Japanese surface force, for not long after Halsey threw his cap to the deck of the *New Jersey*, Kurita decided that he had pressed his luck far enough. Rather than push forward into Leyte Gulf, he gave the order to retire northward. It was a decision that has left historians scratching their heads.† Consequently, when the lead elements of Task Force 34 arrived at the eastern end of San Bernardino Strait after steaming all night, what

––––––––––––

‡ Kurita may have calculated that many, if not most, of the American support ships in Leyte Gulf would have departed by then, which was correct. Still, the destruction of the fifty or so ships that remained would have seriously crippled American sealift capacity. After the war, both Kurita and his chief of staff, Tomiji Koyanagi, suggested that they had turned north to attack another (non-existent) American carrier force. Most scholars, however, believe that Kurita was simply exhausted and confused.

remained of Kurita's force had already passed through it into the Sibuyan Sea heading west. Lee's Task Force 34 expended their frustration by sinking a lone straggling Japanese destroyer.

IT WAS AFTER 6:00 P.M. and growing dark when news arrived in Pearl Harbor that the crisis had passed, though the events of the day left everyone uneasy and troubled about what might have been. Nimitz later wrote to King, "It never occurred to me that Halsey . . . would leave San Bernardino Strait unguarded." He might also have wondered about his own role in the near catastrophe. That night at dinner, as he discussed it with Spruance and McMorris, Chet asked what orders Halsey had been given. When his father told him those orders gave Halsey the latitude to make the destruction of the enemy fleet "his primary goal," Chet recalled later that he had said to his father, "It's your fault." His father did not argue, merely saying, "That's your opinion."[26]

That in the end it was an American victory after all was due not only to Kurita's baffling decision to retire, but also to one of the great heroic naval actions of the entire war. When Kurita's big ships had first appeared over the horizon that morning, Ziggy Sprague had ordered his escorting destroyers to attack them—beagles charging elephants. In what has been dubbed the Battle off Samar (October 25, 1944), their headlong assault caused Kurita to slow down and maneuver. That bought Sprague's little carriers precious minutes to launch planes, make smoke, and take evasive action. Three of the American destroyers making that sacrificial charge were quickly sent to the bottom with heavy losses. In addition, pilots from the jeep carriers carried out harassing attacks on Kurita's big ships, even to the point of making strafing runs after they had exhausted their ammunition. Collectively, they convinced Kurita that he was facing a stronger force than he was. That, and his exhaustion, likely convinced Kurita to retire.[27]

Tragic and sobering as the American losses were, Japanese losses were catastrophic. Counting the ships sunk by *Darter* and *Dace*, those destroyed in the Sibuyan Sea by Halsey's aircraft, those sunk in Surigao Strait by Oldendorf's heavies, and those sunk by Halsey's strike against the decoy force, the Japanese lost no fewer than twenty-nine warships, including four aircraft carriers, three battleships, and six heavy cruisers. For all meaningful purposes, the Imperial Japanese Navy had ceased to exist as a credible fighting force. As Halsey put it in a triumphal message to Nimitz and copied to all task groups: "It can be announced with assurance that the Japanese Navy has been beaten, routed, and broken by the 3rd and 7th Fleets."[28]

N IMITZ BARELY HAD A CHANCE TO EXHALE before he had to decide what—if anything—to do about Halsey. Clearly, Bull had
seriously misjudged the operational circumstances at Leyte Gulf, and the
U.S. Navy avoided disaster largely because of a providential blunder by the
Japanese commander. Nimitz issued a triumphant communiqué announcing "an overwhelming victory" in what he called "The Second Battle of the
Philippine Sea." Intended for public distribution, the declaration obscured
the confusion of Halsey's run northward, noting only that Third Fleet pilots
had inflicted serious damage on the Japanese carriers and that "the engagement was broken off to proceed to the assistance of Seventh Fleet carrier
escort groups then under attack off Samar Island."[1]

That might have been the end of it but for Halsey's unwillingness to acknowledge that he had made an error at all. His efforts to justify himself
afterward were both clumsy and embarrassing. He wrote Nimitz that it
would have been "childish" for him to remain by San Bernardino Strait,

and in his after-action report he insisted that Kurita's force had been "too heavily damaged" in the Sibuyan Sea to constitute a threat to U.S. forces off Leyte Gulf, though events had clearly proved otherwise. Halsey attributed any misunderstandings during the battle to MacArthur's requirement that messages between the fleet commanders had to pass through the communications center at Manus, though an additional problem was his own decision to employ the short-range TBS system to announce the delay in forming Task Force 34.[2]

Halsey also refused to accept the fact that Ozawa's carrier force had been a decoy, because that would mean he had been duped. Even after the war was over and Ozawa stated publicly and explicitly that his whole purpose had been to decoy the American carriers away from Leyte Gulf, Halsey denied it. His only regret, he insisted, was that he had given in to the pressure to order Lee's battleships southward, telling King, "It was a mistake to turn south when the Japs were right under my guns." Almost as much as his initial errors, Halsey's refusal to accept reality was worrisome.[3]

Nimitz did not want to lose Halsey; he believed that his strengths greatly outweighed his weaknesses, which in any case consisted mainly of over-zealousness. Then, too, Halsey had become a national hero whose bold, occasionally profane comments had made him a favorite with the American public and the press. For Nimitz to react to, or even acknowledge, Halsey's failures at Leyte Gulf could turn the matter into a public issue that could hurt both the Navy and the war effort.

In 1942, when Nimitz had to decide how to respond to Pete Mitscher's spurious report on the Battle of Midway, he had maintained an official silence about what happened even as he quietly removed Mitscher from command of a task force. He remained officially silent again about Halsey's blunder during the Battle of Leyte Gulf. This time, however, he did not remove Halsey from his command. From the first days of the war, Halsey had been his most aggressive and reliable strike force commander—Davout to his Napoleon, Jackson to his Lee. It was Halsey who had provided the nation with its first Pacific victories back in 1942. So Nimitz said nothing publicly about what some were calling "Bull's Run," and Halsey kept command of the Third Fleet. At the same time, however, Nimitz also decided that he could no longer give Halsey quite as free a hand as he had done previously.

Immediately after the battle, Halsey planned to take the Third Fleet to Ulithi Atoll, twelve hundred miles east of the Philippines. Nimitz had ordered the occupation of Ulithi as a fleet base, and he sent repair ships, oilers, and even a floating drydock to its commodious lagoon. The Seabees added buildings and an airfield ashore, plus picnic areas, athletic fields, and a 1,200-seat theater on the island of Mogmog, which was designated as a recreation center for the men so that they could have some down time between missions. The extensive American base was supposed to be a closely held secret. All the ships that anchored there maintained radio silence, and the word "Ulithi" was not allowed to appear in the press. Nimitz called Ulithi his "secret weapon."[4]

A group of Navy officers enjoy a few beers on Mogmog Island, part of Ulithi Atoll, which Nimitz established as both a fleet base and a recreation area. The Higgins boats just off the beach are waiting to carry the men back to their ships, visible on the horizon. (U.S. Naval Institute)

Halsey explained his move to Ulithi by telling Kinkaid that his air groups were "exhausted" after sixteen days of "unprecedented fighting" and needed a respite. Previously, Nimitz might not have intervened, but monsoon-like weather in the Philippines had slowed construction of new landing fields on Leyte, and Kinkaid reported that he needed continued air support from the carriers. Nimitz therefore ordered Halsey to maintain a "heavy combat air patrol" over Leyte with at least one, and preferably two, of his carrier groups. Halsey sent two of his carrier groups to Ulithi and kept the other two on station in the Philippines, planning to rotate them at appropriate intervals.[5]

In another message two weeks later, on November 13, Nimitz reminded Halsey that the carriers "must be kept in state of material readiness not only for current operations but to carry on throughout the war." In pursuit of that, he ordered Halsey to send the *Bunker Hill* and the *Enterprise* to Pearl Harbor, and laid out a schedule for rotating the big carriers between Pearl Harbor and the forward area. Such issues would ordinarily have been within Halsey's command discretion, yet he did not object to either order. A third issue, however, proved more contentious. It was connected to an entirely new threat in the war, one that neither Nimitz nor anyone else had foreseen.[6]

On the day after the Battle off Samar, Sprague reported that Japanese "suicide crash planes" had struck three of the American jeep carriers off Leyte Gulf. One of them, the *St. Lô*, sank; the other two had to return to the United States for lengthy repairs. Here was a terrifying new development in the war, both because of the self-evident peril of human-guided missiles and because it was further proof of the intensity of Japanese determination.[7]

Halsey's carriers bore the brunt of this new terror. Between October 29 and November 1, Japanese suicide planes—the kamikaze—hit four of his big carriers: *Intrepid, Franklin, Belleau Wood,* and *Lexington*. None of them was lost, but two had to be sent stateside for repairs. Halsey's response was to advocate for a change in the mix of planes on American carriers. With the Japanese surface navy all but toothless, he planned to move many of the dive-bombers and torpedo planes to shore bases and replace them with additional fighters that could intercept and shoot down the kamikazes. Nimitz approved the idea in general. He nonetheless cautioned Halsey that due to a shortage of fighter pilots, the change would have to be made incrementally. He noted pointedly that "no change has yet been authorized."[8]

Halsey persisted. "Time is short," he radioed, "and things are already moving." He insisted that choosing the kind of planes on carriers was an issue for the local commander, like a battleship captain choosing whether to use HE or AP ammunition. It was not, in other words, an issue for the theater commander to decide. "Please advise by urgent dispatch."[9]

Nimitz did not accept Halsey's analogy. Nor did he simply pull rank. Instead, he explained the situation in pragmatic terms. He told Halsey that he was free to employ the fighter planes that he had any way he wanted. Adding additional fighter squadrons, however, was problematical because there were only forty surplus fighter pilots in the theater and, because of that, it would be impossible "to maintain the expanded fighter strength" that Halsey wanted. Halsey insisted he could assign bomber pilots to fly fighters. To that, Nimitz responded, "The conversion of bomber pilots to fighter pilots will take place in the Hawaiian area rather than the forward area." Less confrontational than simply saying no, it made the point that the issue was one for the theater commander to determine.[10]

ON NOVEMBER 21, NIMITZ AGAIN FLEW to San Francisco to talk with King. Though it was a short visit, Nimitz got to spend Thanksgiving with Catherine and Mary, who were living in nearby Berkeley. Catherine was delighted. "I get so lonely for him," she wrote a friend. "His visits are so few and so short and always filled with conferences so I see little of him." In the professional part of his visit, he and King discussed the recent battle, including Halsey's role in it. King agreed with Nimitz that it would be counterproductive now to confront Halsey openly. They also considered other issues, among them how to handle the British.[11]

British prestige in East Asia had suffered a near-fatal blow in 1942 when the Japanese drove them out of their Asian colonies, including Hong Kong and Singapore. To Churchill, the British Empire was a tangible and vital thing, and he was determined to reestablish Britain's standing on the far side of the world. With the war in Europe—and particularly the naval war—winding down, he wanted to dispatch a British Pacific Fleet to partic-ipate in the war against Japan.

King didn't want it. First, especially after the Battle of Leyte Gulf, the U.S. Navy did not need additional support. Indeed, by then, the Navy had such a surplus of planes that hundreds of brand-new aircraft were simply parked on empty fields and left there to rust. In addition, accommodating a British fleet in the Pacific would complicate the logistics and supply systems. King first tried to avoid saying no by repeatedly declaring that it was under con-sideration. Churchill was not to be put off, asking Roosevelt bluntly, "The offer has been made, is it accepted?" Roosevelt could hardly refuse. Thus Nimitz learned that a delegation headed by the commander in chief of the British Home Fleet, Admiral Sir Bruce Fraser, would visit his headquarters in December to work out the details.[12]

King recruited Nimitz to help delay or deflect the inevitable. With King virtually—if not literally—looking over his shoulder, Nimitz wrote to Fraser from San Francisco to tell him, "I will be delighted to have you as my guest at Pearl Harbor." In that same letter, however, he also sought to narrow the role a British fleet might play by suggesting that it should focus on Sumatra and the Malay Peninsula rather than operate in the Central Pacific. He added that King "fully supports above views." In fact, King prob-ably dictated them.[13]

Over the ensuing several weeks, King did his best to circumscribe British participation in the Pacific war by denying Fraser and his ships access to U.S. shore establishments and the use of U.S. oil resources, directing that any support provided them would be on a "not to interfere" basis. Once again, Nimitz played the role of fixer as he sought to buffer these challenging, if not openly hostile, declarations. He asked King's permission to allow the British Pacific Fleet to use Manus as an anchorage, explaining that by the time the British arrived there in March 1945, his own forces would be using Leyte Gulf as a base and Manus would be underutilized. Grudgingly, King consented. Soon after, Nimitz radioed Fraser: "Welcome to service in the Pacific."[14]

MEANWHILE, NIMITZ RETURNED TO PEARL HARBOR on November 27 and spent the rest of the day catching up with dispatches. His ability to fulfill

Nimitz poses with Royal Navy Admiral Sir Bruce Fraser in this 1945 photograph.
A former Commander of the Home Fleet, Fraser assumed command of the British
Pacific Fleet in December 1944 with a headquarters in Sydney. (U.S. Naval Institute)

such quotidian demands, however, was jeopardized by the need to play host to more groups of VIP visitors. As the war lengthened, the number of visitors multiplied to the point where taking care of them threatened to overtake running the war.

Some visitors were welcome, including Joseph Grew, the former U.S. ambassador to Japan, who stopped in Hawaii en route to his new job in Washington as Undersecretary of State. Nimitz hosted him in his quarters for several days and enjoyed Grew's take on the political and diplomatic aspects of the war. Grew told him it was important to signal to the Japanese some flexibility about retaining the position of emperor after the war since otherwise the Japanese were likely to fight to the bitter end. Other welcome guests included Frank Jack Fletcher, who showed up for a four-day visit in late November, and J. O. Richardson, Kimmel's predecessor as CinCPac, who arrived soon afterward. Nimitz put them up as well, though it meant that Doc Anderson and Soc McMorris had to double up. Nimitz had always enjoyed Fletcher's company, and though Admiral Richardson could be "severe and grouchy," Nimitz told Catherine that "he is very pleasant when you get to know him."[15]

Entertaining larger groups, such as the fifteen members of the House Naval Affairs Committee who were scheduled to arrive on December 7, was another matter. In addition to the time Nimitz devoted to playing host, there was the problem of where to put them all. The massive influx of military and civilian personnel to Hawaii meant that housing in Honolulu was, as Nimitz described it to Catherine, "deplorable." Nor was it likely to get better soon since "relief can come only with large lumber shipments and imported labor and there is not enough of either for war purposes."[16]

In fact, the housing shortage had already triggered another tiff with Robert Richardson, the Army commander. General Richardson (who was no relation to Admiral Richardson) continued to nurse a grudge about Holland Smith's treatment of Ralph Smith on Saipan. When he learned that Nimitz had billeted Army soldiers on trawlers offshore, he was furious. Richardson insisted that Nimitz had no business giving orders to Army personnel, much less assigning them to ships. In that, Richardson was entirely incorrect. As theater commander, Nimitz had authority over all of the forces, of every service and every nationality, throughout the Pacific Ocean Area—including, for that matter, Richardson himself. Nimitz's usual response to this kind of complaint was to be conciliatory. Not this time. As he wrote to Catherine, "I can never live eternally at peace with the General, so I might as well have it out now." He did not quite "have it out" with Richardson, though he did inform the general that the housing shortage on Oahu meant that the soldiers would simply have to adjust.[17]

He could not put the congressmen on trawlers, however. Nimitz himself would host the committee chairman, James J. Heffernan of New York, which was difficult enough since both Fletcher and J. O. Richardson were still in residence. He asked several of his senior staff members to accommodate the others. The exception was Margaret Chase Smith of Maine. It was obvious to Nimitz that the "lady congressman" (as he called her) could not be billeted with one of his male officers, so he used his influence to get her a room at the Moana Hotel.

Then he learned that the group would arrive a day early. The Moana Hotel insisted that it had no rooms available for that night, not even for a congresswoman sponsored by the theater commander. What saved the day was the presence of the first contingent of WAVES. As noted previously, Nimitz had opposed having WAVES in Hawaii at all on the grounds that it was a forward area. That argument was less convincing in the fall of 1944, and a delegation of WAVES personnel was en route. To prepare for their arrival, Lieutenant Commander Eleanor Rigby (whom Nimitz called "Mrs. Rigby") had already arrived, and Nimitz prevailed upon her to host Congresswoman Smith for the duration of her visit. The next day, he entertained Heffernan, Rigby, and Smith at a dinner along with Fletcher and J. O. Richardson. Afterward, Nimitz reported to Catherine that Smith was "a charming person."[18]

The House Naval Affairs Committee controlled the purse strings for Navy budgets. In his role as fixer, Nimitz was therefore determined to ensure the members had a pleasant and productive visit. In addition to briefings and tours of both the Navy Yard and the island, he arranged for a day at sea on an aircraft carrier so that they could observe flight operations. It all went off splendidly. Nimitz was sure it was "a sight they will never forget."[19]

The congressional delegates left Pearl Harbor on December 10 to continue their tour of Pacific bases, though they were scheduled to return again just before Christmas at about the same time that the delegation of British officers was due to arrive. During both visits, Nimitz had to rise early and skip his usual walk in order to do his normal office work in the morning so that he could play gracious host in the afternoon. He was often exhausted by the end of the day. With as much irony as frustration, he wrote Catherine, "What a way to carry on a war!"[20]

Almost the moment the British left, another crisis erupted in the western Pacific, and once again Halsey was at the center of it.

THE GROUND BATTLE FOR LEYTE had been fierce. Krueger's Sixth Army lost nearly 3,000 killed and 10,000 wounded, while 60,000 Japanese had died. Soon afterward, MacArthur moved on to the island of Mindoro, which was to be the springboard for his move to Luzon. On December 15 Halsey's carriers provided air cover for the landings on Mindoro, and the admiral scheduled another air strike for December 19. Before that, however, he needed to refuel his ships, especially the gas-guzzling destroyers, some of which were down to only 15 percent of capacity. He therefore directed the fleet to a refueling rendezvous east of the Philippines.

As the scores of ships headed for the rendezvous, the weather turned ugly. Halsey noted "a moderate cross swell" that would "make fueling difficult," but, eager to complete the refueling so that he could return to station, he ordered it to proceed anyway. Determination and perseverance, however, could not conquer the weather, which soon blew up into a full-scale typhoon. Reluctantly, Halsey postponed the refueling. Rather than take the fleet farther from the Philippines by heading south, Halsey ordered it to head west, unaware that by doing so he was moving with the storm and prolonging his ships' exposure to the conditions. To Nimitz, he radioed: "Baffling storm pursues us."[21]

The storm pounded the ships of the Third Fleet all day on December 18. Winds gusted to over 100 miles an hour, and waves crashed over the top of carrier flight decks; airplanes on carrier hangar decks broke loose from their restraints and smashed into one another, igniting fires. By the nineteenth, the day when Halsey had hoped to conduct a strike against ground targets on Mindoro, the surviving ships of his command were scattered all over the Philippine Sea. There was no choice now but to direct them all to Ulithi. Total losses during the typhoon—which was ever after known as "Halsey's Typhoon"—were equivalent to a major defeat: eight hundred men had been killed, two hundred planes wrecked, and three ships sunk.[22]

Back in Pearl Harbor, news of the disaster was a shock. Doc Anderson remembered that even though Nimitz spoke "quietly, as if he were discussing the weather" (which in this case he was), his criticism of Halsey was "very severe." In addition to the three ships that sank, nearly every ship had suffered significant damage to its radar system, which was especially critical in light of the kamikaze threat. Nimitz's first act, therefore, was to send civilian contract engineers and spare parts to Ulithi to repair the radars, and a few days later he flew there himself along with Forrest Sherman.[23]

Navy regulations required an official enquiry whenever a ship was lost or damaged, and Nimitz knew that the enquiry would focus on Halsey. Since it could not be conducted by any of Halsey's subordinates, Nimitz also brought along Vice Admiral George Murray, the former CO of the *Enterprise* who was now Commander Air Forces Pacific, and during a fuel stop on Guam he added Vice Admiral John C. Hoover to his entourage. Neither was in Halsey's chain of command, and they had sufficient rank to act as investigators.[24]

Nimitz and the others arrived at Ulithi on Christmas Eve, 1944, and all of them immediately went on board Halsey's flagship, *New Jersey*. Nimitz did not arrive empty-handed. In honor of the season, he had brought a full-sized decorated Christmas tree, which had been cut in Washington State and shipped nearly six thousand miles. It was the first time Nimitz and Halsey had met face-to-face since August, and if there was any tension after Halsey's decisions at Leyte Gulf or his actions during the typhoon, it was not evident. In fact, the mood was mostly celebratory. Nimitz wrote Catherine, "I had an enjoyable dinner with Halsey & his staff, some 30 at the table, and they were all in high spirits, which they have every right to be." The next day—Christmas Day—the celebrations continued as Halsey hosted a large buffet lunch on the *New Jersey* that included dozens of flag officers, many of them old friends of Nimitz.[25]

Afterward, Nimitz went ashore on Mogmog Island to get some exercise. When he landed, he was welcomed by a sailor dressed up as Santa Claus who cheerfully greeted one and all. Nimitz was delighted to see "literally thousands of young men, officers & sailors," playing games, swimming, or simply having a beer (rationed at two cans per sailor, though many found ways to avoid the rationing). "They had been cooped up aboard hot ships [for] weeks, and some for months," he wrote to Catherine, "without setting foot ashore."[26]

The court of enquiry began the next day on board the destroyer tender *Cascade*. Nimitz did not stay for it. Instead, he flew to Leyte to talk with MacArthur. There, he met briefly with President Osmeña, and he accompanied MacArthur on a tour of the island. There was a bit of excitement at dinner when a lone Japanese plane flew over and dropped a bomb. It did no damage. That night, Nimitz listened from his bed to a heavy tropical rainstorm, and as he wrote Catherine, he thought about "the poor troops in the mud in tents with no floors."[27]

Nimitz was back in Pearl Harbor when he received a summary of the court's verdict regarding the typhoon. After hearing more than fifty witnesses over nine days, the court concluded that "the preponderance of responsibility" for the devastating losses on December 18 "falls on Commander Third Fleet, Admiral William F. Halsey, U.S. Navy." Nimitz read the lengthy transcript with care before accepting the official finding. In his endorsement, however, he expressed his "firm opinion that no question of negligence is involved" and, mirroring the court's language, declared that Halsey's "errors in judgment" were a product of the "stress of war operations" that stemmed "from a commendable desire to meet military commitments." Because of that, he ruled, "no further action is contemplated or recommended."[28]

His endorsement was consistent with his earlier decisions about Mitscher at Midway, Holland Smith on Saipan, and Halsey after the Battle of Leyte Gulf. In each case, Nimitz took care to ensure that personnel disputes, inter-service rivalries, or even errors in judgment did not interfere with progress in the war. The important thing was not to find fault or to apportion blame, but to sustain the momentum. King concurred, and later told Halsey (as Halsey remembered it), "You've got a green light on everything you did." Others were less certain. Gerald Bogan, who commanded one of Halsey's four carrier groups, believed that both at Leyte Gulf and during the typhoon, the main problem was Halsey's "plain, goddam stubbornness." Stubbornness was unquestionably one of Halsey's salient characteristics and at times it had proved to be a virtue. Yet as recent events demonstrated, it could also be a weakness.[29]

NIMITZ FLEW BACK TO HAWAII via Saipan and Kwajalein. He spent part of the long trip reading *Mrs. Miniver,* a novel about the impact of war on a British family in a London suburb. He told Catherine that it was even better than the movie, which they had both seen. Flying through pitch darkness on New Year's Eve put him in a reflective mood. In a long letter to Catherine, he recalled that it was three years ago to the day that he had assumed command of the Pacific Fleet. Despite occasional problems, he wrote, things had mostly "gone well," for which he credited "the help of many people." Of course, the job was still unfinished, and the road ahead remained perilous. Still, he wrote, "with proper planning & preparation we will move ahead, sometimes with bigger losses, and sometimes with less, but definitely always closer to the Japs and closer to final victory." He mourned the losses at Leyte Gulf and in the typhoon, yet he remained convinced that neither should interfere with progress. As he summarized it to Catherine, "Our Pacific War goes on by halts and jerks but ever forward."[30]

When he arrived back in Hawaii, he took a shower, changed his uniform, and went straight to the office, where he found a daunting pile of dispatches waiting for him. More happily, there was also a pile of mail from Catherine and a number of Christmas presents. Staff members had bought him several recordings of classical music, and President Roosevelt had sent him "a handsome leather suitcase" that clinked enticingly. It subsequently proved to be several bottles of scotch. Alas, since there was no key to open the case, his appreciation of that particular gift would have to wait.[31]

He also learned of his promotion. When he had been named CinCPac back in 1941, he had become a four-star admiral, the highest rank then available in the United States Navy, just as general was the highest rank in the Army. In mid-December 1944, however, Congress passed a law authorizing the president to appoint four individuals in each service to five-star rank, to be designated as either "general of the Army" or "fleet admiral." In the Army, Marshall, MacArthur, Eisenhower, and Hap Arnold were so designated. In the Navy, Leahy, King, and Nimitz were selected; the fourth Navy slot was left vacant.* In his new rank, Nimitz was two

---

* There was some controversy about who the fourth 5-star admiral should be, and for a full year the position remained unfilled. Though Nimitz did not speak publicly about it, he almost certainly believed that Spruance was the logical candidate for that honor. In the end, however, it went instead to Halsey, who became a fleet admiral on December 11, 1945.

days junior to King, one day junior to MacArthur, and one day senior to Dwight Eisenhower. He received a telegram from Churchill offering "every congratulations" for his "well deserved promotion." As Nimitz wrote to Catherine, "It was nice of the old boy to send me a message." Yet for all that, one of the first things Nimitz did, pragmatist that he was, was to calculate how much of a pay bump it meant. The promotion would increase his pay package from $10,200 a year to $13,000 a year. "If I am lucky enough to get 5 stars," he wrote Catherine, "we will have an increase of $2,800 annually or $233.33 per month." He suggested that she could use it either to buy more war bonds or save it to buy a home for their eventual retirement.[32]

IT WAS A MOMENT TO TAKE STOCK. The Central Pacific Drive had lasted a full year. In that time, forces under Nimitz's direction had advanced nearly four thousand miles across the Pacific from Tarawa in the Gilberts to Kwajalein in the Marshalls, Saipan in the Marianas, and Leyte in the Philippines. In the process, those forces had all but annihilated Japanese naval and air power. The principal reason for that was that Nimitz had by far the bigger hammer, thanks to the astonishing productivity of American industry.

Still, he had wielded that hammer with skill and subtlety—and modesty. MacArthur had made headlines by accompanying the invasion forces to several invasion beaches, including Hollandia, Los Negros, Morotai, and of course Leyte. Nimitz, by contrast, chose not to seek the spotlight, flying to each captured island only after the battle was over to congratulate the soldiers, sailors, and Marines, and to talk with the officers. While MacArthur was invariably the star of each performance, Nimitz assumed the role of director behind the scenes, guiding and supporting the actors who executed his orders. Like many great actors, those subordinates were both talented and temperamental, their very nicknames suggesting their disposition: "Terrible" Turner, "Howling Mad" Smith, even "Bull" Halsey. Keeping them focused on a clear objective and all pulling in the same direction was a central aspect of Nimitz's command leadership. He had championed bold and aggressive actions—in the Coral Sea and at

Midway, Kwajalein, Eniwetok, Truk, and Leyte. Even more than his audacity, however, it was his steady hand on the helm that was the key to success. Though he never conned a ship, dropped a bomb, or stormed a beach, he was the essential element of American victory in the Central Pacific campaign.

PART IV

DÉNOUEMENT

We will all of us put our shoulders to the wheel & finish the job as soon as
we can.

— Chester W. Nimitz to Catherine Nimitz, December 31, 1944

*By 1945, Japan was a defeated nation. Her invasion of China remained
a quagmire; the vast empire she had seized in 1942 was swiftly disap-
pearing; her navy had all but ceased to exist; American bombers savaged
her cities; and American submarines cut off her vital imports so effectively
that mass starvation loomed as a genuine possibility. Yet Japan's leaders
clung to a belief that they could avoid the humiliation of defeat. In these
circumstances, the problem for the United States was how to bring the war
to an end. Would it be necessary to invade Japan's home islands and physically occupy them? Would it then be necessary to land an American army
in China to confront the Japanese army there? Japan's decision to embrace
"body crash" attacks suggested that ending the war might be as fraught
and as painful as fighting it.*

A S THE WAR MOVED WEST, so did Nimitz, who shifted his headquarters from Oahu to Guam in January 1945, a move he had been
planning for some time. Guam is about half the size of Oahu, with a much
smaller population; there were no true cities like Honolulu or great natural
ports like Pearl Harbor. Most of the roads were dirt or crushed coral, and
the principal harbor, Apra, was clogged with coral heads and reefs. What
made Guam a likely headquarters was its location. It was only one time
zone away from Tokyo, and close to future battlefields, including Luzon,
fifteen hundred miles to the south, and Iwo Jima, eight hundred miles to
the north. From Guam it was possible, as Nimitz told Catherine, to "pack
up staff members and visit important places in a very few hours." Almost at
once, the Seabees began transforming the island, working seven days a week
and around the clock building roads, installing power and water plants,
and improving the harbor. They blew up rocks and coral heads, dredged
the bottom, and extended the breakwater, a process they called "harbor

stretching." Eventually, Nimitz brought in a huge floating drydock that could repair damaged warships on-site so they did not have to go back to Pearl Harbor. The drydock was so large, it could lift a battleship right out of the water.[1]

Like Hawaii, Guam was an American territory, and, like Wake, the Japanese had seized it during their string of victories back in December 1941. American forces recaptured it in the summer of 1944, landing there on July 21, two weeks after Saipan fell. That date is still celebrated in Guam as Liberation Day, though the island was not secured until August 10, on which day Nimitz flew there, as he did to all Pacific battlefields. While touring the island in a jeep, he kept an eye out for a location for an advance headquarters.[2]

The site he picked was on a high plateau, 650 feet above sea level, that overlooked the small village of Agana and the harbor of Apra on the western side of the island. The location was known locally as Fonte Plateau, though soon enough everyone began to refer to it as Nimitz Hill. It offered what Nimitz described as "a magnificent view" of the beach and the Philippine Sea. Almost immediately, the Seabees got to work turning the bare hillside into a sprawling complex of housing and office spaces. Four months after Liberation Day, Nimitz stopped in Guam en route to visit Halsey in Ulithi and checked on progress. He saw how the site had been transformed. The work was not complete, but Nimitz decided that it was sufficiently far enough along for him to make the move, and elements of his staff began moving there soon after Christmas.[3]

Nimitz's main reason for moving to Guam was to be closer to the front. It was also farther from Washington. Presumably that would discourage at least some of the VIP visitors who arrived expecting Nimitz to house, feed, and entertain them. In the weeks before the move, Nimitz confessed to Catherine that he had failed to send her one of his daily letters because "my time was completely taken up with . . . the visiting delegation from Washington." As always, he offered the visitors ("26 top ranking officers") briefings, tours, lunch, and dinner. One group had barely left when the next arrived, this one headed by "another big shot" (Nimitz's phrase) "with a delegation of *six*" (Nimitz underscoring the number), who spent the next two days with him. He did not resent the visitors themselves. "All these visitors are very considerate and very pleasant," he wrote Catherine, "but it does take time to look after them, particularly if they are VIPs." He knew he would have visitors on Guam, too, but hopefully not as many, and not as often. Nimitz was a hands-on commander who liked to walk around from section to section and talk to the staff officers to see how work was progressing. Yet by the end of 1944 he had begun to feel trapped in his office, "more and more isolated." Commander Eller remembered that "Admiral Nimitz wanted to get out of all the hubbub of Pearl Harbor and all the folderol" that went with it.[4]

There was a third benefit to the move. While Nimitz planned to bring his closest advisers with him—including McMorris, Sherman, Anderson, and Lamar—Jack Towers would remain behind. From the moment he had arrived in Hawaii, Towers had been a contrary voice on almost every command issue, from personnel decisions to grand strategy. In addition to that, Towers simply "rubbed a lot of people the wrong way," according to Captain George Anderson. In writing Towers's fitness report, Nimitz gave him high marks for initiative and responsibility, but graded him lower on the ability to work with others. The decision to leave Towers at Pearl Harbor was not punitive. He was, after all, Deputy CinCPac, and it was appropriate that he should supervise logistical and administrative matters in the rear area while Nimitz coordinated operations at the front. Still, it would be a great relief not to have to deal with the vexatious Towers on a daily basis.[5*]

That January, Nimitz's staff acquired a 15-ton Chris-Craft runabout with four bunks, a small cabin, and a galley—perfect for deep-sea fishing. "It was a beautiful thing," a sailor recalled, with "varnished hardwood decks and a lot of polished brass." Nimitz named it the *Catherine* ("for my sweetheart," he wrote her) and planned to take it with him to Guam to be available for staff officers and visiting dignitaries. That month, too, he learned that Chet had been awarded the Navy Cross and promoted to full commander. He

---

* Even from four thousand miles away, Nimitz found reasons to be annoyed with Towers. He wrote Catherine on February 4 that "my friend Jack Towers is still trying to introduce WAVES into my P.H. headquarters, but I will not let him do so."

sent his son a silver belt buckle with a submarine on it. Another pleasant surprise was learning that his name was on King George's New Year's Day honors list. He informed Catherine that he was to be made "Honorary Knight Grand Cross of the Bath," adding, "whatever that means." He teased her that he was going to make Lamar call her "Lady Catherine" from then on.[6]

THE WAR CONTINUED EVEN AS NIMITZ planned his move. In the second week of January MacArthur was poised to invade Luzon, home to Manila. Nimitz attended a dinner at Schofield Barracks on January 9 (an event he described as "rather dull"), but, aware that MacArthur's move was in the offing, he went to his headquarters afterward and stayed late hoping to hear some news. There were no reports that night, though MacArthur issued a communiqué the next day announcing a successful landing. Nimitz was relieved to learn that American casualties were "exceptionally light," and he was gratified as well that subsequent newspaper accounts acknowledged the role played by the ships that Nimitz had contributed, characterizing the invasion as a cooperative effort. "I have gone out of my way in order to produce good relations and cooperation with D.M.," he wrote Catherine that night, so it was "particularly pleasing" that, this time at least, the papers did not portray them as adversaries.[7]

There was news from Halsey, too. For months, Halsey had urged Nimitz to allow him to conduct a sweep of enemy targets in the South China Sea. In particular, Halsey wanted to find and sink the two hermaphrodite battleship/carriers, *Ise* and *Hyuga*, that had escaped him during the Battle of Leyte Gulf. Up to this point, Nimitz had denied him permission, but as MacArthur was now moving toward Luzon, Nimitz gave Halsey the green light. Not long afterward, Halsey reported sinking 15 ships and destroying 42 airplanes near Formosa, and another 41 ships and 112 enemy planes in the South China Sea. He did not, however, find either of the Japanese battleships. Nimitz congratulated Halsey on the destruction of "about 200,000 tons of merchant shipping." Privately, however, he admitted to Catherine that he was "terribly disappointed" that Halsey had not eliminated the two warships. At the end of his sortie, Halsey proposed exiting the South China Sea via San Bernardino Strait, the route Kurita had used back in October. Nimitz told him no, though because Halsey maintained his usual radio silence, there was no answer from him. A year before, Nimitz might have let that go. This time he radioed Halsey to tell him "to acknowledge his dispatch." Halsey did so, and returned around the north cape of Luzon.[8]

Nimitz followed MacArthur's campaign on Luzon closely. He hoped for a quick victory there so that some, at least, of the ships he had lent to MacArthur for the landings could be returned to Spruance in time for the invasion of Iwo Jima, now only two weeks away. That began to appear unlikely when those ships became targets of relentless kamikaze attacks. Twenty-nine ships were hit by kamikazes during the landings—three of them sank, and thirteen others were so badly damaged they had to withdraw. MacArthur insisted that he needed to keep the rest. Spruance suspected that the general was simply unwilling to release any elements of his command. Nimitz did not complain about it either to MacArthur or to King. Instead, he adjusted. To replace the ships MacArthur kept, Nimitz ordered two of the fast battleships in Mitscher's screen, *Washington* and *North Carolina*, to shift their ordnance package to high explosives so that they could augment the shore bombardment mission at Iwo Jima.[9]

As he prepared for the move to Guam, Nimitz tied up loose ends in Pearl Harbor. He had a physical, after which the doctors pronounced him in "excellent physical condition," though his visit to the dentist proved more complicated. He ended up returning multiple times, and by the end of the week, he had what he described to Catherine as "a brand new set of 'store' teeth," which were "quite comfortable." He also carried out a number of professional and social calls that week, including one to the Walkers, who surprised Lamar with a birthday party at which pretty Hawaiian hula dancers presented a blushing Lamar with leis and small gifts.[10]

Packing up the office, Nimitz found that he had accumulated a surprising amount in three years. In addition to the piles of paperwork, both official and private—some of which could be boxed up and forwarded—there were scores of gifts and mementos from well-wishers. Much of that he simply tossed out, though he did keep his favorite items, including a recording that Catherine and Mary had made of their own voices, which he played "over and over again." In one section of it, Catherine played the piano and their cocker spaniel Freckles did his old trick of leaping up onto the piano bench to howl in accompaniment. When Nimitz played it for Anderson, Mak, who had been sleeping nearby, heard Freckles's howls and became "intensely interested."[11]

NIMITZ MADE THE MOVE TO GUAM on January 27, a week after Franklin Roosevelt took the oath of office for a fourth term as president. His new residence was large and comfortable, with four bedrooms (each with its own bath), a combined living and dining room, and a long open lanai facing the ocean, all of it on one floor. At 650 feet above sea level, there was often a cool breeze to mitigate the heat, and Lamar arranged to have a horseshoe pit built outside. As Truman Hedding put it, it was "a nice way to fight a war if you had to fight one." Nimitz, Anderson, and Lamar each got a bedroom, leaving one empty for VIP guests. Sherman moved into a smaller cottage nearby, as would McMorris when he returned from stateside, where he was visiting his sick wife. In time, what Nimitz called his "regular mess" stabilized at seven: himself, McMorris, Sherman, Anderson, Commodore William R. Carter (the ops officer), and Army Brigadier General Harold C. Mandell, plus Lamar, who served as mess treasurer.[12]

Nimitz told Catherine that the officers on his extended staff were "greatly pleased with their new housing," though that was not entirely true. Many occupied what were essentially double-decker Quonset huts that were "not too comfortable," as Truman Hedding put it. And because it was the rainy season, the humidity was stifling. Eller described his quarters as "damp, humid, and moldy," recalling that "your shoes would mildew" overnight and "your clothes would be soggy when you put them on" the next morning. Even worse, when the Seabees bulldozed the hillside to create the building sites, they had unearthed scores of dead Japanese soldiers who had been hurriedly buried after the battle six months earlier. As a result, "there was a horrible smell around the place."[13]

Nimitz retained his regular daily schedule at his new headquarters, including the 9:00 staff meeting and the afternoon walks. In the busy weeks

McMorris, Sherman, and Nimitz employ captured Japanese "big eyes" to examine the shipping in Apra Harbor outside Nimitz's new headquarters on Guam. (U.S. Naval Institute)

before he left Hawaii, he had been feeling an almost desperate need for exercise, and the day after he arrived in Guam, he, Sherman, and Anderson all set off for a long hike. Mak, who nearly always accompanied Nimitz on his walks, stayed behind this time because Nimitz worried about him in a strange place with lots of traffic.[†] If Nimitz worried about Mak, the governor of the island, Marine Corps Major General Henry Larsen, was

† He was right to be concerned. Three months later, Mak disappeared and (as Nimitz put it in a letter to Chet) was "AWOL" for more than two months. When a Marine guard finally cornered him, recognized him, and brought him back, he was covered with cuts and bruises. Nimitz took him to the 3rd Marine Division Dog Hospital for their "War Dogs," and after a week of good care and regular meals, he was back sleeping under Nimitz's desk. (Nimitz to Chet Nimitz, July 26, 1945, Chester Nimitz Papers, Center for Pacific War Studies, NMPW.)

An aerial shot of the headquarters complex on Fonte Plateau above Apra Harbor on the eastern side of Guam. While Nimitz, McMorris, and Sherman each occupied comfortable cottages on the crest of the hill, most of the staff took up quarters in Quonset huts. (U.S. Naval Institute)

nervous about Nimitz striding around on his own when there were still an unknown number of armed Japanese soldiers on the island, so he sent an armed Marine to guard him. Told he would be escorting the theater commander, the Marine wore his Class A uniform. Not long into the hike, it began to rain, and within minutes the Marine was a sodden mess. Nimitz stopped, asked him for his pistol, assured him he could defend himself if necessary, and ordered him back to his quarters. The pistol proved an inconvenient dead weight as the stalwart hikers marched on for the next two hours, during which the only danger they encountered was from traffic, with trucks and jeeps speeding past on various errands.[14]

Nimitz returned from that walk "soaked to the skin." Refreshed after a bath, he was just sitting down to the first meal in his new quarters when Rear Admiral John W. Reeves, who commanded one of the Fifth Fleet carrier groups, arrived to pay his respects. Of course Nimitz invited him to dinner. Nimitz had moved his headquarters four thousand miles in part to reduce the number of guests at his table, but as he wrote to Catherine that night, he could see that "there will be very few days when guests of one kind or another [will] not be with us." In fact, it was soon evident that, as in Hawaii, he could expect, as he put it, "a profusion of visitors from now on."[15]

ON THE SAME DAY NIMITZ ARRIVED in Guam, Spruance relieved Halsey in command of the Big Blue Fleet at Ulithi Atoll four hundred miles to the southwest. The Third Fleet once again became the Fifth Fleet. Nimitz was eager to visit Spruance. Indeed, the ability to do so quickly had been a main justification for moving his headquarters. To facilitate his travel, the Navy had provided him with a trio of new command aircraft, all of them modified two-engine DC-5s. Each had a private cabin with a table and two bunks so that he could either work or sleep en route to meetings, plus a separate section with seating for sixteen. Nimitz was enthusiastic about the planes and confided conspiratorially to Catherine that his plane had a bathroom that was "larger than the one in the SECNAV plane." The planes were distinguished from one another by their interior upholstery of gray, blue, and salmon. The first two were immediately christened the "Gray Goose" and the "Blue Goose," and the one with salmon upholstery, which Nimitz used as his command plane, became "the Pink Lady."[16]

On February 2, Nimitz and seven of his staff members boarded the Pink Lady for a two-and-a-half-hour flight to Ulithi. Once there, Nimitz, Sherman, and Lamar all slept on board Spruance's flagship Indianapolis, while the others berthed on the new battleship Missouri, anchored nearby. Spruance invited all the flag officers at Ulithi to a reception. With most of the Fifth Fleet in the lagoon, it was quite a crowd. Nimitz enjoyed seeing a number of old shipmates, and he was pleased to note that their morale appeared high and they were "looking forward to the next move with enthusiasm." Now reunited, Spruance and Nimitz went ashore, and the old hiking companions took a long walk during which they had what Nimitz called "a very satisfactory exchange of ideas" about the forthcoming campaign.[17]

Old walking companions, Nimitz and Spruance here walk the deck of Spruance's flagship, the heavy cruiser *Indianapolis*. Later, they went ashore on Mogmog Island to continue their discussion. (U.S. Naval Institute)

With MacArthur making rapid progress on Luzon, the prospects for Spruance's assault on Iwo Jima (Operation Detachment) were promising. He would command an armada of nine hundred ships including Mitscher's Task Force 58, now composed of five carrier groups with more than twelve hundred airplanes. Marine Corps Major General Harry Schmidt would command an invasion force of a hundred thousand men in four divisions (three Marine, one Army).[18]

Though Spruance had been an early advocate of invading Iwo Jima rather than Formosa, additional pressure to do so came from the Army Air Forces. Almost from the beginning of the war, the U.S. Army's air arm had sought a way to conduct a strategic bombing campaign against Japan's homeland, similar to the one being unleashed on Germany. The capture of the Mariana Islands provided the necessary airfields, and the champions of strategic bombing also had a new weapon to execute it. It was the Boeing B-29 Superfortress bomber, which could carry five thousand pounds of bombs more than three thousand miles at thirty thousand feet, which was above the effective range of Japanese fighters. Air Force leaders were confident that with this sleek new bomber and the super-secret Norden bombsight, which they believed could direct bombs to pinpoint targets, they could compel a Japanese surrender without having to invade the home islands.

In order to ensure that the B-29s focused on the strategic mission, Hap Arnold convinced the JCS that the planes should be exempt from oversight by the theater commanders. That meant that neither Nimitz nor MacArthur could order them to support their movements. On the other hand, the Navy had to support the bombers by positioning submarines as rescue boats, and by carrying from the States all the bombs, spare parts, and especially fuel used by the big airplanes. Each B-29 burned up 6,400 gallons of aviation fuel per round trip, and all of it had to be brought to Saipan from the United States by sea.[19]

Yet for all that, the initial B-29 raids against Japan, which began in November 1944, were disappointing. High winds and cloud cover over Japan rendered the highly touted Norden bombsight largely ineffective, and from thirty thousand feet, the bomb loads fell almost randomly over the Japanese countryside. By January when Nimitz moved into his Guam head-quarters, many objective observers considered the strategic bombing campaign to be, as one air group commander put it, "a complete failure."[20]

Seeking a way to change that dismal record, the Army Air Force decided to add fighter escorts to the bombing raids, though it was unclear how that would improve bombing accuracy. The problem was that even with external belly tanks, Army fighters like the P-51 Mustang could not make it to Tokyo and back from Saipan. They could, however, do so from Iwo Jima, whose capture came to be seen as a way to rescue the disappointing strategic bombing campaign. King, who had never favored the Iwo Jima option, groused that the "sole importance" of the island was to improve "the performance of the long range aircraft of the Army Air Corps," though an additional benefit was that Iwo could serve as an emergency landing field for crippled bombers returning from the raids.[21]

All that was grist to the conversation between Nimitz and Spruance as they walked together, first on board the *Indianapolis*, then ashore on Mogmog Island. Nimitz wanted the attack on Iwo Jima to be a tactical surprise, and a key question was how best to ensure that. Spruance suggested that the Japanese could be distracted by a carrier raid against their home islands a week before the invasion. In addition to providing a diversion, it could accomplish what the B-29s had not: wrecking the Japanese airplane factories near Tokyo. After all, Spruance declared, it was far better to destroy enemy airplanes on the factory floor than to confront them in battle. It might even reclaim the strategic bombing mission for the Navy. However Spruance framed it, Nimitz gave his approval.[22]

On February 11, the seventeen carriers of Task Force 58, escorted by battleships and cruisers, including Spruance's *Indianapolis*, headed north. After refueling at sea, they bypassed Iwo Jima and struck at Tokyo on the sixteenth. Japanese resistance was feeble. The Japanese had no shortage of airplanes, but they lacked both the fuel to propel them and the pilots to fly them. The real enemy that day, as Spruance described it, was the "extremely difficult flying conditions." Pilots returning from the strikes claimed the destruction of 350 enemy planes to 32 American planes lost, and they had also struck two airplane factories, thus claiming bragging rights over the B-29s. Still, heavy cloud cover made it difficult to determine the extent of the damage. With the weather showing no sign of improvement, Spruance called off additional strikes the next day and headed south to support the Iwo Jima landings, now only two days away.[23]

It was the first time planes from U.S. Navy carriers had hit the Japanese capital since the Doolittle Raid in April 1942, and Mitscher called it "the greatest air victory of the war." In a public statement, Nimitz proclaimed that Spruance's fleet had "achieved a decisive victory over the enemy," and

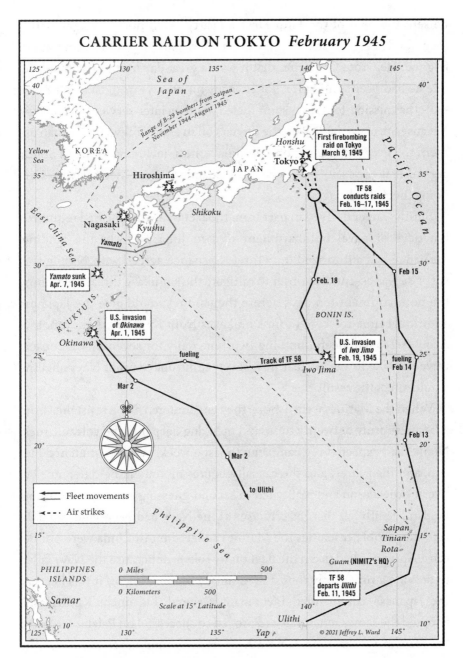

Map 14: Carrier Raid on Tokyo, February 1945

he sent the men of the Fifth Fleet a hearty "Well done," congratulating them for dealing the enemy "a crushing blow." Nimitz's enthusiasm was not feigned. He wrote Catherine that it was "a great day for the Pacific Fleet," one he had been waiting for "for so many months, years in fact." Yet for all that, the mission to Tokyo soon fueled another inter-service controversy. Because Spruance had taken the carriers off to attack Tokyo rather than use them to cover the landing on Iwo Jima, critics, including Holland Smith, argued that the Navy had once again abandoned the Marines who were doing the real fighting.[24]

Smith's anger derived in part from the fact that while he had requested ten days of naval bombardment of Iwo Jima prior to the landing, Spruance had authorized only three. Spruance agreed with Nimitz that surprise was essential in order to mitigate the kamikaze threat. Beginning the bombardment ten days before the landing would give the Japanese additional time to stage more kamikazes from Kyushu. Then, too, U.S. Army B-24s had been bombing Iwo Jima daily for seventy-two consecutive days, so it was unclear how seven additional days of Navy shelling would affect the result.

When the Marines went ashore, they encountered fierce resistance from a Japanese army of twenty thousand men dug deep into the volcanic rock. Nimitz had expected the campaign to last a week. When it stretched into two, and then three, and the casualty figures mounted, the difference between expectation and reality led to second-guessing and finger-pointing. Holland Smith felt that his criticism of the Navy had been vindicated. In fact, the terrible casualties the Marines suffered on Iwo Jima were not because Spruance had taken the fleet off to Tokyo, or because the Navy failed to provide a sufficiently robust preliminary bombardment. It was because the Japanese commander, Lieutenant General Tadamichi Kuribayashi, adopted the same tactics that had proved so successful on Peleliu: ordering his men to stay in their labyrinth of underground caves and force the Marines to come and get them. As on Peleliu, there was no alternative other than to fight the battle on the ground, yard by yard, and suffer the cost of having to kill virtually all of the defenders with grenades and flamethrowers. That explanation did not satisfy Smith, who remained disgruntled, though part of his dissatisfaction was because, as at Tarawa, he had to remain aboard Turner's flagship throughout the battle, and he spent much of that time brooding in his cabin.[25]

FEBRUARY 23, 1945, WAS A MILESTONE day on two fronts in the Pacific. On Luzon, MacArthur entered the wrecked and smoking ruins of the Philippine capital, Manila, where the Japanese had carried out a holocaust of murder and rape comparable to the German sacking of Warsaw half a world away. On that same day on Iwo Jima, a half dozen Marines replaced a small American flag on the crest of Mount Suribachi with a larger flag from an LST offshore. Associated Press photographer Joe Rosenthal captured the moment in an image that was destined to become both iconic and immortal. When he saw it, Nimitz asked Lamar to find out the names of the Marines and send copies of the photo to all their hometown newspapers.

The flag-raising did not mark the end of the violence. The next day, the Running Summary at Nimitz's headquarters reported that the Marines were still "encountering stiff enemy resistance." The enemy defenses, it noted, "including block houses, pillboxes, and caves were mutually supporting and built of concrete, in some instances four feet thick."[26]

February 24 was Nimitz's sixtieth birthday. It was the fourth birthday he had observed since becoming CinCPac. He received a number of gifts from family and friends, including several classical record albums from Catherine, a "lovely leather box" from Chet, a bottle of scotch from Bernard Austin, and "a whole box" of items from Sandy and Una Walker. In his thank-you note to the Walkers, he noted that their son Henry (nicknamed "Hanko"), with whom Nimitz had frequently gone fishing and sailing at Muliwai, was now a junior communications officer on the *Missouri* and had taken part in the Tokyo Raid. "How we all envy him the active participation in these interesting operations," Nimitz wrote. "With us back here in the safe rear area, life runs along smoothly, and we have settled into a routine of work—food—exercise—sleep & then repeat." It was characteristic of him to make light of the burden he bore, largely to soothe the concern of friends. It was not a measure of his emotional disengagement. As ever, his mind turned frequently to the men who were doing the "actual fighting."[27]

The next day, Secretary of the Navy Forrestal arrived in Guam after having visited Iwo Jima. Nimitz turned the morning staff meeting over to him, and Forrestal related what he had seen on Iwo Jima. He reported that progress was steady despite horrific conditions.

Four days later, Nimitz, Sherman, and the ever-present Lamar flew the eight thousand miles from Guam to Washington. At San Francisco, Catherine once again joined her husband for the cross-country trip. For three days in Washington, Nimitz met with the Joint Chiefs, briefing them on progress on Iwo Jima as well as plans for the imminent invasion of Okinawa. Looking beyond that, the Chiefs wanted to discuss the invasion of the Japanese homeland. Nimitz was a full participant in those talks, though he hoped and believed that an invasion would not be necessary. He was convinced that the loss of her empire, the interdiction of her supply lines (mostly by American submarines), and the destruction of her cities by American bombers would compel a surrender before an invasion was needed.

While in Washington, Nimitz had lunch with the president in the White House. He was shocked to see how rapidly Roosevelt had declined since their last meeting—his gray pallor and slurred speech were an unmistakable harbinger of his approaching mortality. Nimitz did not support many of the president's domestic initiatives, yet he admired both his diplomatic prowess and his stalwart support of the Navy. His loss would be devastating.

On a much happier note, Nimitz's brief presence in Washington allowed him to be present at his daughter Kate's marriage to James Lay, a Navy officer to whom she had been engaged for some time. It had not been scheduled for that week, but with both of her parents in D.C., Kate decided that it was an opportunity not to be missed. The young couple were wed in the Fairfax Hotel suite where her parents were staying. Later, Nimitz wrote her to tell her that both he and Catherine had "high regard and great esteem for our son-in-law. You could not have picked anyone we could like more." He wished them "a long and wonderful life, just as Mother's and mine has been."[28]

By mid-March, Nimitz was back in Guam, where the usual pile of mail and dispatches waited for him. Among them were too many letters like those he had received after Tarawa signed "A Marine Mother," holding him responsible for the death of a son on Iwo Jima. It was sufficiently painful that it led Nimitz to review his decisions. Could he have done anything differently to minimize the losses? "I am just as distressed as can be over the casualties," he wrote to Catherine, "but don't see how I could have reduced them."[29]

The Marines on Iwo Jima eventually secured the island. On March 16, the day after Nimitz returned to Guam, he announced publicly that "the Battle of Iwo Jima has been won," though, in fact, pockets of resistance on the island were still being overcome. He visited the island a week later, on March 24, and was appalled by its desolate landscape worthy of Dante's *Inferno*. "Iwo must be seen to be appreciated," he wrote Catherine. There was not a single growing thing on the island, and sulfuric steam issued from vents in the ubiquitous volcanic dust. Within minutes of landing, Nimitz and his entire party were covered with black dust so thick that "we all looked like coal heavers." He went forward to observe some fighting in a ravine where two hundred or so Japanese soldiers were still holding out. On the plane back to Guam, he mused, "By now they are all dead or sealed up in caves where death will come soon."[30]

The cost of the victory had been staggering. American casualties totaled 26,038, with 6,821 killed. Japanese numbers are less certain, but most authorities agree 19,000 soldiers were killed, with another thousand taken prisoner. It was the only battle of the Pacific war in which the Americans suffered more total casualties than the Japanese. Afterward, the president awarded twenty-seven Medals of Honor to veterans of Iwo Jima—twenty-two of them to Marines, and fourteen of those posthumously. Almost certainly that represented only a fraction of the total number of heroic deeds performed on that barren volcanic island. As Nimitz said in his March 16 communiqué, "Among the Americans who served on Iwo Island, uncommon valor was a common virtue."[31]

OKINAWA WAS NEXT. Indeed, it was almost a seamless transition from one campaign to the other given that Mitscher's carriers began a series of air strikes on Okinawa even as the fighting on Iwo Jima continued. Those air strikes were so persistent and relentless that within a few days the Japanese stopped sounding the air raid alarm.[1]

Okinawa is the largest of the Ryukyu Islands, which extend southward from Kyushu like the tail of a kite. It is a long and narrow island: sixty-six miles north to south, and only three to fifteen miles wide. Still, at 463 square miles, it was the largest island the Fifth Fleet had targeted so far. It had a civilian population of as many as half a million, and the largest Japanese garrison outside the Philippines: 75,000 soldiers—three times as many as on Iwo Jima—plus another 20,000 local militia. Though the native population on Okinawa was not ethnically Japanese, the island had been formally annexed by Japan in 1879 and was considered one of the five home islands. Thus when the Americans landed, it would mark the first time an enemy boot desecrated Nippon's sacred soil.[2]

The armada assembled for the invasion (code-named Operation Iceberg) was enormous. It was, in fact, the largest naval fleet ever assembled, outstripping in combat power the invasion fleets for both Normandy and the Marianas. In addition to Mitscher's seventeen carriers and Willis Lee's eight "fast" battleships, Turner commanded another ten battleships for fire support. Turner also commanded 433 transport and cargo ships loaded with equipment and supplies. The landing force consisted of five combat divisions (three Army and two Marine) of what was labeled the Tenth Army. Because the soldiers outnumbered the Marines, the overall ground commander was an Army lieutenant general. Simon Bolivar Buckner was certainly aware of the pitfalls of exercising effective joint command, since he had presided over the board that Richardson had assembled the year before to evaluate the Smith vs. Smith Controversy.[*]

The size and complexity of Iceberg created more than the usual number of logistical puzzles for Nimitz and his staff. Troop ships and cargo ships would load up at Ulithi, Guam, and Saipan. Hundreds more embarked at Eniwetok, Leyte, the Russell Islands, and even the West Coast of the United States, more than seven thousand miles away. Coordinating all those various elements was challenging. The success of any invasion depends on the timely arrival of reinforcements and supplies, so post-invasion support convoys had to be scheduled to depart at planned intervals. Those from the West Coast would leave every ten days for as long as the operation lasted. Steaming at an average speed of 10 knots and zigzagging most of the way, it took a California convoy twenty-six to thirty days to get to Okinawa; then, after unloading, it had to steam back again. At any given moment, therefore, there could be as many as six California convoys at sea at the same time— three laden convoys heading west, and three more empty convoys heading east—with all of them requiring escorts.[3]

It became clear at once that the invasion of Okinawa would absorb virtually all of the available shipping in the Pacific Theater. American shipyards

---

[*] Buckner's father, also named Simon Bolivar Buckner, had been a Confederate general, and MacArthur's father had been a Union officer. In those two families there was but a single generation between the Civil War and World War II.

turned out 2,710 Liberty ships and another thousand so-called Victory ships during the war. Even so, the logistical demands of Iceberg threatened to outstrip supply. Some of the units and equipment designated for the first wave had to be bumped to the second or third wave, and of course every such change had a ripple effect among the hundreds of planners working in scores of offices across Nimitz Hill.[4]

Nevertheless, by the end of March, just two weeks after Nimitz announced victory on Iwo Jima, some 1,300 ships carrying 180,000 soldiers and Marines plus three-quarters of a million tons of supplies were assembled off the western beaches of Okinawa. With the near-annihilation of the Imperial Japanese Navy, the greatest threat to that fleet came from kamikaze attacks from Kyushu, five hundred miles to the north, and from Formosa, four hundred miles to the south. As if to demonstrate that, on March 31, the eve of D-Day, a lone kamikaze came almost straight down out of the clouds and smashed into the fantail of Spruance's flagship, *Indianapolis*. The bomb it carried tore through the hull and exploded underneath the ship. The damage was too great for a local repair, and Spruance and his staff had to transfer to the older battleship *New Mexico* while the *Indianapolis* limped back to the United States.[†]

At 5:30 the next morning, Easter Sunday, the *New Mexico* was one of ten battleships—plus nine cruisers and twenty-three destroyers—that opened up on the landing beaches. They fired nearly fifty thousand shells and more than thirty thousand rockets in the heaviest concentration of pre-invasion naval gunfire during the war. When the bombardment lifted, planes from Mitscher's carriers swooped in to saturate the beaches with napalm. At 8:00 a.m. the landing craft began heading for the shore, the 1st and 6th Marine Divisions on the left, and the 7th and 96th Army Divisions on the right.[5]

BACK ON GUAM, NIMITZ FOLLOWED EVENTS by reading the lengthy and detailed reports sent in by Kelly Turner. From the first of them he learned that the invaders encountered only "very light opposition" during the landing.

---

† The presence of the *Indianapolis* on the West Coast that summer is why it subsequently got the assignment to carry the atomic bombs from California to Tinian.

In fact, there was almost no opposition at all. That was certainly good news. It was also puzzling. Later that day, Turner reported that the troops were advancing inland "standing up." As Robert Sherrod of *Time* magazine wrote, "Nothing stranger has occurred in the Pacific war than the Tenth U.S. Army landings on Okinawa."[6]

The explanation for this mystery was that the Japanese commander, Mitsuru Ushijima, had made a deliberate decision not to contest the landings. Adopting the tactics that had frustrated the Americans on both Peleliu and Iwo Jima, he concentrated his defenses in the southern half of the island around a fourteenth-century Shinto shrine known as Shuri Castle (see Map 15). There, in an elaborate warren of caves and tunnels surrounded by tank traps and mine fields, Ushijima put his best troops and ordered them to fight to the death.[7]

For now, though, the news from Turner was reassuring. The invaders had seized the principal airfield at Yonton and were crossing the narrow waist of the island against "negligible resistance." On April 3, they reached Okinawa's eastern shore, effectively cutting the island in half. That night, Nimitz wrote Catherine that "the Okinawa operation is going along splendidly and with light losses so far." He also told her that he suspected the real fighting still lay ahead.[8]

Meanwhile, he carried on with the other aspects of his job. As always, he sought to keep tabs on the various elements of his headquarters command. At Pearl Harbor, he had walked from office to office; on Guam he drove. He kept a jeep outside his headquarters office, and when the paperwork slacked off, he would ask his orderly to drive him to one or another unit. Sometimes he drove himself. A signalman whose office was halfway up a tower that overlooked Apra Harbor recalled watching a jeep coming down to the base of the tower. As it got closer, he could see that the driver was Nimitz, in khaki shorts and an open-collar shirt. The jeep stopped at the base of the tower, and Nimitz climbed the stairs to the platform. "He would say hello to us," the signalman recalled, "and then go digging around in the cabinets looking for his coffee cup." Coffee in hand, he then took a spot by the telescope in the corner to look around the harbor "just to see what was going on."[9]

Such opportunities were relatively few, however. Visitors continued to arrive. In early April, a dozen labor leaders showed up. Nimitz welcomed the visit despite the timing because he knew their support was crucial for military success. For the most part, organized labor did not strike during the war, especially at defense plants, though there were exceptions. The most notorious was the United Mine Workers strike in May 1943, which had so angered Roosevelt that he ordered the Army to take over the mines and threatened to draft the mineworkers. The defiant miners declared, "You can't dig coal with bayonets." In the end a compromise ended the strike. More such labor stoppages could disrupt the supply chain that sustained the war effort. Nimitz hoped to co-opt the labor leaders by showing them how critical it was to maintain a secure and reliable line of supply, thus making them partners in the war effort. He even referred to them in a letter to Catherine as "my Labor Leaders," telling her that "they are most appreciative of the friendly reception they have had here, and I am confident the visit will help us."[10]

After they left, an equally large group of congressmen arrived. A subcommittee of the House Naval Affairs Committee, the group included Nimitz's Texas hill country neighbor Lyndon Johnson. The congressmen all stayed in Nimitz's house, though since there weren't enough beds, some of them slept on cots. "These visits do take my time," he wrote to Catherine, "but as I think they will help the Navy, we will do our best for them."[11]

There were more visitors after that, "a string of them," Nimitz reported to Catherine: "French correspondents, trade magazine publishers, newspaper publishers, etc." In an effort to limit such visits, Nimitz issued an instruction that all applications to travel to Guam should be disapproved unless the visit directly supported ongoing operations. It had little effect. A month later he sent another, nearly identical message restricting visits to "those whose presence is necessary for the prosecution of the war."[12]

Secretary of the Navy Forrestal was exempt from Nimitz's edicts, of course, and in furtherance of his campaign to elevate the Navy's public profile, he issued hundreds of passes and free transportation to reporters, publishers, and editors, who regularly showed up at Nimitz's headquarters. Nimitz found most of them "interesting but time consuming." He went out of his way to accommodate them when he could, though Forrestal was no doubt horrified to learn that Nimitz had rejected a request by Henry Luce, publisher of the two most popular magazines in the country, *Time* and *Life*, to visit Okinawa, declaring that it was "impracticable to authorize [a] visit to Okinawa at this time by Mr. Luce."[13]

Another one of Forrestal's initiatives that Nimitz resisted was the secretary's insistence that in order to boost morale—and the Navy's public profile—he should produce both a daily newspaper and a weekly magazine. Forrestal was frustrated by the more robust publicity being secured by the Army and Army Air Forces. Nimitz told Catherine that although Forrestal was "hell bent" on his producing a newspaper, he found the idea absurd. He was perfectly willing to provide the necessary information, and he was dedicated to ensuring that the men at the front got regular newspapers and magazines from home, but writing, editing, publishing, and distributing both a newspaper and a magazine was, in his view, "just too much when we are trying to run a war." Forrestal marked it down as another example of Nimitz's uncooperativeness.[14]

Meanwhile, there was alarming news from Okinawa. Five days after the American landing, the Japanese unleashed a massive kamikaze attack against the invasion fleet. Mitscher had raided the airfields in southern Kyushu in March in an effort to suppress the number of planes the Japanese had for such attacks. His pilots had claimed the destruction of more than five hundred Japanese planes, most of them on the ground. Nevertheless, on April 6, some seven hundred planes, half of them kamikazes, assailed Spruance's Fifth Fleet. Hundreds were shot down and others crashed into the sea, but twenty-six ships were hit, some of them by multiple kamikazes. The destroyers that were assigned to picket duty as an early warning system took the brunt of that attack. Three of them were sunk and ten others damaged. The kamikazes also sank two Victory ships, a minesweeper, and an LST. Given the size of the attack, though, it could have been worse. "If this is the best the enemy can throw at us," Turner opined, "we can sustain our losses." Indeed, the light opposition ashore and the failure of the kamikazes to do more serious damage made Turner almost giddy. "I MAY BE CRAZY," he wrote to Nimitz in an all-caps message, "BUT I THINK THE JAPS

HAVE QUIT THE WAR AT LEAST FOR THE TIME BEING." Nimitz wrote back: "Delete all after 'crazy.' "[15]

Of course, the Japanese had not quit the war. The kamikazes returned on April 12, April 16, and April 21, each time claiming more ships. By the end of the month, the attrition had become alarming. Turner changed his tune, writing, "The losses incurred to date have made this situation even more critical." The Japanese hoped it would compel the Americans to call off the invasion, though Nimitz never considered that.[16]

Japanese admirals, meanwhile, were embarrassed, if not humiliated, that while the Imperial Army was fighting to the death on land and kamikaze pilots were sacrificing their lives in the air, the massive *Yamato* sat idly at anchor in the Inland Sea. More out of pride than with any expectation of affecting the battle, they ordered her to sea on April 7 along with an escort of a light cruiser and eight destroyers, practically all the combat ships that were left. It was a futile, suicidal gesture, evident from the fact that she sailed with only 60 percent of her fuel capacity. Her commander was supposed to run the *Yamato* aground on the island, expend all his ammunition against targets of opportunity, and then order surviving crewmembers to go ashore and join the ground battle. It was an absurd scenario. Without air cover it was all but certain the *Yamato* would never make it to Okinawa. When a report of her approach reached Mitscher, he flashed a message to Spruance: "Shall you take them or shall I?" Spruance responded, "You take them."[17]

And he did. That afternoon (April 7) the *Yamato* became the focus of hundreds of American bombers and torpedo planes. Struck by dozens of bombs and torpedoes, the *Yamato* absorbed brutal punishment until 2:30 p.m., when she spectacularly exploded, the black cloud from the blast rising twenty thousand feet into the air. That cloud marked the end of the Imperial Japanese Navy. "Wasn't it grand news?" Nimitz wrote to Catherine. He wondered how the members of the Japanese cabinet would react. "I'll wager the new Cabinet at Tokyo feels lots worse than I did on 25 Dec. 41 when I arrived at P.H. to take over the Fleet."[18]

Throughout the fighting at sea and ashore, Nimitz maintained close oversight of other units in his enormous command theater. He sought to sustain goodwill with MacArthur by sending him formal thanks for the support his bombers provided in attacking Japanese airfields on Formosa, and he expressed thanks to Bruce Fraser, commander of the British Pacific Fleet, for its contributions. King had fought hard to keep the Royal Navy out of the Pacific altogether; having failed in that, he had mandated that it be assigned tasks ancillary to the main effort. Nimitz gave the British the job of suppressing Japanese airfields on the islands south of Okinawa, as well as on Formosa. British planes flew 4,691 sorties against those targets, and Nimitz sent his praise and thanks for their support.[19]

TWO DAYS LATER AND EIGHT THOUSAND miles away in Warm Springs, Georgia, Franklin Roosevelt was sitting for a portrait when he told the artist, "I have a terrible pain in the back of my head," and slumped in his chair. He never regained consciousness and was pronounced dead later

The Japanese super-battleship *Yamato* explodes in a giant fireball on April 7, 1945.
Her destruction marked the virtual end of the once dominant Imperial Japanese Navy.
(Naval History and Heritage Command)

that day. Nimitz got the news when he awoke on April 13. "I for one feel a deep sense of personal loss," he wrote to Catherine. He knew that not everyone in his family agreed with FDR's policies, but the president had always been a strong champion of the Navy and "always most cordial and friendly to me." "Truman faces a most stupendous task," he wrote, "and I hope and pray he will be well advised and guided."[20]

To the fleet, he issued a general message: "The world has lost a champion of democracy who can ill be spared by our country and the Allied cause. The Navy which he so dearly loved can pay no better tribute to his memory than to carry on in the tradition of which he was so proud." The firing of salutes, he added, would be dispensed with "in view of war conditions."[21]

ONCE THE AMERICAN INVADERS HAD CUT Okinawa in half, the two Marine divisions turned north, and the two Army divisions turned south. The Marines made rapid progress and within a week had secured the northern two-thirds of the island. The Army divisions, however, ran smack into Ushijima's citadel of caves and tunnels near Shuri Castle. It was not a surprise. Based on aerial photographs, Mitscher had described the area to Turner as "honeycombed with caves, tunnels and gun positions." His pilots reported seeing tanks and trucks actually driving into the cave entrances. Turner relayed that information to Spruance and to Nimitz, telling them that the Japanese held "strong defensive positions in depth." As Army Major General John R. Hodge put it, "I see no way to get them out except blast them out yard by yard."[22]

Buckner sought to do exactly that. On April 19, following an air assault and what the U.S. Army official history called "the greatest concentration of artillery ever employed in the Pacific War," all three Army divisions, including the 27th, which had been at the center of the controversy on Saipan, assailed Japanese positions near Shuri Castle. For five days the fighting was nearly continuous. The Americans were supported by gunfire from three battleships and three heavy cruisers offshore, yet Japanese defenses were such that the Americans could advance only a few yards at a time.[23]

By then, the battle for Okinawa was nearly a month old and seemed likely to last another month—at least. That was worrisome not only because of the

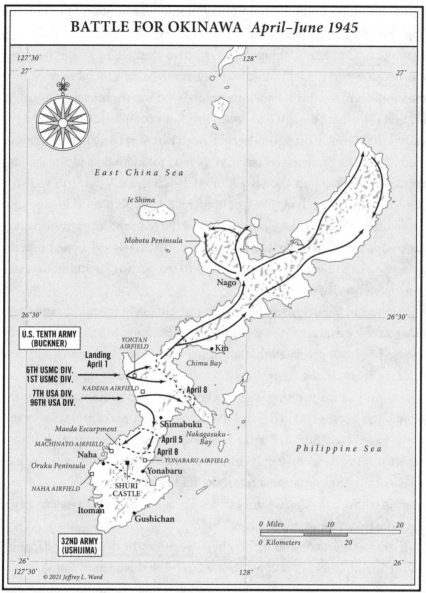

MAP 15: Battle for Okinawa, April–June 1945

casualties on the ground but also because it kept Spruance's ships loitering off the coast, where they remained vulnerable to the relentless attacks of the kamikazes.

In the midst of all this, Nimitz received a visit from Archer Vandegrift, Commandant of the Marine Corps. Nimitz greeted him warmly and invited him to stay in his home. When Vandegrift said that he planned to visit the front on Okinawa, however, Nimitz told him no. Partly it was because, as he wrote to Catherine, "things are very active up there now," but mainly it was because Nimitz did not want a four-star Marine general looking over the shoulder of the three-star Army general who was running the campaign. He told King that he wanted to avoid "invidious comparisons" between the Army and Marine Corps. Vandegrift flew to Iwo Jima to inspect operations there. When he returned on April 21, Nimitz told him he had changed his mind. He was going to Okinawa himself, he said, and Vandegrift was welcome to come along. It may be that upon reflection, Nimitz decided against peremptorily keeping the Commandant of the Marine Corps from visiting his troops in the field. In addition, however, he likely calculated that his presence as a five-star admiral was likely to temper any latent inter-service tension such a visit might create.[24]

Nimitz and Vandegrift arrived at Yonton Airfield in the middle of yet another kamikaze attack. While Nimitz thought the island itself was "really lovely," he also appreciated that capturing it would be a long and ugly slog since, as he put it, the enemy was "cleverly dug in and never expose themselves." Still, at his meeting with Buckner, he urged him to accelerate the ground war because every day that passed risked the loss of more Navy ships to the kamikazes. Buckner replied somewhat stiffly that tactical decisions ashore were an Army matter. Nimitz acknowledged that. Still, in an uncharacteristically confrontational retort, he told Buckner that "if this line isn't moving within five days, we'll get someone here to move it so we can all get out from under these stupid air attacks."[25]

There was discussion about how best to employ the two Marine divisions on the island. Buckner said he planned to bring them south to join in the assault on Shuri Castle. Vandegrift suggested that the Marines could execute an amphibious landing on the south coast of Okinawa behind Japanese lines. Buckner replied that his staff had explored that option, but the southern coastline was dominated by sheer cliffs and it would be difficult, if not impossible, to get ashore there. Even if it could be done, the Marines were likely to be trapped there in "another Anzio"—a reference to the Allied effort the year before to get around German defenses in Italy. That gambit not only had failed but had trapped the invaders in a bloody cul-de-sac for months. After some discussion, Nimitz accepted Buckner's analysis and approved his plan to bring the Marines south, though he reiterated the importance of "early results."[26]

Instead of early results, the front remained mostly static and the damage to ships continued. On May 11, two kamikazes hit Mitscher's flagship, *Bunker Hill*. The big flattop survived, but Mitscher had to transfer his flag to the *Enterprise*. Three days later, the *Enterprise*, too, was hit. Mitscher transferred again, this time to the *Randolph*. Spruance himself nearly became a casualty on May 12, when a kamikaze crashed into the bridge of the *New Mexico*. Spruance had been on his way to the bridge when he heard the anti-aircraft batteries open up, and he stopped. Had he continued, he likely would have become a casualty.[27]

Army Lieutenant General Simon Bolivar Buckner commanded the U.S. Tenth Army on Okinawa. Reluctant as Nimitz was to micromanage commanders in the field, he pressed Buckner to bring the campaign to a swift conclusion to halt the kamikaze attacks on American ships offshore. (U.S. Naval Institute)

In an attempt to destroy the kamikazes at the source, Nimitz ordered Mitscher to renew the air strikes on Kyushu. He also reached out to Curtis LeMay, commander of the 21st Bomber Command, to ask if he was willing to use his B-29s to hit the Kyushu airfields. LeMay had arrived on Guam the same week Nimitz did and initially had been unimpressed with the Navy way of doing things. He was annoyed, for example, that the Seabees seemed to spend more time building recreation centers "and every other damn thing," rather than focusing on his air bases. He was also surprised by what he saw when Nimitz invited him to dinner. At the time, LeMay was still living in a tent, and when he showed up at the designated time, he found "a splendid house, way up on the highest peak of the island," where the guests were supplied with "cocktails and highballs and hors d'oeuvres such as you might find at an embassy in Washington."[28‡]

LeMay was not officially in Nimitz's chain of command and did not have to take orders from him about what to target. Still, when Nimitz asked him to divert at least some of the B-29s to the Kyushu airfields "on an emergency basis," he agreed to do it. Over the next several weeks the high-flying bombers cratered the airfields. It did not, however, stop the kamikazes. The Japanese simply pulled the airplanes off the runways and hid them in the trees. After a few weeks of this, LeMay went to Nimitz and told him, "Look, we have done everything we can do. Turn us loose so we can go back to our primary mission." According to LeMay, Nimitz threw an arm around his shoulders and said, "Yes, you have done a fine job. I agree with you, but let's check with Sherman." Nimitz knew full well what Sherman's reaction would be. He not only said no, he said "Hell, no." So the B-29s kept at it for another few weeks until, as LeMay put it, "there was nothing left to bomb." Yet the kamikaze attacks continued.[29]

On the ground, the constant pressure against the Japanese citadel around Shuri Castle finally compelled Ushijima to order a staged retreat to another defensive line farther south. He executed a stealthy evacuation on the night

---

‡ Sometime later, LeMay invited Nimitz to dinner at his HQ and, to make a point, had him stand in the chow line with everyone else. Nimitz took the point and was gracious about it.

of May 27. That same night, at precisely midnight, Halsey relieved Spruance in command of the Fifth Fleet, which once again became the Third Fleet. Spruance had commanded it during four months of virtually continuous combat: the raid on Tokyo, the invasion of Iwo Jima, and now the campaign on Okinawa. He had endured relentless kamikaze attacks, including two strikes on his own flagship. Though Spruance had maintained his Zen-like demeanor throughout, Nimitz, a stoic himself, understood the strain his colleague was under, and he decided to rotate the command team now instead of waiting until the island was declared secure. Spruance did not protest, which suggests that for all his composure, he was worn down if not actually worn out. The change of command took place in the midst of yet another prolonged kamikaze attack. Afterward, Spruance headed for Guam to occupy a guest room in Nimitz's house.[30]

BY THEN, THE WAR IN EUROPE WAS OVER. Hitler had killed himself in the Führer Bunker on April 30, and representatives of the German Army, acting under orders from Hitler's designated successor, Admiral Karl Dönitz, met with Allied representatives in Reims on May 7 to sign an instrument of surrender. Nimitz was elated. He hoped that the arrival of more Allied support from that theater would allow him "to turn full blast on Japan."[31]

First, however, he had to deal with yet another issue involving Halsey, who had been back in command for barely a week before he was again victimized by a major typhoon. Nimitz had defended Halsey's questionable behavior during the first typhoon back in December, attributing his decisions to determination rather than negligence. It was harder to make that case when it happened a second time. The chain of events began on June 3 when Nimitz ordered Halsey to use the Third Fleet carriers (TF 38), now commanded by Slew McCain, to conduct raids against "Japanese naval and air forces, shipping, shipyards, and coastal objectives." The goal, Nimitz told Halsey, was "to maintain and extend unremitting military pressure against Japan." Halsey was just the man to do it.[32]

Two days later, Halsey was preparing to carry out those raids when some of his task group commanders requested permission to change course to the east—that is, away from the Japanese coast—to avoid an approaching storm. Halsey turned them down. "Do not approve of going east," he radioed, "which will only keep us in front of storm area." Instead he ordered a course to the northwest. That was closer to the targets in Japan, but it also took the fleet directly into the path of the storm. The winds increased to 120 knots, and the smaller ships began rolling dangerously. The task group commanders appealed to McCain, who referred the question to Halsey. He ordered everyone to maintain position.[33]

The storm lasted for two days, and once again the Third Fleet took a terrible beating. On a few of the big carriers, the steel beams supporting the flight decks gave way; the bow of the heavy cruiser *Pittsburgh* was completely ripped off. She managed to stay afloat, though she had to avoid colliding with her own bow. Altogether, a total of thirty-two ships were severely damaged. As before, the losses were the equivalent of a major defeat. Halsey blamed it on the lack of "accurate and timely [weather] information," and because of that, he declared, "I can not accept responsibility."[34]

The court of inquiry disagreed. This time, it recommended that both Halsey and McCain should be assigned to other duties—essentially dismissed from their commands. Navy secretary Forrestal was prepared to compel Halsey to retire from the Navy altogether. With King's support, Nimitz intervened. He argued that Halsey was so closely associated with the war against Japan that to retire him now not only would be a personal humiliation, but would hurt the war effort. Halsey was spared, and McCain became the scapegoat. He was relieved of duty and ordered back to the United States to become deputy head of the Veterans Administration. He never actually took up that job. Only a few days after the end of the war, he died of a heart attack. He was sixty-one. His friends insisted that he died of a broken heart.[35]

MEANWHILE, THE INTERMINABLE CAMPAIGN ON OKINAWA provoked criticism in the press. One critic was Homer Bigart of the *New York Herald Tribune*, a respected veteran reporter who had filed stores from London during the Blitz, ridden B-17 bombers over Germany, and reported from North Africa, Italy, and southern France. Now in the Pacific, he heard from many on Okinawa, including a number of Marines, that Japanese resistance there could be quickly overcome by conducting an amphibious landing on the south coast of the island. The *Herald Tribune,* a Republican paper, printed Bigart's criticism, and, based on his reporting, the columnist David Lawrence wrote a syndicated editorial about the "faulty" tactics being employed on Okinawa. Quoting at length from Bigart's reports, Lawrence declared that "an amphibious operation should have taken place." Nimitz had failed to order it, Lawrence surmised, mainly because of "the custom" of "letting the local commander" make all the decisions. Whatever the reason, Lawrence concluded, the circumstances warranted a formal inquiry "by some competent military tribunal."[36]

Nimitz might have ignored criticism of himself, but Lawrence doubled down. In subsequent columns he declared that Okinawa was a "fiasco" that was "a worse example of military incompetence than Pearl Harbor." Such claims had the potential to drive a wedge between Army and Marine Corps leaders. Nimitz had fought hard, often against strong political headwinds and in the face of tribal allegiances, to sustain a joint command system in which soldiers and Marines worked together, or at least cooperated. Determined that nothing should undermine that, Nimitz felt obligated to respond to Lawrence's accusations.[37]

He called a rare press conference for all the reporters on Guam, at which he offered a full-throated defense of Buckner's command leadership. He issued a lengthy statement in which he declared that Lawrence was "badly misinformed" about Okinawa—so misinformed, Nimitz asserted, that it was possible he was being used by others who did not have "the best interests of the United States" at heart. Nimitz told the reporters that he had personally flown to Okinawa and had discussed the idea of an amphibious attack with Buckner. They had agreed that such landings "would have involved heavy casualties and would have created unacceptable supply problems." Buckner's decision not to do it, he said, "had my concurrence and that of the senior naval commanders." More generally, Nimitz proclaimed that the kind of comparison that Lawrence made between the services was "out of place and ill-advised." "Malicious gossip should not be permitted to undermine the confidence of our people in the fighting service or the pride and confidence fighting men here in the Pacific have in each other."[38]

Lawrence was taken aback by the intensity of Nimitz's response. He expressed "the highest respect and admiration" for Nimitz and asserted that all he had done was summarize what others, including Bigart, had reported. For his part, Bigart confirmed that he still believed "a landing on the south of the island would have been a better employment of the marines." He also said that Lawrence's use of the word "fiasco" was "absurd." He had been at Anzio, Bigart wrote, and knew what a fiasco looked like.[39]

The unseemly public squabble might have continued, but on the same day that Nimitz's statement and Lawrence's reply appeared in the *New York Times*, Buckner himself was killed on the front line. Creeping up to a forward observation post, he was peering out between two boulders when a Japanese artillery shell smashed into one of the boulders, killing him. Buckner was the highest-ranking American officer killed by enemy fire during World War II. His death ended the public controversy: now that he was a martyr, no one had any appetite for accusing him of tactical errors.

Within days, the campaign for Okinawa was over. Ushijima killed himself three days after Buckner died. Marine Corps Lieutenant General Roy Geiger completed the conquest of the island. It had been grueling. Both the Army (4,675 killed) and Marines (2,928 killed) had suffered terribly, yet due to the kamikazes, mortal casualties among Navy personnel (4,907) were greater than either. The numbers paled in comparison to Japanese losses (more than 90,000 killed), plus the death of as many as 150,000 Okinawa civilians. Many feared that it was a foretaste of what to expect in an invasion of the Japanese home islands.[40]

THE SAME DAY BUCKNER WAS KILLED on Okinawa, President Harry S. Truman wrote in his diary, "I have to decide Japanese strategy, shall we invade Japan proper or shall we bomb and blockade?" Truman had put his finger squarely on the key question. Having advanced the breadth of the Pacific Ocean, U.S. forces had arrived on Japan's doorstep. Would it be necessary now to invade the homeland? Or could Japan be compelled to surrender by cutting the island nation off from the outside world, starving her of imports, and bombing her cities? There was no doubt how Nimitz would answer that question. When he had discussed end-of-the-war strategy with King in San Francisco, they had agreed that an invasion of Japan was "not necessary" and that it would be far better to—as Truman put it—"bomb and blockade."[1]

In the wake of the fighting on both Iwo Jima and Okinawa, Nimitz's opposition to an invasion had hardened. On May 25, with the battle for Okinawa at full flood, he sent an "eyes only" message to King arguing that "where Japanese troops occupy prepared defenses," American forces could advance "only slowly" while suffering "numerous casualties." It was "unrealistic," he wrote, to think that Japanese soldiers would fight any less hard for the homeland than they were fighting now for Okinawa. Besides, he wrote, an invasion was unnecessary because once he released Task Force 38 from responsibility for covering Okinawa it would conduct raids along Japan's coast. That would augment the pressure already being applied to Japan's economy by American submarines and aerial bombing. Collectively, the subs, carriers, and bombers could ensure "the complete destruction of Japanese industry and shipping." "I believe that the long range interests of the U.S. will be better served," he concluded, "if we continue to isolate Japan & to destroy Jap forces & resources by naval and air attack."[2]

Not everyone in Washington agreed. The day after Truman made his diary entry, he met with the Joint Chiefs as well as his two service secretaries, Forrestal and Stimson, plus Assistant Secretary of War John J. McCloy, to discuss the next step. Marshall was ready with a recommendation. The plan, he told the new president, was to invade Kyushu (Operation Olympic) in November, and then Honshu (Operation Coronet) in the spring of 1946. It was, he said, "the least costly" option. Truman wanted to know just how "costly" it was likely to be. Marshall was equivocal. He suggested that losses might mirror those on Luzon, which were 31,000. Leahy challenged that. American losses on Okinawa, he pointed out, had been 35 percent, and applying that percentage to the proposed Kyushu invasion force of 766,000 would produce a number much larger than 31,000. Marshall rejected the analogy. On Okinawa, he said, the character of Japanese defenses had made it necessary to pry the enemy out of their caves. Kyushu would be a battle of maneuver and firepower, which would give the advantage to the Americans.[3]

Like Nimitz, King had never favored an invasion of the home islands. In his post-war memoir, he wrote that "naval officers in general," including himself, had "always" believed that "the defeat of Japan could be accomplished by sea and air power alone." And yet at the June 18 meeting, he expressed conditional support for Marshall's plan to invade Kyushu. He was more guarded about following that up with an invasion of Honshu. At the end of the discussion, when Truman asked if the minutes should reflect that the Joint Chiefs agreed unanimously that an invasion was the best option, King remained silent. When Truman asked if that was also the view of the Pacific commanders—MacArthur and Nimitz—the Joint Chiefs assured him that it was. While that was certainly true of MacArthur, who strongly advocated "a direct attack on the Japanese mainland," King knew full well that it was not true of Nimitz, though he again remained silent. The final official record of the meeting, therefore, indicated that everyone present agreed that "invading and seizing objectives in the Japanese home islands would be the main effort," though "sea and air blockades of Japan were to be maintained."[4]

Roosevelt had declared back in December that Douglas MacArthur would exercise Supreme Allied command of any invasion of Japan. Rather than express satisfaction at that designation, MacArthur proposed a different arrangement: "I do not recommend a single unified command," he wrote Marshall. "I am of the firm opinion that the Naval forces should serve under Naval Command and that the Army should serve under Army command."[5]

On April 3, the Joint Chiefs adopted MacArthur's proposal, designating him as Commander in Chief, U.S. Army Forces, Pacific, which yielded the acronym CINCAFPAC. Nimitz would retain command of naval forces and his original acronym of CINCPAC. Under the new arrangement, MacArthur and Nimitz would command only the forces of their own services. Nimitz would gain control of the Seventh Fleet, but he would lose oversight of Army forces, including Army Air Forces, within his command theater. MacArthur wanted the change to take place without delay, while Nimitz believed that it should be done—if indeed it had to be done at all—slowly and carefully.[6]

To work out the details, MacArthur sent Sutherland and Kenney to Nimitz's headquarters in Guam. As usual, Nimitz welcomed them warmly and invited them to stay in his house. The ensuing discussions, however, quickly stalled. Sutherland informed Nimitz that MacArthur would take command of all Army units in the Pacific "as soon as possible," adding, somewhat gratuitously, that the previous command arrangement had been "unsatisfactory" from the start, and that the whole idea of a joint command was a "shibboleth"—useful mainly to distinguish tribal loyalties. Once Okinawa was secured, Sutherland declared, Army troops would no longer be allowed to serve under an admiral.[7]

Nimitz listened respectfully and replied that he was ready to turn all "disposable assault troops" over to MacArthur's supervision once operations on Okinawa were completed. On the other hand, he insisted that the garrison forces throughout the Pacific Ocean Area "must remain under my operational control as long as I am responsible for those areas." More generally, he asserted that an immediate abolition of unified theater command would result in chaos. Nimitz told Sutherland bluntly that he would not do it.[8]

Sutherland was astonished. Such a hard line was out of character for Nimitz, who was famous for supporting accommodation and compromise

Army Major General Richard K. Sutherland was MacArthur's chief of staff and right-hand man throughout the war. Marshall wrote that Sutherland, who was utterly loyal to MacArthur, was "totally lacking in the facility of dealing with others." (U.S. Naval Institute)

over confrontation. Not in this instance. Nimitz was convinced that tearing apart existing protocols in the midst of war was a terrible mistake. As one staffer put it, separating Army and Navy logistical systems would be "like unscrambling eggs." In addition, he was annoyed by Sutherland's imperious tone. Later that night, after the Army generals went to bed, Nimitz sent a message to King outlining what he had told Sutherland, to ensure that King was not blindsided in Washington if news of the exchange got to Marshall via MacArthur. King's reply was immediate: "I am in complete agreement with your views."[9]

Thus bolstered, Nimitz was even more assertive the next day. He informed Sutherland that:

A. He would *not* "transfer any important shore positions from the Pacific Ocean Areas to the Southwest Pacific Area."

B. He would *not* "relinquish operational control of any Army forces, ground, air, or service, now under his control, which he considers essential to the functioning, development, of defense of the Pacific Ocean Areas."

C. He would *continue* to "exercise operational control over the major forces assigned to operate from shore positions in the Pacific Ocean Areas unless otherwise directed by the Joint Chiefs of Staff."

D. He would *retain* "coordinating authority over logistic matters"—that is, shipping.

E. He would *not* "assume direct control of naval forces [the Seventh Fleet] involved in the amphibious phases of operations directed to be conducted by CINCSWPA."[10]

McMorris and Sherman were nearly as astonished by their boss's hard line as Sutherland and Kenney were, and they subsequently convinced him to moderate his position to the extent of agreeing to "reconsider" elements of it after Okinawa was secured. Nevertheless, Nimitz had hurled down a gauntlet. As he wrote to Catherine that night, "the other side knows we are tough and no push-overs." The very fact that he referred to MacArthur's command team as "the other side" was itself significant.[11]

Also significant was the fact that during Sutherland's visit they had not discussed the invasion plans at all. Nimitz speculated to King that "the SWPA party was apparently not prepared for such discussion." Planning for Olympic, however, could not be postponed indefinitely. Nimitz suggested to Sutherland that MacArthur's staff should prepare an invasion plan, and that he and his staff would do the same. At some point they would get together to adjudicate any differences.[12]

MAY 7, 1945, WAS THE DAY German generals signed the instrument of capitulation in Reims that ended the war in Europe. That same day, Nimitz notified MacArthur that he had a draft plan for Olympic and suggested that they confer to ensure that their plans fit together. He invited the general to come to Guam for that discussion, but, aware that MacArthur was likely to refuse, he also volunteered to go to Manila, which he did a week later, on May 15.[13]

He was distressed to see what the Japanese had done to the once-grand city. "All buildings of any grace or value [were] completely destroyed," he wrote to the Walkers. As before, he carried gifts for MacArthur's family, including a box of "Midway peanut candy" for Arthur. He advised Mrs. MacArthur to ration the candy to one bar a day, though Arthur managed to circumvent that and ate so many that he "tossed his cookies," as Nimitz put it. Nevertheless, Nimitz considered the meeting "very successful." Encouraged by Marshall to resolve their differences, MacArthur was his most charming self. *Of course* Nimitz would continue to command the garrison forces in his theater, and *absolutely* the Navy would be a full partner in the invasion. Nimitz was accommodating, too. He expressed "regret" for any misunderstanding with Sutherland, and in two days of conversations the theater commanders appeared to reach complete agreement. Naval officers would be in charge during "the naval phases and also the amphibious phases," and Army commanders would assume responsibility for "the land campaign in Japan." Nimitz felt the visit had gone well, though of course the details still had to be worked out by their respective staffs.[14]

On the way back to Guam, Nimitz looked over the operational plan MacArthur had given him (Operation Downfall). At this stage, it was only a blueprint, but Nimitz identified several problems. One concerned shipping, which had been a bottleneck since the beginning of the war. In late 1944, the JCS had endowed Nimitz with control of virtually all shipping in the Pacific in order to support Operations Detachment (Iwo Jima) and Iceberg (Okinawa). Army leaders had resented that, and General Richardson in particular had complained about it. Richardson assumed, as did MacArthur, that when the two theaters merged for the invasion of Japan, the Army—specifically MacArthur—would assume control of shipping. Nimitz feared that overturning the complex shipping protocols that had been worked out over three years would result in chaos.[15]

Another area of potential friction concerned command protocols during the landings. In Manila, MacArthur had agreed that the actual amphibious assault would be conducted by the Navy, yet the plan his staff had produced indicated that MacArthur would command the landings. In every amphibious operation since 1942—in both the Atlantic and the Pacific—the Navy commander had remained in overall command until the Army general established himself on the beach. To make sure there was no confusion, Nimitz had his staff prepare what amounted to a memorandum of understanding outlining these protocols and sent it to MacArthur.[16]

MacArthur fired back a terse note that the arrangement Nimitz described "is not concurred in." Despite his agreeableness in Manila, MacArthur now insisted that putting a *Navy* admiral in charge of an *Army* invasion was absurd. He made it clear how he envisioned the command protocols: "I will accompany the troops and will exercise *at all times* [emphasis in the original] the command responsibility."

Nimitz thanked MacArthur for his thoughtful and helpful message and expressed regret that he had been "misunderstood." He assured MacArthur that he had "no desire to exercise any command or control over Army forces in the OLYMPIC Operation except as necessitated by their being embarked in naval vessels." When Army forces were on board Navy transports, he wrote, "as is customary in amphibious operations, they would remain under the control of amphibious commanders until the appropriate Army commanders are willing to assume their normal command responsibilities." As a gesture of conciliation, he added: "Any procedure which you can propose to shorten this period will be welcomed." He ended with the hope that this would allay all of MacArthur's concerns.[17]

It did not. MacArthur appealed the issue to Marshall, and the Joint Chiefs ordered Nimitz to find a way to transfer "responsibility for, and control of, all Army and Air Force" units to MacArthur no later than August 1. Since that was three months before the projected landings on Kyushu, MacArthur would command the amphibious landings. Nimitz thought it was a formula for confusion and misunderstanding, if not disaster.

IN THE MEANTIME, NIMITZ'S PREFERRED OPTION of defeating Japan *without* an invasion gained significant momentum in large part due to the ongoing success of American submarines. The arrival of more, newer, and larger American submarines in 1944, and the replacement of the troublesome Mark XIV torpedo with the more efficient Mark XVI, meant that by 1945, American submarines were annihilating Japan's trade. They cut off imports from the Japanese-controlled islands in the former Dutch East Indies; they hovered off the exits from Japanese harbors, sowed mines, and even penetrated the previously inviolate Sea of Japan—"the emperor's bathtub." Soon Japan was running out of everything: coal, iron ore, and especially oil, which became so scarce, the Japanese began using soybean oil for propulsion. They confiscated the rice crop of Vietnam and turned it into biofuel, causing widespread starvation. Though American submariners constituted only 2 percent of naval personnel, submarines accounted for 55 percent of all Japanese ships sunk in the war. By May 1945, Japan had resorted to using barges and rafts to bring in food and supplies by night.[18]

Nimitz was happy to leave management of the submarine campaign in the hands of Charlie Lockwood, who had also moved his headquarters to Guam. But occasionally he had to intervene when the submarine war had political ramifications. A few days before the landings on Okinawa, Lockwood came to Nimitz's office to ask if his subs could sink the Japanese transport *Awa Maru*. He asked because the *Awa Maru* was carrying donated supplies for American POWs in China and U.S. State Department had granted it safe passage. Lockwood insisted that the Japanese had also loaded the ship with munitions, aircraft parts, even Japanese troops. Nimitz heard him out, then turned down his request. The Japanese might indeed be taking advantage of the circumstances, he said, but at least some of the cargo was for the relief of American POWs, and in any case the word of the American government was at stake.[19]

Despite that, on April 1 (D-Day on Okinawa), Commander Charles Loughlin, in the submarine *Queenfish*, sent four torpedoes into the *Awa Maru*, discovering only afterward that it had been sailing under a protection agreement. Lockwood characterized it as a "tragic accident" and asked Nimitz to overlook it. Accident or not, Loughlin had violated a pledge made by the U.S. government, and Nimitz couldn't ignore it. He agreed to reduce the charges against Loughlin to "inefficiency in the performance of his duty," and in the end, the court found Loughlin guilty only of "negligence," sentencing him to receive a letter of admonition from the Secretary of the Navy. Nimitz approved the verdict, though he thought the sentence was too light. The U.S. government subsequently acknowledged Loughlin's error, offered to replace the ship, and promised "full indemnification."[20]

While Lockwood's submarines cut off Japan's trade, Halsey's carriers pounded her coastline. By midsummer they were running out of worthwhile targets. Halsey launched thousands of sorties against Japanese cities, airfields, factories, and harbors. Nimitz ordered him to focus on shipping, but there was so little of it left that the pilots took to hitting whatever targets of opportunity they could find. In July, Halsey reported that in addition to destroying more Japanese planes on the ground, his pilots inflicted damage on a picket boat, seven luggers, a junk, and six fishing smacks.[21]

All that time, Army Air Forces B-29 bombers were attacking Japanese cities from the air. Although at Nimitz's request, LeMay had targeted the Kyushu airfields in April, his primary mission remained strategic bombing, and throughout May and June hundreds of B-29s fulfilled his directive to "burn the place to the ground." Having discovered that high-altitude daylight bombing with the Norden bombsight produced disappointing results, and aware that Japanese cities were particularly vulnerable to fire, LeMay ordered the planes to attack at night from low altitude with incendiaries. In the first of those nighttime raids in March, 279 bombers dropped half a million small napalm-filled canisters on Tokyo. The result was apocalyptic.

Sixteen square miles of downtown Tokyo were incinerated; more than a hundred thousand people died; more than a million were made homeless. Over the next several months, the B-29s conducted similar raids against fifty-eight other Japanese cities. With the submarines cutting off imports, Halsey bombarding the coastline, and B-29s destroying her cities, Japan faced starvation and destruction.[22]

And worse was to come.

ON JUNE 3 NIMITZ WAS VISITED by Army Air Forces Colonel William P. Fisher, who arrived from Washington with a hand-carried top-secret message about the "special weapon" that was being developed in secret labs in New Mexico. Nimitz had known about the Manhattan Project since his visit to Washington in March, though at that time no one had known for sure whether the device would work. Now, Fisher told him that while the "special weapon" still had not been tested, Nimitz should begin "to facilitate arrangements for initial delivery of [the] weapon." Nimitz had always sought to minimize civilian loss of life in the war, and here clearly was a non-discriminating weapon of unprecedented power and lethality. On the other hand, it was alien enough that Nimitz wondered if it might give the Japanese "a way out," as he put it, to justify to themselves why a surrender was necessary.[23]

Two weeks later, on June 14, Nimitz and MacArthur each received a cryptic message from the Joint Chiefs. They should make plans, the message read, "to take immediate advantage of favorable circumstances, such as a sudden collapse or surrender, to effect an entry into Japan proper for occupational purposes."[24]

Planning for an invasion went on nonetheless, and so did the reorganization of forces in the Pacific. In the end, the restructuring was not as draconian as MacArthur had initially proposed or Nimitz feared. MacArthur kept control of the Seventh Fleet, and Nimitz retained control of shipping, though he did relinquish command of the Army forces on Okinawa and elsewhere. In doing so, he sent a message to those units that had served under him for the past three years thanking them for "their magnificent record of achievement." He would always remember the soldiers who had fought at Attu, Makin, Kwajalein, Eniwetok, Saipan, Guam, Palau, and Okinawa. They had, he wrote, demonstrated "a standard of unity of purpose and of integrated effort which will not be forgotten."[25]

In the first week of August, the whole issue of reorganizing American forces in the Pacific became moot. On August 6, Nimitz was in his office hosting Captain Paul D. Stroop, who was visiting from King's planning staff. Stroop noted that Nimitz was distracted and kept looking at his watch. When Stroop asked what was afoot, Nimitz asked Stroop if he had been briefed on the "special weapon." He had not. Nimitz nodded and said, "Well, there's a special event that's going to occur" soon. The first atomic bomb detonated over Hiroshima that morning at 8:15 (Tokyo time). Though no one knew it yet, that event, plus a Soviet declaration of war against Japan two days later and the explosion of a second atomic bomb on Nagasaki on August 9, would make an invasion unnecessary.[26]

The day after the explosion of the second atomic bomb, Admiral Bruce Fraser invited Nimitz to a dinner party celebrating Anglo-American unity on board his flagship, Duke of York. At the dinner, Fraser presented Nimitz with the sash and medallion of the Knight's Cross of the Order of the Bath. Later, during the meal, a junior officer entered discretely and quietly handed Nimitz an "eyes only" message from King. A Japanese surrender was "imminent."[27]

At 7:20 in the morning on August 14, Layton came running into Nimitz's office clutching a teletype. As he trotted past Lamar's desk, he said, "This is the hottest thing we've ever had." Nimitz already knew, having received a private message from King just minutes before. When Layton told him the war was over, "he didn't get jubilant or jump up and down," Layton remembered. Instead, he smiled broadly, leaned back in his chair, and put one booted foot up on his desk, which was uncharacteristic of him. Then he dictated a short directive to the fleet: "Cease offensive operations against Japanese forces."[28]

The next day, he sent another all-hands message, one that can be considered an epitaph for his command tenure in the Pacific. Throughout the war, Nimitz, like everyone else, had routinely referred to the enemy with the convenient, but nevertheless dismissive and insulting, term "Japs." Not

On August 10, 1945, one day after the second atomic bomb detonated over Nagasaki, Nimitz was the guest of honor at a formal dinner on board the British battleship *Duke of York*. There he was presented with the trappings of the Knight's Cross of the Order of the Bath. (U.S. Naval Institute)

any more. In a message addressed to ALPAC (all Pacific Area personnel), he wrote:

> With the termination of hostilities against Japan, it is incumbent on all officers to conduct themselves with dignity and decorum in their treatment of the Japanese, and their public utterances in connection with the Japanese. The Japanese are still the same nation which initiated

the war by a treacherous attack on the Pacific Fleet, and which has subjected our brothers in arms who became prisoners of war to torture, starvation, and murder. However, the use of insulting epithets in connection with the Japanese as a race or as individuals does not now become the officers of the United States Navy. Officers of the Pacific Fleet will take steps to require all personnel under their command [to enforce] a high standard of conduct in this matter. Neither familiarity and open forgiveness nor abuse and vituperation should be permitted.[29]

EPILOGUE

ON THE MORNING of September 2, 1945, Tokyo Bay was crowded with more than 250 Allied warships. One of them was Halsey's flagship, the battleship *Missouri*, moored near the spot where Matthew C. Perry had anchored in 1853 when he had "opened" Japan to the West. Though the *Missouri* flew the American flag at the gaff, she also flew the national flags of Great Britain, the Soviet Union, and China. Her crew was busy scrubbing the decks and polishing up the brass in preparation for the ceremony that would formally end the war.

Fleet Admiral Chester Nimitz was on board the battleship *South Dakota*. He had hoped that the surrender ceremony would be held there, but in homage to President Truman, the *Missouri* had been chosen. MacArthur would preside, and he insisted that when he boarded the *Missouri* his red five-star flag should appear at the main. Navy policy reserved such an honor for the senior naval officer on board. Hal Lamar, who was charged with protocol issues, asked Nimitz what he should do. Unwilling to involve himself in a protocol spat with MacArthur's staff, Nimitz told him to figure it out. Lamar conferred with the *Missouri's* skipper, Captain Stuart Murray, and they decided to fly MacArthur's red flag and Nimitz's blue flag side by side.

Nimitz arrived on the *Missouri* first, and after greeting Murray and several others, he went to Halsey's flag quarters, where Ensign Henry "Hanko" Walker, the son of Sandy and Una, and a communications officer on the *Missouri*, was waiting. Nimitz had taken the trouble to ensure that Walker got a pass to watch the ceremony. Before Walker could greet him, Halsey entered, and Hanko discreetly retreated into the background. He watched as the two admirals shook hands. Then MacArthur walked in. By prior agreement, all three men wore open-collar khaki uniforms. While Nimitz might have preferred service dress uniforms to honor the occasion, it had been MacArthur's idea to wear the uniforms in which they had fought the war, and Nimitz had acquiesced.

Hanko watched as MacArthur strode up to Nimitz and gripped his proffered hand, saying simply, "Chester." Then, still holding Nimitz's right hand, he reached over with his left to grab Halsey's hand and put it on top. "My friends and comrades," he said, "this is the day toward which we have been looking for a long time." The three of them stood there unmoving for what seemed to Walker like a long moment. MacArthur, having created the tableau, prolonged it; Nimitz went along so as not to spoil the moment. Finally, Halsey broke the spell, disengaging himself and suggesting that they move to his cabin.

En route, Nimitz noticed Walker. "Henry," he said, "I'm glad to see you." Then, leaning closer, he saw that Walker was not wearing his ensign's bars. "Henry, where are your collar bars?" Walker had been so excited by the summons to flag quarters, he had forgotten to put them on. "Go get your collar bars," Nimitz said. "We may sign this surrender without neckties, but we sure as hell will wear the insignia of our rank."[1]

At five minutes before 9:00, the Japanese delegation came alongside in an American destroyer. The party was headed by Japan's foreign minister, Mamoru Shigemitsu, who was wearing formal morning dress with top hat and tails. Shigemitsu ascended to the deck haltingly; he had a prosthetic leg, the result of an assassination attempt by a Korean nationalist in 1932.

After all eleven members of the Japanese delegation had climbed the ladder to the deck of the *Missouri*, they stood with frozen expressions while official photographers recorded the moment for history. Only then did MacArthur and Nimitz, walking side by side with Halsey behind them, emerge from Halsey's cabin to take up their places. Behind them, and in a long row to their left, were more than two score Allied officers, most of them in khaki, a few in other uniforms. Bruce Fraser stood out in white shorts and knee socks, as did the Russian representative next to him in his dark sack coat covered with medals. All around them, standing or sitting anywhere space allowed, were hundreds of Navy sailors and members of the ship's Marine detachment; some sat atop the *Missouri*'s giant gun turret, their legs dangling over the edge. No doubt the Japanese Army representative, General Yoshijiro Umezu, thought this was disgraceful. How could the Japanese Empire have lost to such an undisciplined mob?

MacArthur began the ceremony by announcing that this was not a parley. The issues had been decided on the battlefield. He then called upon the Japanese representatives to "sign the Instrument of Surrender at the places indicated." At precisely 9:04, Shigemitsu walked to the table and signed. Then one by one, amid complete silence, the other Japanese representatives did so as well, affixing their names in elaborate kanji characters.

Then it was MacArthur's turn. He signed on behalf of all the Allied powers. Nimitz signed next on behalf of the United States of America. Others followed in turn: representatives of China, Britain, the Soviet Union, Australia, Canada, France, Holland, and New Zealand. Once everyone had signed, MacArthur stepped back to the microphone and spoke in his steady baritone: "Let us pray that peace be now restored to the world, and that God will preserve it always."

Moments later, the planes arrived. More than four hundred B-29 Army bombers flew overhead, followed by fifteen hundred Navy carrier planes. It was the largest flyover in the history of aviation and a powerful reminder of why capitulation had been Japan's only option.

NIMITZ'S NAVAL CAREER DID NOT END with the coming of peace. Ever since his days as a junior officer, he had aspired to the Navy's top job as Chief of Naval Operations. King, who held that position throughout the war, had begun his tenure unsure whether Nimitz possessed the toughness necessary to command the Pacific Fleet. Now he insisted that Nimitz was the only logical candidate to succeed him. Most of the Navy thought so, too. Navy secretary Forrestal, however, disagreed. Remembering Nimitz's unwillingness to publish a Navy newspaper on Guam, Forrestal described Nimitz to Truman as "a stubborn Dutchman." Tired of doing battle with independent-minded

Navy admirals like King and Nimitz, Forrestal wanted to promote King's deputy, Vice Admiral Richard A. S. Edwards.[2]

Edwin S. Pauley took up Nimitz's cause. Nimitz had gotten to know Pauley in the 1920s during his days at the University of California at Berkeley, when Pauley had been a regent of the university. Since then, Pauley had become the chief fundraiser for the Democratic Party and a close friend of Truman. While talking with Nimitz about the CNO job, Pauley picked up the phone and called the president. Whether or not that tipped the scales, Forrestal eventually yielded. He agreed to Nimitz's appointment as CNO, but only if he consented to serve a single two-year term. Nimitz accepted the condition and became CNO when King retired on December 15, 1945.[3]

Nimitz believed his good friend Raymond Spruance was the logical candidate to succeed him as CinCPac. Spruance, however, told Nimitz he preferred the job of president of the Naval War College in Newport, Rhode Island, and he relieved Pye in that position in March 1946. As president of the college, Spruance instituted a new program based on what he called an "Operational Planning Model" that emphasized the importance of logistics in strategic planning. After leaving the Navy in 1948 Spruance served as U.S. ambassador to the Philippines. He then retired to Pebble Beach, California, where he lived until 1969, dying at the age of eighty-three.

Halsey became the Navy's fourth fleet admiral in December 1945 and retired two years later. In retirement, he served on several corporate boards and kept an office in downtown Manhattan. He accepted a large advance from McGraw-Hill to write his memoirs, which he dictated to Joseph Bryan, the son of a friend. Alas, the self-serving tone of the book—*Admiral Halsey's Story*—did little to enhance and much to tarnish his reputation, and Halsey later concluded that it had been a mistake to write it. He died in 1959, ten years before Spruance, at the age of seventy-six.

When Spruance went to Newport, John H. Towers succeeded him as commander of the Fifth Fleet—the operational command he had long coveted. A year later, he became commander of the newly unified Pacific Command. After a short tour as Chairman of the General Board, he retired from the Navy in 1947 and died of pancreatic cancer in 1955 at the age of seventy.

Marc "Pete" Mitscher, whom Nimitz had put in Coventry for his missteps at Midway and then resuscitated in 1943, became Deputy Chief of Naval Operations for Air, again serving under Nimitz. In February 1947, while commanding the Atlantic Fleet, he suffered a massive heart attack and died at the age of only sixty.

Holland M. Smith, who had fired Ralph Smith on Saipan and caused Nimitz a number of major and minor headaches, retired as a lieutenant general (three stars) in May 1946. He moved to La Jolla, California, and, contrary to his nickname and in defiance of his reputation, spent much of his time quietly puttering in his garden. He did, however, find time to work with Percy Finch to create an opinionated and cantankerous memoir— *Coral and Brass*. He died in 1967 at the age of eighty-four.

Una Walker was even more long-lived than Howling Mad Smith. Though Sandy died in 1969, partly as a result of the ravages of Guillain-Barré syndrome, his wife outlived him by eighteen years and died just shy of her one hundredth birthday, in 1987. She continued to host events at Muliwai right to the end, counting among her guests Dwight Eisenhower, Chiang Kai-Shek, and the king and queen of Thailand, as well as a number of flag officers. The guest house where Nimitz had spent many nights during the war continued to be known as the "Admiral's Cabin."[4]

Charles Lockwood, Nimitz's Pearl Harbor neighbor and close friend, served as the Navy's Inspector General for two years before he retired in 1947 to Los Gatos, California, only an hour or two down the coast from Berkeley. He wrote half a dozen books about the war and served as technical adviser on several movies, working with stars like John Wayne and Ronald Reagan. He died at seventy-seven on the twenty-third anniversary of D-Day, June 6, 1967.

After handing over the conn of the Navy to Nimitz in December 1945, Ernest J. King retired to Washington, D.C., where he accepted the post of president of the Naval Historical Foundation. It was not merely an honorific. He was an enthusiastic advocate of the study of naval history and personally endowed a chair in maritime history at the Naval War College. He suffered a debilitating stroke in 1947, and though he was able to assist Walter Muir Whitehill in the writing of a memoir (*Fleet Admiral King: A Naval Record*), he never fully recovered his health. He died of a heart attack in 1956 at the age of seventy-seven.

Douglas MacArthur performed the greatest service of his life as the Supreme Allied Commander (SCAP) during the occupation of Japan. The qualities that many found aggravating in a commander—his imperial demeanor and his acts of public drama—served him well in this role. He reformed land ownership, democratic processes, and health and safety regulations, and was perceived as, and likely fancied himself, a modern shogun. He had another moment of military prowess overseeing the daring landing at Inchon during the Korean War. Yet his imperiousness did not serve him well in Korea, and President Truman felt compelled to dismiss him in 1951. He remained a popular hero with a large segment of the American public and was widely mourned when he died in 1964 at the age of eighty-four.

AS FOR NIMITZ, HIS SHORTENED TOUR as CNO took place at a critical time for the Navy. He spent much of his tenure defending the Navy's independence amid an acrimonious debate about unifying the armed services into a single Department of Defense. As strong a champion as he was of joint service and joint command, he fought hard to prevent the Navy from being subsumed altogether. Only days after taking the job, he described his activities in a letter to Sandy and Una: "I find myself in a maelstrom of speeches, dinners, conferences, visits to Congressmen, Senators and plain downright lobbying." In all these venues, he insisted that it was not the atomic bomb or Russian intervention that had won the war against Japan; it was the persistent application of American naval power that had stripped away Japan's empire, destroyed her navy, ravaged her maritime commerce, and left her a wrecked nation. His calm, non-confrontational manner acted as a balm to the fierce and sometimes bitter inter-service rivalries concerning unification, budgets, and national policy.[5]

As promised, he left the CNO's job after two years, retiring to Berkeley, where he and Catherine bought a house at 728 Santa Barbara Road, overlooking San Francisco Bay. The unification controversy continued to fester. It was resolved in 1947 with an independent Air Force joining the Navy and Army as separate services, though all three were part of a unified Department of Defense. Forrestal became the first Secretary of Defense, though he left that job after two years in March 1949. Two months later he leapt to his death from the window of a hospital where he was undergoing treatment for severe depression. Not long after that, his successor as Defense Secretary, Louis Johnson, cancelled the Navy's planned 60,000-ton aircraft carrier. In response to that, Nimitz's successor as CNO, Admiral Louis Denfeld, was sharply and publicly critical. Truman fired him, and then called Nimitz to ask if he would return as CNO. Nimitz responded that it was a bad precedent to bring back former CNOs and urged him to appoint a younger man. When Truman asked for a recommendation, Nimitz named his former deputy chief of staff, Forrest Sherman, who became CNO in October 1949 at the age of only fifty-three.

In retirement, Nimitz continued to walk, play horseshoes, and do card tricks with his grandchildren. He read military history—especially histories of the Civil War. He acquired a set of "big eyes"—those oversize binoculars that had given the Japanese an early advantage in night fighting in the Solomon Islands—and set them up in his back garden. From there he could watch ships entering and leaving San Francisco Bay, and in the evening watch the sun set between the pillars of the Golden Gate Bridge.

Pleasant as all that was, for a man who had spent literally all his adult life in service, it was not enough. His daughter Nancy thought it was hard for him to wake up each day without a challenge, a project, a job to do, a cause to serve. He was bored and frustrated, and his default sunny disposition occasionally gave way to a grumpy surliness. He was, she believed, "monstrously unhappy."[6]

Almost certainly, that was why he agreed to accept an appeal from the United Nations to supervise a plebiscite in Kashmir to determine whether it would become part of India or Pakistan. It was a thankless job. The centuries-old dispute was so deeply rooted in rival cultures and religions that it resisted his best efforts to find a solution. After working at it for two years, Nimitz decided that it was hopeless as well as thankless, and he resigned. Kashmir remains divided and disputed to this day.

He had other offers: corporate boards, a university presidency, chancellor of UCLA. The only one he accepted was the invitation from the University of California to serve as a regent, a job he held for eight years.

Unlike King, Halsey, and Holland Smith, Nimitz did not write a memoir, though he did agree to work with historian E. B. "Ned" Potter to edit the portion of Potter's work on naval history that covered World War II. He took the task seriously, contributing both substantive suggestions and even editorial corrections. The book, titled *Sea Power*, was published in 1961 and served as a textbook at the Naval Academy for more than two decades.

In 1963, after a dozen years in their Berkeley home, he and Catherine moved to Quarters One, a vacant Navy property on Yerba Buena Island in the middle of San Francisco Bay, partly because it had an elevator. Walking had become more difficult, especially after Nimitz fell that summer and broke a hip. Arthritis set in, and he also underwent back surgery. Walking now with two canes, he found his activities severely restricted, which was a kind of torture for a man who had walked hundreds of miles for pleasure. He was unable to attend the funeral of Douglas MacArthur in Norfolk in April 1964. His health steadily deteriorated. He had a series of small strokes in 1965 and developed congestive heart problems. Early in 1966, he slipped into a coma.

On February 20, 1966, four days short of Nimitz's eighty-first birthday, Catherine was sitting next to his bed when she noticed he was shivering. The nurse went to get another blanket, but it was not a chill. Catherine reached over and put her hand on his, and he stopped shaking. Chester Nimitz had died, quietly and without fuss, as was his wont.[7]

He was buried with full military honors in Golden Gate Cemetery in San Bruno, California, just over the city line from San Francisco. He had been offered space at Arlington, but Nimitz wanted to be closer to the Pacific, where he, and the thousands who had served with him and under him, had fought. Years earlier, in the midst of the war, Nimitz, Spruance, and Lockwood had all agreed to be laid to rest near one another. They agreed, too, that their headstones should be plain white markers, indistinguishable from the thousands of other veterans' graves in the national cemeteries. Never a religious man, Nimitz asked that his headstone be inscribed with the five-star emblem of his rank as a fleet admiral rather than the Christian cross. He purchased a plot with space for six graves for himself, his two friends, and their wives. Kelly Turner learned of the plan and purchased a plot of his own nearby.

It is noteworthy that Nimitz's principal lieutenants wished to immortalize their association with their wartime commander, and he with them. They had shared much together—the war in the Pacific was, after all, the great adventure of their lives. In addition to that, however, there is in their decision a recognition that Nimitz was the centerpiece of that adventure—the pole around which everything orbited. In 1941, King had feared that Nimitz wasn't tough enough for command. Over the ensuing four years, Nimitz had demonstrated that humility, careful listening, calm assessment, patience, and the ability to recognize when to accept calculated risk, brought military success as well as the admiration of those who executed his orders.

Nimitz's greatness lay less in his ability to do great things than in his facility to convince others that they could do great things. Spruance, Lockwood, and Turner were better commanders because of their association with Chester Nimitz, and they knew it. That was true as well of Halsey and Mitscher, even Holland Smith. In that respect, Nimitz was a force multiplier in the Pacific war, and the Allied victory in that war is his legacy.

THE NIMITZ GRAYBOOK

T HE "COMMAND SUMMARY of Fleet Admiral Chester W. Nimitz," consisting of eight fat volumes in the archives of the Naval History and Heritage Command in the Washington Navy Yard, and universally referred to as the "Graybook," is a principal primary source for this narrative. It is referenced literally hundreds of times in what follows. Many of the entries refer to the "Running Summary" that was kept at headquarters, which constitutes part of the Graybook; other references are to the official messages, sent by radio, between and among the principal commanders. In the originals of those messages, both the sender and the recipient are identified by their command acronym, as in "COMINCH TO CINCPAC." In many histories, the messages are cited this way, often along with their date-time signature, such as 021718, meaning that it was sent on the second day of the month (02) at 1718 Greenwich Mean Time (5:18 p.m.). Rather than require the reader to internalize these references and decode the date-time signatures, I have cited all of them using the principals' names and the date. The message just mentioned, for example (cited in note 9 of chapter 2) is rendered as "King to Nimitz, Jan. 2, 1942," and Nimitz's reply as "Nimitz to King" rather than "CINCPAC TO COMINCH." The ensuing numbers (1:122) refer to the volume and page number in the digitized version of the Graybook where the message can be found. I hope readers will find this more user friendly.

Abbreviations Used in Notes

AHC	American Heritage Center, Laramie, Wyoming
BOMRT	Battle of Midway Roundtable, online at www.midway42.org
ECU	Joyner Library, East Carolina University, Greenville, North Carolina
FDRL	Franklin Delano Roosevelt Presidential Library, Hyde Park, New York
Graybook	Command Summary of Fleet Admiral Chester W. Nimitz, USN, Naval History and Heritage Command, Washington Navy Yard, Washington, D.C.
NARA	National Archives and Records Administration, College Park, Maryland
NHHC	Naval History and Heritage Command, Washington Navy Yard, Washington, D.C.
NMPW	Center for Pacific War Studies, National Museum of the Pacific War, Fredericksburg, Texas
NWC	U.S. Naval War College Archives, Newport, Rhode Island
UMD	Hornbeck Library, University of Maryland, College Park, Maryland
USNA	Nimitz Library Special Collections, U.S. Naval Academy, Annapolis, Maryland

NOTES

Chapter 1

1. Craig C. Felker, *Testing American Sea Power: U.S. Navy Strategic Exercises, 1923–1941* (College Station: Texas A&M University Press, 2007), 131; Gordon W. Prange with Donald F. Goldstein and Katherine V. Dillon, *At Dawn We Slept: The Untold Story of Pearl Harbor* (New York: Penguin, 1982), 39–41, 47.

2. E. B. Potter, *Nimitz* (Annapolis: Naval Institute Press, 1976), 9.

3. Nimitz to Catherine Nimitz, Dec. 20 and 21, 1941 (Nimitz Diary), NHHC; H. Arthur Lamar, *I Saw Stars* (Fredericksburg, TX: The Admiral Nimitz Foundation, 1975), 2.

4. Nimitz to Catherine Nimitz, Dec. 22, 1941, Michael Lilly Collection.

5. Frank DeLorenzo, "Admiral Nimitz Arrives at Pearl Harbor," BOMRT; Craig L. Symonds, *The Battle of Midway* (New York: Oxford University Press, 2011), 7; E. B. Potter, *Nimitz* (Annapolis: Naval Institute Press, 1976), 16.

6. S. S. Murray oral history (May 15, 1971), "A Cluster of Interviews," 5:614, USNA.

7. Chester Lay to the author, March 11, 2021. I am grateful to Richard Lay, who generously shared with me the original dental records of his grandfather.

8. Waldo Drake oral history (June 15, 1969), "A Cluster of Interviews," 2:5, USNA. The senior officer was Raymond Spruance in an interview with Gordon Prange (Sept. 5, 1964), Prange Papers, box 17, UMD. The longtime friend was Joseph Wilson Leverton Jr., *Nimitz: A Good Humored Leader of Men* (Cary, NC: The Leverton Family, 1975), 1.

9. 1905 *Lucky Bag*, USNA; Henry A. Walker, "Memoirs," courtesy of Sam King, 2; Joseph Rochefort oral history (Oct. 5, 1969), 1:223, and William Callaghan oral history (June 30, 1969), 1:11, both in "A Cluster of Interviews," USNA. Nimitz's daughter Nancy claimed later that she knew her father was genuinely upset when he let loose with "Gosh all hemlock!" Nancy Nimitz oral history (June 7, 1969), "A Cluster of Interviews," 3:32, USNA.

10. The visitor was British LCDR F. M. Beasley, cited in John B. Lundstrom, *Black Shoe Carrier Admiral: Frank Jack Fletcher at Coral Sea, Midway, and Guadalcanal* (Annapolis: Naval Institute Press, 2006), 124.

11. Joseph Rochefort oral history (Dec. 6, 1969), 225, USNA; Richard Misenhimer oral history (June 23, 2009), 34, NMPW.

12. Robert L. Sherrod, *On to Westward: War in the Central Pacific* (New York: Duell, Sloan and Pearce, 1945), 234.

13. S. S. Murray oral history (May 15, 1971), "A Cluster of Interviews," 5:630, USNA.

14. Nimitz to Catherine Nimitz, Jan. 19, 1945 (Nimitz Diary), NHHC.

15. David W. Plank oral history (Jan. 19, 1970), 5:9, and William Callaghan oral history (June 30, 1969), 1:10, both in "A Cluster of Interviews," USNA.

16. Waldo Drake oral history (June 15, 1969), "A Cluster of Interviews," 2:12, USNA.

17. Odale D. Waters Jr. oral history, 9–10, and J. Wilson Leverton oral history, 7, both in *Recollections of the Late VADM Chester W. Nimitz as Given by Various Officers*, NWC. Also Sam P. Moncure oral history (July 30, 1969), "A Cluster of Interviews," 4:22–23, USNA.

18. George S. Perkins oral history (Sept. 19, 1969), and S. S. Murray oral history (May 15, 1971), both USNA; E. B. Potter, *Nimitz* (Annapolis: Naval Institute Press, 1976), 158–59.

19. Odale D. Waters oral history, 2–3, and J. Wilson Leaverton oral history, 7, both in *Recollections of the Late VADM Chester W. Nimitz as Given by Various Officers*, NWC.

20. H. Arthur Lamar oral history (May 3, 1970), "A Cluster of Interviews," 2:3, USNA.

21. George van Deurs oral history (Aug. 18, 1974), in Buell Papers (King Collection), box 1, folder 12, NWC.

22. Stephen Jurika to Tom Buell, Aug. 22, 1974, and George van Deurs to Buell, Aug. 18, 1974, both in Buell Papers (King Collection), box 1, folders 8 and 12, NWC; Thomas B. Buell, *Master of Sea Power: A Biography of Fleet Admiral Ernest J. King* (Boston: Little, Brown, 1980), 111.

23. Floyd Thorn oral history (Aug. 14, 2000), NMPW; James H. Doyle to Tom Buell, Aug. 12, 1974, Buell Papers (Whitehill Collection), box 1, folder 7, NWC.

24. Patrick Abbazia, *Mr. Roosevelt's Navy: The Private War of the U.S. Atlantic Fleet, 1939–1942* (Annapolis: Naval Institute Press, 1975), 136.

25. Ernest J. King and Walter Muir Whitehill, *Fleet Admiral King: A Naval Record* (New York: W. W. Norton, 1952), 349–51; Running Summary, Feb. 15, 1942, Graybook, 1:216.

26. J. P. W. Vest to Tom Buell, Aug. 2, 1974, Buell Papers (King Collection), box 1, folder 12, NWC.

27. John Lundstrom, *The First Team: Pacific Naval Air Combat from Pearl Harbor to Midway* (Annapolis: Naval Institute Press, 1984), 91–94. Interestingly, in his January 11 message, King identified himself as "CinCUS," apparently forgetting that he had insisted his title be changed to "CominCh." King to Nimitz, Jan. 11, 1942, Graybook, 1:175.

28. Knox to FDR, Feb.14, 1942, Buell Papers (King Collection), box 12, folder 31, NWC.

29. King and Whitehill, *Fleet Admiral King*, 250, 368; King to All Navy, Jan. 10, 1942, Graybook, 1:175.

30. "Admiral Nimitz," interview of Walter Muir Whitehill by Tom Buell (July 31, 1969), Buell Papers (King Collection), box 19, folder 10, NWC.

31. Chester Nimitz Jr. oral history (Apr. 14, 1969), "A Cluster of Interviews," 3:38, USNA; King to Nimitz, Jan. 11, 1942, Graybook, 1:175; Eric Larrabee, *Commander*

in Chief: Franklin Delano Roosevelt, His Lieutenants, and Their War (New York: Harper & Row, 1987), 356.

Chapter 2

1. Nimitz to Catherine Nimitz, Dec. 26, 1942 (Nimitz Diary), NHHC.
2. Thomas C. Anderson oral history (July 5, 1969), 1:17, John R. Redman oral history (June 15, 1969), 2:15, and H. Arthur Lamar oral history (May 3, 1970), all in "A Cluster of Interviews," USNA; Nimitz to Catherine Nimitz, Jan. 4, 1942 (Nimitz Diary), NHHC; David W. Plank oral history (Jan. 19, 1970), 7, USNA.
3. Gordon Prange with Donald F. Goldstein and Katherine V. Dillon, *At Dawn We Slept: The Untold Story of Pearl Harbor* (New York: Penguin Books, 1991), 400–401; Richard B. Frank, *Tower of Skulls: A History of the Asia-Pacific War* (New York: W. W. Norton, 2019), 247.
4. Reminiscences of RADM Ernest M. Eller (Aug. 25, 1977), 533, USNA; Nimitz to Catherine Nimitz, Jan. 4 and 9, 1942 (Nimitz Diary), NHHC; Hal Lamar oral history (May 3, 1970), "A Cluster of Interviews," 2:13, USNA.
5. Nimitz to Catherine Nimitz, Jan. 4, 1942 (Nimitz Diary), NHHC.
6. Thomas C. Anderson oral history (July 5, 1969), "A Cluster of Interviews," 1:5, USNA.
7. Nimitz to Catherine Nimitz, Jan. 21, 1942 (Nimitz Diary), NHHC; H. Arthur "Hal" Lamar oral history, 13, 17, Buell Collection, NWC; Douglas Southall Freeman, *R. E. Lee: A Biography* (New York: Charles Scribner's Sons, 1934), 1:552–53.
8. H. Joseph Chase oral history (Oct. 19, 1969), "A Cluster of Interviews," 1:20, USNA; Nimitz to Catherine Nimitz, Dec. 28, 1941 (Nimitz Diary), NHHC.
9. King to Nimitz, and Nimitz to King, both Jan. 2, 1942, Graybook, 1:122.
10. Nimitz to David L. McDonald, April 3, 1966, "Pearl Harbor Postscript," U.S. Naval Institute *Proceedings* (Dec. 1966), 126.
11. "Employment of Carrier Task Forces," Jan. 2, 1942, Graybook, 1:124.
12. John Jordan, *Warships After Washington: The Development of the Five Major Fleets, 1922–1930* (Annapolis: Naval Institute Press, 2015).
13. Craig L. Symonds, *The Battle of Midway* (New York: Oxford University Press, 2011), 13.
14. Jordan, *Warships After Washington*, 168–79.
15. Symonds, *The Battle of Midway*, 48–49; USNA *Lucky Bag*, 1902.
16. "Admiral Leary, Watchdog of the Anzac Seas," *The Australian Women's Weekly*, Feb. 28, 1942.
17. The newest and best biography of Halsey is Thomas A. Hughes, *Admiral Bill Halsey: A Naval Life* (Cambridge, MA: Harvard University Press, 2016). See also the less reliable but nevertheless revealing autobiography co-written with J. Bryan III, *Admiral Halsey's Story* (New York: McGraw-Hill, 1947).
18. John B. Lundstrom, *The First Team: Pacific Naval Air Combat from Pearl Harbor to Midway* (Annapolis: Naval Institute Press, 1984), 53.
19. John B. Lundstrom, *Black Shoe Carrier Admiral: Frank Jack Fletcher at Coral Sea, Midway, and Guadalcanal* (Annapolis: Naval Institute Press, 2006); Stephen

D. Regan, *In Bitter Tempest: The Biography of Admiral Frank Jack Fletcher* (Ames: Iowa State University Press, 1994).

Chapter 3

1. J. A. C. Gray, *Amerika Samoa: A History of American Samoa and Its United States Naval Administration* (Annapolis: Naval Institute Press, 1960), 240–41.
2. Nimitz to Catherine Nimitz, Dec. 28, 1941 (Nimitz Diary), NHHC.
3. "Employment of Carrier Task Forces," Jan. 2, 1942, Graybook, 1:129–32.
4. William S. Pye, "Additional Considerations Re: Samoa Reinforcement Operation," Jan. 8, 1942, Graybook, 1:146–47.
5. Ibid., 1:152.
6. Handwritten note at end of Pye memo, Jan. 8, 1942, Graybook, 1:153.
7. Nimitz to King, Jan. 18, 1942, Map Room Files, box 36, FDRL.
8. "Appreciation of the Pacific Situation," Jan. 15, 1942, Graybook, 1:167–73; Nimitz to King, and King to Nimitz, both Jan. 5, and King to Nimitz, Jan. 6, 1942, all in Graybook, 1:139–40, 141; "Appreciation Defense of Fiji," Jan. 8, 1942, Graybook, 1:160–66; ANCB to Nimitz, Jan. 27, 1942, Graybook, 1:196.
9. Nimitz to Catherine Nimitz, Jan. 4, 1942 (Nimitz Diary), NHHC.
10. King to Nimitz, and Nimitz to TF commanders, both Jan. 28, 1942, Graybook, 1:193.
11. Thomas C. Anderson oral history (July 5, 1969), "A Cluster of Interviews," 1:23, USNA.
12. Chester W. Nimitz, "Some Thoughts to Live By" (National Museum of the Pacific War, Fredericksburg, TX, 1985), 1.
13. Waldo Drake oral history (June 15, 1969), "A Cluster of Interviews," 2:48, USNA; Nimitz to Catherine Nimitz, Jan. 22, 1942 (Nimitz Diary), NHHC.
14. King to Nimitz, Jan. 20, 1942, Graybook, 1:179.
15. John B. Lundstrom, *Black Shoe Carrier Admiral: Frank Jack Fletcher at Coral Sea, Midway, and Guadalcanal* (Annapolis: Naval Institute Press, 2006), 40. See also memo from C. H. McMorris, Dec. 11, 1942, Graybook, 1:78.
16. Running Summary, Jan. 21, 1942, Graybook, 1:158.
17. Ibid.; Nimitz to TF Commanders, Jan. 21 and 22, 1942, Graybook, 1:180; King to Nimitz, and Nimitz to TF Commanders, both Jan. 28, 1942, Graybook, 1:158, 193. Nimitz's second order to Brown was likely a result of prodding by King, who used identical language.
18. Thomas Wildenberg, *Gray Steel and Black Oil: Fast Tankers and Replenishment at Sea in the U.S. Navy, 1912–1995* (Annapolis: Naval Institute Press, 1996), 130–31.
19. Running Summary, Jan. 23, 1942, Graybook, 1:183.
20. Nimitz to TF Commanders, Jan. 28, 1942, Graybook, 1:193; Running Summary, Jan. 30, 1942, Graybook, 1:188.
21. Halsey to Nimitz, Jan. 31, 1942, Graybook, 1:203; Running Summary, Jan. 31, 1942, Graybook, 1:189; John B. Lundstrom, *The First Team: Pacific Naval Air Combat from Pearl Harbor to Midway* (Annapolis: Naval Institute Press, 1984), 85.
22. Craig L. Symonds, *The Battle of Midway* (New York: Oxford University Press, 2011), 69; Edwin T. Layton with Roger Pineau, *"And I Was There": Breaking the*

Secrets—Pearl Harbor and Midway (Old Saybrook, CT: Konecky & Konecky, 2001), 364; Lundstrom, *The First Team*, 81; William F. Halsey Jr. with J. Bryan III, *Admiral Halsey's Story* (New York: McGraw-Hill, 1947), 96.

23. Halsey and Bryan, *Admiral Halsey's Story*, 93; Edward P. Stafford, *The Big E: The Story of the USS* Enterprise (New York: Random House, 1962), 56–57; Symonds, *The Battle of Midway*, 64–75.

24. Symonds, *The Battle of Midway*, 69–75.

Chapter 4

1. King to Nimitz, Jan. 29, 1942, and Running Summary, Jan. 29, 1942, both in Graybook, 1:197, 187.

2. James Bassett oral history (May 28, 1969), "A Cluster of Interviews," 1:24, USNA; Nimitz to Catherine Nimitz, Jan. 29, 1942 (Nimitz Diary), NHHC.

3. The King-Nimitz correspondence is quoted in E. B. Potter, *Nimitz* (Annapolis: Naval Institute Press, 1976), 41 (italics added); "Briefed Estimate of the Situation," Feb. 2, 1942, Graybook, 1:227–29.

4. King to Nimitz, Feb. 6, 1942, Graybook, 1:220–21.

5. Running Summary, Feb. 21 and Feb. 26, 1942, Graybook, 1:242, 246.

6. King to Nimitz, Jan. 27, 1942, and Nimitz to King, Jan. 29 and 31, 1942, Graybook, 1:204.

7. King to Nimitz, Jan. 31 and Feb. 15, 1942, both in Graybook, 8:204–6.

8. Op Plan R5-1, 1942, Graybook, 1:200.

9. Running Summary, April 3, 1942, Graybook, 1:332.

10. King to Nimitz, Jan. 29, 1942, and April 14, 1942, and Running Summary, Jan. 29 and May 1, 1942, all in Graybook, 1:187, 197, 345, and 432; U.S. Atlantic Fleet Organization, Jan. 29, 1942, NHHC.

11. Handwritten notes in the margin of the "Briefed Estimate," Feb. 5, 1942, Running Summary, Feb. 9, 1942, and Op Plan R5-1, 1942, all in Graybook, 1:200, 238–39. See also "Estimate of the Most Effective Units of Battleship Type in the Near Future," almost certainly prepared by Pye, in Buell Papers (Spruance Collection), NWC.

12. King to Nimitz, and Running Summary, both Feb. 22, 1942, Graybook, 1:252.

13. Running Summary, Feb. 15, 1942, Graybook, 1:216.

14. Marginal note on "Briefed Estimate," Feb. 2, 1942, and Running Summary, Feb. 10 and 15, 1942, Graybook, 1:212, 216, 238; Potter, *Nimitz*, 42.

15. William F. Halsey and J. Bryan III, *Admiral Halsey's Story* (New York: McGraw-Hill, 1947), 97.

16. Running Summary, Feb. 19, 1942, Graybook, 1:240; After Action Report, Jan. 21–March 26, 1942, Brown Papers, USNA; John Lundstrom, *The First Team: Pacific Naval Air Combat from Pearl Harbor to Midway* (Annapolis: Naval Institute Press, 1984), 91–94.

17. Brown to Nimitz, Feb. 20, 1942, Graybook, 1:250.

18. Brown to Nimitz, Feb. 23, 26, and 27, 1942, and Nimitz to Task Force Commanders, Feb. 25, 1942, all in Graybook, 1:253–55.

19. Brown to Nimitz, Feb. 26, 1942, Graybook, 1:255; Craig L. Symonds, *The Battle of Midway* (New York: Oxford University Press, 2011), 84–85.

20. Running Summary, Feb. 23 and 25, 1942, Graybook, 1:242, 244.

21. Edwin T. Layton with Roger Pineau, *"And I Was There": Breaking the Secrets—Pearl Harbor and Midway* (Old Saybrook, CT: Konecky & Konecky, 2001), 371.

22. Running Summary, March 4, 1942, Graybook, 1:262.

23. Running Summary, March 7, 1942, and Nimitz to Halsey, Feb. 25, 1942, both in Graybook, 1:254, 266.

24. Running Summary, March 11, 1942, Graybook, 1:267; Symonds, *The Battle of Midway*, 86.

25. Running Summary, March 13, 1942, and King to Fletcher, March 13, 1942, both in Graybook, 1:269, 288; King to all TF commanders, Feb. 26, 1942, Graybook, 1:256.

26. Thomas Wildenberg, *Gray Steel and Black Oil* (Annapolis: Naval Institute Press, 1996), 170–71.

27. Nimitz to Brown and Fletcher, March 12, 13, and 21, 1942, Graybook, 1:285, 288, 313; Nimitz to King, March 28, 1942, Graybook, 1:257.

28. Nimitz to Fletcher, March 21, King to Fletcher, March 28, Fletcher to King, March 29, and King to Fletcher, March 31, 1942, all in Graybook, 1:313, 320, 322, 324.

29. King to Nimitz and Nimitz to King, both March 31, 1942, Map Room Files, box 37, FDRL.

30. Nimitz to Catherine Nimitz, Dec. 21, 1941, and March 22, 1942 (Nimitz Diary), NHHC; Richard B. Frank, *Tower of Skulls: A History of the Asia Pacific War* (New York: W. W. Norton, 2019), 496. I am grateful to Rich Frank for bringing this memo to my attention.

Chapter 5

1. FDR to Churchill, March 9, 1942, and Churchill to FDR, March 17, 1942, both in Warren F. Kimball, ed., *Churchill and Roosevelt: The Complete Correspondence* (Princeton: Princeton University Press, 1984), 1:398; Ernest J. King and Walter Muir Whitehill, *Fleet Admiral King: A Naval Record* (New York: W. W. Norton, 1952), 370–72.

2. David L. Roll, *George Marshall: Defender of the Republic* (New York: Dutton Caliber, 2019), 171–72.

3. King to Nimitz, April 3, 1942, Graybook, 1:328–30.

4. Ibid.

5. King to Nimitz, April 3 and 4, and Nimitz to King, April 5, 1942, all in Graybook, 1:328, 331.

6. Nimitz to King, April 5, 1942, Graybook, 1:331.

7. John B. Lundstrom, *Black Shoe Carrier Admiral: Frank Jack Fletcher at Coral Sea, Midway, and Guadalcanal* (Annapolis: Naval Institute Press, 2006), 118.

8. King to Nimitz, April 14, 1942, Graybook, 1:345.

9. Running Summary, Feb. 12, 1942, and Leary to Nimitz, Feb. 14, 1942, both in Graybook, 1:214, 223–24.

10. King to TF commanders, info Nimitz, Feb. 26, 1942, Graybook, 1:256.

11. King to Nimitz, March 9, 1942, Graybook, 1:282; Nimitz to ComPhibForPac (Brown), March 31, 1942, Map Room Files, box 37, FDRL.

12. Running Summary, April 16, 1942, Nimitz to King, April 17, 1942, and King to Nimitz, Feb. 22, 1942, all in Graybook, 1:352, 259, 252.

13. King to Nimitz, Feb. 16, 1942; Nimitz to King, March 15 and March 19, 1942; Running Summary, March 12 and 24, 1942, all in Graybook, 1:216, 268, 292, 294, 311.

14. E. B. Potter, *Nimitz* (Annapolis: Naval Institute Press, 1976), 36.

15. Edwin T. Layton with Roger Pineau, *"And I Was There": Breaking the Secrets—Pearl Harbor and Midway* (Old Saybrook, CT: Konecky & Konecky, 2001), 356.

16. Potter, *Nimitz*, 36.

17. King to Nimitz, March 19, 1942, Commanding General Second Marines (Charles Price) to Nimitz, March 24, 1942, Running Summary, May 4, 1942, all in Graybook, 1:311, 316–18, 435.

18. Kim Munholland, *Rock of Contention: Free French and Americans at War in New Caledonia, 1940–1945* (New York: Berghahn Books, 2005), 93–98.

19. Ibid., 103.

20. King to Nimitz, April 11, 1942, Map Room Files, box 39, FDRL.

21. Munholland, *Rock of Contention*, 97; King to Ghormley, May 8, 1942, and Stark to King, May 9, 1942, both in Graybook, 1:448, 450–51.

22. Running Summary, May 15, and Patch to Nimitz, May 18, 1942, both in Graybook, 1:482, 484.

23. King to Stark, May 6, 1942, Running Summary, May 15, Patch to Nimitz, and Ghormley to Nimitz, both May 19, and Nimitz to Patch ("For Admiral d'Argenlieu"), May 22, 1942, all in Graybook, 1:495, 500.

24. Nimitz to Patch, May 22, and Patch to Nimitz, May 29, 1942, both in Graybook, 1:525, 546; Munholland, *Rock of Contention*, 98–102.

25. Stark to King, info Nimitz, July 22, 1942, Graybook, 1:758.

Chapter 6

1. Edwin T. Layton with Roger Pineau, *"And I Was There": Breaking the Secrets—Pearl Harbor and Midway* (Old Saybrook, CT: Konecky & Konecky, 2001), 354.

2. Ibid., 357.

3. Ibid., 359.

4. King to Nimitz, Feb. 6, 1942, Graybook, 1:220–21; Layton, *"And I Was There,"* 268.

5. Layton, *"And I Was There,"* 389.

6. Ibid., 374; Steve Horn, *The Second Attack on Pearl Harbor: Operation K and Other Japanese Attempts to Bomb America in World War II* (Annapolis: Naval Institute Press, 2005), 73–74; Craig L. Symonds, *The Battle of Midway* (New York: Oxford University Press, 2011), 209.

7. Layton, *"And I Was There,"* 378; Running Summary, April 23 and April 29, 1942, Graybook, 1:409, 421.

8. Nimitz to King, March 11, 1942, Graybook, 1:283.

9. John T. Carrell, "Over the Hump to China," *Air Force Magazine*, October 2009, 69.

10. William F. Halsey and J. Bryan III, *Admiral Halsey's Story* (New York: McGraw-Hill, 1947), 101.

11. Running Summary, April 17, 1942, Graybook, 1:364.

12. Edwin Layton oral history (May 30 and 31, 1970), "A Cluster of Interviews," 4:108, 120, USNA.

13. W. J. Holmes, *Double-Edged Secrets: U.S. Naval Intelligence Operations in the Pacific During World War II* (Annapolis: Naval Institute Press, 1979), 72.

14. Running Summary, April 18, 1942, and "Estimate of the Situation," April 22, 1942, both in Graybook, 1:501–5, 373–75.

15. "Estimate of the Situation," April 22, 1942, Graybook, 1:371–79; Annex D of the "Estimate," 407.

16. John B. Lundstrom, "Confrontation in the Coral Sea," in Karl James, ed., *Kokoda: Beyond the Legend* (Cambridge, UK: Cambridge University Press, 2012), 60.

17. Nimitz's orders to Fletcher, April 22, 1942, are quoted in John B. Lundstrom, *Black Shoe Carrier Admiral: Frank Jack Fletcher at Coral Sea, Midway, and Guadalcanal* (Annapolis: Naval Institute Press, 2006), 132–33.

18. "Estimate of the Situation," April 22, 1942, and Nimitz to Fletcher, April 26, 1942, both in Graybook, 1:380, 395, 413.

19. Ernest J. King and Walter Muir Whitehill, *Fleet Admiral King: A Naval Record* (New York: W. W. Norton, 1952), 377; interview of Walter Muir Whitehill (July 31, 1949), Buell Papers (King Collection), box 19, folder 10, NWC; Catherine Nimitz oral history (June 4, 1969), "A Cluster of Interviews," 3:30, USNA.

20. Interview of Walter Muir Whitehill (July 31, 1949), Buell Papers (King Collection), box 19, folder 10, NWC.

21. I am grateful to John B. Lundstrom for illuminating this aspect of Nimitz's decision-making. See his article "Confrontation in the Coral Sea," 60–62, as well as his *Black Shoe Carrier Admiral*.

22. Richard B. Frank, *Tower of Skulls: A History of the Asia-Pacific War* (New York: W. W. Norton, 2019), 492–94.

23. "Minutes of Conversations Between CominCh and CinCPac, April 25–26, 1942," King Papers, Series II, box 10, NHHC.

24. Catherine and Nancy Nimitz oral history (June 8, 1969), 3:13, Lloyd Mustin oral history (March 10, 1970), 4:18, and H. Arthur Lamar oral history (May 3, 1970), 2:5, all in "A Cluster of Interviews," USNA. Lamar claimed that Nimitz hated the gray uniforms "with a passion."

25. Nimitz to King, May 2 and 5, 1942, Graybook, 1:429, 440; Nimitz to Catherine, May 4, 1942 (Nimitz Diary), NHHC.

26. Running Summary, May 4, 1942, Graybook, 1:435; Nimitz to Catherine Nimitz, May 4, 1942 (Nimitz Diary), NHHC.

Chapter 7

1. Running Summary, May 6, 1942, Graybook, 1:443.
2. E. B. Potter, *Nimitz* (Annapolis: Naval Institute Press, 1976), 70–71.
3. Running Summary, May 6, 1942, Graybook, 1:442; David C. Fuquea, "Advantage Japan: The Imperial Japanese Navy's Superior High Seas Refueling Capacity," *Journal of Military History*, Jan. 2020, 224–25, 229–30.
4. John B. Lundstrom, *Black Shoe Carrier Admiral: Frank Jack Fletcher at Coral Sea, Midway, and Guadalcanal* (Annapolis: Naval Institute Press, 2006), 153–55.
5. Running Summary, May 7, 1942, Graybook, 1:443; Potter, *Nimitz*, 74–75; Edwin T. Layton with Roger Pineau, *"And I Was There": Breaking the Secrets—Pearl Harbor and Midway* (Old Saybrook, CT: Konecky & Konecky, 2001), 403.
6. Running Summary, May 8, 1942, Graybook, 1:472; Layton, *"And I Was There,"* 404; Nimitz to Fletcher, April 22, 1942, in Lundstrom, *Black Shoe Carrier Admiral*, 132–33.
7. Running Summary, May 9, 1942, Graybook, 1:473.
8. Nimitz to King, May 10, 1942, Graybook, 1:463 (also in Graybook, 8:275); Samuel E. Morison, *Coral Sea, Midway and Submarine Actions* (Boston: Little, Brown, 1949), 60n.
9. King to Nimitz, May 15, 1942, and Running Summary, May 10, 1942, both in Graybook, 1:468, 475.
10. Fletcher to Nimitz, May 16, 1942, Graybook, 1:468–69.
11. Nimitz to King, June 21, 1942, Graybook, 8:52.
12. Lundstrom, *Black Shoe Carrier Admiral*, 155–56.
13. Nimitz to King, May 20, 1942, Graybook, 1:487.
14. Nimitz to MacArthur, May 17, and MacArthur to Nimitz, info King, May 19, 1942, Graybook, 1:469, 493; MacArthur to Nimitz, and Nimitz to MacArthur, both June 1, 1942, Graybook, 1:549.
15. "CINCPAC Intelligence Briefs, OP-20G file (May 19, 1942)," 75, Special Collections, Nimitz Library, USNA.
16. Nimitz to King, May 14 and May 21, and King to Nimitz, May 15 and May 18, 1942, all in Graybook, 1:465–68, 474, 488, 492.
17. Nimitz to King, May 14, 1942, Graybook, 1:465.
18. Traffic Intelligence Summaries, Combat Intelligence Unit, 14th Naval District, May 15, 1942, USNA; King to Nimitz, May 15, 1942, and Stark to King, May 19, 1942, both in Graybook, 1:468, 499.
19. King to Nimitz, May 15, and Nimitz to King, May 16, 1942, both in Graybook, 1:468–69.
20. Nimitz to Halsey, May 14 ("eyes only") and May 17, 1942, and King to Nimitz, May 17, 1942, Graybook, 8:9, 1:491, 489; Lundstrom, *Black Shoe Carrier Admiral*, 211, 216. As Lundstrom put it, "Nimitz defied Cominch and redeployed his fleet to fight" (p. 212).

21. Nimitz to Halsey, May 14, 1942, Graybook, 8:9; Lundstrom, *Black Shoe Carrier Admiral*, 211.

22. Nimitz to Halsey, May 16, Nimitz to MacArthur, May 17, and Nimitz to Midway Commanders, May 18, 1942, all in Graybook, 1:469, 471, and 496; also Running Summary, May 18, 1942, Graybook, 1:502.

23. W. J. Holmes, *Double-Edged Secrets: U.S. Naval Intelligence Operations in the Pacific During World War II* (Annapolis: Naval Institute Press, 1979), 90; Joseph J. Rochefort oral history (Oct. 5, 1969), "A Cluster of Interviews," 4:211, USNA; Thomas H. Dyer oral history, 241, USNA; author interview with Donald "Mac" Showers (May 4, 2010); Craig L. Symonds, *The Battle of Midway* (New York: Oxford University Press, 2011), 185.

24. Nimitz to King, May 25, 1942, Graybook, 1:530.

25. A printed version of Nimitz's 1923 thesis is available in Chester W. Nimitz, "Naval Tactics," *Naval War College Review*, Nov.–Dec. 1982, 8–13. The quotation is from p. 10.

26. Lundstrom, *Black Shoe Carrier Admiral*, 225. The most complete biography of Spruance is Thomas B. Buell, *The Quiet Warrior: A Biography of Admiral Raymond A. Spruance* (Boston: Little, Brown, 1974 and Annapolis: Naval Institute Press, 1987). See also Symonds, *The Battle of Midway*, 190–91.

27. Robert Oliver to Thomas Buell, Aug. 5, 1971, Buell Papers (Spruance Collection), box 3, folder 12, NWC.

28. Ibid.

29. "Estimate of the Situation," May 26, 1942, Graybook, 1:515, 520. Nimitz's verbal instructions to Spruance, quoted here, are from Spruance's flag lieutenant, Robert J. Oliver, who was present. See Oliver to Buell, Aug. 5, 1971, Buell Papers (Spruance Collection), box 3, folder 12, NWC. See also Nimitz to Commander Striking Group, May 28, 1944, Operational Plan 29–42.

Chapter 8

1. Joseph J. Rochefort oral history (Oct. 5, 1969), "A Cluster of Interviews," USNA, 1:217–19. Curiously, though both Layton and especially Rochefort remembered the occasion vividly, the Running Summary does not mention Rochefort's presence at the May 27 staff meeting.

2. Ibid. As late as May 31, the Office of Naval Intelligence (ONI) in Washington was predicting that the Japanese would have five carriers, declaring that the *Zuikaku* "has been assigned to the Midway Force." Once again, however, Rochefort was right and Washington was wrong. CNO Summaries of Radio Intelligence, May 31, 1942, RG 457, NARA. I am grateful to Elliot Carlson for bringing this to my attention.

3. Running Summary, May 27, 1942, Graybook, 1:544–45.

4. Edward P. Stafford, *The Big E: The Story of the USS* Enterprise (Annapolis: Naval Institute Press, 1962), 72.

5. Nimitz to Navy Yard, May 27, 1942, Graybook, 8:27.

6. John B. Lundstrom, *Black Shoe Carrier Admiral: Frank Jack Fletcher at Coral Sea, Midway, and Guadalcanal* (Annapolis: Naval Institute Press, 2006), 116–17; E. B. Potter, *Nimitz* (Annapolis: Naval Institute Press, 1976), 85–86; Craig L. Symonds, *The Battle of Midway* (New York: Oxford University Press, 2011), 193.

7. Lundstrom, *Black Shoe Carrier Admiral*, 225–26.

8. Running Summary, May 27, 1942, Graybook, 1:543; Nimitz to Navy Yard, Pearl Harbor, and Nimitz to King, both May 28, 1942, Graybook, 8:28.

9. Gordon Prange interview of Fletcher (Sept. 17, 1966), in Prange Papers, UMD; Catherine Nimitz oral history (June 4, 1969), "A Cluster of Interviews," 3:35, USNA.

10. Fletcher to Nimitz, May 28, 1942, and Nimitz to King, May 29, 1942, both in King Papers, series I, box 2, NHHC; Symonds, *The Battle of Midway*, 193–95.

11. Nimitz to Spruance (copy to Fletcher "by hand"), May 30, 1942, Graybook, 8:37.

12. Nimitz to Catherine Nimitz, May 31, and June 2, 1942 (Nimitz Diary), NHHC.

13. John R. Redman oral history (June 5, 1969), "A Cluster of Interviews," 4:7, USNA; Nimitz to Catherine Nimitz, May 31, 1942 (Nimitz Diary), NHHC.

14. Nimitz to NAS Midway, and Nimitz to King, both June 1, 1942, Graybook, 8:52–53.

15. Reid to Gordon Prange, Dec. 10, 1966, cited in Gordon Prange, Donald Goldstein, and Katherine V. Dillon, *Miracle at Midway* (New York: McGraw-Hill, 1982), 162–64; Symonds, *The Battle of Midway*, 413.

16. Nimitz to TF commanders, June 4, 1942, Graybook, 8:92 (commas added for clarity); Symonds, *The Battle of Midway*, 214.

17. Symonds, *The Battle of Midway*, 225–26.

18. "Pertinent Extracts from Communications Logs Relative to Midway Attack," Action Reports, reel 2, USNA; Fletcher to S. E. Morison, Dec. 1, 1947, Fletcher Papers, box 1, AHC; interview of Howard Ady by Walter Lord (April 9, 1966), Walter Lord Collection, box 18, NHHC.

19. Simard to Nimitz, Nimitz to King, and Nimitz to TF commanders, all June 4, 1942, Graybook, 8:102, 107, 113, 115; Nimitz to Potter, May 4, 1975, Buell Papers, box 4, folder 14, NWC; Potter, *Nimitz*, 97; author interview with Donald "Mac" Showers (May 4, 2010).

20. Edwin Layton oral history (March 19, 1970), "A Cluster of Interviews," 4:34, USNA.

21. Samuel E. Morison, *Coral Sea, Midway and Submarine Actions* (Boston: Little, Brown, 1949, 122; Potter, *Nimitz*, 95.

22. Potter, *Nimitz*, 97; Edwin Layton oral history (March 19, 1970), "A Cluster of Interviews," 4:41, USNA.

23. Fletcher's Action Report, June 14, 1942, Action Reports, reel 2, USNA; Lundstrom, *Black Shoe Carrier Admiral*, 242; Fletcher to S. E. Morison, Dec. 1, 1947, Fletcher Papers, box 1, AHC.

24. Richard Best oral history (Aug. 11, 1995), NMPW; Gordon Prange interview of Spruance (Sept. 5, 1964), Prange Papers, box 17, UMD.

25. Spruance to Nimitz, June 4, 1942, Graybook, 8:140.

26. Nimitz to King, June 4, 1942, in Graybook, 8:140; Nimitz to Potter, May 4, 1975, Buell Papers (Spruance Collection), box 4, folder 14, NWC.

27. Fletcher to Nimitz, June 4, 1942, Graybook, 8:128.

28. Fletcher to Nimitz (commas added for clarity), Nimitz to Simard, and Simard to Nimitz, all June 4, 1942, Graybook, 8:138.

29. Fletcher to Nimitz, and Nimitz to Fletcher, both June 4, 1942, Graybook, 8:145, 148.

30. Nimitz to Fletcher, June 4, 1942, Graybook, 8:157; Nimitz's order to the *Vireo* is in Graybook, 8:146.

31. Thomas B. Buell, *The Quiet Warrior: A Biography of Admiral Raymond A. Spruance* (Annapolis: Naval Institute Press, 1987), 154.

32. Spruance to Nimitz (Action Report), June 16, 1942, reel 3, USNA; Buell, *Quiet Warrior*, 154.

33. Nimitz to Potter, April 24, 1965, copy in Buell Papers (Spruance Collection), box 4, folder 14, NWC.

34. Nimitz to King, June 5, 1942, Graybook, 1:552.

35. Oral history of Catherine Nimitz (June 4, 1969), "A Cluster of Interviews," 3:35, USNA.

36. Symonds, *Battle of Midway*, 351–56.

37. Nimitz to Task Force Commanders, June 5, 1942, Graybook, 8:163; *New York Times*, June 6, 7, and 8, 1942.

Chapter 9

1. Nimitz to King, June 8, 1942, and Nimitz to PacFleet, June 16, 1942, Graybook, 1:565, 583; John B. Lundstrom, *Black Shoe Carrier Admiral: Frank Jack Fletcher at Coral Sea, Midway, and Guadalcanal* (Annapolis: Naval Institute Press, 2006), 302–7.

2. Transcript of Spruance interview with Philippe de Baussel (July 6, 1965) for *Paris Match* magazine, Raymond A. Spruance Papers, box 2, folder 14, NWC; H. Arthur Lamar, *I Saw Stars* (Fredericksburg, TX: The Admiral Nimitz Foundation, 1975), 3; Nimitz to Catherine Nimitz, Sept. 20, 1942 (Nimitz Diary), NHHC; George van Deurs oral history (Oct. 12, 1969), 524, USNA.

3. Thomas B. Buell, *The Quiet Warrior: A Biography of Admiral Raymond A. Spruance* (Boston: Little, Brown, 1974), 167n.

4. Craig L. Symonds, *The Battle of Midway* (New York: Oxford University Press, 2011), 287.

5. See the discussion of this event in Symonds, *Battle of Midway*, 245–65. The visitor who thought Mitscher looked "not a day over eighty" (see caption to first figure in chapter 9) was RADM Putty Read, who is quoted in Theodore Taylor, *The Magnificent Mitscher* (Annapolis: Naval Institute Press, 1991), 157.

6. Symonds, *Battle of Midway*, Appendix F, 389–91.

7. Mitscher to Nimitz, June 13, 1942 (Action Report), USNA, reel 3.

8. Buell, *The Quiet Warrior*, 165.

9. Ibid., 168–69; Symonds, *The Battle of Midway*, 331–32.

10. Mitscher to Nimitz, June 13, 1942 (Action Report), USNA, reel 3.

11. Reminiscences of RADM Ernest M. Eller (Jan. 16, 1975), 454–57, USNA; Nimitz's Official Report on the Battle of Midway, June 28, 1942, USNA.

12. Edgar Stanton Maclay, *A History of the United States Navy from 1775 to 1898* (New York: Appleton, 1898), and *A History of the United States Navy from 1775 to 1902* (New York: Appleton, 1902); E. B. Potter, *Nimitz* (Annapolis: Naval Institute Press, 1976), 53.

13. Potter, *Nimitz*, 52–53.

14. Op Plan 29-42, dated May 27, 1942, is available online at http://www.midway42 .org/Features/op-plan29-42.pdf. Nimitz to TF commanders, and Nimitz to King, both June 4, 1942, Graybook, 8:103, 105, 115, 126.

15. Official Report on the Battle of Midway (June 28, 1942), 13, USNA.

16. Interestingly, the correspondence between Nimitz and King on this issue is not in the Graybook. See instead Nimitz to King, June 22, King to Nimitz, June 23, and Nimitz to King, June 24, 1942, in CincPac Secret and Confidential Messages, reel 16, NARA. See also Lundstrom, *Black Shoe Carrier Admiral*, 305.

17. Lundstrom, *Black Shoe Carrier Admiral*, 303–4; Taylor, *Magnificent Mitscher*, 139–40.

18. General Court Martial Order No. 21, Sept. 28, 1908, Disciplinary File, courtesy Richard Lay; Potter, *Nimitz*, 61; Nimitz to Catherine Nimitz, Aug. 10, 1942 (Nimitz Diary), NHHC.

19. Reminiscences of RADM Ernest M. Eller (Aug. 25, 1977), 545, USNA.

20. King to Nimitz, and Nimitz to King, both June 15, 1942, Graybook, 1:586–87; Symonds, *The Battle of Midway*, 60–63, 360–61.

21. Lundstrom, *Black Shoe Carrier Admiral*, 306.

22. Running Summary, June 14, 1942, Graybook, 1:592.

23. Nimitz to King, June 17, 1942, Graybook, 1:585.

24. MacArthur to JCS with copy to Nimitz, June 8, 1942, Graybook, 1:557.

25. King to MacArthur, June 23, 1942, Graybook, 1:601; Ernest J. King and Walter Muir Whitehill, *Fleet Admiral King: A Naval Record* (New York: W. W. Norton, 1952), 387.

26. King to Nimitz, June 23, and Running Summary, June 25, 1942, both in Graybook, 1:601, 670.

27. Medical notes, July 2, 1942, courtesy of Richard Lay; Potter, *Nimitz*, 109–11.

28. Running Summary, June 30, 1942, Graybook, 1:673; "Conversations Between Cominch and Cincpac, July 4, 1942," Buell Papers (King Collection), NWC.

29. Elliot Carlson, *Stanley Johnson's Blunder: The Reporter Who Spilled the Secret Behind the U.S. Navy's Victory at Midway* (Annapolis: Naval Institute Press, 2017); "Conversations Between Comich and Cincpac, July 4, 1942," Buell Papers (King Collection), NWC.

30. "An Offensive for the Capture and Occupation of Tulagi and Vicinity," July 6, 1942, Graybook, 1:709–43; George C. Dyer, *The Amphibians Came to Conquer: The Story of Richmond Kelly Turner* (Washington, DC: Government Printing Office, 1971), 1:273–75.

31. King and Whitehill, *Fleet Admiral King*, 386.

32. "An Offensive for the Capture and Occupation of Tulagi and Vicinity," July 6, 1942, Graybook, 1:722, 728.

Chapter 10

1. Nimitz to Catherine Nimitz, July 11, 1942 (Nimitz Diary), NHHC.

2. Maxwell Oliver, "Vice Admiral Robert L. Ghormley: In the Shadow of the Fleet," student research paper, U.S. Naval War College, 2020.

3. Chester Nimitz, "Naval Tactics," *Naval War College Review*, Nov.–Dec. 1982, 10; Nimitz to Ghormley, July 7 and 9, 1942, Graybook, 1:610, 614.

4. MacArthur and Ghormley to King, info Nimitz, July 8, King to Ghormley, July 9, and Ghormley to King, July 11, 1942, all in Graybook, 1:610–15.

5. Ghormley to Nimitz, info King, July 19, 1942, and "An Offensive for the Capture and Occupation of Tulagi and Vicinity," July 6, 1942, both in Graybook, 1:620, 722, 728.

6. Nimitz to King, July 17, 1942, Graybook, 1:774–75.

7. Running Summary, July 17 and 20, Graybook, 1:772, 777; "Japanese Naval Operations, Estimate of," July 24, 1942, in Graybook, 1:842; Chester Lay to the author, June 9, 2021.

8. Ghormley to Nimitz, July 11, 1942, and Running Summary, Aug. 1, 1942, both in Graybook, 1:617, 791.

9. E. B. Potter, *Nimitz* (Annapolis: Naval Institute Press, 1976), 174–75; H. Arthur Lamar, *I Saw Stars: Some Memories of Commander Hal Lamar, Fleet Admiral Nimitz' Flag Lieutenant* (Fredericksburg, TX: The Admiral Nimitz Foundation, 1975), 4; Henry A. Walker Jr., *Memoirs of Henry Alexander Walker, Jr.*, 32, 50, Michael Lilly Collection; oral histories of Edward Brewer Jr. (Jan. 24, 1970), 1:3, and Joe Wheeler Jr. (Aug. 4, 1969), 5:11, both in "A Cluster of Interviews," USNA.

10. Mell A. Peterson oral history (May 24, 1969), 5:8, Thomas C. Anderson oral history (July 5, 1969), 1:9, and George W. Bauernschmidt oral history (Aug. 9, 1969), 1:8, all in "A Cluster of Interviews," USNA; Robert J. Oliver to Thomas B. Buell, Sept. 17, 1971, Buell Papers (Spruance Collection), box 3, folder 12, NWC; Nimitz to Catherine, Aug. 16, 1942 (Nimitz Diary), NHHC.

11. Nimitz to Catherine Nimitz, July 23, 1942 (Nimitz Diary), NHHC; Edward D. Spruance to E. P. Forrestal, July 16, 1963, Buell Papers (Spruance Collection), box 3, folder 17, NWC.

12. King to Nimitz, copy Ghormley, July 3, and Nimitz to Ghormley, July 9, 1942, both in Graybook, 1:605–7, 613; Lundstrom, *Black Shoe Carrier Admiral*, 327.

13. Lundstrom, *Black Shoe Carrier Admiral*, 321–22; Conference Notes, July 4, 1942, in Buell Papers (King Collection), NWC; Ghormley to Fletcher, July 20, 1942, Graybook, 1:625.

14. Running Summary, July 5, 1942, Graybook, 1:707; Lundstrom, *Black Shoe Carrier Admiral*, 334–37.

15. Ghormley to Fletcher, Aug. 2, 1942, Graybook, 1:631.

16. Jon T. Hoffman, *From Makin to Bougainville: Marine Raiders in the Pacific War* (Washington, DC: Marine Corps Historical Center, 1995), 1–9; George W. Smith, *Carlson's Raid: The Daring Marine Assault on Makin* (New York: Berkley Books, 2001), 79; Nimitz to King, July 30, 1942, Graybook, 1:629.

17. George C. Dyer, *The Amphibians Came to Conquer: The Story of Admiral Richmond Kelly Turner* (Washington, DC: Government Printing Office, 1972), 318. Turner's

August 7 report to Ghormley, which is in the Graybook (1:638), is not in Ghormley's letter book. For a discussion of this, see Lundstrom, *Black Shore Carrier Admiral*, 369–70.

18. Fletcher to Ghormley, July 9, 1942, Graybook, 1:639; Waldo Drake oral history (June 15, 1969), "A Cluster of Interviews," 2:28, USNA.

19. Ghormley to TF commanders, and Ghormley to Nimitz, info King, both Aug. 9, 1942, and Ghormley to MacArthur, Aug. 10, 1942, all in Graybook, 1:640–42.

20. Nimitz to King, info Ghormley, Aug. 9, 1942, King to Nimitz, Aug. 10, 1942, both in Graybook, 1:642–43.

21. Nimitz to Ghormley, info King, Aug. 10 and 11, 1942, Graybook, 1:644, 646.

22. Ghormley to Nimitz, info King, Aug. 10, 1942, and Turner to Ghormley, Aug. 11, 1942, both in Graybook, 1:644, 645.

23. Ghormley to Turner, Aug. 12, 1942, Graybook, 1:646.

24. Nimitz to King, Aug. 12, 1942, Graybook, 1:648.

25. Preston V. Mercer oral history (Oct. 18, 1969), "A Cluster of Interviews," 4:14, USNA; and Reminiscences of Bernard L. Austin, 290–91, USNA.

26. FDR to Nimitz, Aug. 4, 1942, Presidential Personal File (PPF-8541), FDRL; Recollections of Catherine and Nancy Nimitz (June 8, 1969), "A Cluster of Interviews," 26, USNA; Potter, *Nimitz*, 222.

27. Sam P. Moncure oral history (July 30, 1969), "A Cluster of Interviews," 4:31, USNA.

28. Mell A. Peterson oral history (May 24, 1969), and H. Arthur Lamar oral history (May 3, 1970), both in "A Cluster of Interviews," USNA; Lamar, *I Saw Stars*, 11; Robert Allen oral history (Jan. 4, 2015), 3, NMPW.

29. Craig L. Symonds, *World War II at Sea: A Global History* (New York: Oxford University Press, 2018), 326.

30. Fletcher to Ghormley, info Nimitz, Aug. 24, 1942, Graybook, 1:809.

31. The description of Fletcher's "strained expression" is from McCain. See Lundstrom, *Black Shoe Carrier Admiral*, 483–85.

Chapter 11

1. Ghormley to Nimitz, Sept. 1, 2, and 11, 1942, and Nimitz to King, Sept. 1, 1942, all in Graybook, 2:863, 874; Robert L. Ghormley Jr. oral history, reel 1, ECU. Nimitz's August 17 message to the fleet is in Richard B. Frank, *Guadalcanal: The Definitive Account of the Landmark Battle* (New York: Random House, 1990), 204.

2. Running Summary, Aug. 30, 1942, Graybook, 2:839.

3. "Conference Notes," Sept. 9, 1942, included in Graybook, 2:1014–30.

4. Ibid., 2:1027; Clark G. Reynolds, *Admiral John H. Towers: The Struggle for Naval Air Supremacy* (Annapolis: Naval Institute Press, 1991), 370, 378, 396–405; Ernest J. King and Walter Muir Whitehill, *Fleet Admiral King* (New York: W. W. Norton, 1952), 232, 260–61.

5. FDR to Knox, June 12, 1942, Buell Papers (King Collection), box 12, folder 28, NWC.

6. Nimitz to Catherine Nimitz, Sept. 15, 1942 (Nimitz Diary), NHHC.

7. The fellow admiral was Thomas C. Kinkaid. See Gerald E. Wheeler, *Kinkaid of the Seventh Fleet: A Biography of Admiral Thomas C. Kinkaid, U.S. Navy* (Washington, DC: Naval Historical Center, 1995), 301.

8. "Conference Notes," Sept. 9, 1942, Graybook, 2:1029; Jon T. Hoffman, *From Makin to Bougainville: Marine Raiders in the Pacific War* (Washington, DC: Marine Corps Historical Center, 1995), 1–9; George W. Smith, *Carlson's Raid: The Daring Marine Assault on Makin* (New York: Berkley Books, 2001).

9. King and Whitehill, *Fleet Admiral King*, 387–88; George C. Dyer, *The Amphibians Came to Conquer: The Story of Admiral Richmond Kelly Turner* (Washington, DC: Government Printing Office, 1972), 404; Ghormley to King, info Nimitz, Sept. 10, 1942, Graybook, 2:873; "Conference Notes," Sept. 9, 1942, Graybook, 2:1018 (the word "apparently" was added in pen to the typed "Notes").

10. Ghormley to Nimitz, Sept. 11, 1942, and Running Summary, Sept. 13, 1942, both in Graybook, 2:874, 1035.

11. Nimitz to Catherine Nimitz, Sept. 13, 1942 (Nimitz Diary), NHHC.

12. Running Summary, Sept. 13, 1942, Graybook, 2:1035.

13. Craig L. Symonds, *World War II at Sea: A Global History* (New York: Oxford University Press, 2018), 332; Running Summary, Sept. 16, 1942, Graybook, 2:1039.

14. Richard B. Frank, *Guadalcanal: The Definitive Account of the Landmark Battle* (New York: Penguin, 1990), 252; Nimitz to Catherine Nimitz, Sept. 23, 1942 (Nimitz Diary), NHHC; Running Summary, Sept. 14, 1942, Graybook, 2:1036.

15. Potter, *Nimitz*, 189–90.

16. Nimitz to Catherine Nimitz, Sept. 25, 1942 (Nimitz Diary), NHHC; Potter, *Nimitz*, 191; Dyer, *The Amphibians Came to Conquer*, 404–7, 415–17; Henry H. Arnold, *Global Mission* (New York: Harper & Brothers, 1949), 341–42.

17. The staff officer was Nimitz's communications officer, John R. Redman, in his oral history (June 5, 1969), "A Cluster of Interviews," 4:21, USNA; Running Summary, Sept. 23, 1942, Graybook, 2:1043.

18. Arnold, *Global Mission*, 344.

19. Ibid., 327, 342.

20. I am grateful to Elliot Carlson for sharing with me the medical examiner's report of Sept. 17, 1942, in the Robert Ghormley Papers, Collection 1153, ECU.

21. Arnold, *Global Mission*, 347; Potter, *Nimitz*, 191.

22. Potter, *Nimitz*, 192.

23. William Callaghan oral history (June 30, 1969), 1:13–14, USNA.

24. John R. Redman oral history (June 5, 1969), "A Cluster of Interviews," 5:33, USNA.

25. Edwin P. Hoyt, *How They Won the War in the Pacific: Nimitz and His Admirals* (New York: Weybright & Talley, 1970), 141.

26. Running Summary, Oct. 5, 6, and 11, 1942, 2:1079–80, 1088.

27. William Callaghan oral history (June 30, 1969), "A Cluster of Interviews," 1:17, USNA; Edwin T. Layton with Roger Pineau, *"And I Was There": Breaking the Secrets—Pearl Harbor and Midway* (Old Saybrook, CT: Konecky & Konecky, 2001), 461; Potter, *Nimitz*, 196–97.

28. Layton, *"And I Was There,"* 461–62.

29. Nimitz to Ghormley, Oct. 8, 1942, Papers of Fleet Admiral King, box 2, Operational Archives, NHHC. I am grateful to Elliot Carlson for bringing this letter to my attention.

30. Ibid. Italics added.

31. Running Summary, Oct. 12 and 17, 1942, Graybook, 2:1089, 1096; Nimitz to King, Oct. 8, 1942, King Papers, box 2, Operational Archives, NHHC. Nimitz's suggestion to make the Savo Island report public was added in a penciled postscript. In fact, however, King had already been forced to release information about Savo Island the day before Cape Esperance. See Ian Toll, *Twilight of the Gods: War in the Western Pacific, 1944–1945* (New York: W. W. Norton, 2020), 27. See also Symonds, *World War II at Sea*, 341.

32. Ghormley to Nimitz, Oct. 14 and 16, 1942, and Running Summary, Oct. 13 and 15, 1942, all in Graybook, 2:947, 949, 950, 1093; Nimitz to Catherine Nimitz, Oct. 14 and 17, 1942 (Nimitz Diary), NHHC.

33. Nimitz to King, and King to Nimitz, both Oct. 16, 1942, Graybook, 2:895; Nimitz to Robert L. Ghormley Jr., Jan. 27, 1961, in R. L. Ghormley Jr., unpublished memoir in the Joyner Library, ECU. I am grateful to Elliot Carlson for bringing this letter to my attention.

34. Nimitz to Catherine Nimitz, Oct. 14 and 17, 1942 (Nimitz Diary), NHHC.

35. The language used here is from Potter, *Nimitz*, 198. Halsey himself recalled it slightly differently in his memoir: William F. Halsey Jr. with J. Bryan III, *Admiral Halsey's Story* (New York: McGraw-Hill, 1947), 109.

36. Nimitz to R. L. Ghormley, Jr., Jan. 27, 1961, in Ghormley's unpublished memoir in the Joyner Library, ECU; Nimitz to Catherine Nimitz, Oct. 17, 24, and 25, 1942 (Nimitz Diary), NHHC; Potter, *Nimitz*, 199.

37. Nimitz to Catherine Nimitz, Oct. 19, 1942 (Nimitz Diary), NHHC.

Chapter 12

1. William F. Halsey and J. Bryan III, *Admiral Halsey's Story* (New York: McGraw-Hill, 1947), 137–38; Nimitz to Catherine Nimitz, Oct. 30, 1942 (Nimitz Diary), NHHC.

2. Oral history of John R. Redman (June 5, 1969), "A Cluster of Interviews," 5:4, USNA; Frederick D. Parker, "How OP-20-G Got Rid of Joe Rochefort," *Cryptologia*, July 2000, 219.

3. Nimitz to Horne (VCNO), Dec. 8, 1942, Chief Naval Security Group Papers, RG 38, box 94, NARA; Elliot Carlson, *Joe Rochefort's War: The Odyssey of the Codebreaker Who Outwitted Yamamoto at Midway* (Annapolis: Naval Institute Press, 2011), 405.

4. Carlson, *Joe Rochefort's War*, 399–407; Edwin T. Layton with Roger Pineau, *"And I Was There": Breaking the Secrets—Pearl Harbor and Midway* (Old Saybrook, CT: Konecky & Konecky, 2001), 468; Parker, "How OP-20-G Got Rid of Joe Rochefort," 229–30.

5. Oral history of John Redman (June 5, 1969), "A Cluster of Interviews," 4:12, 16, 55, USNA.

6. "Conference Notes," Sept. 9, 1942, in Graybook, 2:1014–30.

7. *New York Times*, Dec. 3, 1925, 12.

8. Clark G. Reynolds, *Admiral John H. Towers: The Struggle for Naval Air Supremacy* (Annapolis: Naval Institute Press, 1991), 371, 399.

9. *New York Times*, June 12, 1940, 6; Reynolds, *Admiral John H. Towers*, 294, 323.

10. Towers to Nimitz, Sept. 21, 1942, quoted in Reynolds, *Admiral John H. Towers*, 407, 294.

11. Waldo Drake oral history (June 15, 1969), "A Cluster of Interviews," 2:16, USNA.

12. Reminiscences of George W. Anderson Jr., 130, USNA.

13. Theodore Taylor, *The Magnificent Mitscher* (Annapolis: Naval Institute Press, 1954), 78.

14. Running Summary, Jan. 4, 1943, Graybook, 3:1268; King to Stark, Oct. 21, 1942, Graybook, 2:897; E. B. Potter, *Nimitz* (Annapolis: Naval Institute Press, 1976), 203; Halsey and Bryan, *Admiral Halsey's Story*, 137–38.

15. *New York Times*, Nov. 19, 1942, 8.

16. Running Summary, Oct. 21 and 22, 1942, Graybook, 2:1100–101; Nimitz to Catherine Nimitz, Oct. 22, 1942 (Nimitz Diary), NHHC.

17. Running Summary, Oct. 24, 1942, Graybook, 2:1103; Nimitz to Catherine Nimitz, Oct. 23 and 24, 1942 (Nimitz Diary), NHHC.

18. Kinkaid to Halsey, Oct. 27, 1942, Graybook, 2:962. See also Craig L. Symonds, *World War II at Sea: A Global History* (New York: Oxford University Press, 2018), 344–45.

19. Nimitz to Catherine Nimitz, Oct. 26, 1942 (Nimitz Diary), NHHC.

20. Kinkaid to Halsey, two messages (0210 and 0440), Oct. 26, and Halsey to Nimitz, info King, Oct. 27, 1942, all in Graybook, 2:960–61.

21. Halsey to Nimitz, Nov. 1, Nimitz to Halsey, info King, Oct. 28, and Halsey to Nimitz, info King, Oct. 29, 1942, all in Graybook, 2:900, 965.

22. Edward P. Stafford, *The Big E: The Story of the USS* Enterprise (New York: Random House, 1962).

23. Halsey to Nimitz, info King, Nov. 1, 1942, Graybook, 2:900; Running Summary, Oct. 31, and Nov. 9, 1942, 2:1111, 1159; Reynolds, *Admiral John H. Towers*, 408.

24. Quoted in Reynolds, *Admiral John H. Towers*, 409.

25. Nimitz to Catherine Nimitz, Oct. 29, 1942 (Nimitz Diary), NHHC; Potter, *Nimitz*, 219.

26. "Estimate of Enemy Capabilities," Nov. 1, 1942, Graybook, 1143, 1147.

27. Running Summary, Oct. 26, 1942, 2:1105; Nimitz to Halsey, Nov. 8, and King to Nimitz, Nov. 12, 1942, 2:902–3.

28. Symonds, *World War II at Sea*, 363–69.

29. Cactus to Halsey, Nov. 13, and Halsey to Nimitz, Nov. 15, 1942, both in Graybook, 2:980, 934; Symonds, *World War II at Sea*, 363–71.

30. Running Summary, Nov. 13, 1942, Graybook, 2:1166. Commas added for clarity.

31. Russell S. Crenshaw Jr., *The Battle of Tassafaronga* (Annapolis: Naval Institute Press, 1995), 76; Jeffery R. Cox, *Blazing Star, Setting Sun* (New York: Osprey, 2020), 264.

32. Richard B. Frank, *Guadalcanal: The Definitive Account of the Landmark Battle* (New York: Random House, 1990), 519–97.

33. Russell Weigley, *The American War of War: A History of United States Military Strategy and Policy* (New York: Macmillan, 1973).

34. Frank, *Guadalcanal*, 601.

Chapter 13

1. The contemporary was LCDR Dashiell Madeira, quoted in Gerald E. Wheeler, *Kinkaid of the Seventh Fleet: A Biography of Admiral Thomas C. Kinkaid, U.S. Navy* (Washington, DC: Naval Historical Center, 1995), 129.

2. Theodore Taylor, *The Magnificent Mitscher* (Annapolis: Naval Institute Press, 1991), 145.

3. "Estimate of the Situation," Dec. 7, 1942, Graybook, 3:1227.

4. Nimitz to King, Dec. 8, 1942, Graybook, 3:1224–35.

5. "Conference Notes," Dec. 12, 1942, Buell Papers (King Collection), NWC (microfilm).

6. Ibid.

7. E. B. Potter, *Nimitz* (Annapolis: Naval Institute Press, 1976), 211.

8. "Conference Notes," Dec. 12, 1942, Buell Papers (King Collection), NWC (microfilm).

9. King to Nimitz, Jan. 2, 1943, and Nimitz to King, info Halsey, Jan. 2, 1943, both Graybook, 3:1376; Running Summary, Jan. 2, 1943, Graybook, 3:1264; and "Estimate of the Situation," Jan. 13, 1943, Graybook, 3:1292 (p. 16 of report).

10. Running Summary, Jan. 2 and 5, 1943, Graybook, 3:1265, 1269.

11. "CINCPAC Examination of Setting Sun Campaign," Jan. 15, 1943, Graybook, 3:1318, 1336.

12. "Estimate of the Situation," Jan. 15, 1943, Graybook, 3:1277–301. Quotations from pp. 1277, 1279, 1284, and 1302.

13. MacArthur to Nimitz and Halsey, Jan. 13, 1943, Graybook, 3:1381–83; Running Summary, Jan. 13, 1943, Graybook, 3:1275.

14. Hal Lamar oral history (May 3, 1970), "A Cluster of Interviews," 2:77, USNA; Potter, *Nimitz*, 214–15.

15. Potter, *Nimitz*, 216.

16. "Notes on the Conference Held at Nouméa," Jan. 23, 1943, Graybook, 3:1343.

17. Ibid., 3:1345.

18. Ibid, 3:1347.

19. Nimitz to Catherine Nimitz, Jan. 29, 1943, Nimitz Diary, NHHC. I am grateful to Michael A. Lilly for helping me pin down the sequence of events here. See his book *Nimitz at Ease* (Apache Junction, AZ: Stairway Press, 2019), 38.

20. Preston V. Mercer oral history (Oct. 18, 1969), 15, USNA; Nimitz to the Walkers, Dec. 15 and 25, 1942, and May 16, 1943, Michael Lilly Collection.

21. Nimitz to Catherine Nimitz, Jan. 29, 1943 (Nimitz Diary), NHHC; Medical History, Feb. 5, 1943, Lay Family Papers, courtesy of Richard Lay; Preston V. Mercer oral history (Oct. 18, 1969), 4:1, and Thomas C. Anderson oral history (July 5, 1969), 1:3, both in "A Cluster of Interviews," USNA.

22. Thomas C. Anderson oral history (July 5, 1969), 1:3, USNA.

23. King to Nimitz and Halsey, Jan. 31, 1943; King to Nimitz, info Halsey, Feb. 13, 1943; and Halsey to Nimitz, info King, Feb. 22, 1943, all in Graybook, 3:1376, 1435, 1424.

24. Waldo Drake oral history (June 14, 1969), "A Cluster of Interviews," 2:30, USNA.

25. Nimitz to King, Jan. 2, 1943, Graybook, 3:1376 (emphasis in the original); Minutes of Conference in San Francisco (Feb. 21–24, 1943), Buell Papers, NWC; Clark Reynolds, *Admiral John H. Towers: The Struggle for Naval Air Supremacy* (Annapolis: Naval Institute Press, 1991), 424.

26. Nimitz to Halsey, info King, March 20, 1943, Graybook, 3:1489; Bruce Gamble, *Fortress Rabaul: The Battle of the Southwest Pacific, January 1942–April 1943* (Minneapolis: Zenith, 2010), 71.

27. William F. Halsey Jr. and J. Bryan III, *Admiral Halsey's Story* (New York: McGraw-Hill, 1947), 54–55.

28. George C. Kenney, *General Kenney Reports: A Personal History of the Pacific War* (New York: Duell, Sloan & Pearce, 1949), 191–92, 312–13, 321–24.

Chapter 14

1. King to Halsey, Nov. 23, 1942, and Nimitz to King, March 24, 1943, both in Graybook, 2:904, 3:1495.

2. Charles A. Lockwood and Hans Christian Adamson, *Hellcats of the Sea* (New York: Greenburg, 1955), 3–23; Charles A. Lockwood, *Sink 'Em All: Submarine Warfare in the Pacific* (New York: E. P. Dutton, 1951), 93–95; Hal Lamar oral history (May 3, 1970), "A Cluster of Interviews," 2:95, USNA.

3. Lockwood, *Sink 'Em All*, 56, 60, 69; Clay Blair Jr., *Silent Victory* (Philadelphia: J. B. Lippincott, 1975), 430.

4. Ernest Eller oral history (Oct. 18, 1977), 555, USNA; Chester Nimitz Jr. oral history (Nov. 6, 2002), 21, NMPW; Lockwood, *Sink 'Em All*, 87; Edwin T. Layton with Roger Pineau, *"And I Was There": Breaking the Secrets—Pearl Harbor and Midway* (Old Saybrook, CT: Konecky & Konecky, 2001), 472.

5. Lockwood, *Sink 'Em All*, 78, 81; S. S. Murray oral history (May 15, 1971), "A Cluster of Interviews," 5:631, USNA.

6. Nimitz to King, info MacArthur, Jan. 5, 1943, Graybook, 3:1377; MacArthur to King, info Nimitz, Jan. 5, 1943, Graybook, 3:1378.

7. Running Summary, March 16, 1943, Halsey to Nimitz, info King, March 18, 1943, and Lockwood to Nimitz, info Halsey, March 19, 1943, all in Graybook, 3:1449, 1488.

8. Layton, *"And I Was There,"* 475.

9. Hal Lamar oral history (May 3, 1970), "A Cluster of Interviews," 2:91, USNA.

10. Craig L. Symonds, *World War II at Sea: A Global History* (New York: Oxford University Press, 2018), 411, 411n.

11. John C. McManus, *Fire and Fortitude: The U.S. Army in the Pacific War, 1941–1943* (New York: Caliber, 2019), 371–87.

12. Ibid.

13. Nancy Nimitz oral history (June 7, 1969), "A Cluster of Interviews," 3:15, USNA.

14. Michael A. Lilly, *Nimitz at Ease* (Apache Junction, AZ: Stairway Press, 2019), 9–15.

15. Ibid., 17, 78; James T. Lay oral history (Feb. 16, 1970), 4:93, George Bauernschmidt oral history (Aug. 6, 1969), 1:5, and Mary Nimitz oral history (June 4, 1969), 3:36, all in "A Cluster of Interviews," USNA.
16. Lilly, *Nimitz at Ease*, 120–21.
17. Waldo Drake oral history (June 15, 1969), "A Cluster of Interviews," 2:9, USNA.
18. H. Arthur Lamar, *I Saw Stars* (Fredericksburg, TX: Admiral Nimitz Foundation, 1975), 16; James T. Lay oral history (Feb. 16, 1970), 4:17, and Hal Lamar oral history (May 3, 1970), 2:97, 98, both in "A Cluster of Interviews," USNA.
19. King to U.S. Fleet, Feb. 19, 1943, CominCh Tenth Fleet, RG 38, box 35, NARA.
20. Running Summary, June 30, 1943, Graybook, 4:1613.
21. Running Summary, July 5, 1943, Graybook, 4:1615.
22. Halsey to Nimitz, July 7, 1943, Graybook, 4:1764.
23. Halsey to Nimitz, July 9, and Nimitz to King, July 10, 1943, both in Graybook, 4:1765–66.
24. King to Nimitz, July 14, and Aug. 5, 1943, Graybook, 3:1768, 1783.
25. Nimitz to Halsey, July 14, 19, and 21, Graybook, 4:1767, 1768, 1769; Nimitz to Halsey, July 21, 1943, Graybook, 4:1769; Running Summary, July 8, 1943, Graybook, 4:1617.
26. Halsey to Nimitz and others, July 26, 1943, Graybook, 4:1729.
27. Halsey to Nimitz, July 26 and 27, 1943, both in Graybook, 4:1729; Halsey to MacArthur, July 10, 1943, and Halsey to Nimitz, July 11, 1943, both in Graybook, 4:1720, 1766; Running Summary, July 19, 1943, Graybook, 4: 1618.
28. Nimitz to Kinkaid, Aug. 3 and 5, 1943, and Kinkaid to Nimitz, Aug. 5, 1943 (two messages, same date), all in Graybook, 4:1782, 1783.
29. Running Summary, Aug. 19, 1943, Graybook, 4:1639.
30. Kinkaid to Nimitz, Aug. 22, 1943, Graybook, 4:1796.
31. Nimitz to King, Aug. 15 and 20, 1943; King to Nimitz, Aug. 21, 1943, Graybook, 4:1790, 1793–94; Running Summary, Aug. 22, and Sept. 7, 1943, Graybook, 4:1641, 1651; Nimitz to Kinkaid, Aug. 25, 1943, Graybook, 3:1798; E. B. Potter, *Nimitz* (Annapolis: Naval Institute Press, 1976), 246.
32. JCS to MacArthur and Nimitz, Oct. 2, Graybook, 4:1816.
33. Nimitz to Una Walker, Oct. 22, 1943, Michael Lilly Collection.

Chapter 15

1. Edward S. Miller, *War Plan Orange: The U.S. Strategy to Defeat Japan, 1897–1945* (Annapolis: Naval Institute Press, 1991), esp. Chap. 9, "The Through Ticket," 86–99.
2. King to Nimitz, Oct. 22, 1943, Graybook, 4:1819; Richard B. Frank, *Tower of Skulls: A History of the Asia-Pacific War, July 1937–May 1942* (New York: W. W. Norton, 2020), 436–38.
3. See, for example, Walter R. Borneman, *MacArthur at War: World War II in the Pacific* (New York: Little, Brown, 2016), 214–18.
4. MacArthur to Marshall, June 30, 1943, quoted in D. Clayton James, *The Years of MacArthur* (Boston: Houghton Mifflin, 1975), 2:318–19; King to Nimitz, Oct. 22, 1943, Graybook, 4:1819.

5. Philip A. Crowl and Edmund G. Love, *War in the Pacific: Seizure of the Gilberts and Marshalls* (Washington, DC: Office of the Chief of Military History, 1955), 3–17.

6. Andrew Faltum, *The Independence Light Aircraft Carriers* (Baltimore: N&A Press, 2002).

7. John C. McManus, *Fire and Fortitude: The U.S. Army in the Pacific War, 1941–1943* (New York: Caliber, 2019), 510–15. The soldier in the APA was S. L. A . Marshall, who is quoted by McManus on p. 515.

8. Edwin T. Layton with Roger Pineau, *"And I Was There": Breaking the Secrets— Pearl Harbor and Midway* (Old Saybrook, CT: Konecky & Konecky, 2001), 465; Reminiscences of VADM Bernard L. Austin (1971), 275, USNA; William Callaghan oral history (June 30, 1969), "A Cluster of Interviews," 1:9, USNA.

9. James Bassett oral history (May 28, 1969), 3–4, USNA.

10. Catherine Freeman Nimitz oral history (June 5 and 14, 1969), 38 and 40, and H. Arthur Lamar oral history (May 21, 1970), 30, both USNA.

11. H. Arthur Lamar oral history (May 3, 1970), "A Cluster of Interviews," 2:16, USNA; Thomas A. Buell, *The Quiet Warrior: A Biography of Admiral Raymond A. Spruance* (Boston: Little, Brown, 1974), 185 (italics added).

12. Interview of Spruance by Philippe de Baussel (July 6, 1965) for *Paris Match* magazine, Spruance Papers, box 2, folder 14, NWC.

13. Clark G. Reynolds, *Admiral John H. Towers: The Struggle for Naval Air Supremacy* (Annapolis: Naval Institute Press, 1991), 403, 411, 426. Reynolds asserts, "Nimitz had no intention of allowing Towers to go to sea."

14. Conference Notes, May 31, 1943, Buell Papers, NWC (microfilm), 3; Nimitz to Halsey, info King, July 27, 1943, Graybook, 4:1775.

15. Buell, *The Quiet Warrior*, 185; E. B. Potter, *Nimitz* (Annapolis: Naval Institute Press, 1976), 239.

16. Reminiscences of Admiral Bernard Austin (1971), 293, 299, USNA; H. Arthur Lamar oral history (May 3, 1970), "A Cluster of Interviews," 2:16, USNA; Richard Misenhimer oral history (Jan. 23, 2009), 35, NMPW.

17. Conference Notes, May 30–June 4, 1943, Buell Papers, NWC (microfilm), 3–4.

18. Running Summary, Oct. 15, 1943, Graybook, 4:1674.

19. Reynolds, *Admiral John H. Towers*, 428.

20. Ibid., 430–31.

21. Ibid., 432–33, 436.

22. The staffer was Allen G. Quynn in his oral history (Dec. 17, 1969), "A Cluster of Interviews," 5:40, USNA; Bernard Austin oral history (Jan. 16, 1971), 540, USNA; Worrall Reed Carter, *Beans, Bullets, and Black Oil* (Washington, DC: Department of the Navy, 1951), 7.

23. Nimitz to King, info Halsey, Sept. 21, 1943, Graybook, 4:1812.

24. King to Nimitz, Sept. 14 and 21, 1943, Graybook, 4:1808, 1811.

25. Nimitz to King, Aug. 3, 1943, King to Nimitz, Aug. 6, 1943, Nimitz to Newton and Newton to Nimitz, both Aug. 16, 1943, and Nimitz to Halsey, Aug. 19, 1943, all in Graybook, 4:1634, 1782, 1785, and 1791.

26. King to Nimitz, Aug. 11, 14, and 16, 1943, all in Graybook, 4:1789–90, 1792.

27. Michael A. Lilly, *Nimitz at Ease* (Apache Junction, AZ: Stairway Press, 2019), 77–78.

Chapter 16

1. JCS to MacArthur and Nimitz, Oct. 2, 1943, Graybook, 4:1816.
2. Ernest M. Eller oral history (Dec. 13, 1977), 629, USNA; Halsey to Nimitz, Sept. 16, 1943, Graybook, 4:1809–10.
3. Nimitz to King, Sept. 26, 1943, Graybook, 4:1813–14; Ernest M. Eller oral history (Dec. 13, 1977), 629, USNA.
4. Holland M. Smith with Percy Finch, *Coral and Brass* (New York: Charles Scribner's Sons, 1949), 116–17, 140–42.
5. Philip A. Crowl and Edmund G. Love, *The War in the Pacific: Seizure of the Gilberts and Marshalls* (Washington, DC: Office of the Chief of Military History, 1955), 48–49; Smith, *Coral and Brass*, 120. See also Maynard M. Nohrden, "The Amphibian Tractor, Jack of All Missions," U.S. Naval Institute *Proceedings*, Jan. 1946; and Joseph H. Alexander, *Utmost Savagery: The Three Days of Tarawa* (Annapolis: Naval Institute Press, 1995), 84–85.
6. Paul M. Sparrow, "A First Lady on the Front Lines" (Aug. 25, 2016), FDRL. Available at https://fdr.blogs.archives.gov/2016/08/25/a-first-lady-on-the-front-lines/.
7. Eleanor Roosevelt, "My Day," Sept. 25, 1943, The Eleanor Roosevelt Papers Digital Edition (2017); Catherine Nimitz oral history (June 4, 1969), "A Cluster of Interviews," 3:21, USNA.
8. Ernest J. King and Walter Muir Whitehill, *Fleet Admiral King* (New York: W. W. Norton 1952), 490–91; E. B. Potter, *Nimitz* (Annapolis: Naval Institute Press, 1976), 251, 290–91.
9. H. Arthur Lamar oral history (May 3, 1970), 2:48, USNA; Running Summary (Oct. 1 and 5, 1943), Graybook, 4:1666, 1668.
10. Alexander, *Utmost Savagery*, 78.
11. Timothy S. Wolters, *Information at Sea: Shipboard Command and Control in the U.S. Navy from Mobile Bay to Okinawa* (Baltimore: Johns Hopkins University Press, 2013), 200–205; Craig L. Symonds, *World War II at Sea* (New York: Oxford University Press, 2018), 478; Running Summary, Nov. 2, 1943, Graybook, 4:1680.
12. Running Summary, Nov. 7, 1943, Graybook, 4:1682.
13. Alexander, *Utmost Savagery*, 493.
14. Smith, *Coral and Brass*, 122.
15. Crowl and Love, *Seizure of the Gilberts and Marshalls*, 32–33.
16. Joseph H. Alexander, *Across the Reef* (Washington, DC: Marine Corps Historical Center, 1993), 13; Fred H. Allison, "We Were Going to Win . . . or Die Trying," *Naval History*, Oct. 2016, 35; Symonds, *World War II at Sea*, 494–95.
17. H. Arthur Lamar oral history (May 3, 1970), 2:48, USNA; Waldo Drake oral history (June 15, 1969), 2:52, USNA.
18. Waldo Drake oral history (June 15, 1969), 2:20, USNA; John Redman oral history (June 5, 1969), "A Cluster of Interviews," 5:14, USNA.
19. Nimitz to Catherine Nimitz, Nov. 29, 1943 (Nimitz Diary), NHHC; Waldo Drake oral history (June 5, 1969), 2:20, USNA; H. Arthur Lamar oral history (May 3, 1970), 2:40, 59, USNA.

20. H. Arthur Lamar oral history (May 21, 1970), "A Cluster of Interviews," 5:40, USNA; Nimitz to Catherine Nimitz, Nov. 29, 1943 (Nimitz Diary), NHHC.

21. Nimitz to Catherine Nimitz, Nov. 29, 1943 (Nimitz Diary), NHHC.

22. Waldo Drake oral history (June 15, 1969), "A Cluster of Interviews," 2:20, USNA; Crowl and Love, *Seizure of the Gilberts and Marshalls*, 165.

23. Perhaps to avoid being accused of jumping the chain of command, MacArthur entrusted his memo to Brigadier General Frederick H. Osborn with orders to hand-carry it to Secretary Stimson and urge him to show it to the president. See Potter, *Nimitz*, 280.

24. John C. McManus, *Fire and Fortitude: The U.S. Army in the Pacific War* (New York: Caliber, 2019), 529–30; Smith, *Coral and Brass*, 123.

25. Ronald H. Spector, *Eagle Against the Sun: The American War with Japan* (New York: The Free Press, 1985), 315–16; Smith, *Coral and Brass*, 125.

26. Crowl and Love, *Seizure of the Gilberts and Marshalls*, 36; Smith, *Coral and Brass*, 126–28; Ernest Eller oral history (Dec. 13, 1977), 656, USNA; Symonds, *World War II at Sea*, 495–96.

27. Robert Lee Dennison oral history (1974), 60–61, USNA.

28. Ernest Eller oral history (Dec. 13, 1977), 657, USNA.

29. Smith, *Coral and Brass*, 134.

30. The film is available on YouTube under its title. The quotation is from Waldo Drake's oral history (June 15, 1969), 2:26, USNA.

31. H. Arthur Lamar oral history (May 21, 1970), "A Cluster of Interviews," 4:40, USNA. The Frank Capra quotations are from his memoir, *The Name Above the Title* (New York: Vintage Books, 1971), 356–57. Not all of what Capra writes in his memoir is trustworthy. He claimed that Nimitz "beat the table with both fists" and repeatedly yelled "Goddam Sonofabitch of a war!" while sobbing. Such behavior was entirely out of character for Nimitz, whom Capra met only once. Though the movie director may have engaged in cinematic exaggeration, his impression that Nimitz was moved by the losses is credible.

Chapter 17

1. Henry I. Shaw, Bernard Nalty, and Edwin T. Turnbladh, *History of the United States Marine Corps in World War II* (Washington, DC: Headquarters U.S. Marine Corps, 1966), 3:109–11; Ernest Eller oral history (Dec. 13, 1977), 627, USNA.

2. "Naval Gunfire Support, Summary of Recommendations," CTF 53, Operations Narrative, NGF Supplement, RG 38, NARA; Robert D. Heinl Jr., "The Most Shot-At Island in the Pacific," U.S. Naval Institute *Proceedings* (April 1947), 397–99. See also Jeter Isely and Philip A. Crowl, *U.S. Marines and Amphibious Warfare* (Princeton: Princeton University Press, 1951), 232.

3. George E. Mowry, *Landing Craft and the War Production Board, April 1942 to May 1944* (Washington, DC: War Production Board, 1944), 30; Craig L. Symonds, *World War II at Sea* (New York: Oxford University Press, 2018), 509–11.

4. Edwin Layton oral history (March 19, 1970), 90–91, USNA; Spruance to Jeter Iseley, Jan. 14, 1949, Buell Papers, Ms. Coll. 37, box 3, NWC.

5. E. B. Potter, *Nimitz* (Annapolis: Naval Institute Press, 1976), 264; Thomas B. Buell, *The Quiet Warrior* (Boston: Little, Brown, 1974), 232; Edwin P. Hoyt, *To the Marianas* (New York: Van Nostrand Reinhold, 1980), 16.

6. It is not certain that Turner said "dangerous and reckless," but both Potter and Buell, without citation, use that phrase in their books. See Potter, *Nimitz*, 265, and Buell, *The Quiet Warrior*, 232. See also Edwin Layton oral history (March 19, 1969), 91, USNA.

7. Clark G. Reynolds, *Admiral John H. Towers* (Annapolis: Naval Institute Press, 1991), 437–41; Arthur W. Radford, *From Pearl Harbor to Vietnam* (Stanford, CA: Hoover Institution Press, 1980), 21.

8. Radford, *From Pearl Harbor to Vietnam*, 21; Charles A. Pownall oral history (April 12, 1970), 146, and Truman Hedding oral history (Feb. 27, 1971), 48, both USNA.

9. Clark Reynolds, *Admiral John H. Towers*, 452; J. J. Clark with Clark Reynolds, *Carrier Admiral* (New York: David McKay, 1967), 138; Buell, *Quiet Warrior*, 237; Hoyt, *To the Marianas*, 16.

10. Reynolds, *Admiral John H. Towers*, 450–51.

11. Potter, *Nimitz*, 266–67; Thomas A. Hughes, *Admiral Bill Halsey: A Naval Life* (Cambridge, MA: Harvard University Press, 2016), 320.

12. Reynolds, *Admiral John H. Towers*, 452.

13. Ibid.; Charles Pownall oral history (April 12, 1971), 94–95, 150, and Truman Hedding oral history (Feb. 27, 1971), 52, both USNA.

14. Reynolds, *Admiral John H. Towers*, 459.

15. The quotation is from Thomas B. Buell, who writes that Spruance was "angered" by Pownall's exile as well as by Mitscher's elevation. See Buell, *Quiet Warrior*, 237.

16. "Items from Conference on West Coast," Feb. 26, 1944, Notes on King-Nimitz meetings (microfilm), Buell Papers, NWC; Potter, *Nimitz*, 267; Buell, *Quiet Warrior*, 273–75.

17. Philip A. Crowl and Edmund G. Love, *The War in the Pacific: Seizure of the Gilberts and Marshalls* (Washington, DC: Office of the Chief of Military History, 1955), 172.

18. Buell, *Quiet Warrior*, 246.

19. Ibid., 232, 244; Potter, *Nimitz*, 265–66.

20. Una Walker Diary, Jan. 15, 1944, Michael Lilly Collection.

21. Ernest M. Eller oral history (1990), 683, USNA.

22. Una Walker Diary, Jan. 29, 30, 1944, Michael Lilly Collection; Running Summary, Feb. 2, 1944, Graybook, 5:1847.

23. *New York Times*, Feb. 8, 1944, 1, 4.

24. Ibid; Townsend Hoopes and Douglas Brinkley, *Driven Patriot: The Life and Times of James Forrestal* (New York: Alfred A. Knopf, 1992), 194–95.

25. Crowl and Love, *The Seizure of the Gilberts and Marshalls*, 243–44, 246; Symonds, *World War II at Sea*, 513; *New York Times*, Feb. 8, 1944, 4.

26. King to Nimitz, Feb. 17, 1944, quoted in Potter, *Nimitz*, 283–84.

Chapter 18

1. Fitzhugh Lee oral history (July 11, 1970), 160, USNA; Nimitz to Catherine Nimitz, Dec. 5, 1944 (Nimitz Diary), NHHC.
2. George C. Kenney, *General Kenney Reports: A Personal History of the Pacific War* (New York: Duell, Sloan and Pearce, 1949), 348–49.
3. Clark G. Reynolds, *Admiral John H. Towers* (Annapolis: U.S. Naval Institute, 1991), 457; E. B. Potter, *Nimitz* (Annapolis: U.S. Naval Institute, 1976), 281; Gerald E. Wheeler, *Kinkaid of the Seventh Fleet* (Annapolis: Naval Institute Press, 1996), 258; John Miller Jr., "MacArthur and the Admiralties," in Kent Robert Greenfield, ed., *Command Decisions* (New York: Harcourt Brace, 1959), 220–23; Kenney, *General Kenney Reports*, 349.
4. Reminiscences of VADM Bernard L. Austin (1971), 524–25, USNA.
5. King to Nimitz, Feb. 8, 1944, in Potter, *Nimitz*, 283–84.
6. Interview of Spruance by Philippe de Baussel for *Paris Match* magazine (July 6, 1965), Spruance Papers, box 2, folder 14, NWC.
7. Truman J. Hedding oral history (Feb. 27, 1971), 62, USNA; Running Summary, Feb. 17, 19, and 26, 1944, Graybook, 5:1857, 1859, 1864.
8. *New York Times*, Feb. 18, 1944, 5; Potter, *Nimitz*, 278.
9. King to Nimitz, Feb. 17, 1944, in Potter, *Nimitz*, 283–84; Truman Hedding oral history (Feb. 27, 1971), 53, USNA.
10. Running Summary, Feb. 24, 1944, Graybook, 5:1862.
11. Truman Hedding oral history (Feb. 17, 1971), 53, USNA; Running Summary, Feb. 24, 1944, Graybook, 5:1863.
12. John Miller Jr., *The War in the Pacific: Cartwheel: The Reduction of Rabaul* (Washington: Office of the Chief of Military History, 1959), 511; Nimitz to King, March 22, 1943, Graybook, 5:2197; Running Summary, March 8, 1944, Graybook, 5:1869; interview of Julian Smith by Benis Frank, quoted by Ian Toll in *The Conquering Tide* (New York: W. W. Norton, 2015), 434.
13. *Life* magazine, March 6, 1944, quotations on p. 41.
14. Una Walker Diary (Feb. 24, 1944), Michael Lilly Collection.
15. Arthur Herman, *Douglas MacArthur: American Warrior* (New York: Random House, 2016), 498.
16. H. Arthur Lamar oral history (May 21, 1970), 51, USNA.
17. Philip A. Crowl, *The War in the Pacific: Campaign in the Marianas* (Washington, DC: Office of the Chief of Military History, 1960), 18–19.
18. Ibid., 19–20; Potter, *Nimitz*, 287–88.
19. Potter, *Nimitz*, 288.
20. Miller, "MacArthur and the Admiralties," 220–23; Thomas Alexander Hughes, *Admiral Bill Halsey: A Naval Life* (Cambridge, MA: Harvard University Press, 2016), 323.
21. Miller, "MacArthur and the Admiralties," 220–23; Hughes, *Admiral Bill Halsey*, 323; Walter R. Borneman, *MacArthur at War: World War II in the Pacific* (New York: Little, Brown, 2016), 350.
22. William F. Halsey and J. Bryan III, *Admiral Halsey's Story* (New York: McGraw-Hill, 1947), 154–55, 189–90; Borneman, *MacArthur at War*, 355–56.

23. Borneman, *MacArthur at War*, 356–58; Craig L. Symonds, *World War II at Sea: A Global History* (New York: Oxford University Press, 2018), 474–75.

24. Potter, *Nimitz*, 289. Ian Toll suggests that it was Kinkaid who encouraged MacArthur to extend the invitation in the belief that a face-to-face meeting between the two theater commanders would be helpful. See Toll, *The Conquering Tide*, 442.

25. Cato D. Glover, *Command Performance with Guts* (New York: Greenwich, 1969), 45.

26. Potter, *Nimitz*, 290.

27. George van Deurs oral history (Oct. 12, 1969), 455–57, USNA.

28. H. Arthur Lamar oral history (May 3, 1970), 63, USNA.

29. Herman, *Douglas MacArthur*, 501; Kenney, *General Kenny Reports*, 377.

30. Nimitz to King, April 14, 1944, quoted in Phillips Payson O'Brien, *How the War Was Won* (Cambridge: Cambridge University Press, 2015), 399–400; Borneman, *MacArthur at War*, 366–68; Potter, *Nimitz*, 291.

31. Glover, *Command Performance*, 46.

32. Ibid.

Chapter 19

1. Michael A. Lilly, *Nimitz at Ease* (Apache Junction, AZ: Stairway Press, 2019), 109, 111.

2. Gordon Prange with Donald M. Goldstein and Katherine V. Dillon, *At Dawn We Slept: The Untold Story of Pearl Harbor* (New York: McGraw-Hill, 1981), 614–16.

3. Lilly, *Nimitz at Ease*, 112–14.

4. Una Walker Diary, April 1, 2, 3, 4, Michael Lilly Collection; Lilly, *Nimitz at Ease*, 115–20.

5. *New York Times*, April 8, 1944; E. B. Potter, *Nimitz* (Annapolis: Naval Institute Press, 1976), 292; Thomas B. Buell, *The Quiet Warrior: A Biography of Admiral Raymond A. Spruance* (Annapolis: Naval Institute Press, 1987), 272–73.

6. Nimitz to Mrs. Knox, April 28, 1944, Nimitz Papers, box 25, NHHC.

7. Townsend Hoopes and Douglas Brinkley, *Driven Patriot: The Life and Times of James Forrestal* (New York: Alfred A. Knopf, 1992), 178–79; Ernest J. King and Walter Muir Whitehill, *Fleet Admiral King: A Naval Record* (New York: W. W. Norton, 1952), 629; Waldo Drake oral history (June 15, 1969), 4, USNA.

8. Truman Hedding oral history (Feb. 27, 1971), 44, USNA. Italics added for "how." The two-foot-high "stack of paper" is from the oral history of Ernest Eller (May 16, 1978), 679, USNA.

9. Philip A. Crowl, *The War in the Pacific: Campaign in the Marianas* (Washington, DC: Office of the Chief of Military History, 1960), 33–36.

10. William F. Halsey Jr. and J. Bryan III, *Admiral Halsey's Story* (New York: McGraw-Hill, 1947), 201.

11. The characterization of an LST as a bathtub is from Ralph A. Crenshaw oral history and Vernon L. Paul oral history, both NMPW. See Craig L. Symonds, *Neptune: The Allied Invasion of Europe and the D-Day Landings* (New York: Oxford University Press, 2014), 157–59.

12. The witness was Carl Mathews, an Army PFC, who is quoted in Harold J. Goldberg, *D-Day in the Pacific: The Battle of Saipan* (Bloomington: Indiana University Press, 2007), 48.

13. Turner to Nimitz, info Spruance, May 15, 1944, and Nimitz to King, May 23, 1944, both Graybook, 5:2200, 2201.

14. Spruance to Mitscher, June 14, 1944, and J. J. Clark to Spruance, info Mitscher, June 16, 1944, both in Graybook, 5:2208, 2210; Crowl, *Campaign in the Marianas*, 39.

15. Buell goes so far as to claim that "Turner had become an alcoholic." Buell, *Quiet Warrior*, 278.

16. Ibid., 280–81; Goldberg, *D-Day in the Pacific*, 51.

17. Lilly, *Nimitz at Ease*, 137–39.

18. Ibid., 141–43.

19. J. J. Clark (TG 58.1) to Spruance and Nimitz, June 12, 13, 1944, Graybook, 5:2204, 2207.

20. Holland M. Smith with Percy Finch, *Coral and Brass* (New York: Charles Scribner's Sons, 1949), 163–64.

21. Charles A. Lockwood and Hans Christian Adamson, *Battles of the Philippine Sea* (New York: Thomas A. Crowell, 1967), 82; Buell, *Quiet Warrior*, 295; Craig L. Symonds, *World War II at Sea: A Global History* (New York: Oxford University Press, 2018), 543.

22. Spruance's thoughts here are a compendium of several sources, including the oral history of Charles Barber, who claimed to have heard them on the bridge of the *Indianapolis* (Barber oral history [March 1, 1996], 19–20, NWC). Spruance's conversation with Turner is in "Interview of Raymond A. Spruance" (July 6, 1965), by Philippe de Baussel for *Paris Match* magazine, Spruance Papers, box 2, folder 14, p. 17, and in "Notes Made by Admiral Raymond A. Spruance for E. B. Potter," Jan. 4, 1959, in Elmer B. Potter Papers, USNA. See also Buell, *Quiet Warrior*, 296; James D. Hornfischer, *The Fleet at Flood Tide: American at Total War in the Pacific, 1944–1945* (New York: Bantam Books, 2016), 170; and Symonds, *World War II at Sea*, 543.

23. Robert C. Rubel, "Deconstructing Nimitz's Principle of Calculated Risk," *Naval War College Review*, 2015, 1–15; Goldberg, *D-Day in the Pacific*, 92.

24. Buell, *Quiet Warrior*, 295–96.

25. Radio traffic "skips" are discussed by Edwin Layton in his oral history (March 19, 1970), "A Cluster of Interviews," 4:18–20, USNA. Waldo Drake oral history (June 15, 1969), "A Cluster of Interviews," 2:39, USNA; Reminiscences of George W. Anderson Jr., 140, USNA.

26. Clark Reynolds, *Admiral John H. Towers: The Struggle for Naval Air Supremacy* (Annapolis: Naval Institute Press, 1991), 450–51; Hornfischer, *Fleet at Flood Tide*, 172–73; Truman J. Hedding oral history (Feb. 27, 1971), 77, USNA.

Chapter 20

1. The pilot was Alex Vraicu in his oral history (Oct. 9, 1994), 74, NMPW.

2. William T. Y'Blood, *Red Sun Setting: Battle of the Philippine Sea* (Annapolis: Naval Institute Press, 1981), 94–139; Harold J. Goldberg, *D-Day in the Pacific: The Battle*

of Saipan (Bloomington: Indiana University Press, 2007); Craig L. Symonds, *World War II at Sea* (New York: Oxford University Press, 2018), 540–52.

3. Charles A. Lockwood and Hans Christian Adamson, *Battles of the Philippine Sea* (New York: Thomas Crowell, 1967), 92–95; Symonds, *World War II at Sea*, 548–49.

4. Symonds, *World War II at Sea*, 549–50; James D. Hornfischer, *The Fleet at Flood Tide: America at Total War in the Pacific, 1944–1945* (New York: Bantam Books, 2016), 212–14; Y'Blood, *Red Sun Setting*, 148–49.

5. Theodore Taylor, *The Magnificent Mitscher* (Annapolis: Naval Institute Press, 1991).

6. Edwin Layton oral history (March 19, 1970), "A Cluster of Interviews," 4:97–99, USNA.

7. Philip A. Crowl, *The War in the Pacific: Campaign in the Marianas* (Washington, DC: Office of the Chief of Military History, 1960), 181–90.

8. Spruance to Nimitz, June 26 and 29, 1944, Graybook, 5:2330; Crowl, *Campaign in the Marianas*, 191.

9. Holland M. Smith with Percy Finch, *Coral and Brass* (New York: Charles Scribner's Sons, 1949), 177–78.

10. Reminiscences of VADM Bernard L. Austin (1971), 528, and Reminiscences of Ernest Eller (May 16, 1978), 2:685, both USNA.

11. Crowl, *Campaign in the Marianas*, 194; Smith, *Coral and Brass*, 180.

12. E. B. Potter, *Nimitz* (Annapolis: Naval Institute Press, 1976), 308–9.

13. Reminiscences of Bernard L. Austin (1971), 528–29, USNA.

14. Ibid., 527.

15. *San Francisco Examiner*, July 6, 1944; Harry A. Gailey, *Howlin' Mad vs. the Army: Conflict in Command, Saipan 1944* (Novato, CA: Presidio Press, 1986), 10–11; Steven Casey, *The War Beat, Pacific: The American Media at War Against Japan* (New York: Oxford University Press, 2021), 183–84.

16. King to Nimitz (dated July 2 in the Graybook, but actually July 22, 1944), Graybook, 5:2334.

17. Interview of Raymond A. Spruance by Philippe de Baussel (July 6, 1965) for *Paris Match* magazine, Spruance Papers, box 2, folder 14, p. 21, NWC; Ian Toll, *Twilight of the Gods: War in the Western Pacific, 1944–1945* (New York: W. W. Norton, 2020), 55–56.

18. Nimitz to King, July 24, 1944, Graybook, 5:2334. Nimitz later revised these figures upward to 505,000 soldiers, 154,000 Marines, and 61,000 Navy personnel. Nimitz to King, Aug. 18, 1944, Graybook, 5:2342.

19. Walter R. Borneman, *MacArthur at War: World War II in the Pacific* (New York: Little, Brown, 2016), 396.

20. The witness was Douglas E. McVane in "An Historic Voyage with President of the United States Franklin Delano Roosevelt," available at https://fdr.blogs.archives .gov/wp-content/uploads/sites/17/2017/10/macvane-personal-recollections. pdf. See also Symonds, *World War II at Sea*, 554.

21. Toll, *Twilight of the Gods*, 65–72; Nigel Hamilton, *War and Peace: FDR's Final Odyssey: D-Day to Yalta, 1943–1945* (New York: Houghton Mifflin Harcourt, 2019), 312–13; Potter, *Nimitz*, 288; Borneman, *MacArthur at War*, 398. Video footage of the auto tour is available from Pond 5 (item ID 75285169-71).

22. William D. Leahy, *I Was There* (New York: Whittlesey House, 1950), 250–51; Toll, *Twilight of the Gods*, 75.

23. Douglas MacArthur, *Reminiscences* (Annapolis: Naval Institute Press, 2001), 196–98. The historian Phillips Payson O'Brien argues that MacArthur "dazzled Roosevelt with tales of easy victories and grateful Filipinos and American voters." See O'Brien, *How the War Was Won* (Cambridge: Cambridge University Press, 2015), 401.

24. Leahy, *I Was There*, 251–52; MacArthur, *Reminiscences*, 197.

25. H. Arthur Lamar oral history (May 21, 1970), 5:53–54, USNA.

26. Toll, *Twilight of the Gods*, 8–81; Leahy, *I Was There*, 252.

27. H. Harold Lamar, *I Saw Stars: Some Memories of Commander Hal Lamar, Fleet Admiral Nimitz' Flag Lieutenant* (Fredericksburg, TX: The Admiral Nimitz Foundation, 195), 25; Memorandum from Wilson Brown to Grace Tully, July 30, 1944, Map Room Files, OF 18, FDRL.

28. Thomas Alexander Hughes, *Admiral Bill Halsey: A Naval Life* (Cambridge, MA: Harvard University Press, 2016), 333–34.

29. Toll, *Twilight of the Gods*, 116; Clark G. Reynolds, *Admiral John H. Towers* (Annapolis: Naval Institute Press, 1991), 472–73.

30. Taylor, *The Magnificent Mitscher*, 188–89.

31. Reminiscences of Ernest Eller (May 16, 1978), 2:691; Recollections of Chet Nimitz (April 14, 1969), "A Cluster of Interviews," 3:12, both USNA.

32. Interview of Raymond A. Spruance by Philippe de Baussel (July 6, 1965) for *Paris Match* magazine, Spruance Papers, box 2, folder 14, p. 21, NWC.

33. Hughes, *Admiral Bill Halsey*, 338–39.

34. Halsey to Nimitz, Sept. 14, 24, and 27, 1944, Graybook, 5:2229, 2232–33, 2236; Hughes, *Admiral Bill Halsey*, 339; Toll, *Twilight of the Gods*, 93.

35. Halsey's message was dated September 14, but that was the thirteenth in Hawaii. Nimitz to King, Sept. 14, 1944, Graybook, 5:2356; Toll, *Twilight of the Gods*, 121; Joseph A. Alexander, "What Was Nimitz Thinking?," U.S. Naval Institute *Proceedings*, Nov. 1998, 43–44.

36. Nimitz to MacArthur, info King and Halsey, Sept. 13, 1944; Nimitz to King, Sept. 14, 1944; and Nimitz to Halsey, Sept. 13, 1944, all in Graybook, 5:2352, 2253, 2356; Alexander, "What Was Nimitz Thinking?," 44.

37. Toll, *Twilight of the Gods*, 142; Running Summary (Sept. 15, 1944), Graybook, 5:2068. For the experience of the Marines, see Peter Margaritis, *Landing in Hell: The Pyrrhic Victory of the First Marine Division on Peleliu, 1944* (Philadelphia: Casemate, 2018); for the 81st Army Division, see Bobby C. Blair and John Peter DeCioccio, *Victory at Peleliu: The 81st Infantry Division's Pacific Campaign* (Norman: University of Oklahoma Press, 2011). A particularly vivid description of the fighting on Peleliu is in E. B. Sledge, *With the Old Breed at Peleliu and Okinawa* (Novato, CA: Presidio Press, 1981).

38. Ernest J. King and Walter Muir Whitehill, *Fleet Admiral King: A Naval Record* (New York: W. W. Norton, 1952), 542.

39. James H. Belote and William Belote, *Typhoon of Steel: The Battle for Okinawa* (New York: Harper & Row, 1970), 5–7.

Chapter 21

1. See the task organization table in Samuel E. Morison, *Leyte: June 1944–January 1945* (Boston: Little, Brown, 1958), 415–32. The orders to "cooperate" are JCS to MacArthur and Nimitz, Oct. 3, 1944, Graybook, 5:2378.

2. George van Deurs oral history (Oct. 12, 1969), 2:488, USNA; Thomas Alexander Hughes, *Admiral Bill Halsey: A Naval Life* (Cambridge, MA: Harvard University Press, 2016), 345.

3. There are many fine histories of the Battle of Leyte Gulf. Among the best are Thomas J. Cutler, *The Battle of Leyte Gulf* (New York: Harper Collins, 1994); Morison, *Leyte*; John Prados, *Storm over Leyte: The Philippines Invasion and the Destruction of the Japanese Navy* (New York: New American Library, 2016); Evan Thomas, *Sea of Thunder* (New York: Simon and Schuster, 2006); Milan Vego, *The Battle for Leyte: Allied and Japanese Plans, Preparations, and Execution* (Annapolis: Naval Institute Press, 2006); and H. P. Willmott, *The Battle of Leyte Gulf: The Last Fleet Action* (Bloomington: Indiana University Press, 2005).

4. John B. Lundstrom, *Black Shoe Carrier Admiral: Frank Jack Fletcher at Coral Sea, Midway, and Guadalcanal* (Annapolis: Naval Institute Press, 2006), 225.

5. Morison, *Leyte*, 58–60; Dean Moel oral history (Sept. 18, 2004), 4, NMPW. A number of contemporaries recalled that Forrest Sherman was largely responsible for inserting that sentence into Halsey's orders.

6. Craig L. Symonds, *World War II at Sea: A Global History* (New York: Oxford University Press, 2018), 564; Morison, *Leyte*, 142, 156.

7. Morison, *Leyte*, 137; Prados, *Storm over Leyte*, 164, 167; Symonds, *World War II at Sea*, 564–65.

8. John G. Mansfield, *Cruisers for Breakfast: War Patrols of the USS Darter and USS Dace* (Tacoma, WA: Media Center, 1997), 149–63.

9. The messages cited here include the GMT/GCT time signature of the messages as well as the actual date. These two are Halsey to Nimitz, both Oct. 24 (0314, 0612), 1944, Graybook, 5:2242.

10. Kinkaid to Halsey, info Nimitz and King, Oct. 24 (1100), 1944; Sprague to MacArthur, info King, Nimitz, Halsey, Oct. 24 (1057), 1944, and Halsey to Nimitz, MacArthur, info King, Kinkaid, Oct. 24 (1104), 1944, Graybook, 5:2244–45.

11. Halsey to Kinkaid, info King and Nimitz, Oct. 24 (1104), 1944, Graybook, 5:2243, 2244. See also Cutler, *The Battle of Leyte Gulf*, 122–28; Morison, *Leyte*, 177–78.

12. Halsey to Kinkaid, info King and Nimitz, Oct. 24 (1124), 1944, Graybook, 5:2243.

13. Symonds, *World War II at Sea*, 573; Cutler, *Battle of Leyte Gulf*, 160–61, 170–71.

14. Nimitz to Catherine Nimitz, Jan. 7, 1945 (Nimitz Diary), NHHC; Chester Nimitz Jr. to Nimitz, April 27, 1942, Nimitz Papers, box 25, NHHC; Chester Nimitz Jr. oral history (Nov. 6, 2002), 26, NMPW.

15. Bernard Austin oral history (1971), 513 USNA; Chester Nimitz Jr. oral history (Nov. 6, 2002), 26, NMPW.

16. Truman Hedding oral history (Feb. 27, 1971), 44, USNA; E. B. Potter, *Nimitz* (Annapolis: Naval Institute Press, 1976), 337.

17. Truman Hedding oral history (Feb. 27, 1971), 44, USNA; Sprague to Halsey, Oct. 24 (2207), 1944, GB, 5:2246.

18. All six of these messages were sent on the morning of October 25 (Manila time) between 7:07 and 7:39 a.m., though the GMT signatures on all of them are October 24. The GMT time signatures are 2207, 2225, 2229, 2235, 2237, and 2239. They arrived in Hawaii between two and three o'clock in the afternoon on the twenty-fourth (local time). See Graybook, 5:2246. Layton's observations are from his oral history (March 19, 1970), 102, USNA.

19. Truman Hedding oral history (March 14, 1971), 97, USNA. Bernard Austin claimed that he was the one who suggested sending a message, but most evidence suggests it was Sherman.

20. Nimitz to E. B. Potter, Nov. 2, 1958, Elmer B. Potter Papers, USNA.

21. Nimitz to Halsey, info King, Oct. 25, 1944, Graybook, 5:2250. Interestingly, this message appears in the Graybook as simply: "Where is Task Force 34?"

22. Carl Solberg, *Decision and Dissent: With Halsey at Leyte Gulf* (Annapolis: Naval Institute Press, 1995), 154. Solberg was on the bridge of the *New Jersey* and a witness to the events he describes.

23. William F. Halsey and J. Bryan III, *Admiral Halsey's Story* (New York: McGraw-Hill, 1947), 220–21; Solberg, *Decision and Dissent*, 154; Hughes, *Admiral Bill Halsey*, 369–71; Cutler, *The Battle of Leyte Gulf*, 251; Symonds, *World War II at Sea*, 584.

24. Solberg, *Decision and Dissent*, 154.

25. Preston Mercer oral history (Oct. 18, 1969), 53; Truman Hedding oral history (March 14, 1971), 98 (italics added), both USNA.

26. Nimitz to King, Oct. 28, 1944. See Potter, *Nimitz*, 343–44.

27. Kinkaid to Halsey, info Nimitz, Oct. 26 (0710), 1944, Graybook, 5:2259. A particularly evocative telling of this story is James D. Hornfischer, *Last Stand of the Tin Can Sailors* (New York: Bantam Books, 1994). See also Symonds, *World War II at Sea*, 578–83. I cannot resist mentioning that one of the Wildcat pilots who conducted ten "dry" runs against Kurita's battleships was my uncle, LT Paul B. Garrison.

28. Halsey to Nimitz and all Task Group Commanders, Oct. 25 (1226), 1944, Graybook, 5:2256. Commas added for clarity.

Chapter 22

1. "United States Pacific Fleet," Communiqué No. 168, Oct. 29, 1944, Graybook, 5:2276.

2. Halsey to Nimitz and MacArthur, info King, Oct. 29, 1944, Graybook, 5:2279–80; Halsey to King, "Action Report," Nov. 13, 1944, and "Report on Communications," Jan. 26, 1945, both quoted in Thomas Alexander Hughes, *Admiral Bill Halsey: A Naval Life* (Cambridge, MA: Harvard University Press, 2016), 373.

3. William F. Halsey and J. Bryan III, *Admiral Halsey's Story* (New York: Whittlesy House, 1947), 226.

4. Robert W. Coakley and Richard M. Leighton, *Global Logistics and Strategy, 1943–1945* (Washington, DC: Office of the Chief of Military History, 1968), 567; Ian Toll, *Twilight of the Gods: War in the Western Pacific, 1944–1945* (New York: W. W. Norton, 2020), 392.

5. Halsey to Kinkaid, info Nimitz, Oct. 25, 1944; Kinkaid to Halsey, info MacArthur and Nimitz, Oct. 27, 1944; Halsey to Task Group commanders, Oct. 26, 1944; and Nimitz to Halsey, info King, Oct. 27, 1944, all in Graybook, 5:2256, 2260, 2268–69.

6. Nimitz to Halsey, Nov. 13, 1944, GB, 5:2284.

7. Sprague to MacArthur, info Kinkaid, Nimitz, King, Oct. 26, 1944, Graybook, 5:2262.

8. Craig L. Symonds, *World War II at Sea* (New York: Oxford University Press, 2018), 587, 600; Nimitz to Halsey, Nov. 28, 1944, Graybook, 5:2292.

9. Halsey to Nimitz, Nov. 28, 1944, Graybook, 5:2292.

10. Nimitz to Halsey, Nov. 29, 1944, Graybook, 5:2292.

11. Catherine Nimitz to Jean Miller, March 21, 1944, Jean Miller Papers, NMPW.

12. Toll, *Twilight of the Gods*, 417; Ernest J. King and Walter Muir Whitehill, *Fleet Admiral King: A Naval Record* (New York: W. W. Norton, 1952), 569.

13. Nimitz to Fraser, Nov. 25, 1944, Graybook, 5:2290.

14. Nimitz to King, Dec. 19 and 21, 1944, Graybook, 5:2466, 2468; Nimitz to Fraser, Dec. 28, 1944, January 16, 1945, Graybook 5:2479, 6:2743.

15. Nimitz to Catherine Nimitz, Nov. 29, 1944 (Nimitz Diary), NHHC.

16. Nimitz to Catherine Nimitz, Jan. 4, 1945 (Nimitz Diary), NHHC.

17. Nimitz to Catherine Nimitz, Dec. 5, 1944 (Nimitz Diary), NHHC.

18. Nimitz to Catherine Nimitz, Dec. 8, 1944 (Nimitz Diary), NHHC.

19. Nimitz to Catherine Nimitz, Dec. 5, 1944 (Nimitz diary), NHHC.

20. Nimitz to Catherine Nimitz, Dec. 17, 1944 (Nimitz Diary), NHHC.

21. Halsey and Bryan, *Admiral Halsey's Story*, 236; Halsey to Nimitz, Dec. 17, 1944, Graybook, 5:2461.

22. C. Raymond Calhoun, *Typhoon: The Other Enemy* (Annapolis: Naval Institute Press, 1981), 106–7, 209, 216–23; Hughes, *Admiral Bill Halsey*, 382–83; Don McNelly oral history (Sept. 18, 2004), 10–14, NMPW.

23. Thomas C. Anderson oral history (July 5, 1969), 5, USNA.

24. Nimitz to Catherine Nimitz, Dec. 24, 1944 (Nimitz Diary), NHHC.

25. Ibid.

26. Nimitz to Catherine Nimitz, Dec. 24 and 26, 1944 (Nimitz Diary), NHHC.

27. Nimitz to Catherine Nimitz, Dec. 28, 1944 (Nimitz Diary), NHHC.

28. Calhoun, *Typhoon*, 236–37, 164, 167.

29. Halsey and Bryan, *Admiral Halsey's Story*, 226; Gerald Bogan oral history (Oct. 1969), 125–26, USNI.

30. Nimitz to Catherine Nimitz, Dec. 30, 1944 (Nimitz Diary), NHHC.

31. Nimitz to Catherine Nimitz, Dec. 31, 1944 (Nimitz Diary), NHHC.

32. Nimitz to Catherine Nimitz, Dec. 9 and 31, 1944 (Nimitz Diary), NHHC.

Chapter 23

1. Fred Bartel oral history (April 5, 2014), 5, 9, NMPW; Reminiscences of Ernest Eller (May 16, 1978), 2:696, USNA; Allen G. Quynn oral history (Dec. 17, 1969), "A Cluster of Interviews," 5:24, USNA; Ian Toll, *Twilight of the Gods: War in the Western Pacific, 1944–1945* (New York: W. W. Norton, 2020), 535.

2. Nimitz to Catherine Nimitz, Feb. 2, 1945 (Nimitz Diary), NHHC.
3. Nimitz to Una Walker, Jan. 28, 1945, Michael Lilly Collection; Recollections of Ernest Eller (May 16, 1978), 2:695, 714, USNA.
4. Nimitz to Catherine Nimitz, Jan. 5, 14, 16, 17, and Feb. 2, 1945 (Nimitz Diary), NHHC; Reminiscences of Ernest Eller (May 16, 1978), 2:712, USNA.
5. Reminiscences of Ernest Eller (May 16, 1978), 2:712, USNA; Reminiscences of George Anderson (June 9, 1980), 131, USNA; King to NAVOP, Jan. 24, 1945, Graybook, 6:2742; Clark Reynolds, *Admiral John H. Towers* (Annapolis: Naval Institute Press, 1991), 485.
6. Fred Bartel oral history (April 5, 2014), 4, NMPW; Nimitz to Catherine Nimitz, Jan. 3, 13, 1945 (Nimitz Diary), NHHC.
7. Running Summary, Jan. 5 and 9, 1945, Graybook, 6:2499, 2505; Nimitz to Catherine Nimitz, Jan. 9 and 11, 1945 (Nimitz Diary), NHHC.
8. Running Summary, Jan. 12, 13, 14, and 16, 1945, Graybook, 6:2510–13 (the quotation is from 2516); Nimitz to Catherine Nimitz, Jan. 12, 1945 (Nimitz Diary), NHHC; Toll, *Twilight of the Gods*, 428.
9. Toll, *Twilight of the Gods*, 433; Spruance to Jeter Iseley, Jan. 10 and Feb. 3, 1950, Buell Papers, Ms. Coll. 37, box 3, folder 6, NWC.
10. Nimitz to Catherine Nimitz, Jan. 17 and 23, 1945 (Nimitz Diary), NHHC.
11. Nimitz to Catherine Nimitz, Jan. 17, 1945 (Nimitz Diary), NHHC.
12. Nimitz to Catherine Nimitz, Jan. 28, 1945 (Nimitz Diary), NHHC; Nimitz to Una and Sandy Walker, Jan. 28 and Feb. 6, 1945, Michael Lilly Collection; Truman Hedding oral history (May 2, 1971), 106–8, USNA.
13. Nimitz to Catherine Nimitz, Jan. 28, 1945 (Nimitz Diary), NHHC; Nimitz to Una and Sandy Walker, Jan. 28, 1945, Michael Lilly Collection; Reminiscences of Ernest Eller (May 16, 1978), 2:713, USNA.
14. Nimitz to Catherine Nimitz, Jan. 29 and 31, 1945 (Nimitz Diary), NHHC.
15. Nimitz to Catherine Nimitz, Jan. 29, and Feb. 1, 1945 (Nimitz Diary), NHHC.
16. Nimitz to Catherine Nimitz, Jan. 27, 1945 (Nimitz Diary), NHHC.
17. Nimitz to Catherine Nimitz, Feb. 4, 1945 (Nimitz Diary), NHHC.
18. Thomas B. Buell, *The Quiet Warrior: A Biography of Admiral Raymond A. Spruance* (Annapolis: Naval Institute Press, 1987), 352–54.
19. Max Hastings, *Retribution: The Battle for Japan, 1944–45* (New York: Alfred A. Knopf, 2008), 290.
20. Samuel Harris, *B-29s over Japan: A Group Commander's Diary* (Jefferson, NC: McFarland, 2011), 201; Craig L. Symonds, *World War II at Sea: A Global History* (New York: Oxford University Press, 2018), 600–603.
21. Ernest J. King and Walter Muir Whitehill, *Fleet Admiral King, A Naval Record* (New York: W. W. Norton, 1952), 596.
22. Spruance to Jeter Iseley, Jan. 10, and Feb. 3, 1950, Buell Papers, Ms. Coll. 37, box 3, folder 6, NWC.
23. Spruance to Nimitz, Feb. 18, 1945, Graybook, 6:2752; Buell, *Quiet Warrior*, 354–57.
24. Nimitz to Catherine Nimitz, Feb. 16, 1945 (Nimitz Diary), NHHC; Toll, *Twilight of the Gods*, 484; *New York Times*, Feb. 19, 1945; Nimitz to ALPOA, info King, Feb. 19, 1945, Graybook, 6:2753.

25. William S. Bartley, *Iwo Jima: Amphibious Epic* (Washington, DC: Historical Branch, U.S. Marine Corps, 1954); E. B. Potter, *Nimitz* (Annapolis: Naval Institute Press, 1976), 367.
26. Running Summary (Feb. 24, 1945), Graybook, 6:2553.
27. Nimitz to Chet Nimitz, April 3, 1945, Nimitz Papers, NMPW; Nimitz to Una and Sandy Walker, Feb. 19 and 24, 1945, Lilly Collection.
28. E. B. Potter, *Nimitz* (Annapolis: Naval Institute Press, 1976), 366; James T. Lay recited the letter in his oral history (Feb. 16, 1970), "A Cluster of Interviews," 4:74, USNA.
29. Nimitz to Catherine Nimitz, March 17, 1945 (Nimitz Diary), NHHC.
30. Nimitz to Catherine Nimitz, March 27, 1945 (Nimitz Diary), NHHC.
31. CINCPOA Communiqué No. 300, March 16, 1945, *Navy Department Communiqués* (Washington, DC: Office of Public Information, 1945), 369.

Chapter 24

1. Roy E. Appleman et al., *Okinawa: The Last Battle* (Washington, DC: Department of the Army, 1948), 46–49.
2. Craig L. Symonds, *World War II at Sea: A Global History* (New York: Oxford University Press, 2018), 618.
3. Robert W. Coakley and Richard M. Leighton, *Global Logistics and Strategy, 1943–1945* (Washington, DC: Office of the Chief of Military History, 1968), 575.
4. Appleman et al., *Okinawa: The Last Battle*, 36–37.
5. Coakley and Leighton, *Global Logistics and Strategy*, 69.
6. Turner to Spruance, info Nimitz, April 1, 1945, Graybook, 6:2811; Coakley and Leighton, *Global Logistics and Strategy*, 69–74; Sherrod is quoted in Nicholas E. Sarantakes, "Warriors of Word and Sword: The Battle of Okinawa, Media Coverage, and Truman's Reevaluation of Strategy in the Pacific," *Journal of American–East Asian Studies* 23, no. 4 (2016): 343.
7. Appleman et al., *Okinawa: The Last Battle*, 84–96.
8. Turner to Spruance, info Nimitz, April 3, 1945, Graybook, 6:2815; Nimitz to Catherine Nimitz, April 3, 1945 (Nimitz Diary), NHHC.
9. Fred Bartel oral history (April 5, 2014), 9, NMPW.
10. Nimitz to Catherine Nimitz, April 3, 8, and 9, 1945 (Nimitz Diary), NHHC.
11. Nimitz to Catherine Nimitz, April 3, 1945 (Nimitz Diary), NHHC.
12. Nimitz to Towers, Smith, King, and all Type Commanders, April 5, and May 27, 1945, Graybook, 6:2820, 2913.
13. Nimitz to Halsey, April 30, 1945, Graybook, 6:2915.
14. Nimitz to Catherine Nimitz, April 5 and 12, and May 5, 1945 (Nimitz Diary), NHHC.
15. Turner to Spruance, info Nimitz, April 6 and 7, 1945, Graybook, 6:2821–22, 2825.
16. Turner to Spruance, info Nimitz, April 13, 1944, Graybook, 6:2853.
17. Russell Spurr, *A Glorious Way to Die: The Kamikaze Mission of the Battleship* Yamato, *April 1945* (New York: Newmarket Press, 1981), 217–21.
18. Symonds, *World War II at Sea*, 627–29; Nimitz to Catherine Nimitz, April 9, 1945 (Nimitz Diary), NHHC.

19. Nimitz to Towers, April 10, 1945, Graybook, 6:2843; Ernest J. King and Walter Muir Whitehill, *Fleet Admiral King: A Naval Record* (New York: W. W. Norton, 1952), 581; Symonds, *World War II at Sea*, 631.

20. Nimitz to Catherine Nimitz, April 13, 1945 (Nimitz Diary), NHHC.

21. CinCPOA communiqué, April 12, 1945.

22. Mitscher to Turner, March 25, 1945, and Turner to Spruance, info Nimitz, April 8, 1945, both in Graybook, 6:2801, 2829. Hodge is quoted in Appleman et al., *Okinawa: The Last Battle*, 185.

23. Appleman et al., *Okinawa: The Last Battle*, 194, 253.

24. Nimitz to King, April 16, 1945, Graybook, 6:3205; E. B. Potter, *Nimitz* (Annapolis: Naval Institute Press, 1976), 373–74.

25. Nimitz to Catherine Nimitz, April 24, 1945 (Nimitz Diary) NHHC; Nimitz's comment to Buckner is quoted in Potter, *Nimitz*, 375.

26. Potter, *Nimitz*, 375; Ian Toll, *Twilight of the Gods: War in the Western Pacific, 1944–1945* (New York: W. W. Norton, 2020), 564.

27. Symonds, *World War II at Sea*, 625; Thomas B. Buell, *The Quiet Warrior: A Biography of Admiral Raymond A. Spruance* (Annapolis: Naval Institute Press, 1987), 388.

28. Curtis LeMay with MacKinlay Kantor, *Mission with LeMay: My Story* (New York: Doubleday 1965), 340–41.

29. Nimitz to Deputy Commander, 20th Air Force, info King, April 15, 1945, and Nimitz to King, April 15, 1945, both in Graybook, 6:2854; "Strategic Air Warfare," interview of Curtis LeMay and others by Richard H. Kohn and Joseph P. arahan, Aug. 1, 1988, Office of Air Force History, 50–51.

30. Toll, *Twilight of the Gods*, 611, 626; Buell, *The Quiet Warrior*, 391.

31. Nimitz to Catherine Nimitz, April 26, 1945 (Nimitz Diary), NHHC.

32. Nimitz to Halsey, May 29, and June 3, 1945, and Halsey to Task Force Groups, info Nimitz, May 20, 1945, all in Graybook, 6:3235, 3242, 3130–31.

33. J. J. Clark with Clark G. Reynolds, *Carrier Admiral* (New York: David McKay, 1967), 233–35.

34. Ibid., 237; Halsey's endorsement to the court report, September 29, 1945, in C. Raymond Calhoun, *Typhoon: The Other Enemy* (Annapolis: Naval Institute Press, 1981), 208.

35. Calhoun, *Typhoon*, 210.

36. "Critics in Capital Hit Okinawa 'Mistakes,'" *Washington Evening Star*, May 30, 1945.

37. Sarantakes, "Warriors of Word and Sword," 335; Charles S. Nichols and Henry I. Shaw, *Okinawa: Victory in the Pacific* (Washington, DC: U.S. Marine Corps, 1955), 269.

38. Sarantakes, "Warriors of Word and Sword," 349–50; "Nimitz Defends Okinawa Campaign," *New York Times*, June 17, 1945, 3.

39. "David Lawrence Issues Reply," *New York Times*, June 17, 1945, 3. The newspaper actually misprinted Bigart's response as "absurb," but it was clearly a typo, which is silently corrected here.

40. The numbers here are from Richard B. Frank, *Downfall: The End of the Imperial Japanese Empire* (New York: Penguin, 1999), 71–72. See also Max Hastings,

Retribution: The Battle for Japan, 1944–45 (New York: Alfred A. Knopf, 2008), 402, who offers slightly smaller casualty numbers.

Chapter 25

1. Robert H. Ferrell, ed., *Off the Record: The Private Papers of Harry S. Truman* (New York: Penguin, 1980), 47; Ernest J. King and Walter Muir Whitehill, *Fleet Admiral King: A Naval Record* (New York: W. W. Norton, 1952), 598.

2. Nimitz to King, May 25, 1945, Graybook, 6:3232.

3. Richard B. Frank, *Downfall: The End of the Imperial Japanese Empire* (New York: Penguin, 1999), 144–46; J. Samuel Walker, *Prompt and Utter Destruction: Truman and the Use of the Atomic Bombs against Japan* (Chapel Hill: University of North Carolina Press, 1997), 35–37. Leahy did not do the arithmetic at the meeting, but applying 35 percent to 766,000 yields a casualty total of more than 200,000.

4. King and Whitehill, *Fleet Admiral King*, 598; Douglas MacArthur, *Reminiscences* (New York: McGraw-Hill, 1964), 260; Frank, *Downfall*, 146–47; William D. Leahy, *I Was There* (New York: Whittlesey House, 1950), 383.

5. MacArthur to Marshall, Dec. 17, 1944, quoted in Robert W. Coakley and Richard M. Leighton, *Global Logistics and Strategy, 1943–1945* (Washington, DC: Office of the Chief of Military History, 1968), 581.

6. JCS Directive 1259/4, April 3, 1945, quoted in Coakley and Leighton, *Global Logistics and Strategy*, 581.

7. Nimitz to King, April 13, 1945, Graybook, 6:3203.

8. Ibid.; Coakley, *Global Logistics and Strategy*, 583.

9. Marshall is quoted in Walter R. Borneman, *MacArthur at War: World War II in the Pacific* (New York: Little, Brown, 2016), 478; King to Nimitz, April 14, 1945, Graybook, 6:3203.

10. Summarized in Nimitz to King, April 15, 1945, Graybook, 6:3204.

11. Nimitz to Catherine Nimitz, April 16, 1945 (Nimitz Diary), NHHC.

12. Nimitz to King, April 15, 1945, Graybook, 6:3204–5.

13. Nimitz to MacArthur, May 7, 1945, Graybook, 6:3224.

14. Nimitz to Sandy and Una Walker, May 19, 1945, Michael Lilly Collection; Marshall to MacArthur, May 4, 1945, quoted in Borneman, *MacArthur at War*, 478; Nimitz to MacArthur, May 26, 1945, Graybook, 6:3233–34.

15. "Organization of High Command," memo, Richardson to Marshall, Nov. 3, 1944, quoted in Coakley and Leighton, *Global Logistics and Strategy*, 580.

16. MacArthur, *Reminiscences*, 261; Nimitz to King, May 17, 1945, Graybook, 6:3127.

17. Nimitz to MacArthur, May 26, 1945, Graybook, 6:3233.

18. Mark R. Parillo, *The Japanese Merchant Marine in World War II* (Annapolis: Naval Institute Press, 1993), 128–31, 174–77, 209; Max Hastings, *Retribution: The Battle for Japan* (New York: Alfred A. Knopf, 2008), 17, 37; Clay Blair, *Silent Victory: The U.S. Submarine War Against Japan* (Philadelphia: J. B. Lippencott, 1975), 794–96, 799; Craig L. Symonds, *World War II at Sea: A Global History* (New York: Oxford University Press, 2018), 593–95.

19. Roger Dingman, *Ghost of War: The Sinking of the* Awa Maru *and Japanese-American Relations, 1945–1946* (Annapolis: Naval Institute Press, 1997), 51–52.
20. Ibid., 85, 95, 101.
21. Halsey to Nimitz, July 17 and 18, 1945, Graybook, 7:3328.
22. Frank, *Downfall*, 3–19; Hastings, *Retribution*, 296–305; Edwin Layton oral history (March 19, 1970), 4:112–13, USNA.
23. King to Nimitz, May 31, 1945, Graybook, 6:3239.
24. JCS to MacArthur and Nimitz, June 14, 1945, Graybook, 6:3248.
25. Nimitz to Tenth Army, July 26, 1945, Graybook, 7:3336.
26. Paul Stroop oral history (Feb. 2, 1970), "A Cluster of Interviews," 5:214, USNA.
27. Truman Hedding oral history (March 14, 1971), 125–26, USNA.
28. Edwin Layton oral history (March 19, 1970), 4:110–11, USNA; James W. Archer oral history (Aug. 2, 1969), USNA; Nimitz to ALPAC, August 14, 1945, Graybook, 7:3349.
29. Nimitz to ALPAC, Aug. 15, 1945, Graybook, 7:3352.

Epilogue

1. Henry A. Walker, *Memoirs*, 58, courtesy of Samuel P. King; Michael A. Lilly, *Nimitz at Ease* (Apache Junction, AZ: Stairway Press, 2019), 292–93.
2. Waldo Drake oral history (June 15, 1969), "A Cluster of Interviews," 2:34, USNA.
3. E. B. Potter, *Nimitz* (Annapolis: Naval Institute Press, 1976), 407–8.
4. Lilly, *Nimitz at Ease*, 338–41.
5. Nimitz to Sandy and Una Walker, Dec. 7, 1945, Michael Lilly Collection.
6. Nancy Nimitz oral history (June 7, 1969), "A Cluster of Interviews," 3:44, USNA.
7. Catherine Nimitz oral history (June 4, 1969), "A Cluster of Interviews," 3:62–63, USNA.

BIBLIOGRAPHY

Documentary Sources

American Heritage Center, Laramie, Wyoming
Frank Jack Fletcher Papers

Franklin D. Roosevelt Library, Hyde Park, New York
Map Room Files
Secretary's Files

National Archives and Records Administration, College Park, Maryland
Chief Naval Security Group (Record Group 38)
CincPac Secret and Confidential Message Traffic (Record Group 38)

National Museum of the Pacific War, Center for Pacific War Studies
Nimitz Collection
Jean Miller Papers

Naval History and Heritage Command, Navy Yard, Washington, D.C.
Ernest J. King Papers
Marc A. Mitscher Papers
Chester W. Nimitz Letters and Papers
Command Summary of Fleet Admiral Chester W. Nimitz, 7 December 1941–31
August 1945 (Graybook)
Letters of Chester W. Nimitz to his wife, Catherine (Nimitz Diary)
Raymond A. Spruance Papers

Lay Family Papers (Private)
Nimitz Service Records and Medical Records

Captain Michael A. Lilly Collection (Private)
H. Arthur Lamar Letters
Memoirs of Henry Alexander Walker Jr.
Catherine Nimitz Letters

Chester Nimitz Letters
Una Walker Diary

U.S. Naval Academy, Annapolis, Maryland
Wilson Brown Papers
Chester Nimitz, Official Report on the Battle of Midway (June 28, 1942)
Elmer B. Potter Papers
OP-20-G File of CINCPAC Intelligence Bulletins
Traffic Intelligence Summaries, Combat Intelligence Unit, 14th Naval District, 3 vols.
U.S. Navy Action and Operational Reports from World War II, Pacific Theater, Part
    I: CINCPAC (16 microfilm reels)

U.S. Naval War College, Newport, Rhode Island
Thomas B. Buell Papers (King Collection, Spruance Collection, Whitehill Collection)
Notes of Conversations Between E. J. King and C. W. Nimitz at Various Meetings
Recollections of the Late VADM Chester W. Nimitz as Given by Various Officers
Raymond A. Spruance Papers

Newspapers

Honolulu *Star Bulletin*
New York Herald Tribune
New York Sun
New York Times
San Francisco Examiner
Washington Evening Star

Official Histories

Appleman, Roy E., James M. Burns, Russell A. Gugeler, and John Stevens. *The War in the Pacific: Okinawa: The Last Battle*. Washington, DC: Historical Division, Department of the Army, 1948.
Auxier, George W. *Shipbuilding Policies of the War Production Board: January 1942– November 1945*. Historical Reports on War Administration Study, no. 26. Washington, DC: Government Printing Office, 1947.
Bartley, William S. *Iwo Jima: Amphibious Epic*. Washington, DC: Historical Branch, U.S. Marine Corps, 1954.
Carter, Worrall Reed. *Beans, Bullets, and Black Oil: The Story of Fleet Logistics Afloat in the Pacific During World War II*. Washington, DC: Department of the Navy, 1953.
Coakley, Robert W., and Richard M. Leighton. *United States Army in World War II: Global Logistics and Strategy, 1943–1945*. Washington, DC: Office of the Chief of Military History, 1968.
Crowl, Philip A. *The War in the Pacific: Campaign in the Marianas*. Washington, DC: Office of the Chief of Military History, 1960.

Crowl, Philip A., and Edmund G. Love. *The War in the Pacific: Seizure of the Gilberts and Marshalls.* Washington, DC: Office of the Chief of Military History, 1955.

Lowenstein, Francis L., Harold D. Langley, and Manfred Jonas, eds. *Roosevelt and Churchill, Their Secret Wartime Correspondence.* London: Barrie & Jenkins, 1975.

Miller, John. *The United States Army in World War II: The War in the Pacific, Guadalcanal: The First Offensive.* Washington, DC: Historical Division, Department of the Army, 1949.

Miller, John. *The War in the Pacific: Cartwheel: The Reduction of Rabaul.* Washington, DC: Office of the Chief of Military History, 1959.

Mowry, George E. *Landing Craft and the War Production Board, April 1942 to May 1944.* Washington, DC: War Production Board, 1944.

Nichols, Charles S., Jr., and Henry I. Shaw Jr. *Okinawa: Victory in the Pacific.* Washington, DC: Headquarters, U.S. Marine Corps, 1955.

Shaw, Henry I., Bernard Nalty, and Edwin T. Turnbladh. *History of United States Marine Corps Operations in World War II,* vol. 3, *Central Pacific Drive.* Washington, DC: Historical Branch, USMC, 1966.

Oral Histories

At National Museum of the Pacific War, Fredericksburg, Texas
Robert Allen (January 4, 2015)
Fred Bartel (April 5, 2014)
Richard Best (August 11, 1995)
Ralph A. Crenshaw (n.d.)
Keith D. Healy (November 11, 2004)
Edwin T. Layton (n.d.)
Don McNelly (September 18, 2004)
Richard Misenhimer (January 23, 2009)
Dean Moel (September 18, 2004)
Chester W. Nimitz Jr. (November 6, 2001)
Vernon Paul (n.d.)
Floyd Thorn (August 14, 2000)
Alex Vraicu (October 9, 1994)
At East Carolina University, Greenville, North Carolina
Robert L. Ghormley Jr. (October 13, 2010)
At U.S. Naval Institute, Annapolis, Maryland
Gerald Bogan (October 1969)
At U.S. Naval Academy, Annapolis, Maryland
"A Cluster of Interviews on Fleet Admiral Chester W. Nimitz, U.S. Navy," 5 vols.
George W. Anderson (8 interviews, June 9–November 25, 1980)
Bernard L. Austin (16 interviews, August 22, 1969–January 16, 1971)
Hanson Baldwin (8 interviews, February 24–December 8, 1975)
George Bauerschmidt (August 6, 1969)
Edward Brewer (January 24, 1970)

Chester Bruton (June 18, 1969)
William Callaghan (June 30, 1969)
George E. Cozard (January 24, 1969)
Robert Lee Dennison (1974)
Ernest M. Eller (13 interviews, December 19, 1974–August 22, 1978)
Truman J. Hedding (3 interviews, February 27–May 2, 1971)
Fitzhugh Lee (July 11, 1970)
Harold R. Miller (May 11, 1970)
Stuart S. Murray (5 interviews, October 10, 1970)
Catherine Freeman Nimitz (June 4 and June 14, 1969)
Charles A. Pownall (April 12, 1970)
Henri Smith-Hutton (41 interviews, August 22, 1974–October 10, 1974)
George van Deurs (October 12, 1969)
At U.S. Naval War College, Newport, Rhode Island
Charles Barber (March 1, 1996)
Chester Bruton (June 18, 1969)
Joseph Wilson Levering (August 22, 1969)
Sam P. Moncure (July 30, 1969)
Lloyd M. Mustin (March 10, 1969)
F. E. M. Whiting (September 19, 1969)
Odale Waters Jr. (July 14, 1969)

Personal Accounts and Memoirs

Arnold, Henry H. *Global Mission*. New York: Harper & Brothers, 1949.

Capra, Frank. *The Name Above the Title*. New York: Vintage Books, 1985.

Clark, J. J., with Clark Reynolds. *Carrier Admiral*. New York: David McKay, 1967.

Glover, Cato D. *Command Performance with Guts*. New York: Greenwich, 1969.

Halsey, William F., and J. Bryan III. *Admiral Halsey's Story*. New York: McGraw-Hill, 1947.

Harris, Samuel. *B-29s over Japan: A Group Commander's Diary*. Jefferson, NC: McFarland, 2011.

Holmes, W. J. *Double-Edged Secrets: U.S. Naval Intelligence Operations in the Pacific During World War II*. Annapolis: Naval Institute Press, 1979.

King, Ernest J., and Walter Muir Whitehill. *Fleet Admiral King, A Naval Record*. New York: W. W. Norton, 1952.

Lamar, Hal. *I Saw Stars: Some Memories of Commander Hal Lamar, Fleet Admiral Nimitz' Flag Lieutenant*. Fredericksburg, TX: The Admiral Nimitz Foundation, 1975.

Layton, Edwin T. *"And I Was There": Breaking the Secrets—Pearl Harbor and Midway*. Old Saybrook, CT: Konecky & Konecky, 2001.

Leahy, William D. *I Was There: The Personal Story of the Chief of Staff to Presidents Roosevelt and Truman Based on His Notes and Diaries Made at the Time*. New York: Whittlesey House, 1950.

LeMay, Curtis, with MacKinlay Kantor. *Mission with LeMay: My Story*. Garden City, NY: Doubleday, 1965.

LeMay, Curtis, and Bill Yenne. *Superfortress: The Story of the B-29 and American Air Power*. New York: McGraw-Hill, 1988.

Lockwood, Charles A. *Hellcats of the Sea*. New York: Greenburg, 1955.

Lockwood, Charles A. *Sink 'Em All: Submarine Warfare in the Pacific*. New York: E. P. Dutton, 1951.

Lockwood, Charles A., with Hans Christian Adamson. *Battle of the Philippine Sea*. New York: Thomas Y. Crowell, 1967.

MacArthur, Douglas. *Reminiscences*. New York: McGraw-Hill, 1964; Annapolis: Naval Institute Press, 2001.

Radford, Arthur W. *From Pearl Harbor to Vietnam: The Memoirs of Admiral Arthur W. Radford*. Edited by Stephen Jurika Jr. Stanford, CA: Hoover Institution Press, 1980.

Rosenman, Samuel I. *Working with Roosevelt*. New York: Harper & Brothers, 1952.

Sherrod, Robert L. *On to Westward: War in the Central Pacific*. New York: Duell, Sloan and Pearce, 1945.

Sledge, E. B. *With the Old Breed: At Peleliu and Okinawa*. Novato, CA: Presidio Press, 1981.

Smith, Holland M., with Percy Finch. *Coral and Brass*. New York: Charles Scribner's Sons, 1949.

Truman, Harry S. *Off the Record: The Private Papers of Harry S. Truman*. Edited by Robert H. Ferrell. New York: Penguin, 1980.

Secondary Sources

Alexander, Joseph H. *Across the Reef: The Marine Assault of Tarawa*. Washington, DC: Marine Corps Historical Center, 1993.

Alexander, Joseph H. *Utmost Savagery: The Three Days of Tarawa*. Annapolis, MD: Naval Institute Press, 1995.

Belote, James, and William Belote. *Typhoon of Steel: The Battle for Okinawa*. New York: Harper & Row, 1970.

Blair, Bobby C., and John Peter DeCioccio. *Victory at Peleliu: The 81st Infantry Division's Pacific Campaign*. Norman: University of Oklahoma Press, 2011.

Blair, Clay. *Silent Victory: The U.S. Submarine War Against Japan*. Philadelphia: J. B. Lippincott, 1975.

Borneman, Walter R. *The Admirals: Nimitz, Halsey, Leahy, and King*. New York: Little, Brown, 2012.

Borneman, Walter R. *MacArthur at War: World War II in the Pacific*. New York: Little, Brown, 2016.

Buell, Thomas B. *The Quiet Warrior: A Biography of Admiral Raymond A. Spruance*. Annapolis: Naval Institute Press, 1987. Originally published in 1974.

Calhoun, C. Raymond. *Typhoon, the Other Enemy: The Third Fleet and the Pacific Storm of December 1944*. Annapolis: Naval Institute Press, 1981.

Carlson, Elliot. *Stanley Johnson's Blunder: The Reporter Who Spilled the Secret Behind the U.S. Navy's Victory at Midway*. Annapolis: Naval Institute Press, 2017.

Casey, Steven. *The War Beat, Pacific: The American Media at War Against Japan.* New York: Oxford University Press, 2021.

Costello, John. *The Pacific War.* New York: Harper Collins, 1981.

Cox, Jeffery. *Blazing Star, Setting Sun: The Guadalcanal-Solomons Campaign, November 1942–March 1943.* New York: Osprey, 2020.

Crewshaw, Russell S., Jr. *The Battle of Tassafaronga.* Annapolis: Naval Institute Press, 1995.

Cutler, Thomas J. *The Battle of Leyte Gulf, 23–26 October 1944.* New York: Harper Collins, 1994.

Dingman, Roger. *Ghost of War: The Sinking of the* Awa Maru *and Japanese-American Relations, 1945–1946.* Annapolis: Naval Institute Press, 1997.

Dyer, George C. *The Amphibians Came to Conquer: The Story of Richmond Kelly Turner.* Washington, DC: Government Printing Office, 1971.

Frank, Richard B. *Downfall: The End of the Imperial Japanese Empire.* New York: Random House, 1999.

Frank, Richard B. *Guadalcanal: The Definitive Account of the Landmark Battle.* New York: Random House, 1990.

Frank, Richard B. *Tower of Skulls: A History of the Asia-Pacific War.* New York: W. W. Norton, 2019.

Gailey, Harry A. *Howlin' Mad vs. the Army: Conflict in Command, Saipan 1944.* Novato, CA: Presidio Press, 1986.

Gamble, Bruce. *Fortress Rabaul: The Battle of the Southwest Pacific, January 1942–April 1943.* Minneapolis: Zenith, 2010.

Goldberg, Harold J. *D-Day in the Pacific: The Battle of Saipan.* Bloomington: Indiana University Press, 2007.

Gray, J. A. C. *Amerika Samoa: A History of American Samoa and Its United States Naval Administration.* Annapolis: Naval Institute Press, 1960.

Greenfield, Kent Roberts, ed. *Command Decisions.* New York: Harcourt, Brace, 1959.

Hamilton, Nigel. *The Mantle of Command: FDR at War, 1941–1942.* New York: Houghton Mifflin Harcourt, 2014.

Hamilton, Nigel. *War and Peace: FDR's Final Odyssey: D-Day to Yalta, 1943–1945.* New York: Houghton Mifflin Harcourt, 2019.

Harris, Brayton. *Admiral Nimitz: The Commander of the Pacific Ocean Theater.* New York: Palgrave, 2011.

Hastings, Max. *Retribution: The Battle for Japan, 1944–45.* New York: Alfred A. Knopf, 2008.

Hoffman, Jon T. *From Makin to Bougainville: Marine Raiders in the Pacific War.* Washington, DC: Marine Corps Historical Center, 1995.

Holwitt, Joel Ira. *"Execute Against Japan": The U.S. Decision to Conduct Unrestricted Submarine Warfare.* College Station: Texas A&M University Press, 2009.

Hoopes, Townsend, and Douglas Brinkley. *Driven Patriot: The Life and Times of James Forrestal.* New York: Alfred A. Knopf, 1992.

Hornfischer, James D. *The Fleet at Flood Tide: America at Total War in the Pacific, 1944–1945.* New York: Bantam, 2016.

Hornfischer, James D. *Last Stand of the Tin Can Sailors: The Extraordinary World War II Story of the U.S. Navy's Finest Hour.* New York: Bantam, 2004.

Hoyt, Edwin P. *How They Won the War in the Pacific: Nimitz and His Admirals.* New York: Weybright and Talley, 1970.

Hoyt, Edwin P. *To the Marianas: War in the Central Pacific: 1944.* New York: Van Nostrand Reinhold, 1980.

Hughes, Thomas A. *Admiral Bill Halsey: A Naval Life.* Cambridge, MA: Harvard University Press, 2016.

Isely, Jeter, and Philip A. Crowl. *U.S. Marines and Amphibious Warfare.* Princeton: Princeton University Press, 2015 [1951].

Jordan, Jonathan W. *American Warlords: How Roosevelt's High Command Led America to Victory in World War II.* New York: Caliber, 2016.

Jordan, John. *Warships After Washington.* Annapolis: Naval Institute Press, 2011.

Lilly, Michael A. *Nimitz at Ease.* Apache Junction, AZ: Stairway Press, 2019.

Lundstrom, John B. *Black Shoe Carrier Admiral: Frank Jack Fletcher at Coral Sea, Midway, and Guadalcanal.* Annapolis: Naval Institute Press, 2006.

Lundstrom, John B. *The First Team: Pacific Naval Air Combat from Pearl Harbor to Midway.* Annapolis: Naval Institute Press, 1984.

Mansfield, John G. *Cruisers for Breakfast: War Patrols of the USS* Darter *and USS* Dace. Tacoma, WA: Media Center, 1997.

Margaritis, Peter. *Landing in Hell: The Pyrrhic Victory of the First Marine Division on Peleliu, 1944.* Philadelphia: Casemate, 2018.

McManus, John C. *Fire and Fortitude: The U.S. Army in the Pacific War, 1942–1943.* New York: Caliber, 2019.

Miller, Edward S. *War Plan Orange: The U.S. Strategy to Defeat Japan, 1897–1945.* Annapolis: Naval Institute Press, 1991.

Miller, John, Jr. *The War in the Pacific: Cartwheel: The Reduction of Rabaul.* Washington, DC: Office of the Chief of Military History, 1959.

Morison, Samuel E. *Coral Sea, Midway and Submarine Actions.* Boston: Little, Brown, 1949.

Morison, Samuel E. *Leyte: June 1944–January 1945.* Boston: Little, Brown, 1958.

Munholland, Kim. *Rock of Contention: Free French and Americans at War in New Caledonia, 1940–1945.* New York: Berghahn Books, 2005.

O'Brien, Phillips Payson. *How the War Was Won: Air-Sea Power and Allied Victory in World War II.* Cambridge: Cambridge University Press, 2015.

Parillo, Mark R. *The Japanese Merchant Marine in World War II.* Annapolis: U.S. Naval Institute Press, 1993.

Potter, E. B. *Admiral Arleigh Burke.* New York: Random House, 1990.

Potter, E. B. *Nimitz.* Annapolis: Naval Institute Press, 1976.

Prados, John. *Combined Fleet Decoded: The Secret History of American Intelligence and the Japanese Navy in World War II.* New York: Random House, 1995.

Prados, John. *Storm over Leyte: The Philippine Invasion and the Destruction of the Japanese Navy.* New York: New American Library, 2016.

Prange, Gordon W., with Donald M. Goldstein and Katherine V. Dillon. *At Dawn We Slept: The Untold Story of Pearl Harbor.* New York: McGraw-Hill, 1981.

Prange, Gordon W., with Donald M. Goldstein and Katherine V. Dillon. *Miracle at Midway.* New York: McGraw-Hill, 1982.

Reynolds, Clark G. *Admiral John H. Towers: The Struggle for Naval Air Supremacy.* Annapolis: Naval Institute Press, 1991.

Rogow, Arnold A. *James Forrestal: A Study of Personality, Politics, and Policy.* New York: Macmillan, 1963.

Smith, George W. *Carlson's Raid: The Daring Marine Assault on Makin.* New York: Berkley Books, 2001.

Solberg, Carl. *Decision and Dissent: With Halsey at Leyte Gulf.* Annapolis: Naval Institute Press, 1995.

Spector, Ronald H. *Eagle Against the Sun: The American War with Japan.* New York: The Free Press, 1985.

Spurr, Russell. *A Glorious Way to Die: The Kamikaze Mission of the Battleship* Yamato. New York: Newmarket Press, 1981.

Stafford, Edward P. *The Big E: The Story of the USS* Enterprise. New York: Random House, 1962.

Symonds, Craig L. *The Battle of Midway.* New York: Oxford University Press, 2011.

Symonds, Craig L. *World War II at Sea: A Global History.* New York: Oxford University Press, 2018.

Taylor, Theodore. *The Magnificent Mitscher.* Annapolis: Naval Institute Press, 1954, 1991.

Thomas, Evan. *Sea of Thunder.* New York: Simon and Schuster, 2006.

Toll, Ian. *The Conquering Tide: War in the Pacific Islands, 1942–1944.* New York: W. W. Norton, 2015.

Toll, Ian. *Pacific Crucible: War at Sea in the Pacific, 1941–1942.* New York: W. W. Norton, 2012.

Toll, Ian. *Twilight of the Gods: War in the Western Pacific, 1944–1945.* New York: W. W. Norton, 2020.

Venzon, Anne Cipriano. *From Whaleboats to Amphibious Warfare: Lt. Gen. "Howling Mad" Smith and the U.S. Marine Corps.* Westport, CT: Praeger, 2003.

Vigo, Milan. *The Battle for Leyte: Allied and Japanese Plans, Preparations, and Execution.* Annapolis: Naval Institute Press, 2006.

Walker, J. Samuel. *Prompt and Utter Destruction: Truman and the Use of Atomic Bombs against Japan.* Chapel Hill: University of North Carolina Press, 1997.

Weigley, Russell, *The American War of War: A History of United States Military Strategy and Policy.* New York: Macmillan, 1973.

Wheeler, Gerald E. *Kinkaid of the Seventh Fleet: A Biography of Admiral Thomas C. Kinkaid, U.S. Navy.* Annapolis: Naval Institute Press, 1996.

Wildenberg, Thomas. *Gray Steel and Black Oil: Fast Tankers and Replenishment at Sea in the U.S. Navy, 1912–1995.* Annapolis: Naval Institute Press, 1996.

Wolters, Timothy S. *Information at Sea: Shipboard Command and Control in the U.S. Navy from Mobile Bay to Okinawa.* Baltimore: Johns Hopkins University Press, 2013.

Wukovits, John. *One Square Mile of Hell: The Battle for Tarawa.* New York: NAL Caliber, 2006.

Y'Blood, William T. *Red Sun Setting: The Battle of the Philippine Sea.* Annapolis: Naval Institute Press, 1981.

Articles

Alexander, Joseph. "What Was Nimitz Thinking?" U.S. Naval Institute *Proceedings,* November 1988, 42–46.

Allison, Fred H. "We Were Going to Win . . . or Die Trying." *Naval History*, October 2016, 32–39.

Carrell, John T. "Over the Hump to China." *Air Force Magazine*, October 2009, 68–71.

Fuquea, David C. "Advantage Japan: The Imperial Japanese Navy's Superior High Seas Refueling Capacity." *Journal of Military History*, January 2020, 224–30.

Giangreco, D. M. "Casualty Projections for the U.S. Invasion of Japan." *Journal of Military History*, July 1997, 521–82.

Lundstrom, John B. "Confrontation in the Coral Sea: Admiral Nimitz's Plan for a Decisive Battle in the South-West Pacific." In Karl James, ed., *Kokoda: Beyond the Legend*, 48–67. New York: Cambridge University Press, 2012.

Nimitz, Chester. "Military Value and Tactics of Modern Submarines." U.S. Naval Institute *Proceedings*, December 1912, 1193–212.

Nimitz, Chester. "Naval Reserve Officers' Training Corps." U.S. Naval Institute *Proceedings*, June 1928, 441–45.

Nimitz, Chester. "Naval Tactics." *Naval War College Review*, November–December 1982, 8–13.

Nimitz, Chester. "An Open Letter to Junior Officers." U.S. Naval Institute *Proceedings*, February 1960.

Nimitz, Chester. "Pearl Harbor Postscript." U.S. Naval Institute *Proceedings*, December 1966, 126.

Nohrden, Maynard M. "The Amphibian Tractor, Jack of All Missions." U.S. Naval Institute *Proceedings*, January 1946, 13–17.

Parker, Frederick D. "How OP-20-G Got Rid of Joe Rochefort." *Cryptologia*, July 2000, 212–34.

Rems, Alan P. "Halsey Knows the Straight Story." *Naval History*, August 2008, 40–46.

Rubel, Robert C. "Deconstructing Nimitz's Principle of Calculated Risk." *Naval War College Review*, 2015, 1–15.

Sarantakes, Nicholas E. "Warriors of Word and Sword: The Battle of Okinawa, Media Coverage, and Truman's Reevaluation of Strategy in the Pacific." *Journal of American-East Asian Relations* 23, no. 4 (2016): 334–67.

Sparrow, Paul M. "A First Lady on the Front Lines: Eleanor Roosevelt's Tour of the South Pacific—August & September, 1943." Franklin D. Roosevelt Presidential Library and Museum, August 25, 2016.

Wildenberg, Thomas. "Chester Nimitz and the Development of Fueling at Sea." *Naval War College Review*, Autumn 1993, 52–62.

Unpublished Sources

Corneil, Cecilia Stiles. "James V. Forrestal and American National Security Policy, 1940–1949." Ph.D. dissertation, Vanderbilt University, 1987.

Hill, James R. "A Comparative Analysis of the Military Leadership Styles of Ernest J. King and Chester W. Nimitz." U.S. Army Command and General Staff College, Fort Leavenworth, 2008–9.

Oliver, Maxwell. "Vice Admiral Robert L. Ghormley: In the Shadow of the Fleet." Student research paper, U.S. Naval War College, 2020.

Stone, Christopher B. "Fleet Admiral Chester W. Nimitz: Leadership Forged Through Adversity." Ph.D. dissertation, University of Nebraska, 2018.

INDEX